Historical Economics

Historical Economics

Art or science?

Charles P. Kindleberger
Professor of Economics Emeritus, Massachusetts Institute of Technology

UNIVERSITY OF CALIFORNIA PRESS
BERKELEY LOS ANGELES

University of California Press
Berkeley and Los Angeles, California

Library of Congress Cataloging-in-Publication Data

Kindleberger, Charles Poor, 1910–
Historical economics: art or science?/Charles P. Kindleberger.
p. cm.
Includes index.
ISBN 0–520–07343–6, — ISBN 0–520–7344–4 (pbk.)
1. Historical school of economics. 2. Economics—History.
I. Title.
HB97.K57 1991 90-11217
330′.09—dc20 CIP

Printed in Great Britain

1 2 3 4 5 6 7 8 9

Contents

Figures

Tables

Introduction

This is the eighth book of my collected papers, each on a fairly narrow range of topics within economics – international economics, international financial questions, financial history and economic history (including some specialized topics such as the multinational corporation and the Marshall Plan). The exercise has strong overtones of narcissism, which makes me uneasy, but may serve a useful purpose in assembling in convenient locations work that would otherwise remain scattered and in part lost (as perhaps it should be). And yet I am a sufficient believer in the market test to defend myself against the charge of vainglory by pointing out that none of the eight has been published by a vanity press, subsidized by me, but each has been more or less willingly taken on, if not fought over, by some commissioning editor.

This collection deals with economic and financial history. The title implies that there is a difference between an economist who deals with historical issues and a historian who studies past economic questions. I come back to this in the Conclusion, which deals with the methodological question of whether history is a necessary dimension of the compleat economist, as I think it is.

The scattered provenance of the separate papers – written for symposia, delivered at conferences, as lectures on special occasions, and one on Spanish silver that appeared as a pamphlet (Chapter 3) produced on my own initiative to satisfy curiosity – is indicated in the first footnote of each chapter. None is the typical paper for a refereed journal that enjoys the highest standing in academic circles. Chapter 2, in fact, was commissioned and then rejected by the editors of an encyclopedia, on the ground that it did not conform to their idea of how the subject should be treated.

I am grateful to Peter Johns of Harvester Wheatsheaf for urging me to proceed with the collection, and to omit a couple of my beloved intellectual offspring which he thought, doubtless rightly, were out of place.

Charles P. Kindleberger
Lexington, Massachusetts
November 1989

PART 1

Economic history or historical economics?

1

Historical economics
A bridge between liberal arts and business studies?

If one looks through the Directory of the American Economic Association for addresses, it will become clear that some economics departments are located in business schools and some in schools of arts and sciences. My brother-in-law was very fond of a *New Yorker* cartoon in which a man returned home, happened to discover an unkempt bearded hippy in his wife's boudoir closet, and elicited the remark "Like, man, everybody's got to be someplace." This, I suppose, is true of economics departments as well as of hippies, but the fact that they choose liberal arts on some occasions, or have it chosen for them, and business schools at other times, emphasizes the ambiguity embodied in the subject. One could perhaps distinguish between technical economics, heavy with mathematics and econometrics, models and *n*-dimensional diagrams, and literary or anecdotal or intuitive economics – the former allied to operations research, statistical inference and sharp-pencil subjects like finance, and belonging really in a business school; the latter flirting with sociology, politics, perhaps even psychology, more comfortable with social science, and, to the extent that it is historical, perhaps with the liberal arts. I say "perhaps" because economic history itself has bifurcated into cliometrics, manipulating statistics and models to try to prove contentions in history, or more generally disprove those of others, and traditional economic history, which is more inductive.

I happen to profess historical economics, rather than economic

---

*A talk to a June 1988 conference supported by the Peat Marwick Main Foundation and sponsored jointly by the Association of American Colleges and the American Assembly of Collegiate Schools of Business. An abridged version was published in *Liberal Education*, vol. 75, no. 1, May – June 1989.

history, using historical episodes to test economic models for their generality. Many economic models are plausible and will fit particular circumstances; the question is how general they are and how much one can rely on them to provide understanding and wisdom in particular circumstances. I do not say prediction: I am a non-believer in positive economics that permits prediction because I take the view that in general-equilibrium models, with scores or perhaps even hundreds of variables, it is difficult to the point of impossibility – what literary people sometimes call infinitely difficult – to be certain that the various arguments in a given function have been accurately specified the first time and replicated the second. Historical economics, as I view it, believes in partial equilibrium, *ceteris paribus*, rather than *mutatis mutandis*, and looks for patterns of some uniformity but is wary of insisting on identity.

I have moved into historical economics from international economics, and in this paper I propose to strike out in the directions of the international aspects of business, on the one hand, and the liberal arts on the other, meaning, I suppose, mostly history, politics, cultural anthropology, sociology, perhaps even a little geography. But first let me suggest that business schools may not have enough, and liberal arts too much, of ambiguity. In mathematics and some business schools, the task is to prove theorems, relationships which are universally true. In the real world, ambiguity is king.

Should one look before one leaps, or is it true that he who hesitates is lost? If it ain't broke don't fix it fits some occasions, but others demand a stitch in time that saves nine. When in Rome do as the Romans do is one rule for the multinational corporation, but there are occasions when it is better to follow Polonius and to thine own self be true. Good, better, best, never let it rest, until your good is better and your better best is the optimistically American rule, but the French remind us that the best is the enemy of the good. Quit while you are ahead often applies but occasionally keep going when you are on a roll, embarked on the:

> tide in the affairs of men
> Which taken at the flood leads on to fortune
> Omitted, all the voyage of their life
> Is bound in shallows and miseries.
>
> (*Julius Caesar* IV,3.)

I could go on, but forbear, reminding you, however, not to stay spellbound before ambiguity, catatonic, like the ass of Bouridon, the French philosopher, which starved to death equidistant between two bales of hay, unable to decide which to go for first. In such circumstances it is important to do something; don't just stand there. On the other hand, there are occasions when it is important to stand there, rather than just do something.

My interest in historical economics most recently has been in the fields of international finance and economic growth and decline. The two subjects occasionally dovetail. Since the Renaissance there has generally been one dominant world financial center – Florence, Venice, Bruges, Antwerp, Amsterdam, London, New York – with economies of scale. Savers wanting to invest money take it to the center to examine various outlets; entrepreneurs and impecunious governments wanting to borrow go to the center because that is not only where the money is, as Woody Allen noted, but also where it is cheapest. The dominance of a center at any one time is never complete because there are costs of information, and diseconomies if all the information on the credit standing of everybody is gathered in a single place. The centers at the national level are sometimes the same as the capitals, e.g. London and Paris; sometimes not, e.g. New York, Toronto, and Zurich. The continuous shifts of the top international financial center follow the change of the fortunes of countries, and in part are the result of accident.

In recent years a number of explanations of the rise and fall of nations has been given. To Cipolla (1970), editing *The Decline of Empires*, the problem is that as a country improves its standard of living, more and more people demand to share the benefits. Incomes increase and extravagances develop. Prosperity spreads to neighboring countries which may become a threat and force the empire into military expenditures. Public consumption has a tendency to rise sharply and outstrip production. Survival of the empire demands new methods of productivity, and in general, empires seem to resist change.

A related view is that of Mancur Olson (1982) and is expressed in terms of distributional coalitions, vested interests in old-fashioned terminology, that lobby in democracies in their own interest, seeking to get protection, resisting taxation thought to bear on them, blocking the national agenda, and edging the country into inflation. When the people's representatives cannot agree on taxation through a budget, the budget remains unbalanced and an arbitrary inflation tax is applied. The burden may differ from case to case – reparations, paying off foreign debt, military expenditure, correcting an import surplus, but inability to agree on its sharing produces decline. A recent book by Paul Kennedy (1987) attributes decline altogether to military expenditure. And an article by Anthony Burgess (1988) writing on Edward Gibbon's *Decline and Fall of Rome* put it in terms of the complacency of successful empires that leads to enervation and fall before barbarian energy.

I do not mean to subscribe to stage theories of economic development, like that of W.W. Rostow – preconditions, followed by take-off, then drive to maturity and high mass consumption – but no category provided for decline in the optimistic 1950s when *The Stages of Economic Growth* was written. The contingent often overwhelms the systematic. In the first edition of *International Economics* (1953, p. 375), I wrote:

> Brazil, for example, has had separate booms in sugar, rubber, cotton and coffee, each of which under different circumstances might have been expected to lead to a "natural" process of economic growth. However many times the plane went down the runway, it had not, prior to World War II, effected a takeoff.

Many of the processes of economic and natural life follow in broad outline an S- or Gompertz curve, starting slowly, picking up speed, and then slowing down. But the shape of any one curve, and the fact that new curves may grow out of others, makes the generalization almost useless for prediction. By the same token, we have in international economics a series of stages a country is supposed to go through in the course of development: young debtor, as it starts borrowing; mature debtor, as it begins to pay back; young creditor, as its claims on the rest of the world exceed its liabilities; and mature creditor, as it stops piling up claims, lives off the income on its foreign assets, or even consumes them. Again the model has little predictive value. The United States went from the first stage to the third stage in four years of World War I and then spent sixty years there as a young creditor. Canada went forward and slipped back time and again between young debtor and mature debtor.

But let me get back to financial centers. They flourish first in trade, and then as the enthusiasm for risk wanes with wealth, shift sometimes into finance, sometimes to high life. Trade needs to be protected, so Venice, Amsterdam, and Britain all had navies. If too many of the successful merchants move into the counting house as bankers, and too many of the successful bankers go in for stately homes or châteaux, hunting, shooting and fishing, and the genteel life, the country slips. Antwerp's decline, however, was a consequence of the blockade of the port in 1585, with the result that the merchants moved to Amsterdam. Amsterdam had a wonderful run, peaked perhaps in 1730, suffered a couple of serious financial crises in 1763 and 1772, and then bet on the wrong horse, going to war with England, and shifting investments to France, which repudiated them in the Revolution. London's decline has been gradual, with a pickup when the Eurocurrency and Eurobond markets more or less concentrated there. I say "more or less" because the advent of satellite communication and giant computers has begun to deprive world markets of any fixed location. The process began with primary markets – underwriting which was first localized, and then undertaken by syndicates gathered worldwide. For a time secondary markets had to remain concentrated to get the economy of market agglomeration for the person who wanted to buy or sell only a few bonds or shares and could not afford to search markets everywhere. Today with distant communication cheap and fast, the fixed location of markets for money and capital is rapidly disappearing.

I emphasize that history is useful for its insistence on change rather than its aid in guiding or predicting it. The world can learn from the past: compare war debts, reparations, German inflation, commercial lending to Germany after the Dawes loan, and its sudden halt in 1928, with Lend-Lease, the British loan, the Marshall Plan, German monetary reform in 1948, and the cooperation of the industrial powers in the OEEC and OECD.

But history exhibits a pronounced tendency of markets, people, ideas to go to excess. Modern economists insist that one ought to treat man (a generic, not the masculine gender) as rational. Most of economics works best when the rationality of men is taken, in Popper's vocabulary, as a pregnant hypothesis, with problems solved on the hypothesis not that man is certainly rational, but that he acts on average as if (*als ob*) he were. But there have been times when this hypothesis plays one false: tulip mania, the Mississippi bubble, the South Sea bubble, canal mania, railway mania, "new eras", and financial crisis after financial crisis where the object of excessive enthusiasm was more general, such as the stock-market boom of 1928–9 and that of 1982–7. The details differ, the pattern has a strong family resemblance: some autonomous event that changes investment opportunities, a response by investors. The first investors make substantial gains, others follow and the gains pyramid, attracting people who may be rational in their daily life, but who are not informed about financial markets, or the particular object of investment – real estate, pork bellies, gold coins, luxury condominia, whatever – and enter late when prices are high. The same kind of faddism and excess can be found in the history of scholarship. I cite from economics only growth theory, core theory, Keynesianism, monetarism, rational expectations, cliometrics, historical explanations based on property rights, the agency problem, transaction costs, information costs, etc.

I have just finished reading, as I write, Martin Mayer's new book, *Markets* (1988), in which he has some rather sharp asides about academic observers of security markets in stocks, bonds, options, futures, Standard & Poors indexes, interest-rate hedging and the like. Most of the book deals with national rather than international markets, though he does discuss Tokyo and London along with Chicago and New York. His criticism of modern markets can be put in terms of the familiar distinction of Isaiah Berlin between the hedgehog and the fox, the fox who knows many things and the hedgehog that knows one thing. This remark is usually used by people who favor the hedgehog, but I suspect that Mayer would believe that business schools try to teach the tricks of hedgehogs, when life is more ambiguous and complex than that approach. I have often quoted a physicist colleague of mine at the Massachusetts Institute of Technology, Robley Evans, who said that "Everything is more complicated than most people think." If the liberal arts can help with the education of our future business leaders, it perhaps should make them stop from time to time and play the role of the fox.

Let me illustrate some of this complexity with the theory of international trade and protection. In graduate school at such a university as Yale, it used to be taught in two sections, one for economists, rigorous, mathematical, with theorems and lemmas (but few dilemmas), and the other for students from other disciplines, not so rigorously. The latter course was called secretly by the students of economics, "international trade for idiots." But there is something of a question in my mind, perhaps disloyally, as to which was the more valuable approach to a rounded view.

The Heckscher–Ohlin–Samuelson theorem, for example, states that under certain restrictive assumptions with two factors, two commodities and two countries, each country will export the product of its relatively abundant factor and import the product that uses the scarce factor intensively. The abundant factor will favor free trade, the scarce factor protection. It works like that to a considerable extent historically, but by no means universally. Sometimes both factors, labor and capital, in the exporting industry will favor free trade, or both factors in the import-competing industry will lobby for tariffs, as Stephen Magee (1980) has shown. In addition, tariff choices are sometimes predicated on pure politics: Napoleon III favored the Anglo-French Treaty of Commerce of 1860 – also known as the Cobden–Chevalier treaty – against the pressure of his dominant manufacturing interests in France because he wanted to gratify Britain and gain her neutrality in the war he was about to wage against Austria to liberate Italy. Bismarck was for low tariffs so long as they embarrassed Austria, and for high ones after the defeat of Austria in 1866. And the political economists work their way into the act, suggesting, for example, that to gain protection commodities must be somewhat concentrated, but not too concentrated (Pincus, 1977). Economics may be axiomatic and Cartesian, but in the real world there is much to take into account.

Further examples: more exports can stimulate growth, and more trade can hinder growth; more imports may hurt growth, or more imports can stimulate growth. I could run through the exercise for less exports and less imports, but leave it to the reader. More exports stimulate growth through the familiar export-led growth model which is back in fashion again after some discouragement with the import-substitution model. But more exports can also be a bane rather than a boon, as the British learned as they continued to push exports of cotton textiles, coal, rails, and galvanized iron sheets toward the end of the nineteenth century when they should have been shifting their energy and attention to other industries, such as electricity, chemicals, and automobiles. It is sometimes exhilarating to go fast, but it is not salubrious if it happens to be in the wrong direction. That more imports can hurt is obvious enough from the histories of India and Ireland, which were overwhelmed by British cotton textiles in the early part of the nineteenth century, the hand-loom industry being wiped out by machinery and its workers left with no obvious new industry into which to shift. More imports can also stimulate. William Huskisson's most famous speech in the House of Commons in 1822 when he was President of the Board of Trade dealt with the stimulus to the production of silk in Spitalfields from a lower tariff which produced the French competition to which the local industry responded vigorously. But when Britain was thinking of joining the Common Market to elicit the competition needed for growth, one civil servant told Professor, later Dean, Abraham Siegal of the Sloan School of Management, MIT, that not every kick in the tail stimulated; some just hurt.

There are in economics a number of models with great explanatory power, models perhaps but close to laws. The law of supply and demand is one such. In 1980 I gave some lectures in Italy published as *Economic Laws and Economic History* (1989), one lecture each on Engel's law, Gresham's law, the Lewis model of growth with unlimited supplies of labor, which might be called the iron law of wages, and the law of one price, which, if a person's name is wanted for it, could be called Adam Smith's law. My point was and is that there are a lot of uniformities or quasi-uniformities in the way people behave in earning a living, but none is good for all times and places, and that the choice of the time and place to apply a given tendency is a matter for art, rather than science. Economics is a toolbox and which tool to use at which time is partly a matter of science, partly clinical training, to borrow a metaphor from medicine, and often to a very considerable extent a question of instinct, of determining what is the most plausible in a given situation.

Technical economics and much of the method taught in business schools – at least those that do not use the case method – take a different view. In reviewing a series of books on economic development, Jan Tinbergen (1984, p. 112), the distinguished Dutch econometrician, economist and Nobel laureate, took exception to the rather loose techniques used by the authors and stated that "policy planning required an econometric approach – that is, the systematic and integrated use of theoretical and empirical knowledge, also known as model building." He divided the approach into five steps:

1. Drawing up a list of variables to be considered.
2. Formulating a list of relationships assumed to exist between the variables.
3. Collecting empirical data on the variables.
4. Testing the assumed relationships and changing them until they have become statistically reliable.
5. Using the model so obtained to find the optimal policy.

Literary economics, Tinbergen goes on, stops at the first stage. Intuition and implicit tests for plausibility are involved, to be sure, at many of his stages, but it is clearly possible for this sort of exercise to go wrong, especially at stage two where relationships are assumed. It is of course true that literary economics, sometimes called "touchy-feely," can be mushy. But it is better, I believe, to err on the side of an artistic feel for the relationships and the data than to rely on strong prior beliefs about the assumed relationships.

In an article in the *Journal of Economic Literature* about the Chicago school in economics, Melvin Reder (1982) stressed the fact that Chicago economists approach a problem with a strong view of how the world works. If the facts do not bear out the theory, they are disposed to struggle for a protracted period, gathering more facts, dismissing the particular set of facts as an outlier or exception, rejecting the facts, and the like, before they are willing to abandon, or even in some cases modify, the theory in question. In a collection on mercantilism the editor, D.C. Coleman (1969), and English economic historian, stated in an aside that economists (read also most professors of business schools) are interested in theories, while historians are interested in evidence. One is reminded of Thomas Carlyle's remark on hearing Margaret Fuller assert on a lecture platform "I accept the universe": "By God, she'd better."

I suspect I may be saying no more than the banal cliché that one must use the inductive as well as the deductive method, and that to the extent that business schools use texts, rather than the case method, in statistics, finance, accounting, and the like, it may be useful to have their international economics with a considerable historical orientation to help make the point that the application to problems of tight models often goes wrong. I believe in models, but, like diapers, in changing them frequently.

In conclusion, a story that makes one wary of any and all methodology. In 1939 the young diplomat came to the old diplomat to complain and ask: "People are coming to me every day to ask whether there is going to be a war. What shall I tell them?" The old diplomat thought for a minute and said: "Tell them 'No.' I have been telling them 'no' for forty years and I have been wrong only once."

References

Burgess, A. (1989), "Two Hundred Years Ago," in *New York Times Book Review*, February 28, pp. 1, 24–5.

Cipolla, C.M., ed. (1970), *The Economic Decline of Empires*, London: Methuen.

Coleman, D., ed. (1969), *Revisions in Mercantilism*, London: Methuen.

Kennedy, Paul (1987), *The Rise and Decline of Great Powers: Economic Change and Military Conflict from 1500 to 2000*, New York: Random House.

Kindleberger, Charles P. (1953), *International Economics*, Homewood, Ill.: Irwin.

Kindleberger, Charles P. (1989), *Economic Laws and Economic History*, New York: Cambridge University Press.

Magee, Stephen (1980), "Three Simple Tests of the Stolper–Samuelson Theorem," in Peter Oppenheimer, ed., *Issues in International Economics*, London: Oriel Press, pp. 138–53.

Mayer, Martin (1988), *Markets*, New York: Norton.

Olson, Mancur (1982), *The Rise and Decline of Nations: Economic Growth, Stagflation and Social Rigidities*, New Haven, Conn.: Yale University Press.

Pincus, Jonathan J. (1977), *Pressure Groups and Politics in Antebellum Tariffs*, New York: Columbia University Press.

Reder, Melvin (1982), "The Chicago School," *Journal of Economic Literature*, vol. XX, no. 1, pp. 1–30.

Tinbergen, Jan (1984), "Optimal Development Policies: Lessons From Experience", *The World Economy*, vol. 7, no. 1, March, pp. 112–16.

2

Economic history

As a field of learning, economic history grew up at the end of the nineteenth century, drawing partly on the tradition of historical economics in Germany, with Gustav Schmoller as its leading exponent, and partly on the profuse use of historical illustrations by Adam Smith, Karl Marx, Alfred Marshall, and others as they expounded economic theory. History itself had become more rigorous in the nineteenth century, and the theory of evolution attracted economists interested in tracing the development of economic institutions. While some statistical material had been gathered since the times of William Petty and Gregory King, the production of statistics grew rapidly in the nineteenth century, particularly the last third, providing economists and historians with expanding material for analysis. By the end of the century, economic history had become a distinct subject in British universities, with its own professors. In the United States a few scholars professed themselves economic historians and were located generally in departments of economics, occasionally in departments of history. German universities organized seminars in economic and social history, and the economic aspects frequently dominated the social.

Economic history, M. M. Postan maintained, was produced, like the mule, by cross-breeding between economics and history, though he felt

*Unpublished. This article was commissioned by an economic encyclopedia but rejected on the ground that the editors wanted an entry focused on the role of economic theory in economic history. It has benefited from comments from William N. Parker, W. W. Rostow and Peter Temin, all of whom, however, urged the inclusion of more material on American economic historians than my background in European research has been able to provide.

under no compulsion to indicate which of the parents was asinine, nor to judge whether the outcome was sterile (quoted in Pollard, 1964, p. 291). The economics from which it derives rests on the wide definition of that subject by Alfred Marshall, who called it the study of mankind in the everyday business of life, rather than on Lord Robbins's narrower definition as the study of choices among ends using scarce means with alternative uses. The broader definition encompasses the "impurities" of technology, law, sociology and politics, which play significant roles in economic life, not to mention such vagaries of nature as the weather (Hancock, 1946). Economic history differs from history, moreover, in wanting to go beyond narrating what actually happened in the past to explaining why. In a debate over economic growth in Italy in the nineteenth century, the historian Rosario Romeo lamented that he was interested in finding out merely what happened in Italy, whereas his opponent, the economic historian Alexander Gerschenkron, was searching for general laws applicable to all growing economies (Gerschenkron, 1968, p. 121). While some economic historians go so far as to say, with Fernand Braudel (1984, p. 619), master of the rhetorical question, "Is not the secret and underlying motive of history to explain the present?", or even further – "The purpose of history is to enable man to understand the past and to increase his mastery over the society of the present" (E.H. Carr, quoted in S. Checkland, 1971, p. 308) – A. W. Coats (1966, p. 332) has warned against such an intention: "Those who study history in the hope of relieving present discontents are apt to distort the past".

In addition to uncovering generalizations about economic life and informing current policy, economic history has been put to another use: to test economic models for the extent of their applicability. Economic theories are frequently deduced from axioms, and sometimes from observation of one case or a small number of cases. The record of the past is a laboratory in a social science largely prevented from experimenting, in which theories can be tested for generality. The Stolper and Samuelson (1941) theorem, for example, based on two countries, two factors of production, and each producing two goods, explaining why the relatively scarce factor in each country wants protective tariffs on imports, while the abundant factor favors free trade, is helpful in combination with information on the political strengths of the separate factors in explaining the choice between tariffs and free trade in some countries on some occasions, but only some, as historical studies show (Kindleberger, 1978, chs 2, 3). Other tariffs are explained by public-choice theory (Pincus, 1977) and some tariff wars by game theory (Coneybeare, 1984). Leland Yeager, a theorist with a strong prior commitment to the purchasing-power-parity theory, makes a distinction between using economic theory as a tool of historical research, which he applauds, and appealing to history to discriminate between correct and incorrect economic theories – in the instant case dealing with the gold standard. In Yeager's (1985, p. 662) view the facts underlying or informing economic theory "ought" to be more basic, dependable and enduring than the contingent facts or specific historical conditions and episodes.

G.R. Elton denies that general laws emerge from economic history, offering the example derived from English, French and Russian revolutions that political revolutions are engineered by social groups that have benefited from recent improvement in their economic position and status, claiming that there are many other revolutions in which the energizing force came from groups that were really destitute (Fogel and Elton, 1983, pp. 96–7). A more narrowly economic example comes from R. Cameron and a number of colleagues, testing the hypothesis that banks played a major role in the economic development of Europe after the industrial revolution in England. A series of case studies of Scotland, France, Germany and Belgium supported Gerschenkron's thesis on economic backwardness – that banks could substitute for missing entrepreneurship (Cameron, 1967). An extension of the original study to Austria, Italy and Spain, however, made clear that while banks such as the Crédit Mobilier founded in France in 1851, may be one means to vigorous growth in backward countries, they are not always sufficient to achieve it (Cameron, 1972).

Subject matter

The subject matter of economic history has been shaped partly by the availability of materials for study, and partly by contemporary concerns. Among the earliest statistical series most easily accessible were those on prices, wages and money and banking. Thomas Tooke and William Newmarch wrote *A History of Prices and the State of Circulation*, in six volumes, the first two appearing in 1838. Thorold Rogers planned an eight-volume *History of Agriculture and Prices in England*, publishing two volumes in 1866, two more covering the period 1401–1583 in 1882, and volumes 5 and 6, dealing with 1584–1702, in 1887. He had collected material for two more volumes to bring the account to 1793 before his death. A popular version of the longer work was issued in 1884 as *Six Centuries of Work and Wages*. Studies of prices in France were produced by Labrousse (1933) and Hauser (1936), in Germany by Elsas (1936; 1940; 1949), for the Netherlands by Posthumus (1935), in Denmark by Friis and Glamann (1958), in Sweden by Jörberg (1972), and for many other countries. Earl J. Hamilton's (1965) study of the "price revolution" of the sixteenth century, written in 1934 and based on the influx of silver from the New World after the discovery of America, has given rise to a notable debate (Outhwaite, 1969). As interest turned to working conditions, historical studies shifted to real wages, using nominal wages deflated by price series. In this area the work of Henry Phelps-Brown and Sheila Hopkins (1955, 1956, 1957, 1959) on wage rates, especially in the building trades of England, of François Simiand (1932) on France, and Gerhard Bry (1960) on Germany, deserve mention.

The central topics in the twentieth century up to World War II were the industrial revolution, a phrase made popular by Arnold Toynbee in lectures given in 1872 and published in 1884, and business fluctuations in prices and output. A variety of cycles of varying periodicity was claimed to have been discovered – one of 39 months, representing accumulations and run-offs in inventories, the so-called Kitchin cycle, named after its discoverer; another of eight to nine years associated with waves of investment in plant and equipment, the Juglar; a 20-year cycle associated with house construction, identified by Simon Kuznets; and a 50-year cycle in prices, but not in output, due to Kondratieff (for discussion, see Schumpeter, 1939). Kondratieff was unable to provide an explanation for the 50-year cycle, with peaks in 1817, 1873, 1920 (or 1929) and 1951, and troughs in 1848, 1896, 1936, and perhaps 1972. Rostow (1978), who provides the later dates, attributes the cycle to pressures of population against resource availability, and their relaxation, while J.W. Forrester (1989) ascribes it to periodic overinvestment in capital equipment. A simple explanation would lie in the random periodicity of major wars, but a recent study by a political scientist has sought to prove that the wars themselves have economic origins, and are endogenous (Goldstein, 1988). An even longer cycle of 150 years, with peaks in 1350, 1650, 1817 and 1974, had been adduced by Braudel (1984, pp. 76ff.) who relates it to major structural changes in the world economy. One of the first studies in economic history to use economic theory rigorously was Rostow's (1948) dissertation on Juglar cycles.

A major concern of economic history, in addition to prices, wages and cycles, has been the study of economic growth and development. Adam Smith's *Wealth of Nations* focused on the question. The historical school in Germany in the nineteenth century, incorporating Darwinian notions of evolution, propounded theories of economic evolution by stages, in which economies grew in per capita income and developed institutionally. Marx's theory, tracing the development of economic life from feudalism to capitalism, and projecting its ultimate arrival at socialism, is the most widely known, but there are others. List traces a development from savagery, through pastoral life, agriculture, agriculture and manufactures, to agriculture, manufactures and trade, Bücher, from household economy, through town economy, national economy to international economy; Hildebrand, from barter, through money, to credit; the British historian, W.J. Ashley, set out a pattern that evolved from household to guild, the domestic system and factory; in the United States, N.S.B. Gras's system ran from village through town to nation and the world. In the postwar period, the notion of stages was revived by W.W. Rostow (1960). Rostow's system has five stages: traditional society, the development of preconditions, takeoff into sustained growth, the drive to maturity, and high mass consumption. Takeoff is the great watershed in his system. A similar conception comes from Gerschenkron (1968), who insisted, however, that substitutability among various types of institutions in fulfilling preconditions was possible; banks and/or government might substitute for individual industrial entrepreneurs, depending on a country's degree of backwardness. His concept, analagous to Rostow's takeoff, was that of a "big spurt." Without explicitly adopting the concept of stages, Sir John Hicks (1969), tracing history up to the start of the industrial revolution, outlined how traditional economies based either on custom or command developed into market economies, first centered around city-states and then expanding to fill out large nations when these grew to become political units with effective administration.

Hildebrand's scheme of whole economies evolving along a path from barter through money to the use of credit was sharply attacked by the medieval economic historian M.M. Postan (1973, pp. 2–6), who observed that credit was well developed institutionally, though circumscribed in use, at the times that barter and money flourished. A wider attack on the German concept of stages comes from Braudel (1981; 1982; 1984). He argues that the materialism of the household, largely self-contained and using little money, all of it copper, existed side by side in Europe with the market economy of towns which used silver money, and with the world economy of what Adam Smith called "distant trade," using silver, gold, and especially credit in the form of bills of exchange. A similar view is set out in Edward Whiting Fox (1971), distinguishing the France of the ports and the gateway cities of Paris and Lyons, from "the other France" of the interior. It is further illustrated in Eugen Weber (1976), who describes the changes in thought and practice produced by the French revolution in Paris and the larger towns of France as they penetrated slowly into the countryside, with peasants taking a century to become "Frenchmen" with the help of conscription in 1870 and of universal education.

A prominent role in the takeoff in Rostow (1960) is taken by so-called "leading sectors", although it is not completely clear whether the designation is based on a growing sector's size, its speed of growth, or its impact in transmitting rapid growth to other sectors with which it is linked. A debate has taken place in the theory of economic development between, on the one hand, proponents of balanced growth who held that because of Say's Law, stating that supply creates its own demand, an economy had to grow in all sectors simultaneously at rates determined by the income elasticities for the products in question, since otherwise a sector that grew ahead of the others would be unable to sell its output (Nurkse, 1953), and those, on the other hand, who denied such necessity. The theory of balanced growth implicitly assumed a closed economy in which excess supply could not be sold abroad as exports, or deficiencies in inputs or consumption made up through imports. Even assuming a closed economy, however, the opposing theory argued that a sector or industry far in advance of others would stimulate them in one of two ways, either by creating a demand for other sectors' outputs as inputs in the leading sector – a backward linkage – or by making a supply of cheap inputs available to other industries – a forward linkage (Hirschman, 1959). This insight has been used to explain how an innovation in one industry or branch, such as the flying shuttle that increased productivity in weaving, created an enormous increase in demand for cotton yarn that led to innovations in spinning. This is part of the basis of the cliché that necessity is the mother of invention, with an additional element, discussed below, that invention may respond to scarcities in factors of production – resources, manpower or capital – that create a different sort of bottleneck. That invention and innovation respond to economic pressures of this sort is undeniable (Schmookler, 1966), but they can also occur, like resource discoveries, exogenously. One brand of economic history has attributed critical significance in economic advance to a few crucial innovations: hay that enabled cattle and other livestock to be better fed in winter and emerge stronger in springtime; the rudder which allowed the Venetians to build larger ships beyond the capacity of an oar to steer; the lateen fore-and-aft sail that made it possible for the Portuguese in the fifteenth century to extend the range of their ships by enabling them to tack home against the trade winds; or the horse collar which substituted the horse for the ox and sped the process of ploughing. These and similar innovations were presumably developed in response to economic need. But the metallurgist Cyril Stanley Smith (1970), has indicated that many innovations are the work of artists in search of better or more beautiful materials rather than necessity – for example, sculptors working with metal alloys such as bronze, or builders of cathedrals developing the extrusion process to make lead channels to hold stained glass. And some inventions, such as Berthollet's discovery of the process for producing chlorine, were undertaken solely in response to a demand for beauty, a luxury attribute in a commodity, rather than a necessity. The kings of England wanted their linens white, and sent them to Holland for bleaching in whey and sunlight. Chlorine enabled the bleaching to be done anywhere.

A highly original Canadian economic historian, Harold Innis (1930), has woven the history of the development of his country about the relations of different commodities to their economic environment. Canadian development, for example, was advanced hardly at all by the export of beaver pelts to Britain as raw material for the making of felt hats: production of beaver fur required large amounts of land, and little labor or equipment, and accordingly did not lead to settlement. The cod fisheries, on the other hand, had a differential effect, turning on whether the fishermen from Europe did or did not have access to cheap salt. Those with salt, notably the Portuguese and the French, could salt down their catches on board and had no reason to go ashore in the New World; those without, the British, were forced to land to dry the cod in the sunshine, formed settlements and established a colony. The major stimuli to Canadian development, however, were the timber industry and mining, both of which required large amounts of labor and then agriculture to feed the workers. The spread of agriculture to the Plains ultimately led to railroads. Through similar linkages the gold rush in California induced the development of agriculture to feed the miners; in due course agricultural development outstripped mining. Innis's staple theory of economic development can be extended to the recruitment of entrepreneurs, with merchants in the putting-out system readily becoming manufacturers of cloth, and locksmiths, clockmakers, wheelwrights, and the like, going into the mechanical industries, and apothecaries into chemicals.

Various historians have emphasized different aspects of the growth process. David Landes pays particular attention to technology, both in his discussion of the industrial revolution and subsequent development (Landes, 1968), and in his study of clocks and watchmaking, which also treats the increasing preoccupation with time in the modernization process (Landes, 1983). Schumpeter (1949) concentrated on entrepreneurs, including their background in class, national character, and like. The impact of religion on the development drive has been treated by Weber (1904) and Tawney (1952), while a Swedish economic historian (Samuelsson, 1961) casts doubt on their conclusion that the Protestant parts of Europe responded to development stimuli more fully than the Catholic. The question of attitudes arises especially in the question whether there has been entrepreneurial failure, and the beginnings of economic decline – a stage not included in Rostow's model. In writing on economic dynamics, Burton Klein (1977) makes a distinction between the "happy-warrior" type of entrepreneur who breaks out of constraints, takes risks, and produces "fast history," exchanging micro-stability, with many firms failing, for macro-economic growth, and middle-class rationality which avoids risks, makes for micro-economic stability for firms, but slow overall growth and slow history. At one time David Landes (1951) and John Sawyer (1951) each ascribed the slower growth of France than that of Britain between the French revolution and 1940 to the dominance in the former of the family firm, interested in avoiding risks and preserving the family fortune for future generations.

Economic historians have long attributed importance in economic growth to natural resources, in explaining, for example, why the industrial revolution came first in Britain instead of Holland or northern Italy, which were richer than Britain at the end of the seventeenth century. Habakkuk (1962) believes that British inventions in the industrial revolution tended to economize on natural resources, in which that country was less well endowed than the United States, whereas US inventions tended to be labor-saving because labor was the scarce factor there. Two difficulties confront this view: first, that if the comparison runs between Britain and France, rather than between Britain and the United States, Britain with its abundant coal was resource-rich, not resource-poor; second, that in static equilibrium, though perhaps not in a dynamic model, the marginal return to a currency unit's worth of input of any factor of production should be the same as that of any other.

Still related to factor endowments and country growth is the Lewis (1954) model of growth with unlimited supplies of labor, with its affinity to the Marx model of capitalism's exploitation of the mass reserve army of the unemployed, the lumpenproletariat, after the primitive accumulation of capital from the enclosures that drove labor off the land into the city. In the Lewis model, excess labor holds down wages, and ensures that any exogenous increase in the marginal-revenue product of labor goes to land or capital as rent or profits. To the extent that the rent and profits are reinvested and yield still higher potential returns to labor, the process becomes self-reinforcing until the supply of labor runs out. At this point further investment raises wages and dampens or reverses the rise in profits and rents. It has been hypothesized that this model helps explain the rapid rise in British growth after the industrial revolution, and the failure of wages to rise from the 1770s to 1850, but the suggestion has been denied (Pollard, 1978). Agriculture's failure to release peasant labor tied to the land has been blamed for slow French growth, although questions have lately been raised whether both the speed of British growth and the leisurely pace of French have not been exaggerated. The United States, on the other hand, can be said to have grown with an analogous model of growth with unlimited supplies of land, with improvements in productivity going to labor rather than to agriculture with its free land until the frontier was finally fully exploited.

Much study of economic growth is statistical in character, the investigators seeking to measure inputs and outputs with great care and to range the resulting data against various theories of growth and development. The pioneering effort among contemporary economists was perhaps that of Colin Clark (1957), but the outstanding efforts, for which he received the Nobel prize, were those of Simon Kuznets (1966). Major studies on leading countries have been prepared under the editorship of Moses Abramovitz and Kuznets (e.g. Carré *et al.*, 1972; Matthews *et al.*, 1982). Mathias and Postan (1978) consists of 1500 pages devoted to a study of particular inputs in particular countries in recent years. A number of individual scholars pursue work along these lines, notably Paul Bairoch, Edward Denison, and Angus Maddison. In virtually all these investigations, however, after great ingenuity has been expended in attributing fractions of economic growth to one or another input, or to such factors as economies of scale, investment in human capital (education), and the like, there remains an unexplained residual of sizeable proportions that is ascribed, somewhat unsatisfactorily, to technical progress or some other unmeasurable aspect of the process.

Studies of economic growth, prices, wages and cycles have focused primarily on countries. There are, of course world studies such as Braudel's *Civilization and Capitalism, 15th–18th Century* (1981; 1982; 1984) and Wallerstein's *The Modern World System* (1974; 1980; 1989), or Woodruff's *Impact of Western Man* (1966), studies of continents and subcontinental areas, such as Latin America, the Middle East, the Pacific Rim, and of areas within single countries. To celebrate the 1960 centennial of Italian unification, the Banca Commerciale Italiana commissioned an overall economic history of Italy, only one volume of which was finished before the author's death (Luzzato, 1963), plus some 20 regional studies covering separate provinces as a whole or more limited sectors or functional aspects such as agriculture, banking and industry in particular provinces. A few economic historians compare one country with another: France with Germany (Clapham, 1953), industrial Belgium with late industrializer Holland (Mokyr, 1974), and especially France and Britain (Kindleberger, 1964; Crouzet, 1972; O'Brien and Keyder, 1978). Occasional studies concentrate on bilateral relations between countries in a given function over a specific time period (Wilson, 1941; Ferns, 1960). Still more narrowly focused comparisons have run between the cities of Hamburg and Frankfurt am Main in West Germany (Böhme, 1968) and between Antwerp and Amsterdam (Van Houtte, 1972).

National studies have been criticized as too narrow, and, with transport continuously cheaper and economic integration under way, perhaps even anachronistic (Parker, 1984, p. 184). As already noted, Braudel and Wallerstein adopt world frameworks. On the other hand, Crouzet and Pollard regard the country as too big a unit for the analysis of the industrial revolution because of the diversified experience of various regions, affected, say, by the presence or absence of guilds. Parker concedes that the nation is a conventional accounting unit, and that economic history must make room for state policy, on the one hand, and national character, on the other. He insists, however, that attitudes, techniques and practices are not identical within given countries, and spread from parts of one nation to parts of another. He is particularly taken by the impact of the coal deposit running from the Pas de Calais in France, through Walloon Belgium to South Holland and the Ruhr. Significant differences exist, however, between the mining laws, entrepreneurial attitudes and the education of mining engineers in France and West Germany so that it is difficult to escape entirely from the national framework (Parker, 1984, ch. 5).

Lord Acton, quoted by W. Ashworth (1971), urged historians to study problems, not periods, and his advice has been widely followed in economic history. A.P. Usher participated with co-authors in an economic history of Europe (Bowden *et al.*, 1937) and wrote a textbook on the industrial history of England. His major contributions, however, were made through monographs: on the grain trade of France (Usher, 1913); the history of mechanical inventions (Usher, 1929, rev. 1954); and early deposit banking in the Mediterranean area (Usher, 1943). Such a reach was wide. Most scholars of given economic functions and processes specialize, and particular branches of economic history have grown up around technology, demography, management and industrial organization, money and banking, particular industries, including agriculture, individual companies, shipping, migration and the like. Financial history has been characterized as falling into four broad categories: the orthodox that explains the development of money and banking generally, or in a given country, and traces the evolution of financial instruments and techniques of commercial or central banking for some considerable distance; the heroic that assigns a leadership role, usually in economic growth, to banks and bankers; the populist that emphasizes how bankers, merchants and their political allies have exploited the common run of people in their own countries or in foreign countries or colonies; and the statist that underlines the role of central and commercial banks in support of the state (Jones, 1982). The orthodox is illustrated by Pierre Vilar (1976), or by the detailed studies of the Bank of England by Andréadès (1909), Clapham (1945) or Sayers (1976). Notable among the heroic is Cameron's (1961) monograph claiming that the Crédit Mobilier of France facilitated the development of all of Europe, either by its own lending or by example. Volume 3 of Braudel's *Civilization and Capitalism* (1984) furnishes a populist view of merchants and bankers. Connections of banks with the state become especially clear in connection with war: the Bank of England was established in 1694 in the Nine Years War, the Bank of France during the Napoleonic wars, and the National Bank Act in the United States during the Civil War. In all instances, the new institutions or legislation provided help for the state's finances.

Many topics in economic history become the subjects of intense discussion, to such an extent that a British publisher, Methuen, has published a series of small books covering "Debates in Economic History." These deal with such issues as the role of agriculture in British growth, the causes of the industrial revolution in England, the growth of English overseas trade in the seventeenth and eighteenth centuries, and the like. Many hardy perennials are posed and debated as problems: the economic bases of the enclosures in Britain, produced by changes in the relative prices of wheat and wool, by the reduced need for real insurance against crop failure inherent in the three-field system, or by the demand for defining property rights to stimulate output; whether the inflation in Germany after World War I was the consequence of monetary expansion by the Reichsbank or had its origin in balance-of-payments problems, arising in the first instance from reparations payments, and then from the need to restock the economy; the decline of the British aristocracy in the seventeenth century; the standard of living in Britain during the Napoleonic wars and afterwards; whether the origin of the price revolution of the sixteenth century was monetary – the influx of American silver – or real – the faster growth in population than in agricultural output; the Poor Laws in England up to 1832; the capital shortage in Germany in the mid-nineteenth century; and so on.

New interest in a topic or the development of new theories can lead to renewed study and new interpretations. The German inflation from 1914 to 1923 was widely analyzed in the 1920s and 1930s; with the revival of the quantity theory of money after World War II and the inflation of the 1970s, the topic aroused new interest and a series of monographs and symposia appeared (e.g. Holtfrerich, 1980). Jacob Viner (1924) studied the balance of payments of Canada from 1896 to 1913, a period of heavy borrowing from London, testing, and to his own satisfaction proving, the price-specie-flow mechanism under the gold standard as an effective means for transferring capital from one country to another in real goods and services. His interpretation was questioned at the time by R.H. Coats (1915), the Dominion statistician. With the development of the Keynesian foreign-trade multiplier, G.M. Meier (1953) reworked the Viner material to assign a higher role to income movements than to gold movements and prices. Still later, J. Ingram (1957) went over the record again, incorporating a Harrod-Domar growth model that allowed for the growth of output and explained some phenomena that Viner left unresolved. More recently a new monetary interpretation of balance-of-payments adjustment, relying on prices held steady by worldwide arbitrage under purchasing-power parity, has undertaken a fresh assault on the Viner interpretation (Rich, 1984).

Causation in economic history

Some purely random or accidental events produce significant effects in economic history: crop failures, extremes of weather, plant diseases, and perhaps war, discoveries and epidemics. The "perhaps" is required especially for the last two sets of accidental causes, since it has been suggested that plagues, such as the Black Death in the fourteenth century, were the result of improvements in transport which brought people with diseases held in check by antibodies built up over years into contact with other peoples without such resistance (McNeill, 1976); and Pierre Vilar (1976) has propounded the theory that the search that led to Columbus's discovery of the New World was caused by the lack of money in Europe as a consequence of the drain of specie to the Levant and the Far East, and a conscious search for gold. War is usually regarded as the product of political factors and exogenous to economics. In the Marxian lexicon, on the other hand, war is an endogenous outcome of the struggle for markets under capitalism.

Apart from accidental factors with economic consequences, the search for causes in economic history poses great difficulty. In general equilibrium many causes tend to be necessary to a given outcome, none sufficient. In partial-equilibrium analysis, when a few factors are studied and all others, including feedbacks, are impounded under the head of *ceteris paribus*, there is danger of abstracting from one or more necessary causes. Occam's razor and the principle of parsimony call for simplicity and elegance, especially the elimination of as many trivial contributing causes as possible. Some economic historians believe that in economic history one must seek economic causes for economic outcomes to the greatest extent possible (Hobsbawm, 1965, p. 157), but

Hicks (1969, p. 23) views economic history as a forum where economists, political scientists, lawyers, sociologists and historians can talk with one another. Parsimony has led many economic historians to move, if not all the way to mono-causality, at least to a position that emphasizes a single cause above others. Major causes singled out by various economic historians include money and banking (Cameron, Gerschenkron, Hoselitz, Vilar, etc.); property rights (North and Thomas); resources (Parker); technology (Landes); widening of the market (Adam Smith); capital accumulation (Ashton); population growth as a response to a series of bumper crops (Deane); and so on. Ashton (1949, p. 167) objects to economic historians who go to great length to systematize economic history, noting that facts are stubborn, and can be viewed either logically or chronologically, but seldom both at the same time. He further objects to the coiners of phrases such as commercial revolution, industrial revolution, Great Depression, Juglars, proto-industrialization, etc., in which, he claims, rhetoric is substituted for thought (Ashton, 1949, p. 163).

A typical problem involves many causes, all to some degree necessary, none sufficient, taking the form:

$$E = f(C_1, C_2, \ldots C_n)$$

where E is the effect and the Cs are contributing causes. McClelland (1975) points to the difficulty of knowing whether the list of Cs is complete, and suggests that it is virtually impossible to say that the effect E is "always" or "necessarily" ahead of the function f. In this case causation becomes little more than observed correlations. The new "scientific" economic history seeks to build models along the lines above and to calculate weights for the various Cs by the device of the "counterfactual," removing one cause at a time and calculating the outcome without it. The social saving of the railroad in US economic growth was deemed to have been small, using a model that had growth dependent on various forms of transport – horse and wagon, canals and railroads – all, however, with constant-cost functions over the full range of possible output, and all in use simultaneously (Fogel, 1964). In theoretical terms, of course, any one form of transport in these circumstances can be dispensed with and the others expanded to take its place. One economic historian, contrasting the economist's approach to that of the historian, insists that causation can be found only in models, since it is unobservable in real life. He contrasts the formal, optimizing behavioral models of the economist, however, with the vague, multidisciplinary heuristic models of the historian, presumably to the derogation of the latter (Fleisig, 1985, p. 352).

Much of the so-called new scientific history has a revisionist cast to it, taking some cliché of history and seeking by rigorous methods to turn it on its head. In addition to the standard view that the railroad was central to US economic growth that Fogel sought to dismiss, Fogel and Stanley Engerman (1971) set out of disprove that slavery was a dying institution before the US Civil War, demonstrating with ingeniously derived data, manipulated with statistical sophistication, that slave agriculture was as efficient as that of whites in the north. Donald McCloskey, Peter Temin, Lars Sandberg and others undertook to demonstrate that the British entrepreneur was not responsible for the relative decline of the British economy after about 1875, as widely held, by "proving" that entrepreneurs were maximizing profits within the limits of available supplies and existing demand, but using static models in which entrepreneurs have no capacity to break bottlenecks, penetrate into new markets, or innovate (slow history). Patrick O'Brien and Caglar Keyder (1978) try to establish with assorted statistical material that France was richer per capita in 1785 than Britain, this in the face of the general view to the contrary. A growing number of historians are attacking the view that there was an industrial *re*volution, as opposed to an *e*volution, in England (Cameron, 1989, pp. 163–5). A German economic historian has lately attempted to subvert the general view of the Marshall Plan's importance by maintaining that the Federal Republic had sufficient land, labor and capital to grow at the rate achieved with Marshall Plan aid (Abelshauser, 1990). His model, however, assumed an absence of bottlenecks.

A scholarly but sharp confrontation between a "cliometrician", skilled in the use of economic theory and sophisticated econometrics in writing economic history, and a traditional historian, relying on a wide range of evidence from archives, reports, contemporary accounts, biographies and the like and "vague, multidisciplinary, heuristic models", suggests that neither approach has a marked advantage over the other, and that each must be employed by its practitioners with great care. "Scientific" history runs the risk of embodying its conclusions in its assumptions; traditional history the danger that its evidence may be unrepresentative, with the historian smuggling untenable assumptions into an apparently straightforward narrative (Fogel and Elton, 1983, p. 124). The scientific historian claimed that his method called attention to important processes, hitherto ignored, and yielded findings that proved strikingly different from those of the old research. At the same time it was admitted that the statistical method substituted an ahistorical stereotype for real individuals who behaved often in different ways, and that cliometrics has failed to produce timeless generalizations or coherent accounts of given economies over extended periods of time (Fogel and Elton, 1983, pp. 63, 68).

Is economic history necessary?

Scientific economic history is sometimes said to be merely applied economics using historical data, but with most of the history removed. As graduate curricula in economics become more sophisticated in the mathematical theories they use, and in econometric and statistical techniques, economic history may be left to be picked up along with applied economics in general, and economic history in the traditional sense will be squeezed out of the curriculum altogether to make room for more and more high-powered mathematics. Economic historians for the most part resist this development, claiming that the past has useful economics, and that broad economic history, as opposed to narrow cliometrics, develops more facts, better facts, better economic theory, better economic policy and better economists (McCloskey, 1976). A panel of theorists and historians went beyond this in insisting that economic history honed the intuition, needed, along with analytical skill, in making an economist, helping develop alertness in allowing for the contingent as well as the systematic. Economic history, it was concluded, while certainly not sufficient to train an economist, was surely necessary to the education of one (Parker, 1986).

Bibliography and references

Abelshauser, W. (1990), "The Economic Role of the ERP in German Recovery and Growth after the War: A Macroeconomic Perspective," in C. S. Maier and G. Bischof, eds, *The Marshall Plan and Germany*, New York: St Martin's Press.

Andréadès, A. (1909), *History of the Bank of England*, London: P. S. King.

Ashton, T. (1949), "The Relation of Economic History to Economic Theory," in N.B. Harte, ed., *The Study of Economic History*, London: Frank Cass, pp. 161–79.

Ashworth, W. (1971), "Inaugural Lecture," in N. B. Harte, ed., *The Study of Economic History*, London: Frank Cass, pp. 204–18.

Bloch, M. (1953), *The Historian's Craft: Reflections on the Nature and Uses of History and the Techniques and Methods of the Men Who Write it*, New York: Vintage Books, translated by Peter Putnam.

Böhme, H. (1968), *Frankfurt und Hamburg, Des Deutsches Reiches Silber- und-Goldloch und die Allerenglischte Stadt des Kontinents*, Frankfurt: Europäische Verlagsanstalt.

Bowden, W., M. Karpovich, and A. P. Usher (1937), *An Economic History of Europe since 1750*, New York: American Book Company.

Braudel, F. (1981), *Civilization and Capitalism, 15th–18th Century*, vol. I: *The Structures of Everyday Life*, New York: Harper & Row.

Braudel, F. (1982), *Civilization and Capitalism, 15th–18th Century*, vol. II: *The Wheels of Commerce*, New York: Harper & Row.

Braudel, F. (1984), *Civilization and Capitalism, 15th–18th Century*, vol. III: *The Perspective of the World*, New York: Harper & Row.

Bry, G. (1960), *Wages in Germany, 1871–1945*, Princeton, NJ: Princeton University Press.

Cameron, R. (1961), *France and the Economic Development of Europe, 1800–1914*, Princeton, NJ: Princeton University Press.

Cameron, R., ed. (1967), with the collaboration of Olga Crisp, H. T. Patrick and R. Tilly, *Banking in the Early Stages of Industrialization: A Study of Comparative Economic History*, New York: Oxford University Press.

Cameron, R., ed. (1972), *Banking and Economic Development; Some Lessons of History*, New York: Oxford University Press.

Cameron, R. (1989), *A Concise Economic History of the World*, Oxford: Oxford University Press.

Carré, J.-J., P. Dubois and E. Malinvaud (1972), *La Croissance française: un essai d'analyse causale de l'après-guerre*, Paris: Seuil.

Checkland, S. (1971), "Inaugural Lecture," in N. B. Harte, ed., *The Study of Economic History*, London: Frank Cass, pp. 301–13.

Clapham, Sir John (1953), *The Bank of England: A History*, 4th edn, 2 vols, Cambridge: Cambridge University Press.

Clark, C. (1957), *The Conditions of Economic Progress*, 3rd edn, New York: St Martin's Press.

Coats, A.W. (1966), "Economic Growth: The Economic and Social Historian's Dilemma," in N. B. Harte, ed., *The Study of Economic History*, London: Frank Cass, pp. 329–48.

Coats, R.H. (1915), *The Rise of Prices and the Cost of Living*, Ottawa: Canada, Dept. of Labor, Statistical Branch.

Coneybeare, J.A.C. (1984), "Public Goods, Prisoners' Dilemmas and the International Political Economy," *International Studies Quarterly*, vol. 28, pp. 5–22.

Crouzet, F. (1972), "Western Europe and Great Britain: 'Catching Up' in the First Half of the Nineteenth Century," in A. J. Youngson, ed., *Economic Development in the Long Run*, London: Allen & Unwin.

Elsas, M.J. (1936), *Umriss einer Geschichte der Preise und Löhne in Deutschland*, vol. I, Leiden.

Elsas, M.J. (1940), *Umriss einer Geschichte der Preise und Löhne in Deutschland*, vol. II, Leiden.

Elsas, M.J. (1949), *Umriss einer Geschichte der Preise und Löhne in Deutschland*, vol. III, Leiden.

Ferns, H.S. (1960), *Britain and Argentina in the Nineteenth Century*, Oxford: Clarendon Press.

Fleisig, H.W. (1985), "Comment" on McGouldrick, "The German Central Bank and The Rules of the Gold Standard," in M.D. Bordo and A.J. Schwartz, eds, *A Retrospective on the Classical Gold Standard, 1821–1931*, Chicago: University of Chicago Press.

Fogel, R.W. (1964), *Railroads and American Economic Growth: Essays in Econometric History*, Baltimore, Md: Johns Hopkins University Press.

Fogel, R.W. and S. Engerman (1971), *Time on the Cross: The Economics of American Negro Slavery*, Boston: Little Brown.

Fogel, R.W. and G.R. Elton (1983), *Which Road to the Past: Two Views of History* New Haven, Conn.: Yale University Press.

Forrester, J.W. (1989), "The System Dynamics National Model: Macrobehavior from Microstructure), unpublished paper, System Dynamics Group, MIT.

Fox, Edward Whiting (1971), *History in Geographic Perspective: The Other France*, New York: Norton.

Friis, A. and K. Glamann (1958), *A History of Prices and Wages in Denmark, 1660–1800*, London: Longmans, Green.

Gerschenkron, A. (1962), *Economic Backwardness in Historical Perspective*, Cambridge, Mass.: Harvard University Press.

Gerschenkron, A. (1968), *Continuity in History and Other Essays*, Cambridge, Mass.: Harvard University Press.

Goldstein, Joshua H. (1988), *Long Cycles, Prosperity and War in the Modern Age*, New Haven: Yale University Press.

Habakkuk, H.J. (1962), *American and British Technology in the Nineteenth Century*, Cambridge: Cambridge University Press.

Hamilton, E.J. (1965), *American Treasure and the Price Revolution in Spain, 1501–1650*, New York: Octagon Books; first published 1934.

Hancock, W.K. (1946), "Economic History at Oxford," in N. B. Harte, ed. *The Study of Economic History*, London: Frank Cass, pp. 143–59.

Hauser, H. (1936), *Recherches et documents sur l'histoire des prix en France de 1500–1800*, Paris: Les Presses Modernes.

Hicks, Sir John (1969), *A Theory of Economic History*, Oxford: Clarendon Press.

Hirschman, A.O. (1959), *The Strategy of Economic Development*, New Haven: Yale University Press.

Hirschman, A.O. (1985), "Against Parsimony: Three Easy Ways of Complicating Some Categories of Economic Discourse," *Economics and Philosophy*, vol. 1, no. 1, pp. 7–21.

Hobsbawm, E.L. (1965), "The Crisis of the Seventeenth Century," in T. Aston, ed., *Crisis in Europe, 1560–1660*, London: Routledge and Kegan Paul.

Holtfrerich, Carl-Ludwig (1980), *Die deutsche Inflation, 1914–1923*, Berlin: de Gruyter. Published in English as *The German Inflation, 1914–1923*, New York: de Gruyter (1986).

Ingram, J.C. (1957), "Growth and Canada's Balance of Payments," *American Economic Review*, March, pp. 93–104.

Innis, H.A. (1930), *Problems of Staple Production in Canada*, Toronto, University of Toronto Press.

Jones, C. (1982), "The Monetary Problems of Export Economies Before 1914," paper presented to the Symposium on "Argentina, Australia and Canada, Some Comparisons, 1870–1950," at the 44th International Congress of Americanists, Manchester, England, September 8.

Jörberg, L. (1972), *A History of Prices in Sweden, 1732–1914*, 2 vols, Lund: CWK Gleerup.

Kindleberger, C.P. (1964), *Economic Growth in France and Britain, 1851–1950*, Cambridge, Mass.: Harvard University Press.

Kindleberger, C.P. (1978), *Economic Response: Comparative Studies in Trade, Finance and Growth*, Cambridge, Mass.: Harvard University Press.

Klein, B.W. (1977), *The Elements of Dynamic Economics*, Cambridge, Mass.: Harvard University Press.

Kuznets, S. (1966), *Modern Economic Growth*, New Haven, Conn.: Yale University Press.

Labrousse, C.E. (1933), *Esquisse du mouvement des prix et des revenues en France au XVIIIe siècle*, Paris: Dalloz.

Landes, D.S. (1951), "French Entrepreneurship and Industrial Growth in the Nineteenth Century," in E.M. Earle, ed., *Modern France*, Princeton, NJ: Princeton University Press, pp. 334–53.

Landes, D.S. (1968), *The Unbound Prometheus: Technological Change and Industrial Development in Western Europe, from 1750 to the Present*, Cambridge: Cambridge University Press.

Landes, D.S. (1983), *Revolution in Time: Clocks and the Making of the Modern World*, Cambridge, Mass.: Harvard University Press.

Lewis, W.A. (1954), "Development with Unlimited Supplies of Labor," *The Manchester School*, vol. XXII, May, pp. 139–91.

Luzzato, G. (1963), *L'Economia italiana del 1861 al 1914*, vol. 1 (*1861–1894*), Milan: Banca Commerciale Italiana.

Maddison, A. (1982), *Phases of Capitalist Development*, Oxford: Oxford University, Press.

Matthias, P. and M.M. Postan, eds (1978), *The Cambridge Economic History of Europe*, vol. VII, *The Industrial Economies: Capital, Labour and Enterprise*, Cambridge: Cambridge University Press.

Mathews, R.C,O., C.H. Feinstein and J.G. Odling-Smee (1982), *British Economic Growth, 1856–1973*, Oxford: Clarendon Press.

McClelland, P.D. (1975), *Causal Explanations and Model Building in History, Economics and the New Economic History*, Ithaca, NY: Cornell University Press.

McCloskey D.N. (1976), "Does the Past have Useful Economics?" *Journal of Economic Literature*, vol. XIV, June, pp. 434–61.

McNeill, W.H. (1976), *Plagues and People*, Garden City, NY: Anchor Books.

Meier, G.M. (1953), "Economic Development and the Transfer Process, 1895–1913," *Canadian Journal of Economics and Political Science*, February, pp. 1–19.

Mokyr, J. (1974), *Industrialization in the Low Countries, 1795–1850*, New Haven, Conn.: Yale University Press.

Nurkse, R. (1953), *Problems of Capital Formation in Underdeveloped Countries*, Oxford: Blackwell.

O'Brien, P.K. and C. Keyder (1978), *Economic Growth in Britain and France, 1780–1914; Two Paths to the Twentieth Century*, London: Allen & Unwin.

Outhwaite, R.B. (1969), *Inflation in Tudor and Early Stuart England*, London: Macmillan.

Parker, W.N. (1984), *Europe, America and the Wider World: Essays on the Economic History of Western Capitalism*: vol. I, *Europe and the World Economy*, New York: Cambridge University Press.

Parker, W.N., ed. (1986), *Economic History and the Modern Economist*, Oxford: Blackwell.

Phelps-Brown, E.H. and S.V. Hopkins (1955), "Seven Centuries of Builders' Wages," *Economica*, New Series, vol. 22, pp. 195–206.

Phelps-Brown, E.H. and S.V. Hopkins (1956), "Seven Centuries of the Prices of Consumables Compared with Builders' Wage Rates," *Economica*, New Series, vol. 23, pp. 296–314.

Phelps-Brown, E.H. and S.V. Hopkins (1957), "Wage Rates and Prices: Evidence for Population Pressure in the Sixteenth Century," *Economica*, New Series, vol. 23, pp. 289–306.

Phelps-Brown, E.H. and S.V. Hopkins (1959), "Builders' Wage Rates, Prices and Population: Some Further Evidence," *Economica*, vol. 26, pp. 18–36.

Pincus, J.J. (1977), *Pressure Groups and Politics in Antebellum Tariffs*, New York: Columbia University Press.

Pollard, S. (1964), "Economic History – A Science of Society?" in N.B. Harte, ed., *The Study of Economic History*, London: Frank Cass.

Pollard, S. (1978), "Labour in Great Britain", in Peter Mathias and M.M. Postan, eds, *The Cambridge Economic History of Europe*, vol. VII, part I, pp. 289–312.

Postan, M.M. (1973), *Medieval Trade and Finance*, Cambridge: Cambridge University Press.

Posthumus, N. (1943), *Nederlandische Prijsgeschiedenis*, 2 vols, Leiden: E.J. Brill.

Rich, G. (1984), "The Experience of Canada without a Central Bank: The Price-Specie-Flow Mechanism, 1872–1913," in M. Bordo and A.J. Schwartz, eds, *A Retrospective on the Classical Gold Standard, 1821–1931.*

Roehl, R. (1976), "French Industrialization: A Reconsideration," *Explorations in Economic History*, vol. XIII, pp. 233–81.

Rogers, J.E.T. (1884) *Six Centuries of Work and Wages*, London: W.S. Sonnenschein.

Rogers, J.E.T. (1866–87), *History of Agriculture and Prices in England*, 8 vols, New York: G.P. Putnam's Sons.

Rostow, W.W. (1948), *British Economy of the Nineteenth Century*, Oxford: Clarendon Press.

Rostow, W.W. (1960), *The Stages of Economic Growth: A Non-Communist Manifesto*, Cambridge: Cambridge University Press.

Rostow, W.W. (1978), *The World Economy: History and Prospect*, Austin, Texas: University of Texas Press.

Samuelsson, K. (1961), *Religion and Economic Action*, London: Heineman.

Sawyer, J.E. (1951) "Strains on the Structure of Modern France," in E.M. Earle, ed., *Modern France*, Princeton, NJ: Princeton University Press, pp. 293–312.

Sayers, R.S. (1976), *The Bank of England, 1891–1944*, 3 vols, Cambridge: Cambridge University Press.

Schmookler, J. (1966), *Inventions and Economic Growth*, Cambridge, Mass.: Harvard University Press.

Schumpeter, J.A. (1939), *Business Cycles: A Theoretical, Historical and Statistical Analysis of the Capitalistic Process*, 2 vols, New York: McGraw-Hill.

Schumpeter, J.A. (1949), *The Theory of Economic Development*, Cambridge, Mass.: Harvard University Press.

Simiand, F. (1932), *Le Salaire: l'évolution sociale et la monnaie*, 3 vols, Paris: Alcan.

Smith, C.S. (1970), "Art, Technology and Science: Notes on their Historical Interaction," *Technology and Culture*, vol. II, October.

Stolper, W.F. and P.A. Samuelson (1941), "Protection and Real Wages," *Review of Economic Studies*, November, pp. 58–73.

Tawney, R.H. (1952), *Religion and the Rise of Capitalism*, New York: Harcourt, Brace and World.

Tooke, T. and W. Newmarch (1838–57) *A History of Price and the State of Circulation from 1792 to 1856*, 6 vols; reprinted New York: Adelphi (1928).

Toynbee, A. (1937), *Lectures on the Industrial Revolution in England*, reprinted, New York: Longmans, Green; first published 1884.

Usher, A.P. (1913), *The History of the Grain Trade in France, 1400–1710*, Cambridge, Mass.: Harvard University Press.

Usher, A.P. (1920), *Introduction to the Industrial History of England*, Boston: Houghton Mifflin.

Usher, A.P. (1929, rev. 1954), *A History of Mechanical Inventions, New York*: New York: McGraw-Hill.

Usher, A.P. (1943), *The Early History of Deposit Banking in Mediterranean Europe*, Cambridge, Mass.: Harvard University Press.

Van Houtte, J.A. (1972), "Economic Development of Belgium and the Netherlands from the Beginning of the Modern Era," *Journal of European Economic History*, vol. I, Spring, pp. 100–120.

Vilar, P. (1976), *A History of Gold and Money, 1450–1920*, London: New Left Books.

Viner, J. (1924), *Canada's Balance of International Indebtedness, 1900–1913*, Cambridge, Mass.: Harvard University Press.

Wallerstein I. (1974), *The Modern World-System*, vol. I, New York: Academic Press.

Wallerstein, I. (1980), *The Modern World-System*, vol. II, New York: Academic Press.

Wallerstein, I. (1989), *The Modern World-System*, vol. III, New York: Academic Press.

Weber, M. (1904), *The Protestant Ethic and the Spirit of Capitalism*, translated from the German, 1956, New York: Scribner.

Weber, E. (1976), *From Peasants into Frenchmen: The Modernization of Rural France, 1870–1914*, Stanford Calif.: Stanford University Press.

Wilson, C. (1941), *Anglo-Dutch Commerce and Finance in the Eighteenth Century*, Cambridge: Cambridge University Press.

Woodruff, W. (1966), *Impact of Western Man: A Study of Europe's Role in the World Economy, 1750–1960*, New York: St Martin's Press.

Yeager, L.B. (1985), "The Image of the Gold Standard," in M. Bordo and A.J. Schwartz, eds, *A Retrospective on the Classical Gold Standard, 1821–1931*, Chicago: University of Chicago Press.

PART 2

Europe

3

Spenders and hoarders
The world distribution of Spanish American silver, 1550–1750

Introduction

Anglo-Saxon history of economic thought, which may be ethnocentric, puts the beginning of the end of mercantilism, and especially its bullionist component, about the 1620s with the writings of Thomas Mun (1621; 1664 – the latter written in the 1620s), and the end in the 1750s with David Hume's *Essays* (1752). The picture is not completely accurate. The Italian city-states, especially Venice, permitted the export of precious metals received from central European mines eastward to the Levant in exchange for Middle Eastern and Asian luxuries, well before the flood of silver from Spanish American mines into Europe after 1560. Having liberated itself from the Midas complex (DeVries, 1976, p. 239), Holland in the early seventeenth century was more relaxed than England in allowing bullion and foreign coin to be exported. But the progression from bullionism to the price-specie-flow mechanism – from preoccupation with accumulating gold and silver to the realization that a self-equilibrating mechanism was at work – was confined to Europe over the two centuries it required. At the other ends of the

*Reprinted from a pamphlet published by the Asean Economic Research Unit of the Institute of Southeast Asian Studies, Singapore, 1989. I acknowledge with thanks help from Moses Abramovitz, Arthur Attman, William S. Atwell, Paul Bairoch, Rondo Cameron, John K. Fairbank, Ole Feldbaek, Albert Feuerwerker, Wolfram Fischer, Dennis Flynn, John Hurd, H.C. Johansen, P.W. Klein, William H. McNeill, Peter Petri, Eric Schubert, Barbara Solow, Paul Streeten, Birgit Nuchel Thomsen and Stein Tveite, of whom I asked questions or who provided comments. Since I may lack the background to understand their answers or their observations, they are absolved from the mistakes that follow.

earth, in Spanish America (and Spain) and in the Middle and especially the Far East, different models prevailed.

Potosí in Peru (modern Bolivia), which produced silver in prodigious quantities from 1560, and Mexico to a lesser extent a century later, viewed silver as a commodity rather than money and were ready to part with it. Spain was like the rest of Europe in wanting to keep silver within its borders, but resembled Peru in being unable to hold on to it. In Asia, China and India were sponges that soaked up the streams of silver flowing through Europe (and the Philippines) from Spanish America. Instead of one developing price-specie-flow model, there were three: equilibrium, persistent deficits, and persistent surpluses. Peru, Mexico, and Spain were what are called today "high absorbers," economies that spent heavily for private and public consumption, including, in the last, military expenditure. China and India, on the other hand, were 'low absorbers", with high propensities to save or hoard. The demand for goods at one extreme and for silver and gold at the other was characterized in terms of the human condition: Potosí was "starved for goods" (Borah, 1954, p. 82). India had "a voracious appetite for precious metals" (Richards, 1983, p. 183) or "an ever-thirsty insatiable market" (for silver) (Perlin, 1983, p. 68). China had a "hunger for silver" (Parry, 1967, p. 210), or an "avidity" (Spooner, 1972, p. 77).

There is some question whether India and China were really different from Europe. Chaudhuri, who posed the question, thinks not (1978, p. 156), maintaining that the "role of silver in the commercial life of India may appear on closer examination to have been fundamentally determined by the same type of considerations as elsewhere" (ibid., p. 182). An expert on Chinese monetary history first noted that the Chinese government's silver revenues would normally have been spent in substantial proportion on goods and services and thus re-entered the economy and the monetary system, but that in the late Ming period (1368–1644), they fell into the hands of powerful political and military figures, many of whom chose to hoard. In a subsequent footnote, however, this expert questioned whether the Chinese habitually hoarded a higher percentage of their precious metals than other pre-modern peoples (Atwell, 1982, p. 88).

This paper is addressed to the economic forces that determined the amounts of silver that stayed in various countries or passed through. I write as an economist, not as an economic historian, responsive to Coleman's remark that economists make theories, and historians want evidence (1969, p. 2). The central issue is whether there is one balancing model of the balance of payments – the price-specie-flow model in the period concerned – or three, with persistent surpluses and persistent deficits along with balance. The analysis runs in terms of Alexander's terms of absorption or spending propensities rather than the elasticities implicit in Hume's model based on prices. Several considerations govern the choice. In the first place, after decades of acceptance of the quantity theory of money and the explanation of the price revolution of the sixteenth and seventeenth centuries in Europe as caused by Spanish American silver imports, revisionists have begun to raise doubts. The rise in prices preceded the silver arrivals by several decades, and was much more pronounced in food than in prices in general, suggesting that it was caused more by real than by monetary factors, and especially by the faster comeback of population than of agriculture after the Black Death of the fourteenth century (Outhwaite, 1969). Secondly, price data in the Far East are fragmentary and localized. In India a discussion of "one great rise" of prices between 1610 and the mid-1630s relies on evidence on sugar, indigo, copper, and gold (Habib, 1982, pp. 275ff.); another on copper and indigo alone (Brennig, 1983, pp. 495–6). A discussion of Chinese prices is confined to rice, assumed to be representative of prices in general (Wang, 1972, p. 348). In this paper, it is assumed that gains or losses of specie are based on low or high absorption as much as on low or high prices; of course, the two may be correlated. The monetary approach to the balance of payments under which an excess supply of money, relative to demand, spills over into imports of merchandise and exports of specie, and an excess demand into a merchandise surplus and imports of specie, may have it right for the Far East. In Europe of the sixteenth and seventeenth centuries, however, mercantilist concern for an export surplus to add to the money supply was especially strong because the bullion famine of the fifteenth century had been a consequence of luxury imports from the East that had drained the money supply (Day, 1978).

Among the forces that determined the balance of payments, then, were prices, the money supply, and, of primary concern here, spending and non-spending or hoarding. How much specie and coin were used as money, how much sought as assets for conspicuous consumption or insurance against disasters of one or another sort, and, of the money, how much was retained in the country to help circulate national income, how much spent abroad?

The suggestion that persistent surpluses and deficits can occur alongside the balancing model has some relevance to the present day with dollars (silver) pouring out of the United States (Peru, Mexico, and Spain), circulating into and out of Europe, and ending up – some going directly, to be sure – in the coffers of Japan and Taiwan (India and China). The parallel is inexact because the mining of silver in the earlier period was an economic activity based on costs and selling prices, whereas the dollars in excess supply since at least 1971 have been produced costlessly. The pattern of the world distribution of Spanish silver, therefore, is of interest both in its own right and as a cautionary tale for the United States today.

Crisis

The period from 1550 or 1600 to 1750 in Europe, and various portions of it, are widely described in the historiography in terms of "crisis". Sometimes the crisis is financial, sometimes real. The word "crisis" appears often in the title of histories: DeVries (1976) covering 1600 to 1750, with the emphasis on finance, and a book edited by Aston (1965), covering 1560 to 1660 and dealing largely with real factors, are examples. The latter contains essays by Hobsbawm and Trevor-Roper on crisis in the seventeenth century, both in real terms: Hobsbawm ascribing it to the transition from feudalism to capitalism, Trevor-Roper to the changes taking place between society at large and the emerging nation-state.

Many of the crises pointed to are local. Crisis in Venice is typically thought to have arisen after the Age of Discovery of the fifteenth century because of the diversion of trade with the East from Venice–Aleppo and Venice–Alexandria to direct trade around the Cape of Good Hope, first in Portuguese caravels and, from 1600, in the ships of the Dutch and English East India companies. An idiosyncratic view is that Venetian trade to the Levant continued for a century after 1550, and that the decline of that city-state was rather the result of British competition with Venice, not without deception, in woolen textiles and soap (Rapp, 1976). Trade depression in England in the 1620s has especially been seen in crisis terms, with a variety of not necessarily exclusive causes such as Alderman Cockayne's abortive project for forbidding the export of unfinished, undyed cloth to Holland for dyeing and finishing there, the East India Company's exports of silver to the Far East, and especially the debasement of Polish and German currencies as a result of the Thirty Years War (Gould, 1954; Supple, 1959, ch. 4). Another view suggests that part of the English crisis of 1621 may have been related to a cutoff of Dutch lending to Britain in response to the arrest and trial in Star Chamber of eighteen prominent foreign merchants – mostly Dutch – on charges of exporting £7 million in coin – a large sum for those days (Barbour, 1966, pp. 53, 123). There was occasional crisis in particular markets, as in 1619 when the short Anglo-Dutch war in Asian waters ended and both East India companies brought heavy shipments to Europe, resulting in a pepper glut. Related to the Polish and German currency debasements was a flood of copper over Europe from Sweden as it ransomed the fortress of Alvborg from the Danes in compliance with the 1613 Treaty of Knared – copper used to extend the coins of

Spain as it ran short of silver and to adulterate the outputs of Polish and east German mints in the *Kipper- und Wipperzeit* (period of clipping and debasement).

The connection between real deep-seated change and financial crisis is illustrated by the Polish and East German debasements. The grain-export boom in those countries was the consequence of the rise in populations recovering from the Black Death of 1348, and especially the rise of towns in southern and western Europe faster than agricultural output came back. In the debate between monetarist and real-forces historians, this is the explanation of the latter for the price revolution of the sixteenth century rather than the later sharp increase in silver imports from Spanish America. The comeback of agriculture in the west of Europe in the seventeenth century was critical for east Germany and Poland. The changing structure of agriculture in the west produced a crisis there as well (Ruggerio, 1964). Rice competed with wheat in Italy and Spain as maize did in France. New products of mass consumption were appearing – sugar, maize and tobacco from the New World, calico and tea, to add to the luxuries of pepper, spices, porcelain, and silk, from the Far East. A transition was under way from traditional society based on self-sufficient peasants at the bottom to a market society using money to buy mass consumption goods, not only in food but also in the new instead of the old draperies. As part of this transition, monetization increased, and hoarding decreased. The changes did not come all at once all over Europe, but at different rates in different countries. Postan and Braudel each dismiss theories based on discrete stages which follow one another in succession, for example, that of Hildebrand, postulating stages of natural economy, metallic money and credit, or materialism (self-sufficiency), market economy and capitalism. Postan (1973) and Braudel (1981; 1982; 1984) both claim they overlap. The real aspect of the crisis in Europe between 1550 and 1700 was that these changes – at different rates in different countries – were moving more rapidly.

Crises were not confined to Europe. Two recent articles on seventeenth-century Asia have the word "crisis" in their titles (Atwell, 1986; Wakeman, 1986), in one instance in quotation marks. Atwell (1986, p. 222) calls attention to the literature on crisis in Europe before asking whether there was a little ice age in the seventeenth century in the world as a whole. It is hard to see the connections.

Bullionism

There is a dispute in the literature on mercantilism whether it was largely an issue of money supply, or one of building the national state.

This need not concern us here as my interest is in the monetary aspects. There is something of a tendency today to regard the bullionist aspects of mercantilism as error, based on the failure of observers of the period to understand the self-equilibrating nature of specie movements, later recognized and elaborated by Hume. This negative judgment is being modified. It is recognized that in trading with the East, the self-balancing mechanism did not function well, if at all. In Roman times, the Mediterranean world lost gold to the Middle and Far East (Simkin, 1968, pp. 45–6), and in the late Middle Ages the drain was continuous. The Middle East is called by Ashtor (1971) a sponge economy, soaking up gold and silver. Most of the gold was produced in the Sudan until the Italians and Portuguese diverted it after the sailors of Henry the Navigator made it around Cape Bojador in 1434 to the Gold Coast (now Ghana). The silver came largely from the mines of Central Europe, shipped by Italian merchants, mostly Venetians, with some from Central Asia (Ashtor, 1971, p. 39).

Day (1978) has described the "Great Bullion Famine of the Fifteenth Century" and Vilar (1976, p. 63) explains that the basic purpose of Columbus's voyage across the Atlantic was to obtain gold, a metal that he mentioned at least sixty-five times in his diary during the passage from August 3 to October 12 1492. With metallic coinage shrinking, trade rising, and a lag in the spread of Italian methods of credit, especially bills of exchange, bullionism was not a simple fallacy, like that of misplaced concreteness. "In economies without fully developed credit institutions, central banks and fiat moneys . . . concern about a country's coinage was hardly irrational" (Munro, 1979, p. 176). Such a mercantilist as Thomas Mun, who had been a merchant in Leghorn in the 1590s before joining the East India Company on its creation in 1600, knew about bills of exchange. In a famous passage, he stated that if the exchange in Amsterdam is against London because of an unfavourable balance of trade, the East India Company could obtain guilders to buy Spanish reals in Amsterdam by contemplating the countries where England had a favourable balance, "Spain, Italy, Florence, then next to Frankfurt or Antwerp until at last I come to Amsterdam" (Mun, 1664, p. 167). Mun scorned Maynes's view that country could control its exchange rate – a thought not irrelevant to the world of today – observing:

> I have lived long in Italy where the greatest Banks and Bankers of Christendom do trade, yet I could never see nor hear, that they did, or were able to rule the price of Exchange by Confederacie but still the scarcity or plenty of mony in the course of trade did overrule them. (Ibid., p. 171)

The bill of exchange was spreading rapidly within Europe at this time. In 1585 bills on Amsterdam were traded in Antwerp, Cologne,

Danzig, Hamburg, Lisbon, Lübeck, Middleburg, Rouen, and Seville. By 1634 six more cities had been added, including Frankfurt, London, and Paris; by 1707 nine more (Sperling, 1962, p. 451). By Hume's time (the 1750s) the network had grown to resemble that of the time of Alfred Marshall more than a century later (Price, 1961, p. 273), sharply reducing the necessity for settling bilateral balances in Europe in specie, when overall trade was more or less balanced. But trade between Europe and the East was not in overall balance.

Data on specie and specie flows

I choose not to try to sort out the great variety of estimates of specie production and flows into and out of Europe as a whole, and certainly not country by country. Figures for world production of silver have been produced by Hamilton (1965), reworked and supplemented with those for gold by Vilar (1976) as shown in Table 3.1.

The rise in gold output after 1680 is because of the discoveries at that time in Brazil. After declining from its 1580–1620 highs to 1700, silver production picked up in Spanish America in the eighteenth century since output in New Spain (Mexico) rose higher than it declined in Peru.

Precious metal arrivals at Seville were given by Hamilton by decades (and converted into rixdollars, broadly equal to one piece of eight or *real*, also spelled *rial*, in Arab countries *riyal*, and the plural in French *réaux*) based on the records of the Casa de la Contratación (House of Trade). For a long time these data led to the belief that silver imports

Table 3.1 World average annual production of gold and silver, 1493–1740 (in thousands of ounces)

Period	Gold	Silver
1493–1520	186	1,500
1521–1544	230	2,900
1545–1560	274	10,000
1561–1580	220	9,600
1581–1600	237	13,500
1601–1620	274	13,600
1621–1640	267	12,700
1641–1660	282	11,800
1661–1680	298	10,800
1681–1700	346	11,000
1701–1720	412	11,400
1721–1740	613	13,900

Source: Vilar (1976, p. 351)

from the New World declined from the 1630s. Subsequent investigators have challenged this widely accepted view, noting in part that there was a break after about 1630 when the bar on the Guadalquivir River at San Lucar shifted and larger ships could not make their way to Seville, but unloaded at Cadiz twenty leagues downstream. Cargoes of precious metals were required to be transported intact overland to the Casa de la Contratación in Seville (Haring, 1918, p. 10), but they may not have been. The same was required of the occasional cargo that was unloaded in Lisbon. In addition there was smuggling, and diversion of silver directly from the *flota* to foreign merchants and their ships. Everaert (1973) and Morineau (1985) have challenged the Hamilton figures, the former for a limited number of years on the basis of French consular reports for 1670–90, the latter on the evidence of newspaper reports from 1600. The several estimates are compared by Attmann (1986) in Table 3.2. These data do not include the exports of silver from Peru via New Spain to the Philippines, by way of the Manila galleon, discussed below.

The impact of the precious metals from Spanish America on Europe will be touched upon presently. First observe that most of it was passed through to the East. Charles Wilson asserted that "On balance there seems to be little reason to doubt that over long periods of time, Europe exported at least as much silver as it received" (1967, p. 511). This con-

Table 3.2 Imports of precious metals into Spain, 1530–1700 (in millions of rixdollars per year)

Period	Hamilton (1934)	Everaert (1973)	Morineau (1985)
1531–1540	0.9		
1541–1550	1.7		
1551–1560	2.9		
1561–1570	4.1		
1571–1580	4.0		
1581–1590	8.7		
1591–1600	11.3		
1601–1610	9.1		9.1
1611–1620	8.9		9.2
1621–1630	8.5		9.7
1631–1640	5.5		9.1
1641–1650	4.2		6.9
1651–1660	1.7		7.0
1661–1670	0.9		15.5
1671–1680	1.0	13.8	13.9
1681–1690	0.4	8.2	14.0
1691–1700	0.3	12.4	14.2

Source: Attman (1986, Tables 1.1 and 1.5, pp. 14 and 18).

clusion is broadly supported by the recent estimates of Attman who also states: "The bulk of the supplies of precious metals to Spain and Portugal between 1650 and 1750 were re-exported from Europe to the East" (1986, p. 33). His data show a comparison of precious-metals production with arrivals in Europe and exports East, annual figures for selected years in Table 3.3 and exports by proximate destination, overall in Table 3.4, and by Holland in Table 3.5.

Figures for the separate flows from Europe to the East, by three streams, were estimated in an earlier work by Attman (1983), and the overall figures do not agree exactly. Table 3.4 shows yearly averages about the time of the selected years, Table 3.5 Dutch exports which accounted for somewhere between a half and two-thirds of the total.

In connection with the data on European specie exports to the Baltic (in Table 3.4) Attman insists that the figures are minimal and should not be reduced (1983, p. 12). This certainty reappears in his 1986 discussion of Morineau's work, where he accepts the figures for production but rejects Morineau's resulting estimates for the European monetary stock because Morineau "greatly underestimated the precious metal requirements of the Baltic trade" (Attman, 1986, p. 75 note).

Table 3.3 Circulation of precious metals, 1550–1800 (in millions of rixdollars per year)

Production	1550	1600	1650	1700	1750	1780	1800
In Spanish America	3	11–14	10–13	12	18–20	22	30
In Brazil (gold)	–	–	–	1	9–10	4	3
Supplies from America							
To Spain	3	10	8–9	10–12	10–15	15–20	20–25
To Portugal	–	–	–	0.5	8–10	3	2
Bullion Flow to the East	(2–3)	4.4	6	8.5	12.2	14.7	18

Source: Attman (1986, p. 33).

Table 3.4 Annual exports of precious metals from Europe to the East, 1600–1750 (in millions of rixdollars)

Proximate destination	1600	1650	1700	1750
Levant	(1)	(2)	(2)	(2)
Baltic (incl. Archangel)	1.7–2	2.2–3	2.2–3	2.2–3*
Route around Cape	1	1.7	3.3	5.7
Total	3.7–4	6–6.7	7.6–8.3	10–10.7

* Includes some balancing bills on Leipzig.

Source: Attman (1983, p. 12). The figures in parentheses are less certain.

Table 3.5 Holland's bullion exports, 1600–1780 (in millions of rixdollars)

Proximate destination	1600	1650	1700	1750	1780
The Levant	0.6	0.8	1	(1.5)	(1.5)
Baltic	2	2.5	2	2	3
Eastern Asia	0.3	0.4	2 .	3	3.5
Total	2.9	3.7	5.0	6.5	8.0

Source: Attman (1983, p. 103).

The producers

The flow of precious metals from Europe to the East via the Levant long antedates the Age of Discovery that produced the route around the Cape of Good Hope and the torrent of output in America. Roman gold coins have been discovered in abundance in India, and Pliny complained of the drain thither. Silver from central Europe and central Asia was soaked up before and during the thirteenth century by Eastern countries with a "silver famine" (Ashtor, 1971, ch. 2, quotation from p. 31). But the massive movement begins in the second half of the sixteenth century, well after Columbus, following the discovery in 1545 of Potosí (see Figure 3.1), a mountain rich in silver ore, and the surge in its output in the early 1570s with the introduction of the mercury amalgamation process and production of mercury at not-too-distant Huancavelica, discovered in 1567, eliminating the necessity to bring it from the Almaden mines in Spain (Vilar, 1976, ch. 14).

Vilar (1976, chs. 14–16) sets out a detailed account of the production of silver in Peru and Mexico, and its passage through and around Spain.

Braudel's three magisterial volumes on *Civilization and Capitalism* recur to monetary questions at various places (especially 1981, ch. 7; 1982, *passim*; 1984, pp. 413–25). It suffices here to note that Potosí produced a silver madness, the city growing from nothing in 1545 to a population of 45,000 by 1555, 120,000 by 1585, and 160,000 by 1610. There were 700–800 criminals, 120 white prostitutes, 14 gambling houses, and 14 dance halls. The city spent 8 million pesos to celebrate the succession to the throne in 1556 of Philip II. Indian labour was virtually enslaved. Imported goods were expensive and importing merchants rich. The population was "inordinately given to luxury and display, and recklessly extravagant", and the "heart of the Indies, leading a riotous career of indulgence for which the stream of silver from the *Cerro* furnished abundant means . . ." "A city of feverish life, called by a Portuguese by reason of its riches the most fortunate and happiest of cities" (Schurz, 1939, pp. 365–6).

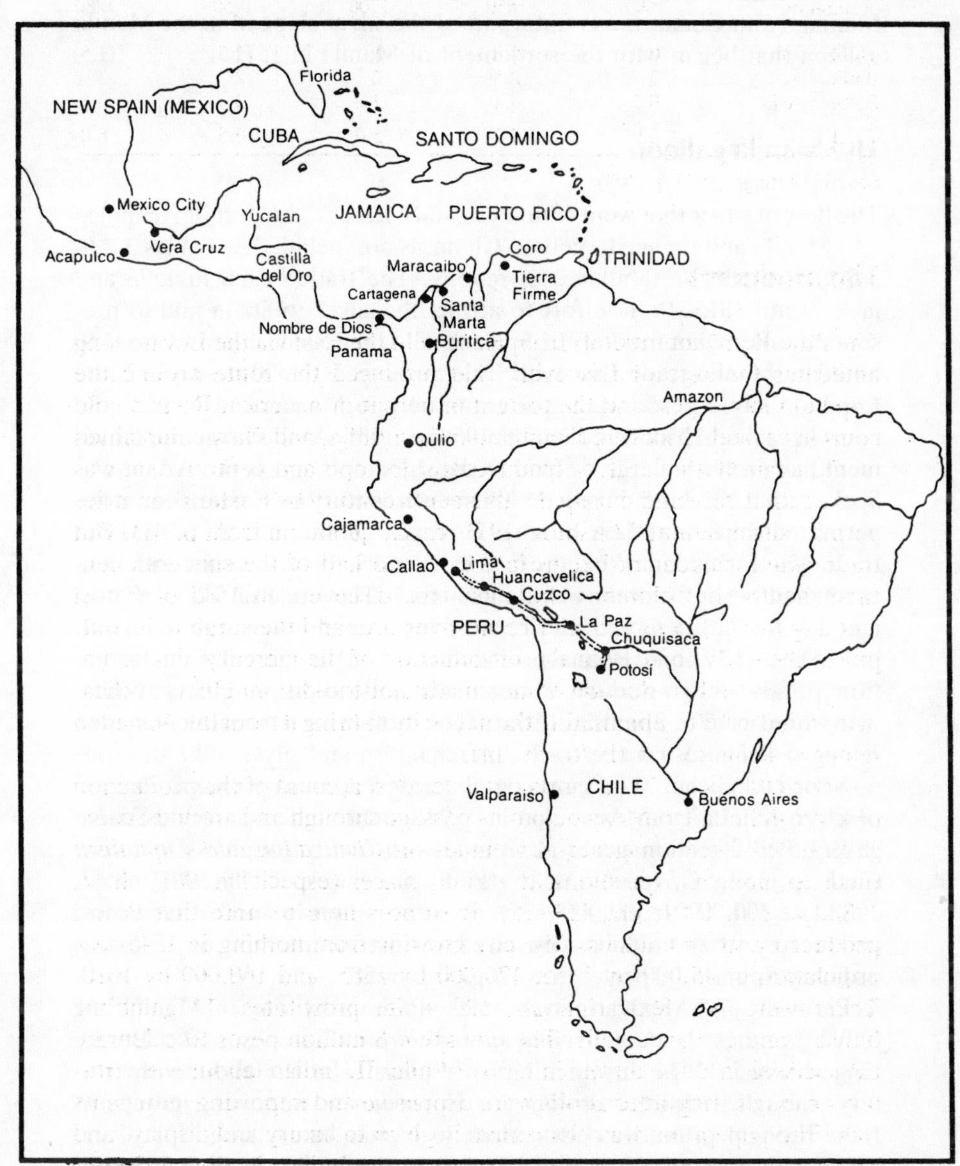

Figure 3.1 Spanish America in the sixteenth and seventeenth centuries

Peru produced little except silver, and imported most of its consumption goods, either in a trickle from Spain, transported from the Atlantic to the Pacific across the Isthmus, or from Mexico and via Mexico and Manila, from China, the counterpart of the silver shipped in the Manila galleon that began with the settlement of Manila in 1571.

The Manila galleon

The flow of silver that went from Peru and Mexico – the port of Acapulco – to Manila and thence largely to China, is not included in Tables 3.2 to 3.5 and cannot be tabulated as readily. The trade began in 1573 and lasted until 1815. In an effort to attract the silver to Spain and to preserve the Peruvian market for Spanish silks, the Spanish crown tried to limit the Manila trade, but with little success. By 1590 between 2 and 3 million silver pesos were going annually to Manila and in 1597 the figures reached 12 million (Borah, 1954, p. 123). At this stage the movement had grown so large – equal to the shipments across the Atlantic to Spain – that the king increased his measures to stop it. The size of the permitted ships, and their number each year, were limited. In 1631 the trade was forbidden altogether, provisionally for five years and then permanently, but success was small (ibid.). The trade lasted in all two and a half centuries, with the regulations a dead letter (Schurz, 1939, p. 185). In 1770 one Boana provided a list of six irregularities in the form of false oaths, perjury, excess loads, and violations of silver limits, with bribes paid to Spanish officials. The motive for concealment was so strong that figures on the trade, merchandise and silver alike, are impossible to believe. Wild rumours abounded. One ship took 2,791,632 pesos to Manila from Acapulco in 1794, and a contemporary estimate gave 1.5 to 2 million pesos per vessel with one to four vessels a year (ibid., p. 189). Governors of the Philippines were said in 1767 to accumulate 300,000 to 500,000 pesos above expenses in four or five years, and merchants and officials conspired to frustrate attempts of the extraordinary Spanish inspectors investigating fraud.

Peruvian and Mexican silver reached China by way of Manila not only by Chinese traders arriving annually from Canton in junks. Beginning slowly in 1644 and picking up especially in the eighteenth century, though with interruptions for European wars, several groups in India brought primarily cotton cloth to Manila to exchange for silver. This "country trade," as it was called to distinguish it from bilateral trade with England, was conducted originally by Company servants, then by English free merchants, Armenians resident in India and finally by the East India Company itself. It is not completely clear from the detailed study of the trade how much of the silver was brought back to Madras, the main seat of the business after the British had been driven out of Bantam by the Dutch, and how much was taken to Canton to be exchanged for such goods as silk, tea, and porcelain for Europe. But it has been estimated under assumptions that in the first half of the eighteenth century 45 percent of the silver reaching Madras, which received approximately half of the East India Company's silver shipment to India as a whole, came from Manila (Quiason, 1966, pp. 75–6). Quiason estimates that the total flow from Manila to China exceeded that to India, but it unable to break it down as between Chinese junks, on the one hand, and the "country trade", on the other. In the first half of the eighteenth century, the total flow from Manila to China greatly exceeded that to China direct from England, but by the middle of the century the two amounts were approximately equal. The "country trade" with Manila came to an end, however, in 1762 when the British captured Manila, killing the goose that laid the silver eggs.

It is not clear from accounts whether Peru was short of money as Spain was, as we shall see, and as was New Spain (Mexico). Mexico was drained of its pesos by the exactions of Madrid, which claimed a large share of mining, state monopolies and state taxes not spent in the colonies (Borah, 1954, p. 83). In addition, Mexican groups complained that the Peruvians bought too much of Spanish and Mexican wares in Mexico City, making goods as well as money scarce (ibid., p. 120). Potosí and Lima were famous for their imports of luxury goods from China via Manila and Acapulco – silks, porcelain, lacquer ware, precious stones and pearls. Imports into Lima from China may have reached 2 million pesos regularly and, in the peak year 1602, 5 million (ibid., p. 123). Mexican merchants made substantial profits from this trade, pouring from Mexico City over the "China Road" to Acapulco when the Manila galleon arrived (Schurz, 1939, p. 381). By no means all goods were sold to Peru. All classes in Mexico wore fabrics of the Far East – cottons of Luzon, silks of China, calicos of India – and both men and women in the early seventeenth century were extravagant in their apparel, for example, wearing a hatband of diamonds in a gentleman's hat, and one of pearls in that of a tradesman. Millions of pesos of gold, silver, pearls, and jewels could be seen in jewelry shops (ibid., pp. 362–3). Attempts to control the quantities and flow of trade were futile as corruption and venality abounded in Mexico, Peru, and Manila (ibid., *passim*, but especially pp. 136, 173, 176, 184–7, 194, 204, 369). Charles V is quoted as having said that it was easier to keep the Flemish from drinking than the Spaniards from stealing (ibid., p. 399). The Manila galleon belongs to the story at the absorbing end, especially China, but our major concern is with the flow around the world counterclockwise.

Spain

Despite smuggling and privateers most silver from America shipped in the *flotas* arrived in Seville and Cadiz. It did not stay long. It remained long enough, however, to produce disaster. A Spaniard in 1650 discussed the ruin brought about by inflation in these terms:

> the possession and abundance of such wealth altered everything. Agriculture laid down the plough, clothed itself in silk and exchanging the workbench for the saddle, went out to parade up and down the streets. The arts disdained mechanical tools . . . Goods became proud, and when gold and silver fell in esteem, they raised their prices. (Quoted in Vilar, 1976, pp. 168–89)

Spain suffered from an acute case of what is known today as the "Dutch disease," in which brilliant success in one activity (silver) raises wages to the point where they stifle the rest of the economy (Forsyth and Nicholas, 1983).

The Habsburgs were forced to rely completely on foreigners in supplying the colonies: five-sixths of the outbound cargoes in the sixteenth century were supplied by foreigners (Haring, 1918, p. 113). In 1702 Cadiz, with a monopoly of Spanish overseas commerce, had 84 commercial houses of which 12 were Spanish, 26 Genoan, 11 French, 10 English, 7 from Hamburg, and 18 Dutch and Flemish. At the end of the eighteenth century, 8,734 foreigners were resident in Cadiz, 5,018 Italian, 2,701 French, 272 English, 277 German and Flemish, etc. (Dornic, 1955, p. 85). Spanish manufacturing had been virtually destroyed, and an immense amount of linens came to Cadiz, a turning table for Europe and the Spanish colonies, from France, Flanders, Holland, and Germany (ibid., pp. 83, 86). Da Silva comments that in Spain as a whole, merchants dominated producers and financiers dominated merchants (1969, pp. 607, 620). The internal trading network was weak as interior bills of exchange were prohibited because of usury. Seville could not count on credit facilities to provision the fleet going to the colonies, and Aragon and Castile found it difficult in consequence to export. Indeed exchanges between Seville and Castile required shipment of gold to the north (ibid., pp. 604, 605). Transport in mountainous Castile was difficult enough; financiers, both domestic and foreign, turned their attention to the market for silver and financial transactions, largely abroad (ibid., p. 620).

One industry flourished: silversmithing. In Seville this was the highest class of artisans, along with pharmacists, and some smiths were rich. In her discussion of Seville society, Ruth Pike mentions silversmiths numerous times, either as individuals of wealth, or members of the upper class (1972, pp. 132, 137, 139, 141, 143, 145, 146, 147). Silversmithing presumably took place elsewhere in Spain on a sumptuous scale. The Duke of Alva of Toledo, who had served as captain general of the Spanish forces in the Netherlands, and again in the court of Philip II in Madrid, a man without a reputation for wealth, on his death in 1582 left 600 dozen silver plates and 800 silver platters (Braudel, 1981, p. 463).

But most of the silver shipped to Spain from America was diverted elsewhere in Europe or passed quickly through. The Spanish tried to restrain the hemorrhaging, but without success. "Scarcely has it come than it disappears." "When a fleet comes in from the Indies with much money, within a month there is no good money to be found for it is all exported in different ways" (quoted by Vilar, 1976, p. 166). Spain ended the seventeenth century relying mainly on *billon*, a compound largely of copper.

The silver left Spain by many routes. Some was paid out immediately to requite bills of exchange drawn on local banks or on foreign representatives for goods delivered to Seville or Cadiz. This might be shipped north to Amsterdam or London; or ships of the East India Company or the Dutch counterpart, the Verenigde Oostindische Compagnie (United East India Company or VOC), would stop at Cadiz to pick up silver for carrying to India and what is now Indonesia (Chaudhuri, 1978, p. 171). A large portion of the silver, however, was required to pay the *asientos* drawn by the Spanish government on German or Genoese banks, or by suppliers of the Spanish troops in Flanders on the Spanish government, to pay the troops fighting in the Spanish Netherlands, and for arming ships of war to fight against France, England, and in the Mediterranean. The problem of the troops in Flanders was particularly exigent. If the troops were not paid they would mutiny or desert as they were largely mercenaries. Spanish soldiers were regarded as superb fighters but as a rule they made up only five or six thousand at a time of armies that reached 84,000 men in 1574 and 300,000 in 1625. The rest were hired in the Spanish Netherlands, Italy and especially Germany (Parker, 1972, pp. 6, 42). Mutinies occurred 45 times between 1572 and 1607, and the more violent of them resulted in the sack of towns (ibid., p. 185).

Asientos were of two types, Spanish and Flemish. The Spanish were negotiated by the Council of Finance in Madrid, though handled at Medina del Campo outside Seville, with businessmen who contracted to provide local funds at given times in foreign places, typically Paris, Lyons, Savoy, Frankfurt or the Genoan fairs of "Besançon" (in Italian transliteration Bizenzone), which for the most part meant Piacenza outside Genoa. Flemish *asientos* originated with the Spanish troops in Flanders when the king's governors or captain generals obtained local moneys, often from German bankers such as the Fuggers and Welsers, against payment in Spain. *Asientos* usually included a license to export silver from Spain (Lapeyre, 1953, pp. 18–19). The silver might be shipped for Spanish account from Barcelona to Genoa, converted into gold and transported via the "Spanish Road" from Piedmont to Savoy, Franche Comté and north through Lorraine to Flanders (Parker, 1972, p. 59). Much of the silver went to Flanders by sea – the so-called "English Road" – from Cadiz to Dover to Flanders, except during outbreaks of war between Spain and England (Attman, 1986, p. 59). Simon Ruiz, the Spanish banker, had a brother in Nantes in France and shipped silver to Flanders through that city and Paris under safe conducts granted by the French with the proviso that one-third of the coin be left in France (Lapeyre, 1953, p. 25). Sometimes silver was used to buy Netherlands currency from the Portuguese, who obtained it with pepper.

The war lasted 80 years, with fighting building up and dying down. In 1572, it cost 1,200,000 florins a month while the Spanish were able to provide only 7,200,000 in all of 1572 and 1573, so that by July 1576 the troops were owed 17,500,000 florins. In September 1575 Philip II declared himself bankrupt, cancelled all licenses to export silver and paid off the *asientos* in *juros*, long-term bonds denominated in reals. By August 1576 the entire army had dissolved in mutiny and desertion (Parker, 1972, pp. 136–7). A more far-reaching bankruptcy occurred in 1596 when the king, attempting to repair his finances, signed *asientos* for a total of 4 million ecus, 280,000 a month, but was unable to make good. He revoked licenses for exporting specie on all earlier *asientos*, and took over revenues that had been assigned as surety to creditors. The pinch in Flanders was so tight that it was said that the captain general did not have enough money for lunch. This was the crisis that crippled the Fuggers of Augsburg and caused the collapse of Genoan credit (Lapeyre, 1953, ch. 4). In due course the debts were settled with the liberal use of *juros* and the resumption of payments in silver arriving from America. There were later royal Spanish bankruptcies in 1607, 1627, 1647, and 1653, with more *asientos* converted forcibly into *juros*. Spain fought long, hard and losing battles with the aid of American silver, but it did not retain it as money.

David Hume thought that there was a sort of inevitability about Spain's inability to hold on to its silver:

> Can one imagine, that it had ever been possible by any laws, or even any art of industry, to have kept all the money in SPAIN, which the galleons had brought from the INDIES? Or that all the commodities would be sold in FRANCE for a tenth of the price they would yield on the other side of the PYRENEES, without finding their way thither and draining from that

> immense treasure? What other reasons, indeed, why all nations, at present, gain in their trade with SPAIN and PORTUGAL; but because it is impossible to heap up money, more than any other fluid, beyond its proper level. (1752, p. 335)

The hydraulic metaphor had other uses, however. An English merchant of Thomas Mun's time, expressing the general concern for the loss of specie to the East, said "Many streams run thither [India], as all rivers to the sea, and there stay" (quoted by Thomas, 1926, p. 8). And Mun himself anticipated Hume's conclusion, if not his rhetoric, in giving Chapter 4 of *England's Treasure by Forraign Trade* the sub-title "The Spanish Treasure cannot be kept from other Kingdoms by any prohibition made in Spain" (1664).

European demand

In his well-known "Digression Concerning the Variation in the Value of Silver," Adam Smith observes that the demand for silver has two components. As wealth increases, the demand for silver as coin increases in order to circulate a greater quantity of commodities. And wealth also leads to the acquisition of more plate, from vanity and ostentation, "like statues, pictures and every other luxury and curiosity" (Smith, 1937, p. 188). Smith elsewhere distinguishes between goods the value of which derives from "use and necessity" and those based on "fashion and fancy" (ibid., pp. 114–15). The demand for precious metals comes partly from utility and partly from their beauty. A silver boiler, for example, is cleaner than one of lead, but the principal merit of silver is beauty, which renders it particularly fit for the ornaments of dress and furniture (ibid., p. 172).

The matter is more complex. Precious metals may be hoarded not for ostentation and display but as insurance, in which case they are often hidden. "In . . . Asia [there is an] almost universal custom of concealing treasures in the bowels of the earth, of which knowledge dies with the person . . ." (ibid., p. 208). Ostentation and insurance can be complements rather than substitutes, as in the case of silver and gold plate, capable of being coined, and war chests may be thought of as insurance if needed for defence, or ostentation if preparatory to conquest. Thomas Mun, a mercantilist and anti-bullionist, thought some national treasure – "by forraign trade" in a country without mines like England – was necessary, but observed that it should not be entirely in bullion. *England's Treasure* should consist not only of specie but also of

> ships of war with all provisions . . . Forts . . . Corn in Granaries of each province . . . and Gunpowder, Brimstone, saltpeter, shot, Ordnance,

> Musquets, Swords, Pikes, Armours, Horses, and in many other such like Provisions fitting War. (1664, p. 188)

The Northern monarchs – Gustavus Vasa, Ivan the Terrible, Charles XI, Frederick William I, for instance – were not so sophisticated but were "hoarders of a type that was disappearing in countries that were advanced economically (Aström 1962, p. 84).

This brings us to the central issue, whether the traditional view that hoarding in India and China was a reflection of financial lack of sophistication or whether their use of precious metals was much the same as that in Europe (see Figure 3.2 for a political map of Europe at this time). Observe that practice in Europe differed widely. In discussing Indian hoarding, Keynes adverts to hoarding in Europe. Of India he says:

> India, as we all know, already wastes far too high a proportion of her resources in the needless accumulation of precious metals. Government . . . ought to counteract an uncivilized and wasteful habit. (1924, p. 99).

Then he states further on:

> There is no one now living in England within whose memory hoarding has been a normal thing. But in countries where the tradition is but lately dead or still lingers, it is apt to revive with astonishing vitality at the least sign of danger. France, Germany and especially Austria during the Balkan wars . . . very remarkable. If this is still the case in Europe, there can not be much doubt as to what would happen in India. (Ibid., p. 165)

These remarks relate to the early part of the twentieth century. In commenting on France, Wicksell refers to the *bas de laine* (woolen stocking) in which the peasant stores gold coins, and went on to quote a witness to the British Gold and Silver Commission of 1887 who thought it remarkable that a hotel owner in southern France with a turnover of a million francs annually would point to his safe, where gold coins were kept, and say "That's my bank." He compared this with the father of Alexander Pope who was said to have retired two hundred years earlier with £20,000 in gold and silver coins which he drew for spending money for the rest of his life (1935, p. 9).

Hobsbawm underlines the fact that, even in the nineteenth century, the French peasant, whether rich or just well-to-do, did not use much money, forming "an uninviting market for mass manufactures". Their wants were traditional. Wealth went into land and cattle, or into hoards, or new buildings, or even into "sheer waste like those gargantuan weddings, funerals and other feasts which disturbed continental princes at the turn of the sixteenth century" (1965, p. 26). Robert Forster, a historian of French families in the eighteenth century, records widely varied attitudes toward money and its use. One command in 1736 was

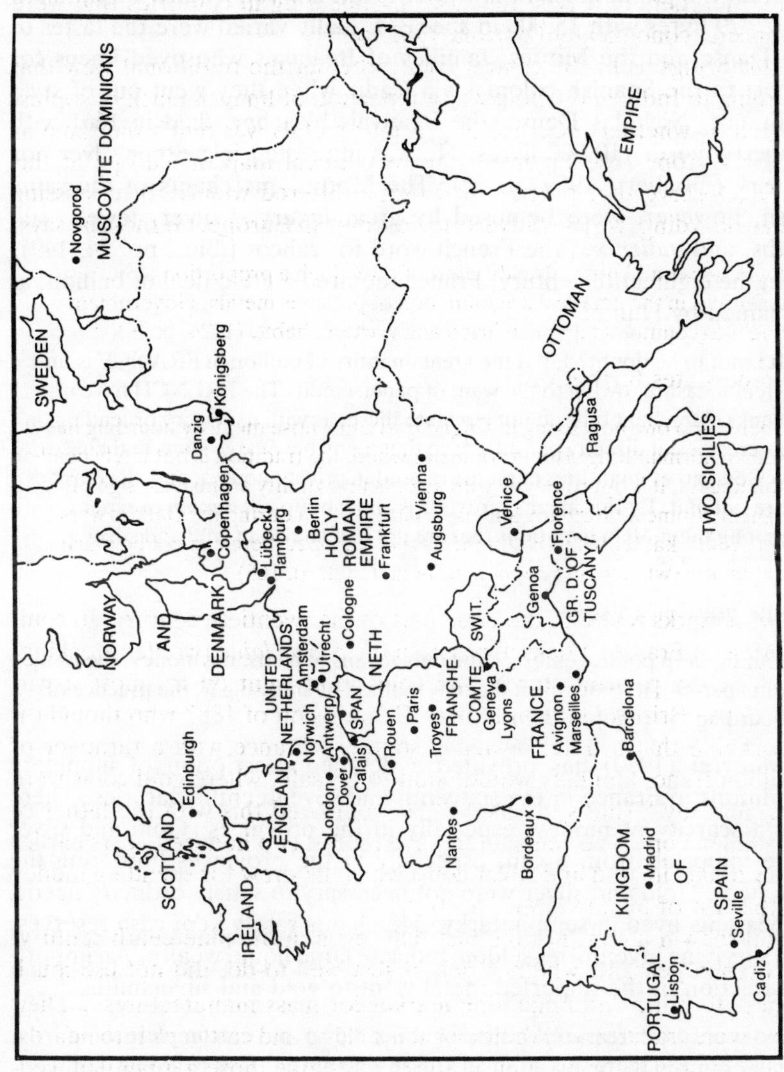

Figure 3.2 Early modern Europe

for sale for 160,000 livres, 60,000 in coin (1971, p. 33); the Marquis de Tesse left 500,000 in cash (*argent comptant*) (ibid., p. 52). On the other hand, the father-in-law of one of the Deponts who died in 1766 left an estate of 653,040 livres, only 1,436 in specie (Forster, 1980, p. 114) whereas the grandfather-in-law in 1748 left an estate which was audited at 42,429 livres with 15,000 in specie. Equally varied were the tastes of the Danse and the Mottes, families of Beauvais who dyed linens for export to the Spanish colonies via Cadiz when they went out of style in France. Nicholas Danse, the Beauvais bleacher, died in 1661 with property worth 110,000 livres. He was interested in neither silver nor jewelry (Goubert, 1959, p. 52). The Mottes, merchants of the same town, however, were bemused by great luxury – silver, jewels, silk cloths, and *indiennes*, the French word for calicos (ibid., pp. 34, 149).

In the eighteenth century, France required a great deal of bullion, as explained by Hume:

> It is not to be doubted, but the great quantity of bullion in FRANCE is, in great measure, owing to the want of paper-credit. The FRENCH have no banks: Merchant bills do not circulate there, as with us: Usury or lending on interest is not directly permitted; so that many have large sums in their coffers; great quantities of plate are used in private houses; and all churches are full of it. By this means, provisions and labour still remain cheaper among them, than in nations that are not half so rich in gold and silver. (1752, p. 338)

Hume goes on to say:

> Our modern politics embrace the only means of banishing money, the using of paper-credit; they reject the only method of amassing it, the practice of hoarding . . . (ibid., p. 343)

Meuvret (1970) has provided a detailed description of monetary conditions in France in the sixteenth and seventeenth centuries. There was a scarcity of money, especially in the provinces. Gold and silver were imported from Spain, especially in the provinces bordering the Pyrenees. Gold and silver were not necessary to satisfy ordinary needs, as peasants lived in semi-autarky. Merchants rarely kept cash reserves, and surviving inventories seldom indicate large liquid wealth. An important fraction of the imported metal went to gold and silversmiths.

> No councillor, treasurer, bishop or abbot did not have a complete set of plate . . . and there was no small artisan who did not seek to have a basin, ewer and cup, or at least a salt cellar and half a dozen spoons.

To this was added a large quantity of precious metals in the chalices, vases, chandeliers, crosses, rods and crucifixes, lamps and reliquaries of churches. This was not totally withdrawn from commercial life as it could be borrowed on and was sometimes melted down on the order of some Huguenot or government official (Meuvret, 1970, *passim*, especially pp. 144–6).

The amount of specie hoarded in a country relative to that which circulated as money is most uncertain, although the ratio probably varied negatively with the state of development. In 1751, Ferdinando Galiani estimated that the hoards of Naples amounted to four times the value of money in circulation. In quoting this observation, Braudel remarks that Naples at the time had a relatively unsophisticated economy (1981, p. 467).

The two most sophisticated economies in Europe were the Dutch and the British, in that order. The British agonized under the currency disturbances of the early seventeenth century; the Dutch did something about them. Supple (1959, p. 178) records the case of one young man leaving college in 1620, unable to sell his furniture because of a shortage of silver, i.e., of money of the appropriate denomination, since the furniture was worth more than copper, less than gold. Legislation limited how much silver the newly founded East India Company could take with it to the East; proclamations forbade the melting, culling or exporting of gold and silver coin. In 1622 a Commission was appointed on abuse of the exchanges, and a lively debate ensued, the origins of which had gone back to the middle of the sixteenth century. Mun was more sophisticated than many of the participants, winning Misselden to his point of view, and scoring over Gerald Malynes who wanted an official exchanger appointed to monopolize all exchange dealings (Wilson, 1967, p. 504). It was in this connection that Mun expressed his views against Confederacie quoted earlier. Mun's basic contention was that shipping specie east brought back goods that could be sold with great profit in Europe and earn more than the original investment in specie. Wilson calls this argument "using a sprat to catch a mackerel" and claims that it did not apply to the specie shipped by the Eastland corporation to buy timber in Norway, since this was rarely re-exported (1949, pp. 154, 155). Other imports from Asia were sold throughout Europe, some even in Italian ports such as Leghorn in competition with the Mediterranean trade to the Levant. Mun insisted that specie was simply one of Britain's commodities. If it were prohibited, the Dutch would take over the trade, charge Britain monopoly prices and cause her to lose bullion in any event (Chaudhuri 1965, pp. 112–13).

For a time, the East India Company paid its dividends in kind, letting its shareholders dispose of pepper, nutmeg, cloves, calico, etc. (ibid., pp. 142ff.). This was stopped in the 1620s, perhaps as a result of the pepper glut of 1619 that followed peace between the Dutch and English in the East.

The nagging worry about loss of specie continued. The Company made continuous attempts to provide British goods to the East but found little demand for its woolens, tin, lead from Britain, or for other products bought in Europe or Africa, such as iron, coral, ivory, and mercury. In due course it learned to engage in triangular trade, in considerable part within the East, taking calicos against silver from Surat on the west coast of India to Bantam to be exchanged for pepper and spices for Europe. There is a variety of estimates of the proportion of goods and specie in the eastward voyages. In the first twenty-three years of the East India Company's operations, bullion made up 75 percent (ibid., Table III, p. 115). Another estimate gives 80 to 90 percent of imports from Asia paid in gold and silver coins (DeVries, 1976, p. 135). It was mostly silver as the price of silver relative to gold was higher in the East than in Europe or America. Silver was bought everywhere it was available, not only in Lisbon, Cadiz, and Seville, as already mentioned, but in smaller ports such as Saint Malo, Calais and Rouen (ibid., p. 126). For the most part, however, it was acquired in Amsterdam.

Amsterdam's sophistication was shown in its responses to the currency debasement in Europe at the beginning of the sixteenth century: it created deposit banks in Amsterdam in 1609, which was followed by similar institutions in Middelburg in 1616 and Hamburg in Germany in 1619 – and then two more in the United Provinces of Holland, Delft in 1621 and Rotterdam in 1635 (Van Dillen, 1934; Sieveking, 1934). Small states, as Adam Smith had noted in a digression on banks of deposit (1937, pp. 446–55), have to use the coin of neighbouring states, and that circumstance, together with the presence of worn or clipped coins, furnished an opportunity for the formation of banks of deposit, to weigh and assay deposits of coin and give receipts for them which, with assured weight and fineness, lowered transactions costs for merchants. Amsterdam had a huge supply of silver, including Spanish reals, bullion, and Dutch minted coins, the total accumulated in its flourishing trade since the collapse of Antwerp in 1585 when the Dutch Navy blockaded the Scheldt. The imperious Spanish demand for goods meant that the Dutch brought to Spain and the Mediterranean the grain, timber products, and naval stores of the Baltic and Norway. In addition, it accumulated silver in the Low Countries by selling herring, cheese, butter, and all sorts of English, German, and French manufactures to the rebels against Spanish authority (Attman, 1983, pp. 31–2). During the Spanish–Dutch truce from 1609 to 1621, silver shipments took place direct. After the Coddington treaty between Britain and Spain, the English road came into play. The peace of Munster in 1648 left Holland free to buy silver not only in Lisbon, which ceased to be part of the Spanish empire in 1640, but also in Seville and Cadiz.

Amsterdam had abundant trade, abundant money and an open market. Attman records that about 1683 the Dutch mintmasters coined the equivalent of 15–18 million guilders, and 13 million of them were exported. By 1699 Dutch opinion favoured freedom of export as well as import for precious metals (1983, pp. 27–8). The point relates to the export of domestic coins, in contrast to foreign coins and bullion. The practice, however, went further back in the century. And in reaching the view that markets for precious metals and all coins should be free, Thomas Mun seems to have been, in the 1620s, well in advance of the Dutch as a whole.

Peace in Europe did not last long. England depended on Holland for the success of its trade but was fiercely rivalrous. In particular, it resented Dutch monopolies in shipping and fishing for herring. The first Navigation Act was passed in 1651 to restrict British cargoes to British ships. Three Anglo-Dutch wars ensued, in 1652–4, 1665–7 and 1672–4. None of these, so far as it has been borne in on my consciousness, had a major effect on world trade in specie.

The three streams

In a memorandum submitted to the English Commission established in 1621 to devise means of coping with the drain of silver, Sir John Wolstenholme, a one-time member of the East India Company's Court of Committees, stated that there were three streams leading east for silver – one by Aleppo for raw silk, one by Mocha in the Red Sea for calicos, and one by Surat and the islands for indigo, pepper, cloves, mace, and nutmeg (Chaudhuri, 1965, p. 120). This is the view of an East Indian merchant (that inadequately takes the Baltic trade into account).

If the focus is on American silver, moreover, there was the stream westward across the Pacific of the Manila galleon. Leaving the last aside, however, but including the Baltic, the streams can be collapsed into three by dividing the trade of Mocha and Ormuz in the Red Sea and Persian Gulf, depending on whether their trade comes around the Cape of Good Hope or north by caravan to Aleppo or Alexandria. It is perhaps anachronistic to take up the Baltic trade ahead of those of the Levant and the Cape route. I do so for geographic reasons, moving gradually eastward.

The Baltic

A number of scholarly debates have sprung up over the need, as seen by the Eastland Company, to export specie to buy imports from the

Baltic countries and Norway. First, it has been held that while bilateral Baltic–British trade needed to be balanced by specie, this was because of the absence of trade in bills of exchange; if they had been available, it might well have been that Britain's import surplus was matched by a Dutch export surplus and that trade could have been balanced all around with adequate financial institutions. This turns out not to have been the case (Heckscher, 1935; 1950; Wilson, 1949; 1951). Wilson (1951) has shown that the Dutch, too, had an import surplus through the Sound, i.e., by sea, in the seventeenth century. In the late eighteenth century, Dutch earnings on invisible transactions covered its negative merchandise balance, and the French accounts were also in surplus. The British deficit remained substantial, however, and outweighed the combined Dutch and French surpluses. As a consequence, bullion continued to flow to the East (Johansen, 1986, p. 140). Direct bilateral estimates of British trade with Scandinavia may be understated, however, on account of exports by sea to Hamburg, by land to Lübeck, and again by sea to Denmark and Norway. It was estimated by the English Hamburg Company in 1737 that its annual sales of woolens to Denmark and Norway by this route were, at between £60,000 and £70,000 a year, of the same order of magnitude as those direct (Thomsen and Thomas, 1966, about p. 60).

The question arose in the earlier period whether the Baltic countries had a large import surplus with Europe by land, large enough to balance the seaborne export surplus with the two major trading companies. Evidence exists of jewelry imports from Leipzig by Eastern nobles, and some imports in the middle of the eighteenth century were paid for with bills drawn on Amsterdam (Jeannin, 1982, p. 18). But the major overland export was livestock, of an amount broadly equal to the export of grain from Poland, Lithuania and East Germany, and in the same direction. Trade of these regions with Western Europe was not thus balanced (ibid., p. 20).

An exception should be noted for Norway, although there is some disagreement. General histories suggest that Norway was traditional in the Hobsbawm sense quoted earlier, importing little in consumption goods, and using the precious-metal proceeds of exports partly as "silver plate and other imported luxuries for want of alternative outlets. Travellers frequently commented on the quality of the houses and furnishings of shipbuilders and merchants" (Milward and Saul, 1973, p. 519). In the sixteenth-century weddings, "We are told how 'the bride was dressed in brown velvet, magnificently arrayed in a crown, and many gold chains around her throat, shoulders and elbows; she had gold chains hanging down toward the ground . . .'" (Larsen, 1948, p. 264).

This view was disputed by Heckscher, insisting that the Baltic was not India (1950, p. 226) and by Scandinavian scholars in recent research covering the timber trade between Norway and England for the period 1640–1710 (Tveite, 1961) and Anglo-Danish trade from 1661 to 1963, for the first part of which, down to the Napoleonic Wars, Norway was part of Denmark (Thomsen and Thomas, 1966). Each study has an English summary, which is all that I can read, although Dr Thomsen was kind enough to translate several pages of her main text commenting on Dr Tveite's study.

Both studies emphasize the large balance-of-payments deficit of England with Norway because of timber imports and their freight, but point to the fact that bullion imports into Norway were supplemented as early as 1630 and commonly from 1660 by bills of exchange drawn in Norway which were discounted in Copenhagen and returned for payment in London via Hamburg or Amsterdam (Tveite, 1961, p. 576). Precious metals continued to be sent in the form of English coins which became the usual means of payment in southern Norway from the middle of the seventeenth century (Thomsen and Thomas, 1966, p. 60). Such coin continued to serve as Norwegian money in the manner described by Adam Smith, already noted, and in 1751 a Norwegian tax collector said he was unable to collect taxes in Norwegian money because merchants paid their workers and creditors in English coin, a practice legalized in 1758 (ibid.).

A Danish student of the Norwegian timber trade, Ole Feldbaek, has privately told me his impression that the notion that Norwegians imported a lot of specie and used it in conspicuous consumption and insurance, in so far as jewelry displays in weddings had such a component, is probably mistaken. In the early trade, with timber cut in south Norway near the water's edge, merchants imported foodstuffs which were traded against timber. As cutting took place further from the ports, and involved cutters away from the sea and specialized haulers, the Norwegian economy had to become both specialized and monetized, and most of the imported specie served this latter purpose. Taxes were paid in money, and the net flow to Copenhagen was partly passed back to Lübeck, Hamburg, and Britain in a loop that did not go continuously east and remain there.

Sweden seems to have been another country that stood aside from the preoccupation with precious metals. For one thing, Sweden's money was initially largely copper, though some silver circulated from time to time when not driven by Gresham's Law. The Stora Kopperberg (copper mountain) at Falun produced half the copper in Europe around 1690, and the awkwardness of the metal as money led the country to issue the first paper money in Europe and to establish the first central bank. The scattered character of the iron and timber industries sustained the natural economy with wages paid in kind longer than elsewhere in Europe. Large inward and outward payments for invisibles took place in the balance of payments – war-tolls collected in Prussia until halted by the Thirty Years War; "feverish" borrowings against the collateral of copper to pay ransom or for conduct of war on the Continent; remittance of profits of the many foreign entrepreneurs in the country, of whom the best known was the ironmaster from Liège, Louis de Geer, transplanted to Amsterdam. The Heckscher account observes that Sweden was only mildly mercantilistic in the period 1600–1720, and gives no indication of preoccupation with gold and silver either for monetary purposes or for ostentation (1954, ch. 4).

Elsewhere in the Baltic, including that honorary Baltic port, Archangel, the precious metals featured prominently. East Germany, Poland, Lithuania, and Russia exported to the West especially grain and timber, grown by peasants on huge noble estates, and brought to the ports down broad rivers that provided cheap transport. Table 3.6 gives an estimate of the export surplus at Danzig and Elbing for median years of decades from the 1560s to the 1640s. The export surplus of the area as measured by this portion of it was variable in response to blockades, wars and bad harvests, but it was on the whole continuous. The question is what happened to the specie counterpart (Maczak, 1974, p. 507).

The important point to bear in mind in this area – I judge from a limited amount of reading – is the skewness of income distribution. The peasants that grew the grain and cut the timber were in effect serfs, while the nobles and the merchants that exploited them were "extremely rich". In a contiguous passage, Braudel claims that prices were dictated from Amsterdam – which seems unlikely – and that the Danzig

Table 3.6 Export Surplus at Danzig and Elbing, 1565–1646 (in thousands of rixdollars)

1565	1,336.5
1575	392.5
1585	82.2
1595	361.7
1605	−277.4
1615	298.0*
1625	−449.0
1635	559.9
1646	−1.1

* Includes land trade.

Source: Maczak (1970, p. 139).

merchants manipulated the magnates by advancing them downpayments on wheat and rye (1984, pp. 254–6). On the land, yields were low but surpluses were obtained "mostly at the expense of peasant consumption" (Bogucka, 1980, p. 7), what are sometimes called "hunger exports".

Some specie was drained to the Middle East through Lwów, or to buy silks, furs, carpets, and jewels from Venice, Leipzig, or Vienna, as well as wines, and Dutch and English cloth through the Sound. The movement of "ready money" (a term for coins of gold or silver) drained to Constantinople was so heavy that robbers in the mountains trimmed their hats with English "nobles" (Maczak, 1976, p. 17). Polish nobles spent heavily on grand tours to the West, and their "greedy and hungry retainers" also lived high, with much more magnificence than servants in Italy and Spain, according to a 1650 remark (ibid., pp. 77, 83). In 1601 Chancellor Zamoyski took 31 sacks of coins, worth 6,000 ducats, on his travels, half his ready money (ibid., p. 80). Precious metals of all kinds were a sign of prestige, still used in the rather medieval way, which, in the West, was slowly giving way to a more economical lifestyle (ibid., p. 82).

How much was spent in the West on luxury goods and travel, how much was drained away to the East in payment for its exotic merchandise, and how much displayed or hoarded at home, the scholar experts on the subject fail to guess. Bogucka twice says that hoarding needs further study (1975, p. 148; 1980, p. 16). In the 1980 paper she says "it seems to have played an enormous role". The crisis of the 1650s and 1660s, she asserts, struck its worst blow at the nobility, which had been accustomed to a lavish lifestyle. The rapid rise in the price of gold (from the depreciation of the currency) cut down the nobles' purchases of cloth, furs, imported wine and fruit from the South, increased the cost of adornment, jewelry, plates, and fancy goods, and reduced the opportunities for hoarding. She quotes one Gostkowski, a nobleman:

> If a nobleman needs to buy anything in silver or gold for himself or his children, such as a jewel, spoon, an inlaid sword or some article of clothing, he now has to cut twice as much corn as he had a few years ago. (Bogucka, 1975, p. 145).

The attitude clashes sharply with that of a nineteenth-century English economist who said:

> No one can feel much commiseration for the richer classes of the community when their expenditure presses inconveniently close to their income. A footman, a horse, a ball or a shooting excursion retrenched during the year will restore the balance without inflicting very great hardship . . . but the poor . . . (Jevons, 1884, p. 93)

It is further observed that the poor burghers and even the peasants tried to lock away valuable ornaments, sometimes a little of the old small coin that was sought after (Bogucka, 1975, p. 148). One is not entitled to a guess, but I gather the impression that of the specie paid to East Germany, Poland, and Lithuania – and doubtless there were differences among them and among different periods – some fraction, perhaps a fifth each, went circulating back to the West, went circulating forward to the East, and stayed in domestic circulation over the long haul, while perhaps two fifths went into hoards.

The Middle East

The further east he goes, the deeper the writer's ignorance, and I venture to say anything at all merely to try to sketch the picture as a whole and to encourage experts to correct and fill it out.

The flow of gold and silver from Europe to the Middle East against luxuries brought to the shore of the Mediterranean by caravan produced the great European bullion famine of the fifteenth century, as noted earlier. But the Middle East itself was said to have experienced a scarcity of precious metals as a regular matter, especially after the wave of silver looted from central and Southern Asia produced by the Muslim conquest of those areas. Gold from the Sudan went regularly to the Middle East as Moslem converts made their pilgrimages to Mecca until the ships of Henry the Navigator penetrated south in the Atlantic to acquire it for Portugal and Christendom from the Gold Coast. This diversion, according to one conjecture, may have dealt a severe blow to the Ottoman Empire of Turkey, Syria, and Egypt (Ashtor, 1971, p. 13).

There was ostentation and display. The sultans sought to win recognition with lavish gifts (Walz, 1983, p. 311; Ashtor, 1971, pp. 100–3). Tribute was paid by Egypt to Istanbul, 600,000 gold coins annually in the sixteenth century, and by Syria, 450,000 ducats each year of which 300,000 came from Aleppo. Tribute was equivalent to taxation and also to protection money (Steensgaard, 1973, pp. 41, 178). But more damaging to the circulation of precious metals as coin, says Ashtor (1971) for the fifteenth century, was hoarding. The *mus-dara* was a contribution arbitrarily levied on the wealthy, especially high dignitaries from time to time to tax away fortunes amassed legally or with fraud. (The practice was widespread in seventeenth- and eighteenth-century France, where it was known as the *Lit de Justice*, in England after the collapse of the South Sea bubble, and even in twentieth-century Argentina, where specialized tribunals were established to tax away "undue enrichment" under the Perón administration.) The threat of such confiscation and pillage that took place frequently led to burying large quantities of gold and silver, jewelry, precious stones, and objects of great value. Ashtor comments that this tendency was more harmful in reducing the quantity of money available for circulation and investment than wasteful spending (1971, pp. 103–5).

In the period of our interest, a substantial movement occurred in silver further east, and some small amount of gold to the West, not as arbitrage but because of the greater profit available by spending the cheaper metal in each direction. Transactions costs were so high, with worn coin, losses, heavy transport charges, and commissions to money changers, that arbitrage in the modern sense was impossible (Munro, 1983, p. 111). The silver going east was used in what Steensgaard calls "the glorious peddling trade" (1973, pp. 47, 196) or "the magnificent but insignificant [peddling] trade" (ibid., p. 205). This was the shipment by camel of silver and some goods to the Indian Ocean by way of Aleppo, Baghdad and Basra to Ormuz on the Persian Gulf, or Alexandria to Mocha on the Red Sea. From Ormuz and Mocha the Gujarati, later the Portuguese, and – after the fall of Ormuz in 1632 – the British and Dutch exchanged calicos, and spices, especially pepper, for silver and Arabian coffee. Some Chinese silks were also brought to the caravan trade, but further loads consisted of Persian silks. It was initially thought that the Portuguese transport of pepper to Europe around the Cape would ruin the Venice–Aleppo and Venice–Alexandria trade, but it survived another century. The decline of the Ottoman Empire was only in part owing to the gradual shift to the sea route, according to Bernard Lewis (quoted by Steensgaard, 1973, p. 78). Other contributing factors were the closing of the European frontier, the price revolution and depreciation of Turkish money, and the shift of the army from feudal cavalry, who contributed their services on the basis of loyalty, to mercenaries who had to be paid. Some part of the decay may be attributable to the neglect of Middle East navies and shipping. Gradually the Moslems stopped importing timber, iron and pitch from Venice, and let their fleets and shipbuilding decay. An Arab soldier who died in 1406 said that in his day the Moslems no longer knew how to build ships (Ashtor, 1976, p. 577). In addition, the taxing authorities in Constantinople tried to raise their returns. Cheap silver killed the Balkan mines of the Empire after 1580 (Richards, 1983, p. 17; Sahillioglu, 1983, p. 284). Ottoman monetary liquidity was offset by an unspecified amount of hoarding (Steensgaard, 1973, pp. 80, 113), but for a great part the Middle East was a stage in the path of silver to the east, and some gold in the opposite direction.

India and China – levels and distribution of income

India and China are thought of as poor today. Such has not always been the case. In the third quarter of the eighteenth century, they were considered rich. Hume wrote:

> China is represented as one of the most flourishing empires in the world; though it has little commerce beyond its borders. (1752, p. 296).

However:

> The skill and ingenuity of EUROPE in general [surpass] perhaps that of CHINA, with regard, to manual arts and manufactures; yet we are never able to trade thither without grave disadvantage. (Ibid., p. 334)

The difficulty lies in the monopolies of the India companies and the distance.

> Nor can any reasonable man doubt but that that industrious nation, were they as near to us as POLAND or BARBARY would drain us of our overplus of specie, and draw to themselves a larger share of WEST INDIAN treasure. (Ibid.)

Adam Smith is equally emphatic:

> China has long been one of the richest, that is, one of the most fertile, most industrious, and most populous countries in the world. (1937, p. 71).

And again:

> China is a much richer country than any part of Europe and the difference between the price of subsistence in China and in Europe is very great . . . In China, a country much richer than any part of Europe, the value of the precious metals is much higher than in any part of Europe. (Ibid., pp. 189, 238)

There are traces of Malthusian doctrine and a belief in the backward-bending supply curve:

> In rich countries, which generally yield two, or sometimes three crops a year, each of them more plentiful than any common crop of corn, the abundance of food must be greater than in any corn country of equal extent. Such countries are accordingly more populous. In them too, the rich, having a greater super-abundance of food to dispose of beyond what they themselves can consume, have the means of purchasing a much greater quantity of the labour of other people. The retinue of a grandee in China or Indostan accordingly is . . . more numerous and splendid than that of the richest subjects in Europe . . . and the same super-abundance of food . . . enables them to give a greater quantity of it for all those singular and rare productions which nature furnishes in very small quantities; such as the precious metals and the precious stones, the great objects of the competition of the rich. (Ibid., p. 205)

The poor, however, are hungry, suffering

> low wages of labour, . . . and the difficulty which a labourer finds in bringing up a family in China. If by digging in the ground all day, he can get what will purchase a small quantity of rice in the evening, he is contented . . . The poverty of the lower ranks of people in China far surpasses that of the most beggarly nations in Europe . . . The subsistence is so scanty that they are eager to fish up the nastiest garbage thrown overboard from any European ship . . . [In] Bengal and . . . some other English settlements in the East Indies . . . three or four hundred thousand people die of hunger in one year. (Ibid., pp. 72–3)

Daniel Defoe, writing half a century earlier in 1728, ascribed the "incredibly cheap manufactures" of China, India, and other Far Eastern countries to the poverty of the labourers:

> The people who make all these fine works are to the last Degree miserable, their Labour is of no Value, their Wages would frighten us to talk of it, and their way of Living raises a horror in us to think of it. (Quoted in Heckscher, 1935, II, p. 171)

Paul Bairoch has estimated that the Third World including Asia was as rich on the average as developed countries in 1750 – about 180 1960 dollars per capita – but in private correspondence grants that averages are not very meaningful when distributions are highly skewed.

India

After the caravans that brought Asian goods to the Levant via Mocha or Ormuz, direct Indian trade with Europe began in the sixteenth century with Portuguese caravels and was followed in the seventeenth with the East India Company of Britain and the United East India Company of Holland. Each chose different modes of operation and different bases (see Figure 3.3). Portugal traded to Goa on the west Indian coast, Ormuz in the Persian Gulf, Malacca in the Straits, and Macao in China. Portugal lost Ormuz in 1632 and Malacca was overtaken about the same time by the Dutch headquarters in Batavia and the British Indonesian centre in Bantam, both trading to Canton in China. In addition to the silver the Portuguese brought from the Iberian peninsula, their ships exchanged Chinese silks for Japanese silver from about 1540 to the 1630s, bringing the silver to Macao, Malacca, and India until the Japanese cut them off because of their attempts to convert the Japanese to Catholicism. Thereafter the Dutch continued to obtain Japanese silver against silks from Canton until 1668 when Japan banned the export of silver for monetary reasons (Yamamura and Kamiki, 1983, pp. 348–50). The

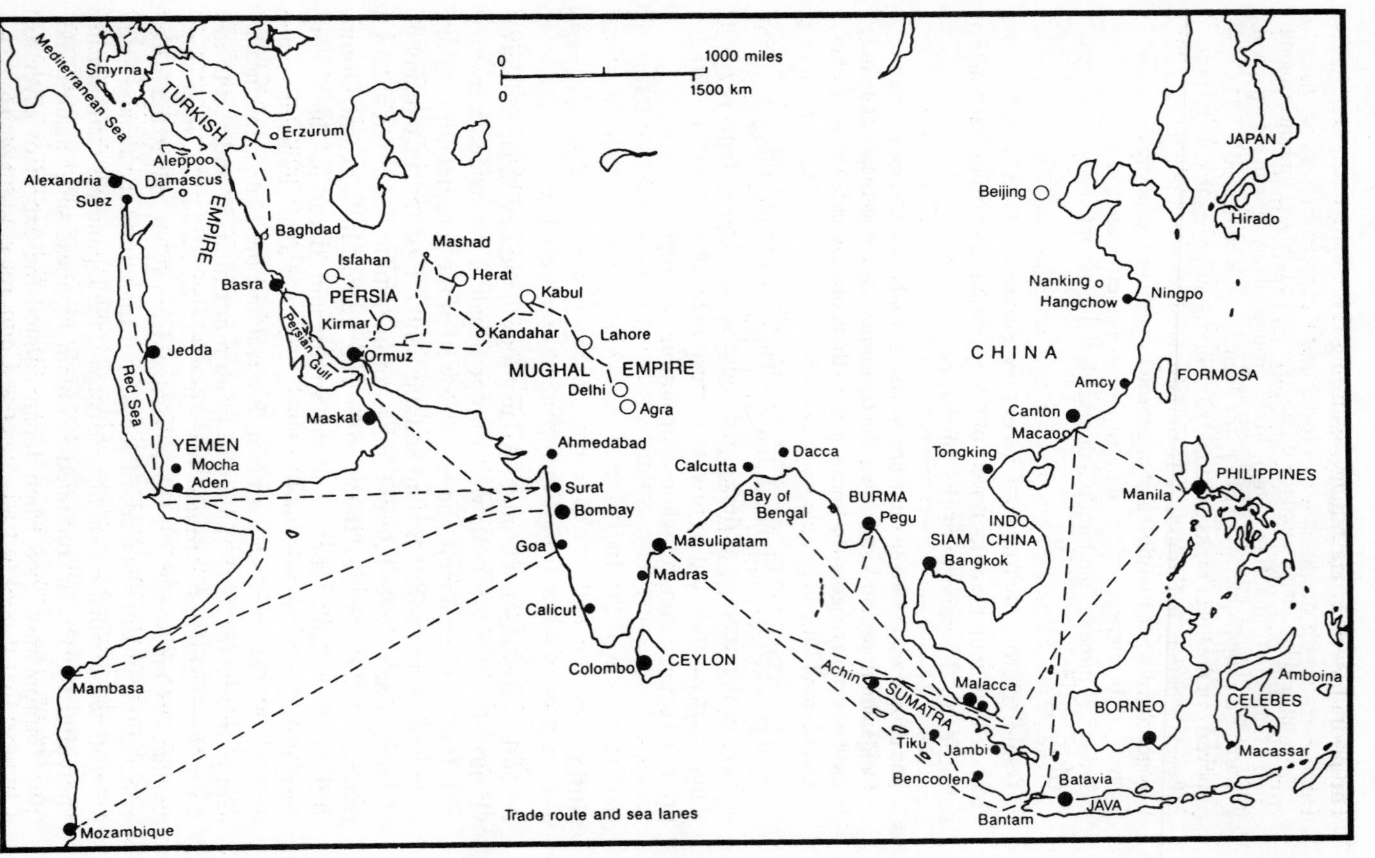

Figure 3.3 Early modern Asia

British had stopped trading in Japan in 1623. Portuguese, Dutch, and English traders brought silver to India and China from Europe directly, from the Red Sea and the Persian Gulf, and from Japan. The importance of the local trade, in which the servants of the East India company traded privately as well, is underlined in a famous 1619 statement by Jan Pieterszoon Coen, the governor-general of the Dutch East India Company (VOC) in Batavia:

> Our wishes we have often repeated before: many ships, good warships, good return ships, medium-size ships for the intra-Asian trade . . . Once we obtain them we can not only procure gold for the Coromandel Coast but also rials for the pepper trade the silver for trade with China without it being necessary to send the bullion from home, but the supplies from the Netherlands must on no account be stopped immediately . . .
>
> Piece goods from Gujarat we can barter for pepper and gold on the coast of Sumatra, rials and cottons from the coast for pepper in Bantam, sandalwood, pepper and rials we can barter for Chinese goods and Chinese gold; we can extract silver from Japan with Chinese goods . . . And all of it can be done without any money from the Netherlands and with ships alone. We have the most important spices already. What is missing then: Nothing else but ships and a little water to prime the pump . . . (By this I mean sufficient money so that the rich Asian trade can be established.) (Quoted in Steensgaard, 1973, pp. 406–7)

European ships had the advantage over the dhows of the Arabs, small sailing vessels of the Indians and the Chinese junks in that they were more seaworthy and carried larger cargoes. But the prospect of cutting off the flow of silver from Europe failed to materialize.

The silver had to keep coming partly because not enough profit could be earned in the intra-Asian trade in competition with local merchants and seamen, and partly because neither the Indians nor the Chinese wanted European goods. The East India Company at least, and presumably the VOC as well, consistently tried to load English woolens for India, but was unable to sell them. There was an initial demand for woolen cloth as a novelty, serving some great men as covering for their elephants or as blankets under their horses' saddles (Chaudhuri, 1965, p. 137). Some tin, lead, ivory from Africa, cowrie shells from the Maldive Islands in the Indian Ocean, and the like could be used, but the limit was low, and silver was needed. When silver from any source was traded against gold, the gold was not shipped home, not because of the high rate of interest and the length of the voyage, as Chaudhuri (1973, p. 181) claims – the interest charges would be the same on gold or merchandise of the same value – but because the profit on Asian luxuries in Europe was higher. The silver/gold ratio was consistently higher in India than in China so that it paid to trade silver to China for gold for India.

Why was there no demand for European goods in India? Some put the explanation in terms of the self-sufficiency of the economy in necessities, and the greater expense of luxuries from Europe as opposed to those available locally (Richards, 1983, p. 183). The same explanation is given of the Chinese lack of interest in imports by one Sir Robert Hart, writing in 1901:

> The Chinese possess the best food in the world, rice; the best drink, tea, and the best clothing, of cotton, silk, furs. Provided with these articles and their innumerable indigenous complements, they have no need to buy for a penny outside themselves. (Quoted by Dermigny, 1964, II, p. 685; see also III, ch. iii, discussing the Chinese lack of need for European products. Simkin, 1968, p. 252, also quotes Hart, noting he might well have added the best pottery.)

In India it was said that the Europeans were surprised to find that the supply of native produce dried up when they raised the prices they were willing to pay, testifying to the presence of a backward-bending supply curve, derived from "satisficing," working to a target income, presumably at the level of subsistence, and being uninterested in maximizing levels of living (Rich, 1967, p. xxiii). This explanation is vigorously denied by Chaudhuri who asserts that it is difficult to accept the hypothesis of an income elasticity of demand for real income of zero (1978, p. 156). The more general view, called "traditional" by Richards (1983, p. 183), is the Indian penchant for hoarding, each generation putting coins down a hole in the ground, well or cistern, not counted, it not being known how much was down in what Smith called "the bowels of the earth". In addition there was the Indian "excessive liking for gold and silver and jewelry" (Richards, 1983, p. 184). Chaudhuri chafes at this, saying that it is hard to accept the argument of an income elasticity of demand for hoarding greater than one (1978, p. 156), although the elasticity of demand for all luxuries is greater than one (by definition). Chaudhuri wants to explain the demand for silver and gold in terms of the need for money – a transactions demand, and a demand for assets, in the absence of alternatives, just as in England (1978). Another scholar who attacks the hoarding thesis is Frank Perlin. He admits that there was an insatiable market for silver, but insists that it was needed for monetization as proto-industrialization – that is, cottage industry organized by merchants – spread through the countryside and required the use of money. Along with cottage industrial workers, peasants in western Deccan in south India participated in fairly frequent if low-level monetary transactions (Perlin, 1983, section vi, especially pp. 68, 73, 75).

Richards has written of the Muslim attack on India from 1000 to 1400 and its plundering of Indian treasure under four Moslem sultans, who looted temples, demanded ransom for captives, instituted payment of tribute, and the like, taking it north and west in one stream, and later in another to Delhi. The amounts of gold and silver were enormous (1983, pp. 186ff.). Later the Emperor Akbar (1572–1607) accumulated a large hoard of precious metals (Brennig, 1983, p. 492), and a sudden drop in the price of gold relative to silver in 1676 was rumored to be the result of a sudden dispersion of the ancestoral gold hoards of the Emperor Auraazeb (1659–1707) who needed money to finance campaigns in western India and Afghanistan (Chaudhuri, 1978, p. 178). This interpretation is disputed by Habib (1982, p. 369), who states that the collapse of the gold price in 1676 (in terms of silver) was the consequence of large imports of Japanese gold, shipped to India by the Dutch. It is worthy of note in the quotation from Jan Pieterzoon Coen on p. xx above that gold was wanted for the Coromandel coast (in India) and silver for trade with China.

It is clearly the case on the reading of the evidence that after 1600 silver was minted into coins in Surat, and used as money as well as hoarded. Jean-Baptiste Tavernier, a French jeweller who travelled in India in the seventeenth century, observes, however, that gold was not coined but sold directly to jewelers (Habib, 1982, p. 365). One Asiza Hasan, whose study I have not seen, working from numismatic finds, concludes that all the silver arriving in India was coined into rupees, and that it tracks closely, with a five- to ten-year lag, the pattern of Hamilton's estimates of American silver arriving in Spain (Habib, 1982). Not all was used as money within India, although monetization was pursued, farm rentals were converted to money payments, and after an initial period when rupees circulated mostly within cities (Brennig, 1983, p. 482) they spread. But Habib's attempts to measure the increase in the Indian money stock based on strong assumptions about all silver arriving being coined and circulated, and no change in the earlier absolute amount of hoarded silver, estimated in 1571 as two-thirds of the total, seem overstated. There was undoubtedly some hoarding of the rupees passed northward along the caravan trail to Agra where the calicos were woven. Perlin states that silver and gold found ready markets in India, silver in the north, gold in the south (1986, p. 1044). There was also a substantial movement of rupees, often recoined when they reached their destination, to Southeast Asia to buy local spices, especially pepper, and Chinese silks, porcelain, and later tea.

The rankest of amateurs is persuaded of the Indian propensity to hoard from the experience of the twentieth century. The appetite for precious metals goes back, as earlier noted, to Roman times, and it comes down to the present day. A *New York Times* article of January 18, 1988 (p. D6) discusses the wedding season and the jewelry expected to adorn many of the 10 to 20 million brides of the season, the 150 to 200 tons of gold smuggled into the country each year from abroad, the 7,000 tons believed to be hoarded in the country. A 1982 study of the world gold position gives a figure of 3,500 tons hoarded in India as of 1968 and well over 4,000 tons at the time of writing (International Gold Corporation Ltd., 1982, p. 15). The report observes that while most of the Indian hoards consist of old jewelry, smuggled exports and imports respond to changes in the outside price so that Indian net demand tends to stabilize the world price (see also *The Economist*, April 30, 1988, p. 85).

Earlier in the century, when the price of gold was raised in the United States from $20.67 an ounce to $35, in 1934 a billion and a half dollars worth of gold poured out of India and China according to Graham and Whittlesey (1939, p. 16). They considered that India was unlikely again to hoard in significant amounts, adding: "If, in these circumstances, the natives of India increase their holdings materially they will not only be failing to show their alleged shrewdness but will be acting against all tradition and common sense" (ibid., p. 125). It is not clear that gold hoarding in India is contrary to tradition there, but as for common sense a United Press International story in the *Boston Globe* of January 31, 1988, discussing a wave of gold buying following a nine-month decline in the stock market in 1987 that reduced the values of portfolios by 25 percent, used expressions like "gold fever," "an age-old lust," "a crazy buying spree," and "madness." One jeweler noted that in India "Gold is considered sacred and auspicious" (*sic*) (*Boston Globe*, February 28, 1988, p. A19). The newspaper account notes that at $29 a gram, equivalent to $812 an ounce, the price of gold in India was 40 percent above the world price, which had recently been $480 in New York (ibid.). The wedge in this instance, of course, was the result of a government ban on private imports of gold, and the need for a large premium to cover the risks involved in smuggling.

Given this fascination with gold, it is hard to accept the experts' opinion – those of Chaudhuri, Perlin, and Richards – that India did not have a strong propensity for hoarding gold, but needed silver imports to use as money, given the spread of small-scale industries and the need for money to pay rents and taxes. The reason is that gold was not used as money in India, money being confined initially to cowrie shells, and then to copper and silver. Much – how much? – of the silver was exported further east to Indonesia against spices, and to China in exchange for gold. The only use of gold in India was ostentation, insurance against a bad monsoon, and for hoarding.

Chaudhuri's most recent statement renews the attack on an Eastern propensity to hoard:

> The huge influx of gold and silver from the New World to Europe from the sixteenth century to the nineteenth was seen by many European historians as one of the fundamental determinants of economic expenditures. But the outflow of the same precious metals to the Middle East, India and China in the paths of an ancient trans-continental trade, we are told, owed its explanation to a totally different reasoning, an eastern psychology which assigned a higher value to stored wealth than to current material consumption. The point has been made many times, by myself and others, that the absorption of gold and silver by the Asian economies in the early modern period had little to do with a "hoarding" social mentality but was grounded on an international pattern of economic specialization, on payments mechanisms, and socially determined demand which had existed for at least a millennium. (1986, pp. 64–5)

The payments mechanism cannot, of course, be said to have produced India's taste for gold over a millennium, especially as gold was not used as money, and monetization of silver to replace cowrie shells is not a thousand years old. Secondly, the pattern of economic specialization and the socially determined demand are consistent with a propensity to hoard. Apart from monetization, the utility produced by gold and silver lies in its possession, rather than in its use and being used up as food, clothing, raw materials. Other objects similar to gold and silver play roles in international trade, for example, paintings. Indian purchases of gold constitute investment, rather than consumption, and it is difficult to accept the argument of the experts that the East is no different from the West when, with millions of poor people, it trades consumption goods – albeit luxuries – against investment goods.

Hoarding in modern times has been studied analytically for Southeast Asia by P.J. Drake who explains it as a transitional stage in very poor countries between saving in real forms such as stores of goods and land, and saving through financial institutions (1980, pp. 124–8). It is thought to be small as a flow, but large as a stock, and the stock further serves to balance consumption cyclically by being borrowed against in bad times. Charles Gamba lists the propensity to hoard first among twelve factors affecting inability to spend and save, following inadequate earnings (1958, p. 35). He notes different hoarding practices – Eastern Indonesians in hollow bamboos, hidden in the walls of houses or buried in the ground; Chinese in Southeast Asia mostly in gold ornaments; rural Indians, particularly the Tamils from Madras, in buried earthenware pots, in the form of gold ornaments and diamonds – and observes the contribution to hoarding of the Muslim prohibition of taking interest on savings (ibid., p. 38). Drake's general discussion of hoarding under the rubric of "informal finance" notes that it gives psychic income, especially when it takes the form of jewelry and ornaments, an attribute of durable consumer goods not obtainable from other stores of value (1980, p. 127). This aspect of hoarding, of course, is not confined to poor villages, in which 90 percent of the people of Asia live, but applies to both rich in poor countries, and some rich countries as a whole.

I end this section with a diversionary aside to note that in Gunnar Myrdal's three-volume work on Asian development, there is no discussion of specie imports, hoarding, or monetization, issues which might have been thought connected with Myrdal's interest in development. He dealt, however, with real rather than with financial factors (1968).

China

The frequent mention of China by Adam Smith and David Hume underlines Heckscher's remark that China to the eighteenth century was idealized as the Netherlands had been earlier, and as China is, to some extent, idealized today (Heckscher, 1935, I, p. 352). A modern historian observes that there was an "India Craze" in the 1680s and 1690s (Brennig, 1983, p. 481). Heckscher says that China was an economic utopia. It was, moreover, full of contradictions, having a disdain of foreign trade based on Confucian philosophy (Richards, 1983, p. 378; Smith, 1776, p. 462, p. 644), but sending its merchants to Manila and the Dutch East Indies to obtain above all else silver. In one view, part of the avidity for silver, at least initially, stemmed from the collapse of its paper money in the second half of the fourteenth century when the silver to gold ratio went from 10:1 to 4:1 between 1346 and 1375 (Atwell, 1982, p. 83; letter of September 15, 1987, and seminar at Harvard University, October 5, 1987). An expert has hypothesized that the movement of silver into the Middle East from Central Asia in the second half of the thirteenth century may have been the result of the introduction of paper money into China (Ashtor, 1971, p. 39).

If both these explanations have merit, a substantial outflow of specie from China during the expansion of paper money, and a return flow when the paper money had collapsed, would constitute a pattern, stretched out over time, such as that followed later in France at the beginning of the French Revolution. The revolution and especially the events leading up to the Terror in 1793 produced a strong outflow of capital that piled up specie in England and contributed substantially to the British canal mania of 1792, whereas the collapse of the *assignats* in 1795 led to an imperious need for money in France. This was so strong that it induced a return flow of specie that depleted the reserves of the Bank of England and led to abandonment of convertibility of sterling in 1797 with the run precipitated by the landing of a handful of Frenchmen on English soil at Fishguard (Hawtrey, 1919, ch. xv). The demand for money continued in the Ming (1368–1644) and Ch'ing (1644–1911) dynasties, and took the form of silver perhaps because of an inbred distrust of paper substitutes, but the experience is unlikely to have dominated Chinese attitudes three centuries later.

Chinese preoccupation with silver does seem paranoid to a Westerner. Atwell puts it in terms that are non-economic: "Foreign silver was so important to the Chinese economy that merchants would do almost anything to procure it" (1982, p. 69). One can find a few traces in the literature of Chinese exports of silver to Japan and to Southeast Asia (Yamamura and Kamiki, 1983, p. 341; Simkin, 1968, p. 98, referring to the period from AD 999 to the twelfth century; Prakash, 1986, p. 84, referring to the sixteenth century; Meilink-Roeloesz, 1962, pp. 40, 168). They were ready to export gold which was not money and they exported money in the form of cash – copper coins, holed, and strung on string – to Japan and the East Indies, "vast quantities" to Bantam, for example (Meilink-Roeloesz, 1962, p. 248). Chinese merchants trading to Manila wanted only silver, and those to Southeast Asia, mostly silver, along with a few spices, sandalwood, an aromatic material available in quantity in Timor and used for ointments, perfumes and especially in cremation ceremonies and sacrifices (ibid., p. 87). Some clockworks were brought from Europe as toys; furs, first from Russia and then the United States, and in the early nineteenth century opium. Another import was rhinoceros horns, an aphrodisiac (Simkin, 1968, p. 98). Silver was clearly money – although it was not minted by the Chinese, but rather used in little "shoes" or "loaves" that could be cut to produce wanted amounts. In due course, the Mexican peso circulated as money, in contrast to Smith's dictum that large countries did not use foreign money. Somewhere between 150 and 500 million dollars flowed into the country between 1700 and 1826 (Wang, 1972, p. 364). Wakeman comments that China drew as much as 20 percent of all silver mined in Spanish America via the Manila galleon, other silver through Central Asian trade at Bokara, as much as half of the silver coming from Spain, plus substantial amounts from Japan. In all, he suggests that at least 250,000 to 265,000 kilograms of silver were imported in the first third of the seventeenth century, and probably much more (1986, p. 3). The amount from Japan to China is estimated at over 112,500 kilograms between 1640 and 1772 (Yamamura and Kamiki, 1983, p. 350).

What needs to be explained is why the silver stops when it comes to China. In other proximate destinations – the Baltic, Levant, India – some is used as money, some as conspicuous consumption or insurance hoards, but some is passed on. China is the end of the line. Not until the opium period of early nineteenth century was silver exported in large amounts, $140 millions from 1827 to 1849 according to Yu-Chien-chi'ung, following a net inflow of $75 millions in 1801–26, and followed by net imports equivalent to $360 millions from 1871 to 1931, as estimated by Charles F. Remer (both quoted by Wang, 1972, pp. 365–6). It would appear that silver was as addictive as opium.

There was lavish use of silver but also of gold, pearls, and precious stones at the court, first in Nanking and after 1421 in Beijing. The emperors ran enormous establishments: 3,000 court ladies, and 20,000 eunuchs (Wakeman, 1986, pp. 10, 11), 5,000 servants in the kitchen alone, and 70,000 overall at the end of the Ming dynasty, most employed in the capital, serving lavish meals on gold and silver vessels, with great banquets four to six times a year (Mote, 1977, pp. 212–13, 220, 243). The court gave gratifications and received presents and tribute. Marco Polo noted that the Great Khan rewarded his captains with fine silver plate, fine jewels of gold, silver, pearls, and precious stones: the officer who was a captain of 100 received a tablet of silver, a captain of 1,000 a tablet of gold or silver gilt, and a captain of 10,000 a tablet of gold with a lion's head on it (Yule, 1903, I, p. 351). On New Year's Day the Great Khan held a festival in which the direction of giving was reversed: from the people who showed him allegiance came "great presents of gold and silver and pearls and gems and rich textiles of all kinds" (ibid., p. 394). Gold and silver came to China regularly from Vietnam in tribute, in the shape of gold men, golden gongs, a gold turtle weighing 90 ounces, silver cranes, etc. (Whitmore, 1983, *passim*, but especially pp. 375–8). Atwell comments that wealth poured into public coffers after the middle of the sixteenth century, leading to imperial extravagances of monumental proportions, illustrated by the weddings and investiture ceremonies of the five sons of Emperor Wan-li costing 450,000 kilograms of silver. This behaviour was emulated by others so that conspicuous consumption became a hallmark of the late Ming period (1986, p. 227). At the same time some poor were starving under the pressure of taxes and labour-service obligations (ibid., p. 228) while others were executed for tax delinquency and anti-government activities (ibid., p. 244 note).

It is hard in the light of this admittedly spotty and anecdotal evidence to share the conclusion of the experts that the Chinese appetite for silver was dominated by monetization and that the notion that the Chinese hoarded more than other countries is questionable (Atwell, 1982, p. 88 note 75). Monetization was important, especially in taxation. Taxes were originally levied in rice, then in paper money, then bolts of cloth, and finally silver (Wakeman, 1986, p. 9). The Imperial Treasury collected its taxes in "silver chests" (Reischauer and Fairbank, 1958, p. 340). Land taxes, labour-service obligations and extra levies were also commuted into silver payments – not exactly monetization since, as already noted, the silver was dealt in as bullion in tael. Taxes were oppressive. The Ming dynasty raised taxes seven times between 1618 and 1636, drawing silver from the economy directly, and increasing the hoarding of warlords (Atwell, 1982, p. 88).

China covers an enormous span of land, and the economies of different areas differed, especially in a monetary sense. The south supplied most of the export products – silk, tea, porcelain, and most of the industrial goods sold internally. The north collected silver in taxes and contributions mainly from the south, spent silver there, and remitted silver south as the private income of officials; local transactions were conducted with cash. The far west was relatively unaffected by monetary changes, but dealt in silver bullion and cash (Wang, 1977, pp. 483–90).

Much of the demand for silver arose from the increase in population from 100–150 million in 1644 to more than 400 million by 1850, along with the commutation of real to money payments. Daily expenses were made in cash, rather than silver, although the use of Spanish dollars started in Canton at the end of the seventeenth century and spread north along the coast. But considerable hoarding must have gone on fairly continuously. Banks had to provide private armies to guard silver shipments (Fairbank *et al.*, 1965, p. 98). Disorder would seem to have been pandemic, and contributed to substantial hoarding. Hoarding is mentioned by Wang, who notes that "a certain percentage [of silver] was channelled into the arts and industry, hoarded or buried under the ground for safekeeping," but offers no guess as to what that percentage was (1977, p. 474).

It would be plausible to believe that the Chinese passion for silver (and the Indian for gold) were no different than those in Europe, except for the fact that the silver seldom left China, and then mainly in payment for the addictive substance, opium, or esoteric items such as spices, incense, and sandalwood.

A final contemporary fact that may or may not be related to a Chinese hoarding phenomenon: the *Boston Globe* reported that in the first few months of 1988, Taiwan bought 186 tons of gold from the United States, worth approximately $600 million, leading a New York commentator to call the country "a major sponge for gold, literally absorbing more gold than is available" (May 23, 1988, pp. A6–7). A traditional Midas complex may not account for the purchases: the metal bought was gold, not silver; it was bought for official, not private account, and it may reflect primarily an attempt to cut down the statistical size of the Taiwanese export surplus by recording the purchases as commodity imports. It may none the less be worth mention.

Gold/silver ratio

Much of the literature on precious metals is devoted to the ratio of the price of silver relative to gold. This is not a particular interest in this discussion, which is directed more to the high deficits settled in silver at one end of the chain and its hoarding or disappearance at the other. A few figures gathered from the handiest sources – largely from a single book on precious metals in the later medieval and early modern world (Richards, 1983) – are useful, however, in illuminating some features of the problem (see Table 3.7). The dates selected from those available in tables by separate authors, covering different periods, are guided on those in the table for China. The drop in the ratio after 1200 and particularly after the collapse of Chinese paper money in about 1360 strongly supports the monetary view favouring silver as money over gold as wealth for ostentation and display, perhaps hoarding and the like. The lower price of silver in India in the early seventeenth century may well reflect the preference of that country for hoarding gold. Increasing trade in modern times helps explain the convergence of ratios, although

Table 3.7 Silver/gold ratio at various centers, 1000–1664

Date	Flanders	Date	Egypt	Date	India	Date	China
						1000	6.3
						1126	13.3
						1134	13.0
		1194–1199	9.3			1198	12.1
1373	10.57					1375	4.0
1384	9.89	1382–1403	9.3			1385	5.0
1416	8.81	1415	8.9			1415	10.0*
1433	10.87	1433	11.1			1436	5.0
1482	10.89	1483	10.3			1481	7.0
1503	11.14	1503	8.5			1502	9.0
						1572	8.0
	Amsterdam			1583	9		
1600–04	11.21						
1620–24	12.17			1621	10	1620	8.0
1635–39	12.25			1633	12.5	1635	10.0
1640–44	13.35			1640	13	1637–40	13.0
1645–49	13.93			1644–45	14		
				1658	16.40		
1660–64	13			1664	14.94/15		

* Authors unable to explain departure from trend.

Source: Flanders: Munro (1983), pp. 148–53.
Amsterdam: Gaastra (1986), pp. 470–1.
Egypt: Bacharach (1983), pp. 170–80.
India: Habib (1982), p. 367.
China: Yamamura and Kamiki (1983), p. 345.

the integration of markets is far from perfect with arbitrage limited in the explanation of Munro (1983, p. 111) already referred to. But our interest is less in the ratio than in the high prices of both precious metals in the East as compared with the West.

Conclusion

Chaudhuri contends that India was not basically different in its response to supplies of precious metals than any other country, and that the movement of silver and some gold eastward was the same as any commodity movement, to be explained along Ricardian principles of comparative advantage (1978, p. 157). Gold and silver were cheap in the West, expensive in the East, and luxury products, the only ones that would bear the cost of transport taking a long time, were cheap in the East and expensive in the West. That is satisfactory as far as it goes, but seems to demand some explanation why the precious metals were so highly prized in India and China. Why did the influx of metal not raise prices, as called for by the price-specie-flow mechanism, and push it out again? Chaudhuri recognizes the problem and says that it is not possible to solve the paradox with available evidence, nor to trace the precise effects of bullion imports on the Indian economy (ibid., p. 160).

Dennis Flynn (1986) attempts to deal with the flow of bullion to the east in micro- rather than macro-economic terms, terms that closely parallel those of Chaudhuri. Instead of the silver being needed to pay for the imports of the West from the East, he claims that the precious metals were the cause of the expansion of intercontinental trade, not the response. This leaves unanswered why the East wanted silver and gold more than it wanted luxury consumers goods. Assume that the East could not have been able to buy food in the West (for it would spoil on the long voyage) or other highly useful but inexpensive goods such as iron, timber for shipbuilding and housing (too heavy and bulky relative to their value), or goods that would be used up in the course of consumption like the exported spices, calico, silks, later tea (but not porcelain, which was durable but could be put to daily use). Perhaps it could be argued that the trade was one in durable consumers goods – say, only porcelain and silver – that yielded utility through aesthetic enjoyment over time. Or the precious metals serving as money could be regarded as highly useful goods, producing utility through lowering transaction costs. I find the explanation unacceptable if it is intended to explain passion, avidity, a voracious appetite, and the like. The West seemed quickly to get sufficient pepper, with gluts leading to sharply lower prices. While the prices of gold and silver shifted against one another in Asia, prices of other goods rose only slightly against the two metals. This is what needs to be explained.

The distribution of income is perhaps a key. The Eastern rich had their necessities cheap, including cheap service, had little taste for Western luxuries, and cultivated the precious metals for their beauty as well as for the insurance they afforded in troubled times. The poor had difficulty in obtaining the cheaper necessities, and no capacity to buy others that were imported. Income distribution was skewed in the West, to be sure, and there was something of the same indulgence in conspicuous consumption. But the tastes of the rich were communicated fairly quickly to the poorer classes in England, at least in the spices, tea, and calico if not in silk and porcelain.

Monetization plays a role, to be sure, especially in the intermediate run, but over the long run money problems can be met through innovation. Wang observes that China developed four types of credit instrument in the eighteenth century: silver notes, cash notes, native bank order drafts, and transfer accounts (1977, p. 480). These made progress at different rates in different places, slowly in the interior such as Yunnan and Sinkiang, more rapidly along the coast. The view that the flow of specie to the East was primarily for monetization encounters the difficulty that India had a voracious appetite for gold and gold was not money, perhaps not even near-money, and that additions of specie were continuous,whereas money plays a balancing role, raising prices and reversing the flow of trade, as explained by Hume in the price-specie-flow mechanism. In China, silver was spent primarily for opium, one addictive substance exchanged for the other. The answer to the puzzle may lie less in economic theory than in psychological and psychoanalytical regions.

Let me return to the present day, and the heavy dollar deficit of the United States, on the one hand, and the surpluses of Japan, Taiwan, and the three other small Asian economies, South Korea, Singapore and Hong Kong, on the other. American high absorption – spending for consumption, investment and government, especially military – and low savings are explained in terms of United States wealth. In writing about the *Decline of Empires*, Cipolla

> points out that improvements in the standard of living brought about by a rising economy lead to more and more people demanding to share in the benefits. Incomes and extravagances develop, as new needs begin to replace those that have been satisfied. (1970, Introduction)

Japanese per capita income has surpassed that in the United States, though the comparison relies on market exchange rates which are often distortionary when real incomes are compared. Japanese savings, however, remain high. A pair of articles in the *Boston Globe* suggests that the Japanese realize that they are in a position to work less hard, consume more, indulge in leisure and save less, but somehow Japanese society finds it difficult to the point of impossibility thus far to do so (February 27, 1988, p. 1; February 28, 1988, p. 1). They export goods with great intensity but find it difficult to buy foreign goods.

I find it difficult to explain the United States deficits by a surplus of money, and the Japanese and Taiwanese trade surpluses by an excess demand for money which could not more readily be otherwise satisfied.

In brief, the explanation that India and China are just like Spain and the rest of Europe, or that Japan and Taiwan today are like the United States and the United Kingdom is implausible, counter-intuitive and unacceptable.

Bibliography and references

Alexander, Sidney, S. (1952), "Effects of a Devaluation on a Trade Balance," *Staff Papers* (of the International Monetary Fund), vol. 2 (April), pp. 267–78.

Aston, Trevor, ed. (1965), *Crisis in Europe, 1560–1660, Essays from Past and Present*, London: Routledge and Kegan Paul.

Ashtor, Eliyahu (1971), *Les métaux précieux et la balance des paiements du Proche-Orient à la basse époque*, Paris: SEVPEN.

Ashtor, Eliyahu (1976), "Observations on the Venetian Trade in the Levant in the XIVth Century," *Journal of European Economic History*, vol. 5 (Winter), pp. 533–86.

Aström, Sven-Erik (1962), *From Cloth to Iron: The Anglo-Baltic Trade in the Late Seventeenth Century*, Helsinki: Centraltryckeriet.

Attman, Artur (1983), *Dutch Enterprise in the World Bullion Trade, 1550–1800*, Gothenburg: Kungl. Vetenkaps- och Vitterhets-Samhallet.

Attman, Artur (1986), *American Bullion in the European World Trade, 1600–1800*, Gothenburg: Kungl. Vetenkaps- och Vitterhets-Samhallet.

Atwell, William S. (1982), "International Bullion Flows and the Chinese Economy, circa 1530–1650," *Past and Present*, no. 95 (May), pp. 68–90.

Atwell, William S. (1986), "Some Observations on the 'Seventeenth-Century Crisis' in China and Japan," *Journal of Asian Studies*, vol. XV, no. 2 (February) pp. 223–44.

Attwell, William S. (1987) "China and the Wider World, 1400–1600," at the "Traditional China" Seminar, Harvard University, 5 October.

Bacharach, Jere L. (1983), "Monetary Movements in Medieval Egypt, 1171–1517," in J.F. Richards, ed., *Precious Metals in the Later Medieval and Early Modern Worlds*, Durham, NC: Carolina Academic Press, pp. 159–81.

Bairoch, Paul (1981), "The Main Trends in National Economic Disparities since the Industrial Revolution," in P. Bairoch and Maurice Lévy-Leboyer, eds, *Disparities in Economic Development since the Industrial Revolution*, New York: St Martin's Press.

Barbour, Violet (1966), *Capitalism and Amsterdam in the 17th Century*, Ann

Arbor, Mich.: University of Michigan Press; first published 1950.

Bogucka, Maria (1975), "The Monetary Crisis of the XVIIth Century and its Social and Psychological Consequences in Poland," *Journal of European Economic History*, vol. 4, no. 1 (Spring), pp. 137–52.

Bogucka, Maria (1980), "The Role of Baltic Trade in European Development from the XVth to the XVIIIth Centuries," *Journal of European Economic History*, vol. 9, no. 1 (Spring), pp. 5–20.

Borah, Woodrow W. (1954), *Early Colonial Trade and Navigation between Mexico and Peru*, Berkeley and Los Angeles, University of California Press.

Braudel, Fernand (1981), *The Structures of Everyday Life*, vol. I of *Civilization and Capitalism, 15th–18th Century*, New York: Harper & Row.

Braudel, Fernand (1982), *The Wheels of Commerce*, vol. II of *Civilization and Capitalism, 15th–18th Century*, New York: Harper & Row.

Braudel, Fernand (1984), *The Perspective of the World*, vol. III of *Civilization and Capitalism, 15th–18th Century*, New York: Harper & Row.

Brennig, Joseph J. (1983), "Silver in Seventeenth-Century Surat: Monetary Circulation and the Price Revolution in Mughal India," in J.F. Richards, ed., *Precious Metals in the Later Medieval and Early Modern Worlds*, Durham, NC: Carolina Academic Press, pp. 477–96.

Chaudhuri, K.M. (1965), *The English East India Company*: *The Study of an Early Joint-Stock Company, 1600–1640*, London: Frank Cass & Co.

Chaudhuri, K.M. (1978), *The Trading World of Asia and the East India Company, 1660–1860*, Cambridge: Cambridge University Press.

Chaudhuri, K.M. (1986), "World Silver Flows, Monetary Factors as a Force of International Economic Integration 1658–1758 (America, Europe and Asia)", in Wolfram Fischer, R. Marvin McInnis and Jürgen Schneider, eds, *The Emergence of a World Economy, 1500–1914*, vol. I, Stuttgart: Franz Steinbar Verlag, pp. 61–82.

Chevalier, Michel (1859), *On the Probable Fall in the Value of Gold, the Commercial and Social Consequences which May Ensue and the Measures which It Invokes*, Manchester: Alexander Ireland.

Cipolla, C.M., ed. (1970), *The Economic Decline of Empires*, London: Methuen.

Coleman, D., ed. (1969), *Revisions in Mercantilism*, London: Methuen.

Da Silva, Jose-Gentil (1969), *Banque et credit en Italie au XVII siècle*: *les foires de change et la dépreciation monétaire*, Paris: Editions Klincksieck.

Day, John (1978), "The Great Bullion Famine of the Fifteenth Century," *Past and Present*, vol. 79, pp. 3–54.

Dermigny, Louis (1964), *La Chine et l'occident*: *Le commerce à Canton au XVIIIe siècle*, 3 vols. Paris: SEVPEN.

DeVries, Jan (1976), *The Economy of Europe in the Age of Crisis, 1600–1750*, Cambridge: Cambridge University Press.

Deyell, John (1983), "The China Connection: Problems of Silver Supply in Medieval Bengal," in J.F. Richards, ed., *Precious Metals in the Later Medieval and Early Modern Worlds*, Durham, NC: Carolina Academic Press, pp. 207–27.

Dornic, François (1955), *L'Industrie textile dans la Maine et ses débouches internationaux (1650–1815)*, Le Mans: Editions Pierre-Belon.

Drake, P.J. (1980), *Money, Finance and Development*, Oxford: Martin Robertson.

Everaert, J. (1973), *De internationale en koloniale handel der Vlaamse firma's te Cadiz, 1670–1700*, Bruges.

Fairbank, John K., E.O. Reischauer, and A.M. Craig (1965), *East Asia: The Modern Transformation*, vol. II of *A History of East Asian Civilization*, Boston: Houghton Mifflin.

Flynn, Dennis O. (1986), "The Microeconomics of Silver and East–West Trade in the Early Modern Period," in Wolfram Fischer, R. Marvin McInnis and Jürgen Schneider, eds, *The Emergence of a World Economy, 1500–1914*, vol. I, Stuttgart: Steiner Verlag, pp. 37–60.

Forster, Robert (1960), *The Nobility of Toulouse in the Eighteenth Century: A Social and Economic Study*, Baltimore, Md: Johns Hopkins University Press.

Forster, Robert (1971), *The House of Saulx-Tavanes: Versailles and Burgundy, 1700–1830*, Baltimore, Md.: Johns Hopkins University Press.

Forster, Robert (1980), *Merchants, Landlords, Magistrates: The Depont Family in Eighteenth Century France*, Baltimore, Md.: Johns Hopkins Press.

Forsyth, Peter J. and Stephen J. Nicholas (1983), "The Decline of Spanish Industry and the Price Revolution: A Neoclassical Analysis," *Journal of European Economic History*, vol. 12, no. 3 (Winter), pp. 601–10.

Gaastra, Femme S. (1986), "The Dutch East India Company and its Inter-Asiatic Trade in Precious Metals," in Wolfram Fischer, R. Marvin McInnis and Jürgen Schneider, eds, *The Emergence of a World Economy, 1500–1914*, vol. I, Stuttgart: Steiner Verlag, pp. 97–112.

Gamba, Charles (1958), "Poverty and Some Socio-economic Aspects of Hoarding, Saving and Borrowing in Malaya," *Malayan Economic Review*, October, pp. 33–62.

Glamann, Kristof (1974), "European Trade, 1500–1700," in Carlo M. Cipolla, ed., *The Fontana Economic History of Europe*, part 2, *The Sixteenth and Seventeenth Centuries*, Glasgow: Collins/Fontana Books.

Goubert, Pierre (1959), *Familles marchandes sous l'Ancient Régime: les Danse et les Mottes*, Paris: SEVPEN.

Gould, J.D. (1954), "The Trade Depression of the Early 1620s," *Economic History Review* (2nd ser.), vol. 7, no. 1 (August), pp. 81–90.

Graham, Frank D. and Charles R. Whittlesey (1939), *Golden Avalanche*, Princeton, NJ: Princeton University Press.

Habib, Irfan (1982), "The Monetary System and Prices," in *The Cambridge Economic History of India*, vol. I, c.*1200–1750*, edited by Tapan Raychaudhuri and Irfan Habib. Delhi: Orient Longman in association with Cambridge University Press, pp. 360–81.

Hamilton, Earl J. (1965), *American Treasure and the Price Revolution in Spain, 1501–1650*, New York: Octagon Books; first published 1934.

Haring, Clarence Henry (1918), *Trade and Navigation between Spain and the Indies in the Time of the Habsburgs*, Cambridge, Mass.: Harvard University Press.

Hawtrey, R.G. (1919), *Currency and Credit*, London: Longmans, Green.

Heckscher, Eli F. (1935), *Mercantilism*, 2 vols. London: George Allen & Unwin.

Heckscher, Eli F. (1950), "Multilateralism, Baltic Trade and the Mercantilists," *Economic History Review* (2nd ser.), vol. 3, no. 2, pp. 219–28.

Heckscher, Eli F. (1954), *An Economic History of Sweden*, Cambridge, Mass.: Harvard University Press.

Hobsbawm, E.J. (1965), "The Crisis of the Seventeenth Century," in Trevor Aston, ed., *Crisis in Europe, 1560–1660, Essays from Past and Present*, London: Routledge and Kegan Paul, pp. 5–58.

Hume, David (1752), *Essays, Moral, Political and Literary*, 2 vols. London:

Longmans, Green (1898 edn).

International Gold Corporation, Ltd (1982), *Above Ground Stocks of Gold: Amounts and Distribution*, New York: International Gold Corporation, Ltd.

Jeannin, P. (1982), "The Sea-borne and the Overland Trade Routes of Northern Europe in the XVIth and XVIIth Centuries," *Journal of European Economic History*, vol. 11, no. 1 (Spring), pp. 5–59.

Jevons, W. Stanley (1884) *Investigations in Currency and Finance*, London: Macmillan.

Johansen, Hans Chr. (1986), "How to Pay for Baltic Products," in Wolfram Fischer, R. Marvin McInnis and Jürgen Schneider, eds, *The Emergence of a World Economy, 1500–1914*, vol. I, Stuttgart: Steiner Verlag, pp. 123–42.

Keynes, John Maynard (1924), *Indian Currency and Finance*, London: Macmillan.

Lapeyre, Henri, (1953), *Simon Ruiz et les "asientos" de Philippe II*, Paris: Colin.

Lapeyre, Henri (1955), *Une famille des marchands, Les Ruiz, Contribution à l'étude du commerce entre la France et l'Espagne au temps du Philippe II*, Paris: Colin.

Larsen, Karen (1948), *A History of Norway*, Princeton, NJ: Princeton University Press.

Maczak Antoni (1970), "The Balance of Polish Sea Trade with the West," *Scandinavian Economic History Review*, vol. 18, no. 2, pp. 107–42.

Maczak Antoni (1974), Review of A. Attman, *The Russian and Polish Markets in International Trade, 1500–1650. Journal of European Economic History*, vol. 3, no. 2, pp. 505–8.

Maczak Antoni (1976), "Money and Society in Poland and Lithuania in the 16th and 17th Centuries," *Journal of European Economic History* vol. 5, no. 1 (Spring), pp. 69–104.

Martin, D.A. (1977), "The Impact of Mid-nineteenth Century Gold Depreciation upon Western Monetary Standards," *Journal of European Economic History*, vol. 6, no. 3 (Winter), pp. 641–58.

Meilink-Roeloesz, M.A.P. (1962), *Asian Trade and European Influence in the Indonesian Archipelago between 1500 and about 1630*, The Hague: Martinus Nijhoff.

Meuvret, Jean (1970), "Monetary Circulation and the Economic Utilization of Money in 16th and 17th Century France," in Rondo Cameron, ed., *Essays in French Economic History*, pp. 140–9. Homewood, Ill.: Irwin; written in 1947.

Milward, Alan S. and S.B. Saul (1973), *The Economic Development of Continental Europe, 1780–1870*, Totowa, NJ: Rowman and Littlefield.

Morineau, Michel (1985), *Incroyables gazettes et fabuleux métaux: Les retours des trésors americains d'apres les gazettes hollandaises (XVIe-XVIIIe siècles)*, Paris: Cambridge University Press/Editions de la Maison des Sciences de l'Homme.

Mote, Frederick W. (1977), "Yuan and Ming," in K.C. Chang, ed., *Food and Chinese Culture: Anthropological and Historical Perspectives*, New Haven, Conn.: Yale University Press.

Mun, Thomas (1621), *A Discourse of Trade from England unto the East-Indies, Answering to diverse Objections which are Usually made against the same*, by T.M. London: Printed by Nicholas Okes for John Pyper.

Mun, Thomas (1664), *England's Treasure by Forraign Trade, or the Ballance of our Forraign Trade is the Rule of our Treasure*, in J.K. McCullogh, ed., *Early*

English Tracts on Commerce, Cambridge: Cambridge University Press (1954).

Munro, John H. (1979), "Bullionism and the Bill of Exchange in England, 1272–1663: A Study in Monetary Management and Popular Prejudice," in Center for Medieval and Renaissance Studies, *The Dawn of Modern Banking*, New Haven, Conn.: Yale University Press.

Munro, John H. (1983), "Bullion Flows and Monetary Contraction in late-Medieval England and the Low Countries," in J.F. Richards, ed., *Precious Metals in the Later Medieval and Early Modern Worlds*, Durham, NC: Carolina Academic Press, pp. 97–158.

Myrdal, Gunnar (1968), *Asian Drama*, 3 vols. New York: Twentieth Century Fund.

Outhwaite, R.B. (1969), *Inflation in Tudor and Early Stuart England*, London: Macmillan (for the Economic History Society).

Parker, Geoffrey (1972), *The Army of Flanders and the Spanish Road, 1567–1659: The Logistics of Victory and Defeat in the Low Countries' Wars*, Cambridge: Cambridge University Press.

Parker, Geoffrey (1974), "The Emergence of Modern Finance in Europe, 1500–1730," in Carlo M. Cipolla, ed., *The Fontana Economic History of Europe*, part 2, *The Sixteenth and Seventeenth Centuries*, Glasgow: Collins/Fontana Books, pp. 527–94.

Parry, J.H. (1967), "Transport and Trade Routes," in E.E. Rich and C.M. Wilson, eds, *The Cambridge Economic History of Europe*, vol. 4, *The Economy of Expanding Europe in the Sixteenth and Seventeenth Centuries*, Cambridge: Cambridge University Press.

Perlin, Frank (1983), "Proto-industrialization and Pre-Colonial South Asia," *Past and Present*, no. 98 (February), pp. 30–95.

Perlin, F. (1986), "Monetary Revolution and Societal Change in the Late Medieval and Early Modern Times," *Journal of Asian Studies*, vol. 14, no. 5, pp. 1037–49.

Pike, Ruth (1972), *Aristocrats and Traders: Seville Society in the Sixteenth Century*, Ithaca, NY: Cornell University Press.

Postan, M.M. (1973), *Medieval Trade and Finance*, Cambridge: Cambridge University Press.

Prakash, Om (1986), "Precious Metal Flows in Asia and World Economic Integration in the Seventeenth Century," in Wolfram Fischer, R. Marvin McInnis and Jürgen Schneider, eds, *The Emergence of a World Economy, 1500–1914*, vol. I, Stuttgart: Franz Steiner Verlag, pp. 83–96.

Price, Jacob M. (1961), "Multilateralism and Bilateralism: the Settlement of British Trade Balances with 'the North', *c.*1700," *Economic History Review* (2nd ser.) vol. 14, no. 2 (December), pp. 254–74.

Quiason, Serafin D. (1966), *English "Country Trade" with the Philippines, 1644–1765*, Quezon City: University of the Philippines Press.

Rapp, Richard Tilden (1976), *Industry and Economic Decline in Seventeenth-Century Venice*, Cambridge, Mass.: Harvard University Press.

Reischauer, Edwin O. and John K. Fairbank (1958), *East Asia: The Great Tradition*, vol. 1 of *A History of East Asian Civilization*, Boston: Houghton Mifflin.

Rich, E.E. (1967), Preface to E.E. Rich and C.H. Wilson, eds, *The Cambridge Economic History of Europe*, vol. 4, *The Economy of Expanding Europe in the Sixteenth and Seventeenth Centuries*, Cambridge: Cambridge University Press.

Richards, J.F. (1983), "Outflows of Precious Metals from Early Islamic India," in J.F. Richards, ed., *Precious Metals in the Later Medieval and Early Modern Worlds*, Durham, NC: Carolina Academic Press.

Ruggerio, Romano (1964), "Encore la crise de 1619–22," *Annales: Economies, Sociétés, Civilisations*, vol. 19, no. 1 (January–February), pp. 31–8.

Sahillioglu, H. (1983). "The Role of International Monetary and Metal Movements in Ottoman Monetary History, 1300–1750," in J.F. Richards, ed., *Precious Metals in the Later Medieval and Early Modern Worlds*, Durham, NC: Carolina Academic Press.

Sanjoy Hazarika (1986), "India's Clandestine Market for Gold," *New York Times*, January 18, p. D6.

Schurz, William Lytle (1939), *The Manila Galleon*, New York: Dutton.

Sieveking, Heinrich (1934), "Die Hamburger Bank," in J.C. Van Dillen, ed., *History of the Principal Public Banks*, The Hague: Martinus Nijhoff.

Simkin, C.G.F. (1968), *The Traditional Trade of Asia*. London: Oxford University Press.

Smith, Adam, (1937), *An Inquiry into the Nature and the Causes of the Wealth of Nations* (Cannan edn). New York: Modern Library; first published 1776.

Sperling, J. (1962), "The International Payments Mechanism in the Seventeenth and Eighteenth Centuries," *Economic History Review* (2nd ser.) vol. 14, no. 3 (August), pp. 446–68.

Spooner, Frank C. (1972), *The International Economy and Money Movements in France, 1493–1725*, Cambridge, Mass.: Harvard University Press.

Steensgaard, Niels (1973), *Carracks, Caravans and Companies: The Structural Crisis of the European Trade in the Early 17th Century*, Copenhagen: Scandinavian Institute of Asian Studies/Chicago: University of Chicago Press.

Supple. Barry E. (1959), *Commercial Crisis and Change in England, 1600–1642: A Study in the Instability of a Mercantile Economy*, Cambridge: Cambridge University Press.

Thomas, P.J. (1926), *Mercantilism and the East India Company: An Early Phase of the Free Trade vs Protection Controversy*, London: P.S. King.

Thomsen, Birgit Nuchel and Brinley Thomas (1966), *Anglo-Dutch Trade, 1661–1963, A Historical Survey*, Aarhus: University Press of Aarhus.

Trevor-Roper, H.R. (1965), "The General Crisis of the Seventeenth Century," in Trevor Aston, ed., *Crisis in Europe, 1560–1660, Essays from Past and Present*, London: Routledge and Kegan Paul, pp. 59–95.

Tveite, Stein (1961), *Engelsk-Norsk Trelasthandel, 1640–1710*. Bergen and Oslo: Universitetsforlaget.

Van Dillen, J.G. (1934), "The Bank of Amsterdam," in J.G. Van Dillen, ed., *History of the Principal Public Banks*, The Hague: Martinus Nijhoff, pp. 79ff.

Vilar, Pierre (1976), *A History of Gold and Money, 1450–1920*, London: New Left Books.

Wakeman, Frederic E., Jr (1986), "China and the Seventeenth Century Crisis," *Late Imperial China*, vol. 7, no. 1 (June), pp. 1–26.

Walz, Terence (1983), "Gold and Silver Exchanges between Egypt and the Sudan, 16–18th Centuries," in J.F. Richards, ed., *Precious Metals in the Later Medieval and Early Modern Worlds*, Durham, NC: Carolina Academic Press, pp. 305–28.

Wang, Yeh-Chien (1972), "The Secular Trend of Prices during the Ch'ing Period (1644–1911)," *Journal of the Institute of Chinese Studies* (Chinese University of Hong Kong), vol. 5, no. 2, pp. 347–68.

Wang, Yeh-Chien (1977), "Evolution of the Chinese Monetary System, 1644–

1850," Paper presented to the Conference on Modern Chinese Economic History, held at the Institute of Economics, Academia Sinica, Taipei, Taiwan.

Whitmore, John K. (1983), "Vietnam and the Monetary Flow of Eastern Asia, Thirteenth to Eighteenth Centuries," in J.F. Richards, ed., *Precious Metals in the Later Medieval and Early Modern Worlds*, Durham, NC: Carolina Academic Press, pp. 305–28.

Wicksell, Knut (1935), *Lectures on Political Economy*, vol. 2, *Money*. New York: Macmillan.

Wilson, Charles (1949), "Treasure and Trade Balances: The Mercantilist Problem," *Economic History Review*; reprinted in *Enterprise and Secular Change: Readings in Economic History*, edited by Frederic C. Lane and Jelle C. Riemersa, pp. 337–49. Homewood, Ill.: Irwin (1953, pp. 337–49).

Wilson, Charles (1951), "Treasure and Trade Balance: Further Evidence," in *Economic History Review*, Second Series, vol. 4, no. 2, pp. 231–42.

Wilson, Charles (1967), "Trade, Society and the State," in E.E. Rich and C.H. Wilson, eds, *The Cambridge Economic History of Europe*, vol. 4, *The Economy of Expanding Europe in the Sixteenth and Seventeenth Centuries*, Cambridge: Cambridge University Press, pp. 487–575.

Yamamura, Kozo and Tetsuo Kamiki (1983), "Silver Mines and Sung Coins – A Monetary History of Medieval and Modern Japan in International Perspective," in J.F. Richards, ed., *Precious Metals in the Later Medieval and Early Modern Worlds*, Durham, NC: Carolina Academic Press, pp. 329–62.

Yule, Sir Henry, ed. (1903), *The Book of Ser Marco Polo, the Venetian concerning the Kingdoms and Marvels of the East*, 2 vols. New York: Charles Scribner's Sons.

4

Introduction to *England's Treasure by Forraign Trade, or The Ballance of our Forraign Trade is the Rule of our Treasure* by Thomas Mun

Thomas Mun's *Discourse of Trade*, published in 1621 as a defense of the East India Company of which he was a director, is a minor classic in political economy of the mercantilist period. Mun's second book, *England's Treasure by Forraign Trade, or The Ballance of our Forraign Trade is the Rule of our Treasure*, has a wider purpose than the defense of the Company and is a major classic. The latter is economic science, applied to the controversies of the day over international trade and payments. Also written in the economically turbulent 1620s, it was not published until 1664 when it was put forth "for the Common Good" by his son, John Mun, as the second Anglo-Dutch war approached. This introduction to *England's Treaure*, also covering Mun's thought in *A Discourse of Trade*, is divided into four sections dealing with the man, the times, his defense of the East India Company, and his wider thought on mercantilism and bullionism.

The man

Thomas Mun was born in 1571 and died in 1641. He is described in the *Dictionary of National Biography* (*DNB*) as an "economic writer"

* Introduction to a facsimile edition of Thomas Mun's *England's Treasure by Forraign Trade* (1664), in the series *Klassiker der National Okonomie* (Classics of Political Economy), edited by Professor Horst Claus Rechtenwald and published by Verlag Wirtschaft und Finanzen, Dusseldorf, Federal Republic of Germany in a separate small volume in German translation with the title "Uber den Handel: Thomas Mun's Ideen im Lichte unserer Epoche" ("A Discourse on Trade: Thomas Mun's Ideas in Contemporary Light"), 1989.

(1921–2, XIII, p. 1183); however, he wrote not to serve party politics but for science (Heckscher, 1935, p. 184, note 7). Son of a mercer, John Mun, he had a stepfather who was also a mercer, and a grandfather and uncle who, as moneyers of the Royal Mint, may have given him an early insight into currency matters. His career as a merchant started about 1596, before the founding of the East India Company in 1600, and he spent some time in Italy, from perhaps 1597 to 1607, where he seems to have failed and absconded because of bankruptcy. In Leghorn, he was known to have been a factor of the merchant William Galloway, who was inscribed on the lists of the Levant Company, trafficking between London and the Eastern Mediterranean, and to have dealt in importing into Italy lead, tin and cloth, while exporting alum. He maintained an account with the bankers Matteo and Lorenzo Galli of Florence (DeRoover, 1957). His Italian experience is mentioned twice in *England's Treasure*, once in recounting that the Grand Duke of Tuscany, Ferdinand the First, had lent him 40,000 crowns and allowed him to export it in specie to import goods from Turkey (pp. 18–19)[1] and again to make the point that exchange manipulation cannot determine the rate of exchange, as Gerard Malynes, an intellectual adversary in London, maintained it did:

> I have lived long in *Italy* where the greatest Banks and Bankers of Christendom do trade, yet could I never see nor hear, that they did, or were able to rule the price of Exchange by Confederacie, but still the plenty or scarcity of money in the course of trade did always overrule them and made the Exchange to run at high or low rates. (p. 51)

Mun returned to London from Italy sometime after 1609, married in 1612, and in July 1615, "as a well known merchant" (*DNB*, 1921–2, XIII, p. 1184) was elected a member of the committee, or a director, of the East India Company. He spent the rest of his life actively promoting the Company's interests and was said to have been "its ablest advocate" (Chaudhuri, 1965, p. 20). He refused, however, certain responsibilities within the Company – in November 1621 to go to India to inspect the Company's "factories," and in March 1624 to serve as deputy governor of the Company. He none the less played a prominent role in the Company's decisions, his name appearing frequently in the Company's minutes, opposing resettlement in Bantam in Java in the 1618–19 war in Asia, advocating instead withdrawal to north India; propounding in 1626 the theory that the Company would have to earn a return three and a half times the original cost of its goods bought in Asia to cover freight, customs, goods exported and other costs and to make a profit; persuading the Court in 1626 to change the manning and stowage of the Company's ships bound for India to another port to lessen the danger from French ships with letters of marque; insisting in 1627 with the governor, but vainly, on the necessity of sending shipping to realize on the Company's assets in India; proposing in 1632 expansion of the investment in Coromandel factories from £15,000 to £20,000 (Chaudhuri, 1965, pp. 67, 68, 71, 102).

Mun's name also turns up among those lending money to Lionel Cranfield, a financier of the early seventeenth century, who borrowed money and received deposits from a wide circle to invest in syndicates formed to take over offices, farm taxes, and buy up properties sold off by the crown (Tawney, 1958, p. 111). The amounts and dates are not stated, but they were probably before 1613 when Cranfield became a minister in James I's government.

Most important for the East India Company, and certainly for economic thought, Thomas Mun was put forward by the East India Company as its representative in the critical times of the 1620s, and to serve on Crown Commissions to make recommendations to the Privy Council on the privileges of the Company in exporting foreign coin. Mun submitted four memoranda to the Commission on Trade appointed in October 1622 that settled down to write its report in the spring of 1623. Their wording follows closely portions of *England's Treasure*, establishing that the origin of that book goes back to the early 1620s, and not, as previously thought, to the last years of the decade (Supple, 1954, pp. 91–2). Other parts have been traced to 1626 or 1627 (DeRoover, 1957). In any event, Mun proved persuasive on these governmental commissions, fighting off proposals that the East India Company be forbidden to export gold and silver coin and bullion to Asia to buy spices, silk, and calicos. In particular, he was one of twelve signatories to the June 1622 Report of the Clothing Committee of the Privy Council – his name misspelled as Thomas Man in the careless orthography of the day – that set out a host of recommendations for overcoming the decay of cloth exports, but explicitly defended the East India Company against the accusation of 'taking away of money to furnish their trade, and return only commodities again' (Thirsk and Cooper, 1972, pp. 210–16). He delayed for some years a proposal by Gerard Malynes to appoint a Royal Exchanger to monopolize all dealings in foreign bills of exchange. Even here, however, he ultimately triumphed because the experiment adopted in 1627 lasted only a short time before it was recognized to have failed.

The times

The period is widely described as one of "crisis," without, however, entire agreement on the nature of the crisis or its duration and extent.

For many historians the crisis covered a century and a half (DeVries, 1976); for others a pair of years (Ruggerio, 1964). In the seventy years of Mun's life there were only twenty-six years of good trade (Hinton, 1975, p. 284, quoting W.R. Scott). Many years were critical because of bad harvests in the Mediterranean, in northern Europe, and especially on occasion in several consecutive years, or because Swedish blockades of Baltic ports in the Thirty Years War from 1618 to 1648 cut off the flow of grain needed in the West. At a more fundamental level, Poland, eastern Germany and Russia lost the prosperity they had enjoyed in the sixteenth century when population had grown faster in the West and Mediterranean than agricultural productivity and rising prices attracted Eastern exports. The early seventeenth-century market for eastern grain was hurt by Italian and Spanish production of rice and French production of maize, as well as by greater agricultural productivity in the West in general.

Crisis further turned on war. In addition to the Thirty Years War, there was the attempt by Spain to crush rebellion of the Dutch in the Netherlands that lasted eighty-odd years from 1572 to 1659, with a truce from 1607 to 1612; religious and dynastic wars between France and Spain, and wars of the British with now Spain, now France, now the Dutch. At times, Spain was simultaneously fighting the Turks in the Mediterranean, the French, English and Dutch. Despite the flow of silver from the New World, Spanish kings were continuously in debt and forced to declare bankruptcy in 1560, 1575, 1596, 1607, 1627, 1647 and 1653, refunding the *asientos*, or finance bills of exchange they had discounted, in long-term *juros* or bonds. Not all Spanish American silver was received in Spain; some was diverted to Lisbon or to Acapulco and the Manila galleon; British and Dutch privateers and even naval forces continuously tried to capture the fleet and occasionally succeeded – Drake in 1573, 1580 and 1586, and Admiral Piet Hein of the Dutch navy in 1628. British exports of woolens were in process of shifting from the old to the "New Draperies," lighter cloth and cheaper, to compete especially with high-quality Venetian woolens and to serve a wider market. One crisis ensued from a bungled attempt in Alderman Cockayne's project of 1614 to persuade the English Crown to forbid the export of cloth to the Dutch for finishing and dyeing there, and to undertake those processes at home. The effort failed, but the crisis in the British export trade that followed was due more to the outbreak of the Thirty Years War and the debasement of Polish and East Germany currency in the so-called *Kipper- und Wipperzeit* (clipping and debasing) which rendered the British pound appreciated. There was also a pepper glut after 1619 when the short war between the Dutch and the British in Asian waters came to an end and both the East India Company and the Dutch equivalent, the Verenigde Oostindisiche Compagnie (VOC), brought heavy cargoes to Europe. Some part of the crisis of 1621 may have been due to the arrest and trial in Star Chamber in 1618–19 of eighteen prominent foreign merchants – most of them Dutch – on the charge of exporting the very large sum of £7 million in coin. This is thought to have been part of an effort to halt the payment of interest to Dutch lenders, which in turn may have contributed to the Dutch withholding new loans and thus accentuating the exchange crisis (Barbour, 1966, pp. 53, 123).

The monetary troubles contributing to crisis were short-run – the flood of copper from Sweden used to ransom the fortress of Alvborg from the Danes as called for by the 1613 Treaty of Knared, copper used by Spain to blacken her coinage when silver became scarce, and by the private mint masters of Poland and Germany to adulterate their coins. Of crucial importance was the long-run decline in the flow of silver from the New World as production slowed down in Peru and Mexico in consequence of the exhaustion of the supply of labor, although Morineau has recently raised a question whether the conventional estimates, based on Seville records, gave Hamilton a wrong impression because of smuggling, and whether, when all records are reconciled, silver imports into Europe did not actually rise from the sixteenth to the seventeenth century (Morineau, 1985; for a chart of the Hamilton and Morineau data see Braudel, 1982, p. 174). Undervaluation of silver relative to gold in Britain at 15 to 1 contributed to a drain of silver, the money in daily use, against gold that circulated less effectively. The shortage of silver for hand-to-hand exchanges was especially acute in 1616–22 (Supple, 1957, p. 244 n.; 1959, pp. 178ff.). The currency debasement throughout Europe led to the establishment of deposit banks to receive and test coin and issue standardized receipts against it used as bank money – the Bank of Amsterdam (1609), of Middelburg (1616), of Hamburg (1619), of Delft (1621) and of Rotterdam (1635).

There is some question whether it is appropriate to regard the silver and gold produced in Spanish America and that hoarded in Asia, and to a lesser extent in Scandinavia, Poland and Russia, as money. In modern economics, prior to free floating in 1973, gold produced in South Africa was a commodity which became transformed into money when it arrived in Europe to be distributed through the gold market. In comparable fashion the Spanish bullion in the sixteenth and seventeenth centuries, some gold but mostly silver, was a commodity on leaving Spanish America, money as it arrived in Europe, and then a commodity again when it was swallowed up in Eastern Europe and Asia.

A certain amount of gold was acquired in the first half-century after Columbus, but the big flow took place in silver, began about 1560 and lasted until about 1600 or 1620 when, according to the orthodox account, it started to decline. The great majority of it escaped capture by English and Dutch privateers, flooded into Spain, and went out again. Spain spent the silver and borrowed against future receipts to provide Peru and Mexico with the supplies needed by the populations there, and to finance its wars in Europe. The New World exchanged silver as a commodity against consumer goods supplied by Spain and especially by the rest of Europe. Some circulated in Europe as money, but most was spent in the East, in the Baltic, the Levant, and the East Indies – for grain and timber as far as the Baltic was concerned, and for luxuries from the Levant and Asia. Much of the specie received by Poland, Russia and Turkey was in turn passed along to Asia for luxuries, though some was hoarded. The New World and Spain were what we would call low absorbers, spending their income fully. Asia was a high absorber, selling luxuries and hoarding the commodity, silver, it received for them. Between stood Europe, exchanging necessities sent to the mining communities in the New World against luxuries received from Asia.

The high spending and low productivity of Spain and its colonies in the field of necessities have been explained. According to a contemporary Spanish source, Spain was ruined by the flood of precious metals:

> the possession of such wealth altered everything. Agriculture laid down the plough, clothed herself in silk and softened her work-calloused hands. Trade put on a noble air and exchanging the work-bench for the saddle, went out to parade up and down the streets. The arts disdained mechanical tools. Goods became proud, and when silver and gold fell in esteem, they raised their prices. (Quoted by Vilar, 1976, pp. 168–9)

Thomas Mun, disapproving of luxury consumption, echoes these sentiments in *England's Treasure*:

> But this great plenty which we enjoy, makes us a people only vicious and excessive, wasteful of the means we have, but also improvident and careless of much other wealth that shamefully we lose . . . we leave our wonted exercises and studies, following our pleasures, and of late years besotting ourselves with pipe and pot, in a beastly manner, sucking smoke and drinking healths . . . As plenty and power doe make a nation vicious and improvident, so penury and want doe make a people wise and industrious." (pp. 72–4)

A more detailed account draws distinctions within the New World. Peru was a purely Spanish community with an avid desire for consumer goods of Spanish, European, Mexican and even Chinese origin, the last imported via Manila and Acapulco in exchange for silver, while the mixed Spanish and Indian community in Mexico exported consumer goods to Peru as well as silver to Spain and Manila (Parry, 1967, pp. 208–10).

The Spanish silver in Europe went initially to those countries that supplied the Spanish army in Flanders and the goods needed for the Iberian empires and domestic consumption (Parker, 1972). As it had not stayed in Spain and Portugal, so most of it did not stay in Holland, Italy, France and England. Three streams took it east, to the Baltic, Levant and East Indies.

Economic historians have explored the specie movements to the Baltic and Levant, noting that some of it was passed further along to Asia in payment for luxuries, some spent again in the West for luxuries and travel, and some hoarded (Maczak, 1976). A controversy turns on whether the bilateral trade of the West through the Sound to the Baltic, settled in specie, was offset by other overland trade with a reverse movement of specie, and on whether the import surplus of one country such as England was balanced multilaterally by an export surplus of others, such as Holland, France or Italy. There was some eastward movement of Western luxuries, such as Leipzig jewelry, silks and spices from the Levant by way of Venice, and similar readily transportable objects of high value and low weight that could move by land. But the main trade overland was in oxen and hides that moved in the same direction as grain and timber (Jeannin, 1982). It seems clear that the gross import surpluses by sea that had to be requited in specie were necessarily balanced bilaterally since all major traders in the West had import surpluses (Wilson, 1949; Heckscher, 1950), and that they were not matched by export surpluses overland. Trade within Europe was multilateral, as Thomas Mun insists, but outside the Continent the opportunity for multilateral balancing through bills of exchange was limited, and specie was necessary to close the accounts.

A question remains: what did the East do with the specie it acquired in exchange for its grain, timber, oxen and luxuries? The answer seems to be that it hoarded it. The distribution of income in Eastern Europe was highly skewed, with rich nobles and largely foreign merchants, and poor peasants. The monarchs of the backward economies of the Baltic hoarded rather than circulated the silver that did not pass on to Asia (Aström, 1962, p. 84). In addition, the Baltic countries, including Russia, insisted on collecting their customs duties in specie. Some hoarding went on in the upland bazaars of India, where the variability of the monsoon made it useful for the risk-averse peasant to accumulate a bridal dowry in silver or gold. Something of the same fashion existed in Norway where in noble or burgher weddings the bride might be magnificently arrayed in a crown and many gold chains around her throat, shoulders and elbows, and many gold chains hanging down toward the ground (Larsen, 1948, p. 264). Poor burghers and peasants in Poland would try to lock away a valuable ornament, a spoon or a coin

(Bogucka, 1975, pp. 145–8). The same mentality existed to a degree in France where no councilor, treasurer, bishop or abbot was without a complete set of tableware in precious metal, and there was no artisan who did not have basin, ewer and cup, at least a salt cellar, belts, rings, or necklace (Meuvret, 1970, p. 146). Mercantilists in Holland and England, while conscious of the function of silver and gold plate serving as a reserve, were interested in specie for circulation, not to gratify a Midas complex. Thomas Mun was disdainful of money as wealth. He was interested in the state having some treasure, but not too much, and he was anxious that it be imported, not drawn from circulation (Heckscher, 1935, p. 212). Harvey's research on the circulation of blood was not published until 1628, but the comparison of blood with money had been made earlier (ibid., p. 217).

Europe was acutely conscious of the loss of specie to the East. An English merchant of the time said "Many streams run thither [to India], as all rivers to the sea, and there stay" (quoted by Thomas, 1926, p. 8). Persistent attempts were made to send goods to India instead of coin, and sometimes gold instead of silver, but factors on the spot resisted. English cloth of wool was unsuitable and expensive. Some arms and ammunition could be provided, some metals, ivory, coral, quicksilver and the like, obtained outside Europe. Mainly the East wanted silver. It has been suggested that one element in the equation was a backward-bending supply curve of labor: satisfied with a target income, and hoarded valuables that protected it against a bad monsoon, increased earnings went into leisure and insurance rather than consumption (Rich, 1967, p. xxiii, quoted by Wallerstein, 1980, p. 47, n. 69). Or income distribution was sharply skewed against the producers of cloth and spice, with precious metals a form of conspicuous consumption for wealthy landlords and *compradores*. There was country trade among the economies of the East, but European goods were not wanted, and the profit for the East India Company and the VOC lay in silver – Venetian ducats before the seventeenth century, Spanish reals for the early days of the chartered companies, then Dutch rixdollars.

When the silver arrived in India it did not go immediately into hoards: some was reminted into rupees, some passed upcountry in purchasing calico and muslin to be hoarded, and some, like the specie received in the Baltic, passed along in country trade. The same occurred in Batavia. To keep its coins in circulation, Batavia, like Spain, raised the prices of undervalued coins (Glamann, 1958, pp. 53–5 and 65–6). Arbitrage took place among various parts of Asia, especially India, Japan and Indonesia trading silver for gold with China. The silver/gold ratio was at times 5:1 in China, and 10:1 or 11:1 not far away in Japan or India (Vilar, 1976, p. 95; Spooner, 1972, p. 77). Chaudhuri suggests that the role of silver in the commercial life of India may be more like that of the Eastern European countries (1978, p. 182). The real sinkhole seems to have been China, with its hunger for silver (Spooner, 1972, p. 77). The highest absorber at the producing end was Peru: the lowest at the receiving end, China.

With a large flow of specie into Europe and out again – in rough balance over long periods of time (Wilson, 1967, p. 511) – the monetary position of Western Europe, and even more of the separate countries, was a matter of some anxiety. There had been a bullion famine in the fifteenth century as German silver mines became depleted, a famine that inspired the voyage of Columbus in search of gold (Day, 1978; Vilar, 1976, ch. 7). "In economies without fully developed credit institutions, central banks and fiat moneys . . . concern about a country's coinage supply was hardly irrational" (Munro, 1979, p. 176). Supple says it bordered on neurosis but was understandable in the light of the drain (1957, p. 246). Controversies had risen over foreign exchange in 1576, 1586, 1600 and 1621. The last particularly raised the question whether the East India Company contributed to the scarcity of money by sending silver to the East in exchange for luxuries. Various measures in 1611 and 1619 forbade the export of gold and silver coin, melting it down, paying prices in excess of the mint, and the like (Supple, 1959, pp. 181–4). Proposals for manipulation of the exchange rate, usually through a Royal Exchanger, abounded. In these circumstances, Thomas Mun came to the defense of the East India Company.

A Discourse of Trade

Mun's defense of the East India Company, and especially of its practice of shipping coin to the East, is divided into parts, answering what he calls four objections to the Company's trade. The first objection is that necessary money is exchanged for unnecessary luxury goods such as spices, dyes, silks and calicos. The second regards the ships of the Company, much larger and more expensive than those used in coastal or Continental commerce, as wasteful, and using up scarce timber. Related to this is a third line of attack on the Company based upon its employment for long periods and at great risk of mariners who consume large amounts of food and are frequently lost at sea, leaving behind widows and children to be cared for. The last criticism returns to the question of money raised in the first, complaining that the Company's export of silver leaves the Mint less than fully employed.

Mun's answer to the first objection rests in part on a defense of consumer sovereignty – that if people want to spend income on drugs, spices, raw silk and calicos they should be allowed to – although in his later argument, both in *A Discourse* and in *England's Treasure*, he criticizes his countrymen for not working as hard as the Dutch, which runs against letting people behave as they choose. He argues further that the East India Company obtains these luxuries in direct trade more cheaply than the previous practice of having them transported overland to Turkey where they were purchased by the Levant Company, or importing them from Dutch, French or Venetian sources. The third part of his reply to the first objection is the principal argument that appears again in his answer to the objection about the Mint. He explains that the East India Company has exported far less foreign silver – it was not licensed to export British coin – than permitted – £548,090 in Spanish reals and some dollars to 1620, as against a permitted amount of £720,000 – and exported £292,286 of British, and some foreign, goods. Moreover, he claims that £100,000 of foreign coin exported annually will produce £500,000 of imports gross, of which England would consume £120,000 annually and re-export £380,000. This last sum is more than three and a half times the original silver exported (pp. 27, 8) and can regain the specie or pay for imports. Thus the East India Company is said to pay out (foreign) specie gross, but earn it net through re-export of the luxury goods bought in the East. He does not make anything of the argument that the United Provinces of the Netherlands, and especially Holland – a more advanced economy than that of England – did not restrict the export of specie and seemed always to have an abundance. In fact, the East India Company bought much of its Spanish silver in Amsterdam.

The second objection that the large ships built for the Indian trade use up British resources and are otherwise useless need not occupy us long. An argument along the lines of opportunity costs is made on the basis of resources – not a cogent one, since the timber and naval stores could be put to use building fishing boats which he calls for in his answer to the fourth objection. For the rest, he argues that the East Indiamen train sailors, and induce a supply of shipbuilders and suppliers that are available to use for the naval defense of the British Isles. Like that of Adam Smith, who upheld the Navigation Acts on the ground that defense is "of much more importance than opulence," the argument is non-economic. It does bear on the question whether mercantilism was more concerned with power than plenty, but Mun devotes only a few pages to the issue and gives it little weight.

The same can be said for the objection that the East India Company wastes sailors and their rations and leaves their wives and children impoverished. The men would have eaten food had they remained at home, much of the grain is imported, rather than home-grown, those that die are replaced, ships are lost in war with the Dutch as well as through perils of the sea, and the Company takes care of the unhappy widows and children resulting from casualties. The fifth part of the third objection is oddly connected with the rest, apparently arguing that for all the losses of men and ships, there has been no saving in the cost of goods imported from the East. This objection is disposed of with tables that compare the cost of imports of spices and indigo from the Levant and Lisbon with those directly from India. The latter route produces a substantial saving. Thus the country gained both employment and wealth.

The fourth objection, that the East India Company takes silver that would otherwise be brought to the Mint and keep it employed, is met in various ways. Both rich and poor continuously complain they do not have enough money. The Mint has been idle some years the Company has exported little silver and busy some years it has exported more. The Company never exported as much silver as it had been licensed to. Moreover, if the East India Company did not trade with India the trade would be taken over by the VOC, which would send the same amount of silver there and sell the same goods to Britain at higher prices. This, of course, is the substitution of a general-equilibrium argument for one of partial equilibrium, following through on the consequences of action to halt shipments by the East India Company, instead of assuming that everything else would remain the same.

The third and last part of the answer to the fourth objection is more general than the earlier and narrower defense of the Company, and sets out a mercantilist concept of trade. Britain could live without trade, but to do well it must trade its superfluities against necessary wares available in other countries and in treasure. This is a theory of trade close to that of Adam Smith in which exports are a vent for surplus. The troubles of the country lie not in the East India Company's dealings but in depreciation abroad (raising the price of foreign coins) and selling England commodities against coin rather than other commodities. He blames goldsmiths for culling and exporting heavy English coin, against the law, and then the authorities for failing to enforce the Statute of Employment, which required foreign exporters to use the proceeds of exports to England to buy English goods, rather than bills of exchange drawn on the Continent (p. 54).

The final suggestion is that the loss of specie may be due to inexperienced British merchants who buy more abroad than they sell, lacking sufficient knowledge of the vocation of merchant. This criticism is directly linked to the opening chapter of *England's Treasure*, listing twelve qualities needed in a good merchant. An export surplus will make a country rich, an import surplus render it poor. Gross imports can be large if a substantial portion of them is re-exported, as the East India Company is wont to do. What is needed is restraint in consumption of imports so as to enable them to be resold abroad for treasure. The country will grow rich if Englishmen increase productivity in the production of the "natural Commodities of the Realme," do not neglect fishing (this is a reference to the strength of the Dutch in the herring fisheries) and avoid excesses of consumption of food and rayment.

England's Treasure

The emphasis in *A Discourse of Trade* is on the East India Company and its innocence of responsibility for Britain being drained of its money. The aim of *England's Treasure by Forraign Trade* is far wider, to make the point that trade should be balanced not bilaterally with each country but overall, that spending specie to acquire valuable goods is a means of getting more specie, that it is a mistake to seek to regulate the level of the exchange rate through manipulation, as Gerard Malynes wanted Britain to do, and that while it is wise to accumulate a treasure it should be a moderate one and in real goods, such as ships and stores, as well as in specie. Mun understood that the balance of trade differed from the balance of payments (on current account) because of payments like those for freight and shipping. He was interested in how to reckon the balance of payments, as were also many early mercantilists. He was, as Viner says, a mercantilist but an anti-bullionist (1937, p. 5) or perhaps more accurately a moderate bullionist.

His greatest contribution is in insisting on the multilateral nature of trade. The East India Company bought some of the silver it shipped to India in Cadiz and Lisbon, but most in Amsterdam. Most again was foreign coin. If the exchange on Amsterdam was low, because of an adverse English balance of trade with the Dutch, florins could be acquired in roundabout fashion, buying bills on Spain, Italy or elsewhere, and with those moneys, assuming that their countries had a surplus of Dutch bills on Amsterdam, with Spanish currency, buying first Florentine, then Venetian, then Frankfurt or Antwerp bills, until at last there is a claim on moneys in Amsterdam (*England's Treasure*, pp. 47, 8).

The specie exported to buy goods for re-export against specie brought back to England was likened to seed-corn, ostensibly thrown on the ground, that produced more corn in good season (*England's Treasure*, p. 21), a simile that pleased both Adam Smith (1937, p. 400) and was noted by Alfred Marshall (1890, Appendix B, footnote quoted in Marshall, 1961, II, p. 752). Charles Wilson characterizes the theory as "using a sprat to catch a mackerel," and notes that it would not apply to the use of specie in the importing of timber from Norway, since heavy timber did not lend itself to re-export (1949, pp. 154–5). Thomas Mun's insistence on the re-exporting of imports to offset the original use of specie in importing marks a way station on the road from barter to well-developed multilateral trade based on bills of exchange. The Hanseatic League traded by bartering, or its close equivalent, selling goods to a country for local money that was then fully spent in acquiring new goods. The use of specie to pay for import surpluses was an intermediate step. A further advance was multilateral balancing through the use of bills of exchange as originally practiced by the Italian bankers. This was spreading rapidly within Europe and Mun was its prophet. Bills of exchange on Amsterdam were traded in 1585 in Antwerp, Cologne, Danzig, Hamburg, Lisbon, Lubeck, Middelburg, Rouen and Seville. By 1634 six more cities had been added, including Frankfurt, London and Paris; by 1707 nine more (Sperling, 1962, p. 451). Silver and gold were still required outside Europe and inside by persistent deficit countries like Spain. But within the West sophistication was increasing, and with it a declining need for settling bilateral balances in specie. While the world of Thomas Mun was not like that of Alfred Marshall, as Eli Heckscher (1950) claimed and Charles Wilson (1957) denied, it increasingly became so after 1700 (Price, 1961, p. 273) when money was again scarce.

Mun has been called the last of the early mercantilists (DeRoover, 1949, p. 157), and one can see his thought changing. In *A Discourse of Trade* he considers that the loss of specie to foreigners who sell goods in England for exported coin is easily remedied by application of the Statute of Employment, requiring that foreigners use the monies earned by their imports into England in buying English goods for export (p. 54). A few years later in *England's Treasure* he concludes that the Statute of "Imployments" cannot increase or preserve England's specie (ch. X). At first blush it seems an efficient way to augment England's treasure. On reflection he argues that bilaterally balanced trade is inefficient, as it distorts channels which might fit into multilateral patterns, that forcing foreign merchants to take English wares reduces the supply that English merchants might export, and that treasure can still be exported by English importers. Thus the multilateral balancing by bills of exchange of *A Discourse* is generalized.

In *England's Treasure* Mun comes close to developing a theory of international trade and specie movements as a self-equilibrating mechanism, but falls just short of the notion of the price-specie-flow mechanism that had to wait for David Hume (1752) to express with great clarity. As Viner points out, however, the essential elements of the theory were already available in previous literature and several fairly satisfactory attempts had been made to bring them together (1937, p. 84).

> As plenty or scarcity of mony do make the price of the exchange high or low, so the over or under ballance of our trade doth effectually cause the plenty or scarcity of mony. (*England's Treasure*, p. 39)

> It is a common saying that plenty or scarcity of mony makes all things dear or cheap; and this mony is either gotten or lost in forraign trade by the over and under ballancing of the same. (Ibid., p. 20)

It is argued that the Spanish treasure cannot be kept from other kingdoms by any prohibition made in Spain (ibid., p. 23) and that no force such as the public authority proposed by Malynes could keep the price of bills at par if the underlying balance of trade is not favorable (ibid., ch. XIV).

Mun's pamphlet was published posthumously in 1664 by his son, as noted earlier, because of the Second Anglo-Dutch War. Large parts of the essay are spent not in detailing the qualities required in a merchant trading abroad – an excursus in which he anticipated Jacques Savary's *Le parfait negociant* (1675) and which differs sharply from Adam Smith (1937, p. 112); in arguing with Misselden against Malynes; or in developing the theory of the balance of trade – so much as in criticizing the British for being too little like the Dutch who work hard, trade industriously, and consume little. He is critical of the Dutch for their weak ships (the flyboat, or *fluitschip*), resents their competition and attacks in Asia, protests that they take too many fish in English waters, and objects that they depend on alliance with England against Spain but reap the rich fruit of British trade "out of our own bosoms" (*England's Treasure*, p. 80). None the less it is clear that he admires the Dutch for having done so much in trade with such limited resources, all the while resisting the Spanish armies, and wishes that the English would reform "our vicious idleness" (ibid., p. 84) and compete with the Dutch in shipping, fish and trade. One can find an echo in these chapters of current American discussion of Japan.

The penultimate chapter touches on the topic of how to draw up a "ballance of trade," including not only merchandise as reported by the customs office's books, but also estimates for freight, duties, losses at sea, travel, remittances such as those of the Church, gifts, etc. As a conclusion he dismisses as unimportant most policies of bilateralism, currency manipulation, exchange-rate intervention and regulation of exports of bullion. Any such attempt to gain money for the kingdom may work for a time, but the important policy is to cherish and promote foreign trade as a whole. The point that a country without mines to produce gold and silver could rely on trade to obtain its money was not original with Mun, although he kept returning to it (*Forraign Trade*, pp. 135, 145). Jean Bodin in the sixteenth century had said that salt, wine and wheat were the mines of France (Wilson, 1967, p. 524) and Antonio Serra had written *A Brief Discourse on a Possible Means of Causing Gold and Silver to abound in Kingdoms where there are no mines* in 1613 (ibid., p. 493). The wealth of every kingdom is partly natural – the product of land and sea such as wool, cattle, corn, lead, tin, fish and many things for raiment and munition (*Discourse*, p. 50) – and partly artificial – cloth. With this wealth, England can acquire the foreign goods it needs and her Treasure by Forraign Trade.

Note

1. Pages cited from *A Discourse* are from the 1622 original text in the Kress Library, Harvard University, Cambridge, Massachusetts. Those from *England's Treasure* are taken from its reproduction in J.R. McCulloch, ed., *Early English Tracts on Commerce*, Cambridge: Cambridge University Press, 1954, from the pagination of the pamphlet at the bottom of the page, not the page number of the book at the top.

References

Aström, Sven-Erik (1962), *From Cloth to Iron: the Anglo-Baltic Trade in the Late Seventeenth Century*, Helsinki: Centraltryckeriet.

Attman, Artur (1983), *Dutch Enterprise in the World Bullion Trade, 1550–1800*, Gothenburg: Kungl. Vetenkaps- och Vittergets-Samhållet.

Barbour, Violet (1966), *Capitalism and Amsterdam in the 17th Century*, Ann Arbor: University of Michigan Press; first published in 1950.

Bogucka, Maria (1975), "The Monetary Crisis of the XVII Century and its Social and Psychological Consequences in Poland," *Journal of European Economic History*, vol. 4, no. 1 (Spring), pp. 137–52.

Braudel, Fernand (1982), *The Wheels of Commerce*, vol. 2 of *Civilization & Capitalism , 15th–18th Century*, New York: Harper & Row.

Chaudhuri, K.N. (1965), *The English East India Company; The Study of an Early Joint-Stock Company, 1600–1640*, London: Frank Cass.

Chaudhuri, K.N. (1978), *The Trading World of Asia and the East India Company, 1660–1860*, Cambridge: Cambridge University Press.

Day, John (1978), "The Great Bullion Famine of the Fifteenth Century," *Past and Present*, no. 79, pp. 3–54.

DeRoover, Raymond (1949), *Gresham on Foreign Exchange: An Essay on Early English Mercantilism*, Cambridge, Mass.: Harvard University Press.

DeRoover, Raymond (1957), "Thomas Mun in Italy," *Bulletin of the Institute of Historical Research*, vol. 30, no. 81 (May), pp. 80–5.

DeVries, Jan (1976), *The Economy of Europe in an Age of Crisis, 1600–1750*, Cambridge: Cambridge University Press.

Glamann, Kristof (1958), *Dutch Asiatic Trade, 1620–1740*, Copenhagen: Danish Science Press; The Hague: Martinus Nijhoff.

Heckscher, Eli F. (1935), *Mercantilism*, authorized English translation by Mendel Shapiro, 2 vols. London: George Allen & Unwin.

Heckscher, Eli F. (1950), "Multilateralism, Baltic Trade and the Mercantilists," *Economic History Review* (2nd series) vol. 3, no. 2 (May), pp. 219–28.

Hume, David (1752), *Political Discourses* in *Essays, Moral, Political and Literary*, Edinburgh, 1875 edn.

Hinton, R.W.K. (1955), "The Mercantile System in the Time of Thomas Mun," *Economic History Review* (2nd series) vol. 7, no. 3 (April), pp. 277–90.

Jeannin, P. (1982), "The Sea-borne and the Overland Trade Routes of Northern Europe in the XVIth and XVIIth Centuries," *Journal of European Economic History*, vol. 11, no. 1 (Spring), pp. 5–59.

Larsen, Karen (1948), *A History of Norway*, Princeton: Princeton University Press, for the American-Scandinavian Foundation.

Maczak, Antoni (1976), "Money and Society in Poland and Lithuania in the 16th and 17th Centuries," *Journal of European Economic History*, vol. 5, no. 1 (Spring), pp. 69–104.

Marshall, Alfred (1890), *Principles of Economics*, London: Macmillan.

Marshall, Alfred (1961), *Principles of Economics*, 9th (Variorum) edn with annotations by C.W. Guillebaud, 2 vols, London: Macmillan, for the Royal Economic Society.

McCullogh, J.R., ed. (1954), *Early English Tracts of Commerce*, Cambridge: Cambridge University Press, for the Economic History Society; first published in 1856.

Meuvret, Jean (1970), "Monetary Circulation and the Economic Utilization of Money in 16th and 17th Century France," in Rondo Cameron, ed., *Essays in French Economic History*, Homewood, Ill.: Irwin, pp. 140–9; written in 1947.

Morineau, Michel (1985), *Incroyables gazettes et fabuleux métaux: Les retours des trésors américains d'après les gazettes hollandaises (XVIe-XVIIe siècles)*, Paris: Cambridge University Press/Editions de la Maison des Sciences de l'Homme.

Munro, John H. (1979), "Bullionism and the Bill of Exchange in England, 1272–1663: A Study in Monetary Management and Popular Prejudice," in Center for Medieval and Renaissance Studies, *The Dawn of Modern Banking*, New Haven, Conn.: Yale University Press, pp. 169–240.

Parker, Geoffrey (1972), *The Army of Flanders and the Spanish Road, 1567–1659: The Logistics of Spanish Victory and Defeat in the Low Countries' Wars*, Cambridge: Cambridge University Press.

Parry, J.H. (1967), "Transport and Trade Routes," in E.E. Rich and C.H. Wilson, eds, *The Cambridge Economic History of Europe*, vol. IV, *The Economy of Expanding Europe in the Sixteenth and Seventeenth Centuries*, Cambridge: Cambridge University Press, pp. 155–219.

Price, Jacob M. (1961), "Multilateralism and/or Bilateralism: the Settlement of British Trade Balances with 'the North', *c.*1700," *Economic History Review* (2nd series) vol. 14, no. 2 (December), pp. 254–74.

Rich, E.E. (1967), Preface to E.E. Rich and C.H. Wilson, eds, *The Cambridge Economic History of Europe*, vol. 4, *The Economy of Expanding Europe in the Sixteenth and Seventeenth Centuries*, Cambridge: Cambridge University Press.

Ruggerio, Romano (1964), "Encore la crise de 1619–22," *Annales, Economies,*

Sociétés, Civilisations, vol. 19, no. 1 (January–February), pp. 31–8.

Smith, Adam (1937), *An Inquiry into the Nature and Causes of the Wealth of Nations*, (Cannan edn), New York: Modern Library; first published 1776.

Sperling, J. (1962), "The International Payments Mechanism in the Seventeenth and Eighteenth Centuries," *Economic History Review* (2nd series) vol. 14, no. 3 (August), pp. 446–68.

Spooner, Frank C. (1972), *The International Economy and Monetary Movements in France, 1493–1725*, Cambridge, Mass.: Harvard University Press.

Supple, Barry E. (1954), "Thomas Mun and the Commercial Crisis, 1623," *Bulletin of the Institute of Historical Research*, vol. 27, no. 75 (May), pp. 91–4.

Supple, Barry E. (1957), "Currency and Commerce in the Early Seventeenth Century," *Economic History Review* (2nd series) vol. 10, no. 2 (May), pp. 239–55.

Supple, Barry E. (1959), *Commercial Crisis and Change in England, 1600–1642: A Study in the Instability of a Mercantile Economy*, Cambridge: Cambridge University Press.

Tawney, R.H. (1958), *Business and Politics Under James I: Lionel Cranfield as Merchant and Minister*, Cambridge: Cambridge University Press.

Thirsk, Joan and J.P. Cooper, eds, (1972), *Seventeenth Century Economic Documents*, Oxford: Clarendon.

Thomas, P.J. (1926), *Mercantilism and the East India Trade: An Early Phase of the Free Trade vs Protection Controversy*, London: P.S. King.

Vilar, Pierre (1976), *A History of Gold and Money, 1450–1920*, London, New Left Books.

Viner, Jacob (1937), *Studies in the Theory of International Trade*, New York: Harper and Brothers.

Wallerstein, Immanuel (1980), *The Modern World-System II: Mercantilism and the Consolidation of the European World-Economy, 1600–1750*, New York: Academic Press.

Wilson, Charles (1949), "Treasure and Trade Balances: The Mercantilist Problem," *Economic History Review* (2nd series) vol. 2, no. 2 (May), pp. 152–61.

Wilson, Charles (1957), "Mercantilism: Some Vicissitudes of an Idea," *Economic History Review* (2nd series) vol. 10, no. 2 (May), pp. 181–8.

Wilson, Charles (1967), "Trade, Society and the State," in E.E. Rich and C.H. Wilson, eds, *The Cambridge Economic History of Europe*, vol. IV, *The Economy of Expanding Europe in the Sixteenth and Seventeenth Centuries*, Cambridge: Cambridge University Press.

5

The historical background: Adam Smith and the industrial revolution

I

An early version of this paper focused on the dispute, if one may call it that, between historians of economic thought who sometimes seek to demonstrate that Adam Smith was fully aware of the industrial revolution taking place around him as he wrote the *Wealth of Nations*, and economic historians who think he was not. It is true, as Samuel Johnson put it, that "in lapidary inscriptions, a man is not upon oath" and piety demands that the guest of honour be given the benefit of the doubt. None the less, I propose to dismiss this question quickly, with an open-and-shut verdict for the economic historians.

It is first necessary to establish that Adam Smith could have known, or should have known, about the industrial revolution. The timing of the industrial revolution is not fully agreed. Rostow, for example, puts "take-off" in 1783 which is too late for a book published in 1776, and even, allowing for publication lag, for the new Chapter VIII of Book IV and the new material of Chapter I of Book V which appeared in the third edition of 1783. But neither the *Wealth of Nations* nor the Industrial Revolution had production functions with point-input/point-output. The former, as we shall see, was 25 years in the writing, and the

* Published in Thomas Wilson and Andrew S. Skinner, eds, *The Market and the State: Essays in Honour of Adam Smith* (Oxford: Clarendon Press, 1976), presented at the Bicentennial Celebration in Glasgow of the publication of Smith's *The Wealth of Nations*. I am indebted for ideas, references, corrections and comments to Mark Blaug, Kenneth Carpenter, Ronald Coase, Larry Neal and Charles Staley.

timing and indicator(s) of the industrial revolution varies among observers, as Charles and Richard Tilly indicate in the following table:[1]

T.S. Ashton	1760s	Major inventions
T.S. Ashton	1782	Cotton exports; Cloth production
Deane and Cole	1740s	Industrial production
Deane and Cole	1780s	Output per head
Walther Hoffmann	1780	Industrial production
W.W. Rostow	1783	Exports and imports
J.A. Schumpeter	1787	Price level

Ashton notes that for those who like to be precise in such matters the lighting of the first furnace at the Carron iron works in 1760 may serve to mark the beginning of the industrial revolution in Scotland.[2] Technology change turned sharply upward in the 1760s. The number of patents, which had seldom been a dozen a year prior to 1760, rose to 31 in 1766 and 36 in 1769, the year in which James Watt took out his patent on the steam engine and Arkwright his on the waterframe.[3] Halévy notes that all the important inventions were crowded into the decade from 1766 to 1775.[4]

Assume for the sake of argument that the industrial revolution was in the making from 1760 to 1782. These are roughly the dates of the *Wealth of Nations*. Dugald Stewart held that its fundamental principles go back to Adam Smith's lectures delivered in Glasgow in 1752–3, in his first year as professor of moral philosophy. W.R. Scott claims that his Edinburgh period from 1748 to 1751 was of the greatest importance for the central principle of his system, and that by 1749 at the latest he had begun to apply the idea of natural liberty – which emerged directly from the Naturalism of the 18th century – to commerce and industry. The lecture of 1755 at the Club dominated by Andrew Cochrane, provost and merchant, contained an important early statement of his ideas. The manuscript of about 1763 discovered by Scott contains a well worked-out version of the opening chapters of Book I on the division of labour, most of it preserved in the final version published 13 years later, but with one alteration in illustration significant for our purpose.[5] In the 13 years between this draft and 1776, Smith spent two years in France, six years at Kirkcaldy in Scotland, and four years in London, the last ten writing, finishing, and publishing the book, as well as, at Kirkcaldy, in studying botany and some other sciences. Writing to Andreas Holt in October 1780, Smith said:

> My own life has been extremely uniform. Upon my return to Great Britain, I retired to a small town in Scotland in the place of my nativity, where I

> continued to live for six years in great tranquility and almost complete retirement.[6]

Scott makes clear that Smith's technique of writing with a closely reasoned argument made revision difficult, as the text would have to be altered for a considerable distance.[7] It may well be true, as Viner says, that "Smith was a keen observer of his surroundings and used skilfully what he saw to illustrate his general argument" – though Viner, puzzled by his unawareness of the bondage of Scottish colliers and salters and by the absence of references to the general economic state of the Highlands, excuses his failure to respond to his immediate Scottish background by saying his loyalties were largely to a wider Britain.[8] But it is surely going too far to say with Max Lerner in his introduction to the Modern Library edition:

> Smith kept his eyes and ears open . . . Here was something that gave order and meaning to the newly emerged world of commerce and the newly emerging world of industry . . . Smith took ten more years. He could not be hurried in his task. He had to read and observe further. He poked his nose into old books and new factories.[9]

The last sentence is half right.

The text of the *Wealth of Nations* supports Smith on "great tranquility and almost complete retirement" against Viner and Lerner on contemporaneous illustrations. There is virtually no mention of cotton textiles, only one reference to Manchester in a list of cities, nothing on pottery, nothing on new methods of producing beer. Canals are dealt with under public works, but illustrated by the canal of Languedoc, finished in 1681, rather than by the Bridgewater canal of 1761, which initiated the spate of canal building and improvement in Britain culminating in the canal mania of the 1790s. Turnpikes are referred to without notice of the fact that travel times were falling rapidly: the first stagecoach from Birmingham to London in 1731 took 2½ days; by 1776 the time had been reduced to 19 hours.

A historian of economic thought argues ingeniously that Smith was "fully aware" of the technical change about him, citing, for example, his text of the use of coal and wood as fuel, and the use of coal in iron and all other metals.[10] But Smith does not discuss the spread of coal in industrial use. Coal is mentioned to illustrate points about rent[11] or consumer taxes,[12] primarily about space heating. From a discussion of producing iron with charcoal in the United States where wood is abundant[13] and a mention of iron in a list – "In some manufactures, besides, coal is a necessary instrument of trade; as in those of glass, iron and all other metals" (825–6; V. ii. k. 12) – I find it difficult to infer that Smith had a full appreciation of Darby's contribution in substituting coke for charcoal. Nor is it credible on the basis of the fact that Smith and Watt were acquainted, even friends, and had close friends in common – Dr Joseph Black, the chemist and Dr John Roebuck, an owner of the Carron Iron Works – to hypothesize a conversation in which Watt explained to Smith the machine-operated devices of the Soho plant of Boulton and Watt.[14] There is no evidence that Watt and Smith met after Smith left Glasgow in 1763, and the evidence for their friendship in Smith's Glasgow period is slight, resting largely on Smiles's *Lives of Boulton and Watt*, unsupported by anything in the surviving papers of Watt or Smith.[15] The minutes of Glasgow University do record that Smith was the chairman of a committee in 1762 to get back from Watt, and from the University printer Foulis, some of their considerable number of rooms.[16] To go from these contacts to a suppositious post-1768 conversation is a heroic leap.

Moreover, Smith's analysis is static. Manufactures using coal were "confined principally to the coal countries; other parts of the country, on account of the high price of this necessary article, not being able to work so cheap" (825; V. ii. k. 12). He recognized the importance of transport costs in the delivered price of coal. What he failed to see was that the high price of coal away from the mines provided a strong incentive to reduce transport costs and to improve efficiency in coal consumption through invention, as in the Watt steam engine. In 1771 James Watt was working to install his new machines in Cornish copper mines where failures were being recorded because of the high price of coal and the inefficiency of the Newcomen engine.[17]

It is unnecessary to labour the point. The *Wealth of Nations* was the work of a literary economist, like some of us, who drew his examples from books, not from the world around him. The steam engine which replaced the plough and grain mills to illustrate the third source of improvement from the division of labour – invention – between the 1763 and the 1776 versions of *WN* I. i was a Newcomen engine, not a separate-condenser Watt, and the story of the invention is said by Cannan to be mythical and drawn from a book published in 1744 (*WN* 9–10). Most of the books Smith relies on, moreover, are fairly old, published in the first quarter of the eighteenth century, and the bulk of his dated illustrations relate to this period as well, e.g. the detailed discussion on public debt in *WN* V. iii (865–7, 868–9 and 874–5 §§13–25, 27–30, 42–6). A detailed and up-to-the-minute discussion in the 3rd edition of 1783 concerns not industrial output but the impact of the herring bounty on the catch (485ff.; IV. v. a. 28–35 and Appendix I). Though it be heretical to say so, when he does go into the real world, he occasionally makes a slip. Smith believed, for example, that higher wages were paid in Birmingham than Sheffield because the former produced goods based on "fashion and fancy", rather than the latter's "use or necessity".[18] Birmingham goods are "continuously changing and seldom last long enough to be considered old established manufactures". This implies that the higher wages are required because of the risks of unemployment, whereas Birmingham workers were paid more because new articles in the "toy trade" – small metal articles, especially buckles and buttons – called for workmen with a capacity to adapt to new tasks, and to a continuous improvement in techniques.[19]

I see no need to make the case that Adam Smith had a thorough understanding of the industrial revolution, and this for two reasons. In the first place, much of the substance of what he wrote was derivative; the division of labour goes back to Henry Martin's *Considerations on the East-India Trade* of 1701, and can be found worked out complete with references to pins in Carl's *Traité de la Richesse des Princes et de leurs états et des moyens simples et naturels* of 1722. Indeed, a powerful case has been made lately that much of the inspiration for Smith's emphasis on the division of labour came from Plato, rather than immediately earlier sources like the *Encyclopédie*, Harris, Locke, Mun or Mandeville (a list which omits Martin and Carl). Strong parallels are drawn between illustrations which Plato puts in the mouth of Socrates, and those used by Smith, along with the observation that the Smith library contained three sets of Plato's complete works.[20] Like Shakespeare who borrowed his plays, his originality was in how vividly and graphically he expressed ideas which were common currency.

Secondly, few are given to recognize the beginnings of great movements at their birth. Smith wrote throughout of "improvements" in an age, as Samuel Johnson said, when the "world was running mad after innovation". A number of the inventors and entrepreneurs had large visions. In his well-known letter to Watt in 1769, Boulton, in reply to the Roebuck suggestion that he buy a licence to make the Watt steam engine for Warwick, Staffordshire and Derby, said that he wanted to make it for the whole world.[21] To James Boswell in 1776 he stated "I sell here, Sir, what the world wants to have, Power".[22] Similar exalted commercial ambition can be found in Josiah Wedgwood, who wrote to his partner, Thomas Bentley, in November 1768: "I have lately had a vision by night of some Vases, Tablets, &c with which Articles we shall certainly serve the *Whole World*".[23] On a more technical level, note Watt's interest in 1769 in a patent for drawing a chaise by steam.[24] The idea had been advanced by his Glasgow colleague in 1759.[25] Boulton and Dr William Small had many conversations on applying steam power to canal boats.[26]

The men associated with nascent industry were many of them caught up in the changes around them. Watt and Boulton visited the Bridgewater canal before undertaking the surveying of canal sites in Scotland in the former case, and the pushing for the Grand Trunk in the latter.[27] Thomas Bentley "participated in the new spirit. Canal-navigation, moss draining, new materials for manufacturers, improved processes for industry, new inventions of all kinds arrested and retained his attention."[28] The "spirit for enterprise and improvement in the arts" of (medical) Dr John Roebuck, friend of Adam Smith and patron of James Watt, inventor of the lead chamber method of making sulphuric acid, entrepreneur of coal mines and the Carron iron works, "was well known."[29] Even Edmund Burke, as Koebner reminds us, in 1769 collected instances of the energies displayed in British manufactures, and praised the "spirited, inventive, and enterprising traders of Manchester."[30] From one viewpoint,

> It was an age in which economic and industrial facts loomed large; they advanced new claims and offered new stimulus . . . a vast change had come over the general mind; the objects of knowledge, study and pursuit were seen in altered perspective and acquired altered values.[31]

Adam Smith, as just noted, wrote continuously of improvements but without suggesting he was aware of their details, on the one hand, or their collective import, on the other. The reason is surely contained in a statement by a colleague of mine at the Massachusetts Institute of Technology, a metallurgist, Cyril Stanley Smith, a statement which both sums up the nature of the industrial revolution and reveals how Adam Smith could have ignored it:

> These and hundreds more materials and uses grew symbiotically through history, in a manner analogous to the S-curve of a phase transformation of the materials themselves. There was a stage, invisible except in retrospect, wherein fluctuations from the *status-quo*, involving only small localised distortion, began to interact and consolidate into a new structure; this nucleus then grew in a more or less constant environment at an increasing rate because of the increasing interfacial opportunity, until finally its growth was slowed and stopped by depletion of material necessary for growth, or by the growing counter-pressure of other aspects of the environment. Any change in conditions (thermo-dynamic = social) may provide an opportunity for a new phase. We all know how the superposition of many small sequential S-curves themselves tend to add up to the giant S-curve of that new and larger structure we call civilisation . . . Because at any one time there are many overlapping competing sub-systems at different stages of maturity but each continually changing the environment of the others, it is often hard to see what is going on. Moreover, nucleation must in principle be invisible, for the germs of the future take their validity only from and in a larger system that has yet to exist. They are at first indistinguishable from mere foolish fluctuations destined to be erased. They begin in opposition to their en-

> vironment, but on reaching maturity they form the new environment by the balance of their multiple interactions. This change of scale and interface with time, of radical misfit turning into conservative interlock, is the essence of history of anything whatever, material, intellectual or social.[32]

Adam Smith has a superb record for forecasting in his remarks on the subject of another revolution, that which started in the same year as the *Wealth of Nations* appeared, unless you take the parochial view of my fellow-citizens of Massachusetts that it started a year and a quarter earlier in the skirmishes at Lexington and Concord. Smith was, moreover, prescient in observing that after freeing the colonies

> Great Britain would not only be immediately free from the whole annual expence of the peace establishment of the colonies, but might settle with them such a treaty of commerce as would eventually secure to her a free trade, more advantageous to the great body of the people, though less so the merchants, than the monopoly which she at present enjoys.[33]

If one takes 1782 or 1783 as the date of ignition of the industrial revolution, the revolution Smith did foresee touched off the one he did not.[34]

II

The industrial revolution is a well-squeezed orange, as Ashton has said, and my friend and former student, Charles Staley, on hearing that I was to write this essay, drew my attention to a quotation from an article on human evolution which he finds applicable to studies of Adam Smith:

> Human paleontology shares a peculiar trait with such disparate subjects as theology and extra-terrestrial biology. It contains more practitioners than objects for study. This abundance of specialists has assumed the careful scrutiny of every bump on every bone.[35]

Despite the danger of strongly diminishing returns, however, it may be appropriate to touch on three aspects of the industrial revolution which currently interest me: the overtaking of Holland by Britain; the role of beauty in technical change; and Stephen Marglin's recent suggestion that the division of labour was practised under capitalism less for efficiency than for lowering the return to labour.

In a curious passage, Adam Smith claimed that England and France consisted in great measure of proprietors and cultivators, whereas Holland and Hamburg were composed chiefly of merchants, artificers, and manufacturers (632; IV. ix. 13). Hollander states that this remark is meant comparatively, but the basis for such a judgment is not evident.[36] Holland, Smith further thought, was a richer country than England in proportion to the extent of its territory and the number of its people (91; I. ix. 10). In a later passage he states that Holland is by far the richest country in Europe, and England perhaps the second richest (354; II. v. 35), which is not completely congruent with a still later passage in which he states that there is no country in Europe, Holland not excepted, whose law is, on the whole, more favourable to the interests of commerce and manufactures, which have been making more rapid progress than agriculture (393; III. iv. 20). Still later, Smith discusses the ruin of manufactures in Holland which is ascribed to high wages (826–7, 857; V. ii. k. 14, 79). This last view of Dutch industry is accepted by modern scholars.[37]

The picture could have been aided by a better historical sense. Holland was the richest country in Europe in 1675, after which its commerce and manufactures decayed and those of Britain advanced rapidly. By 1730, or at the latest 1750, according to modern interpretations, income per capita in Britain had outstripped that in Holland. A successful protectionist policy in Britain had stimulated linen production, especially in Ireland and in Scotland after union in 1707. Dutch potters moved to London to produce their Delftware there to exploit a patent taken out in 1671. Haarlem lost out in bleaching in 1730. Herring fishing and whaling declined. The staple trade of Amsterdam, moreover, had been replaced by direct exchanges of English woolens for German linen and Spanish and Portuguese wine and treasure, without the need for shipment through the intermediary of Amsterdam. Adam Smith was mistaken in relation to stapling. He thought that commerce or at least the carrying trade derived from opulence rather than led to it (354; II. v. 35) and stated elsewhere that merchants exchanging Königsberg corn for Portuguese wine brought both to Amsterdam and incurred the double charge for loading and unloading because they felt uneasy separated from their capital (421–2; IV. ii. 6), thus ignoring the stapling function of grading, packing, storing, and the economies of scale of broader markets.

It is odd that Smith should have thought Britain behind Holland in manufactures in the late 1760s. Josiah Tucker in 1757 wrote:

> Few countries equal, perhaps none excell the English in the Numbers and Contrivance of their Machines to abridge Labour. Indeed the Dutch are superior to them in the Use and Application of Wind-Mills for sawing Timber, expressing Oil, making Paper, and the like. But in regard to Mines and Metals of all sorts, the English are uncommonly dextrous in their contrivance of the mechanic powers . . . Slitting Mills, Flatting Mills, Water Wheels, Steam Engines . . . Yet all these, curious as they may seem are little more than preparation or introduction for further operations . . . at Birmingham, Wolverhampton, Sheffield and other Manufacturing Places,

> almost every Master Manufacturer hath a new Invention of his own, and is daily improving on those of others.[38]

There is the view that it was not the decline of Holland so much as the fact that after 1648 she stood still and let other countries overtake her,[39] or that the Dutch economy did not decline absolutely until 1780.[40] This overlooks the deterioration of Leiden, Haarlem, Delft, and Saandam in shipbuilding, and the loss of the Dutch monopoly in shipping and in the herring catch.

Most of all, however, Smith seems not to have appreciated how much of the advances in commerce and industry in Britain were the result of intervention in the economic process as opposed to the simple and obvious system of natural liberty. The Dutch monopoly in commerce was invaded by the Navigation Acts of the seventeenth century, which Smith more or less approved of on the ground of national defence, though in this respect one view contends that he was being ironic.[41] Smith explicitly objects to the monopoly of the carrying trade with the colonies and insists that Britain was a great nation in trade before the Navigation Acts (563; IV. vii. c. 23). This seems to overlook the basis for Glasgow's prosperity with the monopoly of tobacco trade with Maryland and Virginia; after its loss in 1776 Glasgow fell on hard times. And it especially ignores the position in textiles, where commercial policy was highly effective. It may well be that responsiveness of the economy is more important than the nature of the stimulus; under certain conditions, industry will be spurred either by an increase in a tariff or by a decrease. But the case of cotton textiles is instructive.

At the end of the seventeenth century Indian calicos were beginning to eat into the market for woolens, and the latter interests persuaded Parliament in 1700 to prohibit the import of printed calicos. In the interest of the printing industry, plain muslins were permitted entry under a heavy duty, but as these grew in volume, the woolen and linen interests agitated for an excise tax on calicos printed, stained, painted or dyed, which affected local finishing. This was levied at the rate of 3d. per yard in 1712, and raised to 6d. in 1714. Demand kept rising, and such was the distress among woolen producers that in 1720 an act was passed prohibiting the use or wear of all printed or dyed calicos except muslin, neckcloths and fustians. None of these measures was effective. In 1736 the manufacture of calico was permitted with a linen warp. Walpole's tariff reforms of 1721–42 abolished duties on exports of manufactured goods, and on imports of raw materials, stimulating textile manufacturing of all kinds, though the import of raw cotton did not pick up until after 1748, well after Kay's 1738 invention of the flying shuttle, which could not help, given the yarn bottleneck. When this was broken by Arkwright's waterframe in 1769 and Hargreaves's spinning jenny in 1770, cotton was used first for stockings and then in 1773 for cloth. Arkwright petitioned Parliament to remove the duties, and by 1774 every kind of printed, stained and dyed stuffs made wholly from cotton became lawful.[42] As noted in the 1783 edition of the *Wealth of Nations*, this last year also saw the enactment of a prohibition on the export of utensils used in the cotton, linen, woolen and silk manufacture (624; IV. viii. 43).

Commercial policy equally played a role in the development of linen manufacture in Ireland and Scotland, and in iron.

Policy, as I have noted, was probably less important than the response to it. In the 1820s, Spitalfields would respond positively to a reduction in tariffs as Manchester responded positively to a reduction in imports. The difference between silk and cotton lay in the elasticity of the supply of raw material, low in silk, high (after 1790) in cotton. Entrepreneurs were ready to be stimulated by lower prices or higher, of outputs or inputs.

III

Smith's distinction between fashion and fancy and use or necessity, referred to earlier, had its echo in the division of Josiah Wedgwood's manufactures between Wedgwood and (Thomas) Wedgwood, which produced useful wares at Burslem, and the new plant at Etruria, established for producing ornamental ware by Wedgwood and Bentley.[43] It survives today in Galbraith's distinction between necessities and those goods forced on passive consumers by advertising, and in the lines drawn by developing countries between things they need and those like Coca-Cola and breakfast foods which ignorant consumers waste their substance on. At every epoch it is of doubtful validity.

The usual view is that necessity is the mother of invention, or invention the mother of necessity, or both. Or that inventions leapfrog through disproportionalities, what Hirschman calls unbalanced growth, with expansion at one stage of production putting pressure on improved efficiency upstream in the production of inputs, and downstream in the consumption of its outputs. None of this can be denied. But Cyril Smith makes the point that a very large number of inventions, and particularly the improvement of materials, derive from the attempt to make goods more pleasing – softer, whiter, more brightly coloured, more beautiful,[44] better tasting. A great deal of the effort of merchants and manufacturers is in improving quality, and in standardizing it. Price is important, but so are quality and the assurance of quality which comes from standardization, a point largely missed initially in the Russian revolution and in economic development in the less developed countries, and one which was inherent in capitalist organization under both putting out and the factory system.

In another paper, I make the distinction between the "gains-from-trade" merchant, who largely buys goods where they are cheap, and sells them where they are dear, and the "value-added" merchant, who concerns himself especially with extending the market by insisting that the goods be made better so as to have greater appeal. These are ideal types, of course, since the purest of gains-from-trade merchants, buying spice, silk, or china in the East and selling it in London, will repackage and sort the goods to add some value; at the other extreme, the value-added merchant must still buy cheap and sell dear. The distinction is not quite identical with Adam Smith's separation of the speculative merchant, who exercises no one regular, established, or well-known branch of business, who can sometimes accumulate a considerable fortune by two or three successful speculations, and the slow accumulator in a single industry who seldom makes a great fortune but in consequence of a long life of industry, frugality and attention (113–14; I. x. b. 38). The gains-from-trade merchant leaves goods much as they are, save for sorting, perhaps curing, packing, refining, and the like, relatively simple functions, while the value-added merchant puts pressure on his suppliers to make goods more efficient for the task in hand, and in the cases of textiles, glass, china, and 'toys' more attractive, or cheaper for the same degree of attraction. The chemical industry grew partly from pure science, the investigations of Priestly and Lavoisier which fall within the period of the industrial revolution, and also from pressure of industry to find cheaper methods of bleaching and dyeing, not for "use or necessity" but for "fashion and fancy".

Adam Smith frequently failed to distinguish between commerce and industry, treating them almost as one word, like "damnYankee", and for the purpose of quality improvement and standardization, the differences are minimal. The merchant often retained the finishing stages of textile manufacture in his own hands, or subcontracted them out under rigorous supervision. Such was the case in Manchester,[45] Leeds,[46] Beauvais,[47] Le Mans,[48] Barmen and Elberfeld.[49] In toy-making there was a feverish search for novelties, and designing advances was an important function of the industry.[50] Wedgwood wrote to Bentley in 1770: "I am fully persuaded that the farther we proceed in it [ornament] the richer crop we shall reap of *Fame and Profit*."[51] The hunt for synthetic dyes in the mid-nineteenth century which ushered in the organic chemistry revolution had much the same spur.

It is of particular interest that import substitution and the search for economical beauty go hand in hand. The industrial revolution can be said to have resulted in large measure from the search for substitutes for cottons and china from the East. Calicos in Britain have been discussed. "Siamoises" were a cotton cloth in France devised to imitate the stuffs worn by the wife of the Ambassador of Siam when she was presented to the court of Louis XIV in 1684.[52] China ware was brought from the Orient by the early East India companies at the turn of the sixteenth to seventeenth centuries. Meissen ware in the first decade of the eighteenth century and Sèvres china in the 1750s were early responses. They were both supported by courts, and did not need to meet a market test. Delft provided a less elegant substitute for the earthenware of the ordinary household until Wedgwood took over,[53] in the same way as chemically bleached, dyed and printed cotton took over from unbleached or crudely bleached, and undyed or crudely dyed linens and woolens. Especially in the hot climates of the Mediterranean and Latin America, lighter and brighter were better.

Standardization means value-added in various ways. To the modern consumer, homespun, handcrafted, tailormade is superior to machine-produced goods, but that is because they are made to superior specifications. When all goods were homemade, the lack of standardization was a disability, whether in stacking plates which exerted unequal pressure on one another, and thus broke[54] or the cloth that did not meet specifications and was returned, thus increasing the need for investment in working capital.

One form of standardization is attention to delivery dates. In the eighteenth century this did not seem pressing, but infrequent sailings of ships, the fleet leaving Bristol for Newfoundland once a year, for example, made prompt delivery a capital-saving virtue, as did marketing through semi-annual or annual fairs.

The spectacular inventions in steam, waterframe, spinning jenny, coke, puddling and the like occupy front and centre of the stage of the industrial revolution. Firms like Boulton and Watt capable of contemplating steam-chaises and moving canal boats by steam engine in 1759 and 1770 capture the imagination. But the steady improvement of goods in quality and standardization was a vital part of the action. Search for quality frequently led to breakthroughs such as Wedgwood's creamware, and jaspar, which leads Cyril Smith to hold Wedgwood's science-based, market-oriented industry as a nucleus of English economic growth as much as the better-known contributions of Darby and Cort to iron manufacture or of Watt to power production.[55]

IV

Adam Smith's contribution which is most clearly related to the industrial revolution is doubtless the opening discussion in Book I,

Chapters i–iii. This has recently been praised and damned: praised by Lord Kaldor who asserts that economics went wrong immediately in the middle of Chapter iv when Smith abandoned his examination of the relationship between the division of labour and the extent of the market and moved off into money, the theory of value and the distribution of income, what most think his central contribution to our subject but Kaldor views as irrelevant;[56] damned by Stephen A. Marglin, a radical critic, who contends that the division of labour has nothing to do with efficiency and everything to do with the expropriation of income from the worker by the capitalist.[57] I leave the quarrel with Kaldor to others concerned with resource allocation and income distribution, and address Marglin's proposition. It is, I believe, of interest today because it makes a strong appeal to young people and to non-economist Marxists, such as Johann Galtung, who believe that all dependence, even interdependence, is exploitation.[58] Hierarchical organizations of all kinds are under attack, and the radical faith suggests that foremen and supervisors in a factory should be chosen arbitrarily, by lot, by election, rather than by competitive means, and paid the same as those whom they supervise.

Marglin's argument proceeds along the same lines as Smith's, as he discusses the pin factory and the three sources of improvement: dexterity, the saving of waiting time between tasks, and the devising of inventions which abridge labour by workers concentrating on a single task. The last it is difficult to take seriously, and Marglin does not, pointing out that Smith himself observes that a workman engaged in repetitive tasks has no occasion to exercise his understanding or to exercise his invention in finding out expedients for difficulties which never occur (734; V. i. f. 50). Adam Smith indeed very quickly notes that "All the improvements in machinery . . . have by no means been the inventions of those who had occasion to use the machines" but that

> in the progress of society, philosophy or speculation becomes, like every other employment, the principal or sole task of a particular class of citizens. Like every other employment, too, it is subdivided into a great number of different branches, each of which affords occupation to a peculiar tribe or class of philosophers; and this sub-division of employment in philosophy, as well as in every other business, improves dexterity and saves time. (10; I. i. 9)

Waiting time does not impress Marglin either. A farmer gains from staying with a task long enough to minimize set-up time. A pinmaker could undertake the first of ten operations for a day or days at a time, and then change, to reduce set-up time to an insignificant portion of total work time and then move to the second.[59] In this case, however, Marglin may have missed the point about the extent of the market. He claims that

> if each producer could integrate the component tasks of pin manufacture into a marketable product, he would soon discover that he had no need to deal with the market for pins through the intermediation of the putter-outer. He could sell directly and appropriate to himself the profit that the capitalist derived from mediating between the producer and the market.[60]

The pin producer now performs all the ten manufacturing tasks and markets the product as well. Peasants perhaps can sell their produce above their own sustenance in a local market. It is not clear that the pin market is so organized. The pin is a "very trifling manufacture."[61] Any substantial number produced must be moved in what Smith calls "distant sale."[62] Distant sale requires knowledge of languages, commercial practice, credit standings, modes of transport, etc., forms of dexterity and skill which the home pinmaker may not readily achieve.

The matter is neatly put in a letter of August 23, 1772 to Thomas Bentley by Josiah Wedgwood who sought to lower piece-rates for workers:

> I have had several *Talks* with our men at the Ornamental works lately about the price of our workmanships, and the necessity of lowering it, especially in Flowerpots, Bowpots [boughpots] and Teapots, and as I find their chief reason against lowering their prices is the small quantity made of each, which creates them as much trouble in *tuning their fiddle* as *playing the tune*, I have promised them that they shall make dozens and Groces of Flower, and Teapots, and of the Vases and Bowpots too, as often as we dare venture at such quantities.[63]

Wedgwood, of course, divided functions with the merchant Bentley, and Boulton with the merchant Fothergill. Scale sufficient to handle the waiting-time problem required distant sale, which required merchants. On occasion distant marketing preceded efficient scale in production; often they grew side by side. Colonial trade provided important outlets:

> The process of industrialisation in England from the second quarter of the eighteenth century was to an important extent the response to colonial demands for nails, axes, firearms, buckles, coaches, clocks, saddles, handkerchiefs, buttons, cordage and a thousand other things, "Goods, several sorts."[64]

To this list could be added pottery, both useful and ornamental, produced in the potteries of Staffordshire, the "bulk" of which was exported to the continent and the islands of North America, as well as to every port in Europe.[65] Between Easter 1771 and Easter 1772, at its height, 72 percent of Yorkshire's production of woolens was exported. While output was increasing four times between 1770 and 1780, the export proportion was rising from roughly 40 percent (in 1695) to two-thirds (in 1800).[66] The notion of a producer selling his own output without the aid of specialists seems in these circumstances utopian.

Marglin has most difficulty in maintaining that the division of labour does not add to output per unit of input in improving dexterity. He makes several damaging concessions. Adam Smith would be difficult to counter if he had been dealing with musicians, dancers or surgeons;[67] to the extent that the skills at issue are difficult to acquire, specialization is essential to the division of labour into separate operations.[68] Later he suggests that factory employment can be attractive to men, whereas earlier he had said that whenever it is possible to avoid factory employment, workers had done so.[69] Most of his illustrations are drawn from the cotton-textile industry. In engineering, or in pottery, however, natural ability, training and practice are all needed:

> My idea was to settle a manufactory for the steam engine near to my own by the side of the canal where I would erect all the conveniences necessary for the completion of the engines and from which manufactory we would serve all the world with engines of all sizes. By these means and your [i.e. James Watt] assistance we could engage and instruct some excellent workmen (with more excellent tools than would be worth any man's while to procure for one single engine) and could execute the engine 20 per cent cheaper than it would otherwise be executed and with as great a difference in accuracy as there is between the blacksmith and the mathematical instrument maker.[70]

> I have trained up many and am training up more young plain Country Lads, all of which that betray any genius are taught to draw, from which I derive many advantages that are not to be found in any manufacture that is or can be established in a great and Debauched capital.[71]

> We have not got thirty hands here, but I have much ado to keep the new ones quiet. Some will not work in Black. Others say they will never learn this new business, and want to be released to make Terrines and sauce boats again. I do not know what I shall do with them, we have too many *fresh* hands to take in at once, though we have business enough for them, if they knew, or would have the patience to learn to do it, but they do not seem to relish the thought of a second apprenticeship.[72]

> You observe very justly that few hands can be got to paint flowers in the style we want them. I may add, nor any other work we do – *We must make them* . . . Where among our Potters could I get a complete Vase maker? Nay I could not get a hand through the whole Pottery to make a tableplate without training them up for that purpose, and you must be content to train up such Painters as offer to you and not turn them adrift because they cannot immediately form their hands to our new stile.[73]

> You must have more Painters – You shall, – But remember that there are none *ready made* . . . So please give my respects to Mr. Rhodes, and tell him if any man who offers himself is *sober*, he must make him *everything else*.[74]

A strong case can be made that the division of labour has very little to do with capitalism. Plato's interest in the subject has been referred to earlier. Haley asserts that Dutch shipbuilding in the seventeenth century would have made a better illustration of division of labour than pin-making.[75] Standardized flyboats were built at Saandam using labour-saving machinery – wind-driven saw mills and great cranes which handled heavy timbers; inventories of timber for building four or five thousand ships were kept in hand. In the second war with England, Saandam turned out a ship a day.[76] A century earlier, moreover, in 1574, the Arsenal at Venice, a shipyard under public management, turned out a merchant galley for the edification of Henry III of France in less than an hour:

> Mass production of ships of a standard design became the hallmark of the Venetian Arsenal. Workmen developed unusual skill and efficiency as a result of specialisation; standard replaceable parts made repairs easy; stockpiling such parts allowed the state to maintain a cadre of skilled men always available, who, in case of need, could direct the efforts of a suddenly enlarged workforce, such as might be required for building a new fleet in a hurry.[77]

Marglin admits that evidence in support of his view that the division of labour represents not efficiency but an attempt to divide and conquer is "naturally enough, not easy to come by", and "not overwhelming".[78] He cites in support a cotton textile manufacturer who kept his manager from knowing anything about mixing cotton, or costs, so that he could never take the business away from him.[79] Evidence that care was taken not to furnish industrial secrets to individuals considered as possible candidates for setting up rival establishments is abundant, however. Workmen who had been trained were not encouraged to take their skills elsewhere; on the contrary, manufacturers like Josiah Wedgwood petitioned Parliament to restrict their movement abroad, were wary of imitators, separated the different departments in Etruria and gave each one only outside entrances, so as to prevent workmen in one department from wandering about and picking up proprietary information.[80] At one point (1769) Wedgwood wrote:

> If we get these new painters, and the figure makers, we shall do pretty well in those branches. But these hands should if possible be kept by themselves 'till we are better acquainted with them otherwise they may do us a great deal of mischief if we should be obliged to part with them soon.[81]

It is true enough that owners of proprietary information hung on to it under capitalism as long as they could. It is also true that competition tended to erode its scarcity value. The merchant started out with a monopoly of information, concerning where goods could be found, and where they were wanted. The monopoly over information was related to education, and when education became general, the merchant lost his pre-eminence, except to the extent that he innovated; direct buying and selling replaced him. His efforts to make goods of higher quality, more promptly and cheaper, were part of the innovating process, and generally involved improvements which were unpatentable and insufficiently distinctive to be awarded prizes.

Marglin further insists that the move from the cottage to the factory was prompted by efforts to enforce the division of labour and thereby exploit workers, rather than by application of power, prevention of pilferage and adulteration (the worker's only countervailing tactic, according to Marglin). The view is a familiar one. Charles Bray regarded the ordinary factory as a "cunning device to cheat workmen out of their birthright" and justified the cottage factory which the Quakers set up in Coventry as Owenism.[82] One could equally refer to Karl Polanyi, a Christian socialist, who excoriated the market but exonerated the factory,[83] or Lazlett who embraces the market but rejects the factory.[84] But to pursue these aspects of the industrial revolution would take us too far afield.

Smith was aware that the division of labour could lead to a dead end; in a passage far removed from Book I, he holds:

> The man whose life is spent performing a few simple operations, of which the effects too are, perhaps, always the same or very nearly the same, has no occasion to exert his understanding, or to exercise his invention in finding out expedients for removing difficulties which never occur. He naturally loses, therefore, the habit of such exertion, and generally becomes as stupid and ignorant as it is possible for a human creature to become . . . His dexterity at his own particular trade seems, in his manner, to be acquired at the expense of his intellectual, social and martial virtues . . . In the barbarous societies . . . the varied occupations of every man oblige every man to exert his capacity, and to invent expedients for removing difficulties which are continually occurring. Invention is kept alive, and the mind is not suffered to fall into that drowsy stupidity, which, in a civilized society, seems to numb the understanding of almost all the inferior ranks of people.[85]

This emphasis on the social aspects of the division of labour anticipates a line of argument found in Mary Wollstonecraft, who maintains that:

> The time which, a celebrated writer says, is sauntered away, in going from one part of an employment to another, is the very time that preserves the man from degenerating into a brute . . . The very gait of the man who is his own master is so much more steady than the slouching step of the servant of a servant.[86]

It is also found in John Ruskin, who held that division of labour should be regarded as division of men:

> Divided into mere fragments of men – broken into small fragments and crumbs of life, so that all the little piece of intelligence that is left in a man is not enough to make a pin, or a nail, but exhausts itself in making the point of a pin, or the head of a nail.[87]

These unhappy consequences may result from the division of labour, or what van der Wee refers to as "excessive division of labour," though in the cottage textile industry, rather than the factory.[88] It is a fair point that the social consequences of the division of labour may be untoward, as Smith recognizes. It is quite a different matter to assert that the economic purpose of the division of labour was exploitation rather than efficiency.

Adam Smith's discussion of allocation, distribution, and the division of labour through the market was largely related to what is now called "proto-industrialization", rather than the industrialization into large factories of the industrial revolution. Large-scale production had existed in isolation for centuries, and in Britain for decades. But proto-industrialization, the specialization by merchants, weavers, spinners, nailers, pinmakers, philosophers, and speculators was efficient rather than exploitative. Rudolf Braun has shown for the Zurich Oberland how proto-industrialization raised the level of living of peasants who were overcrowded on limited land, rather than lowering it. Cottage industry did not uproot men. On the contrary, it gave them work and bread and enabled them not to migrate from their homeland.[89] The factory in the Zurich Oberland was a defensive measure to enable the area to meet the competition of British machine-spun.

In cotton textiles in Switzerland, the early factory pioneers were technical people – Wyss, Honneger, Wild, Oberholzer – who worked on making cloth cheaper, and not on impoverishing the workers who were impoverished by improved and cheaper British exports. The less efficient cottage workers moved into the factory and improved their standard. It was the more effective cottage workers, with greater dexterity, who held on in cottage industry too long when the higher efficiency of factories, as revealed by cheaper goods of a given quality, sealed their doom.[90]

Let us permit the division of labour between Adam Smith and, say, Josiah Wedgwood, though both in their way were protean. Wedgwood was a nucleus-maker and a man who understood nucleation;

> I have for some time been reviewing my experiments, and I find such *Roots*, such *Seeds* would open and branch wonderfully if I could nail myself down to cultivation of them for a year or two. And the Fox-Hunter does not enjoy more pleasure from the chace, than I do from the prosecution of my experiments when I am fairly enter'd in the field, and the farther I go, the wider the field extends before me.[91]

Smith was a man of wide interests in law, moral philosophy, criticism, rhetoric, and agriculture.[92] He approached the heart of the industrial revolution with his division of labour, specialization and exchange, and extent of the market, and planted the seed which has developed into the great social science of economics. That surely is glory enough.

Notes

1. Charles and Richard Tilly, "Emerging Problems in the Modern Economic History of Western Europe," unpublished paper (January 1971), 7.
2. T.S. Ashton, *The Industrial Revolution, 1760–1830* (London, Oxford University Press, 1948), 65.
3. Ibid. 90, 68.
4. Elie Halévy, *A History of the English People in 1815*, Book II, Economic Life (Harmondsworth, Middlesex, Penguin, 1937; first published in English, 1924), 102.
5. William Robert Scott, *Adam Smith as Student and Professor* (New York, August M. Kelley, 1965; originally issued 1937 to mark the bicentennial anniversary of Adam Smith's matriculation as a student at Glasgow University), 57, 61, 81, 82, 312–29.
6. Ibid. 283. Letter 208 dated October 26, 1780.
7. Ibid. 423.
8. Jacob Viner, *Guide to John Rae's Life of Adam Smith* (New York, Augustus M. Kelley, 1965), 15, 101. For a debate on another instance in which Smith may or may not have been an astute observer of the contemporary scene, see John Rae, *Life of Adam Smith* (London, Macmillan & Co., 1895), 229ff., in which Rae takes exception to McCulloch's judgment that Smith did not perceive any foreshadowing of the French Revolution in his long stay in France from 1764 to 1766.
9. Max Lerner, 'Introduction' to Adam Smith, *An Inquiry into the Nature and Causes of the Wealth of Nations*, edited with an introduction, notes and marginal summary, with an enlarged index, by Edwin Cannan (New York, The Modern Library, 1937), viii. All text references to the *Wealth of Nations* (*WN*) are to this edition. The London years from 1772 to 1776, however, were devoted to considerable revision. See Rae, op. cit., 256–8. Rae controverts Thorold Rogers's view that the book lay 'unrevised and unaltered during four years in the author's desk." Ginzburg assumes that revisions were required by political events: Smith "must have realised that his prolonged isolation in the small Scottish town was a mistake, in that he had failed to keep informed on many contemporary problems. The sixties and seventies were important decades in English political history" (Eli Ginzburg, *The House of Adam Smith* (New York, Columbia University Press, 1934), 135). The revisions detailed by Rae, however, dealt with a variety of economic matters – the price of hides, the decline in sugar-refining in colonies taken from the French, American wages, extensive additions in the chapter on revenue – but not with methods of industrial production.

   The literature on the Bridgewater canal, on Boulton and Watt's plant at Soho, and on the Wedgwood factory Etruria is replete with accounts of visitors from all walks of life, including such distinguished personages as the King of Denmark, Baron von Stein of Prussia, Samuel Johnson, Benjamin Franklin, the Duke of Buccleugh, etc. but no Dr Smith.

10. Samuel Hollander, *The Economics of Adam Smith* (Toronto, University of Toronto Press, 1973), 105.
11. *WN*, 165–6; I. xi. c. 15, 17–18. Part II of the chapter.
12. Ibid. 825–6; V. ii. k. 12. "Taxes upon Consumeable Commodities."
13. Ibid. 547; IV. vii. b. 37. Part II of the chapter.
14. Ibid., note. A closer reading of this passage indicates that it does not explicitly state that Watt described Soho to Smith in 1767, although that inference was drawn and is possible. It is of interest that in discussing Smith's friends Viner (op. cit., Chapter 2) does not mention Watt, Boulton, Wedgwood, Arkwright, Darby, Wilkinson or any other leader of the industrial revolution, nor do the biographies of Boulton, Watt, and Wedgwood by H.W. Dickinson, Julia Wedgwood and Samuel Smiles (see footnotes 17, 19, 27, 28, 29 and Samuel Smiles, *Lives of Boulton and Watt, Principally from the Original Soho Mss, Comprising Also a History of the Invention and Introduction of the Steam Engine* (London, John Murray, 1865), 201 and Chapter xviii, mention Smith among the industrialists' friends who are explicitly discussed.
15. Rae, op. cit. 98.
16. Scott, op. cit. 149.
17. James Patrick Muirhead, *The Origins and Progress of the Mechanical Inventions of James Watt, Illustrated by Correspondence with his Friends and the Specification of His Patents* (in three volumes, London, John Murray, 1854), vol. ii, 15.
18. *WN*, 114–15; I. x. b. 42. Part I of the chapter.
19. H.W. Dickinson, *Matthew Boulton* (Cambridge, Cambridge University Press, 1937), 62–3.
20. Vernard Foley, "The Division of Labour in Plato and Smith," *History of Political Economy*, vi (1974), 220–42.
21. Dickinson, op. cit. 76.
22. Ibid. 73.
23. *The Selected Letters of Josiah Wedgwood*, edited by Ann Finer and George Savage (London, Cory, Adams and Mackay, 1965), 68.
24. Muirhead, op. cit. i. 53.
25. Ibid. i. lxvii.
26. Ibid. ii. 5.
27. H.W. Dickinson, *James Watt, Craftsman and Engineer* (Cambridge, Cambridge University Press, 1936) 46; Dickinson, *Matthew Boulton*, 50.
28. Julia Wedgwood, *The Personal Life of Josiah Wedgwood* (London, Macmillan, 1915), 29.
29. James Patrick Muirhead, *The Life of James Watt*, with Selections from his Correspondence (London, John Murray, 1858), 95.
30. Cited by R. Koebner, "Adam Smith and the Industrial Revolution," *Economic History Review* (2nd series) xi, no. 3 (August 1959), 386.
31. Julia Wedgwood, op. cit. 28–9.
32. Cyril Stanley Smith, "Metallurgy as Human Experience," the 1974 Distinguished Lectureship in Materials and Society, *Metallurgical Transactions* A, vol. 6A, no. 4 (April 1975), 605.
33. *WN*, 582; IV. vii. c. 66. Part III of the chapter.

34. C.R. Fay notes that Adam Smith was pre-industrial revolution and that his Revolution with a capital R was 1688, adding that incidentally this was the telephone number of Trevelyan in old Cambridge days. *The World of Adam Smith* (Cambridge, W. Heffer, 1960), 81.
35. David Pilbeoni and Stephen Jay Gould, "Size and Scaling in Human Evolution," *Science*, 186, no. 4167 (December 1974), 892.
36. Hollander, op. cit. 97.
37. Joel Mokyr, "Industrial Growth and Stagnation in the Low Countries, 1800–1850" (doctoral dissertation, Yale University, 1974).
38. Quoted in Dickinson, *Matthew Boulton*, 12 and in Koebner, op. cit. 385–6.
39. Charles Wilson, *The Dutch Republic and the Civilisation of the Seventeenth Century* (London, Weidenfeld and Nicholson, 1958), 230.
40. H.R.C. Wright, *Free Trade and Protection in the Netherlands, 1816–1830* (Cambridge, Cambridge University Press, 1955), 9.
41. Larry Neal, "Adam Smith on Defence and Opulence," Faculty Working Paper no. 214, College of Commerce and Business Administration, University of Illinois at Urbana-Champaign (October 22, 1974). Smith's view that Britain was a great nation in trade prior to the Navigation Laws is controverted in Ralph Davis, *Rise of the British Shipping Industry* (New York, Rowman and Littlefield, 1962), ch. 2.
42. Thomas Ellison, *The Cotton Trade of Great Britain* (first impression, 1886, new edition, New York, Augustus M. Kelley, 1968), 11–12; H.R. Fox Bourne, *English Merchants, Memories in Illustration of the Progress of British Commerce* (London, Richard Bentley, 1866), 152.
43. Julia Wedgwood, op. cit. 123. In 1770, Josiah Wedgwood found the distinction between "ornamental" and "useful" ware overdrawn. It was not to be based on fineness, richness, price, colour, enamelling, or gilding, and it was important to avoid disputes such as those in France, where the King forbade the use of gold to ordinary potters, to reserve it for the Royal Pottery at Sèvres. "Useful ware was that made use of at meals" (*Selected Letters of Josiah Wedgwood*, 95–6).
44. Cyril Stanley Smith, "Art, Technology and Science: Notes on their Historical Interaction," *Technology and Culture*, ii, no. 4 (October 1970), 493–549.
45. Alfred P. Wadsworth and Julia de Lucy Mann, *The Cotton Trade and Industrial Lancashire, 1600–1780* (Manchester, Manchester University Press, 1931), 250–2.
46. R.G. Wilson, *Gentlemen Merchants, The Merchant Community of Leeds, 1700–1830* (Manchester, Manchester University Press, 1971), 65–70.
47. Pierre Goubert, *Familles marchands sous l'Ancient Régime: les Danse et les Motte* (Paris, SEVPEN, 1959), 69.
48. François Dornic, *L'Industrie textile dans le Maine et ses débouches internationaux (1650–1815)* (Le Mans, Editions Pierre-Belon, 1955), 44.
49. Wolfgang Köllmann, *Sozialgeschichte der Stadt Barmen im 19. Jahrhundert* (Tübingen, J.C.B. Mohr (Paul Siebeck), 1960), 3.
50. Dickinson, *Matthew Boulton*, 63.
51. *Selected Letters of Josiah Wedgwood*, 97. In an early letter (October 1, 1769) he had put the matter in a more modern economic mode: "Let us begin, proceed, and finish our future schemes, our days and years, in the pursuit of *Fortune*, *Fame*, and the *Public Good*" (ibid. 82). In the pursuit

of fortune, Wedgwood and Bentley sought to keep their designs and materials secret; for the sake of the public good, they would welcome imitation.

52. Pierre Dardel, *Commerce, industrie et navigation à Rouen et au Havre au XVIIIe siècle* (Rouen, Société Libre d'Emulation de la Seine-Maritime, 1966), 117.
53. *Selected Letters of Josiah Wedgwood*, 3.
54. Julia Wedgwood, op. cit. 22.
55. Cyril S. Smith, "Metallurgy as Human Experience," 614.
56. Nicholas Kaldor, "The Irrelevance of Equilibrium Economics," *Economic Journal*, lxxxii (December 1972), 1240.
57. Stephen A. Marglin, "What Do Bosses Do, Part I," *Review of Radical Political Economy*, vi, no. 2 (Summer, 1974), 60–112.
58. Johann Galtung, "The Future of Human Society," *Futures, The Journal of Forecasting and Planning*, 2, no. ii (June 1970), 132–42.
59. Marglin, op. cit. 66–7.
60. Loc. cit.
61. In the 1763 draft, the example is called "a frivolous instance" (reprinted in W.R. Scott, 328). In Carl's *Traité de la Richesse des princes et de leurs états et des moyens simples et naturels*, the pin is called "the least of our needs" (Paris, Chez Theodore Legas, three volumes, 1722), i, 18.
62. *WN* 359, 381, 382, 393 etc.; III. i. 5, III. iii. 17, 19, 20; III. iv. 20.
63. *Selected Letters of Josiah Wedgwood*, 130.
64. Ralph Davis, "English Foreign Trade, 1700–1774," *Economic History Review* (2nd series) xv, no. 2 (May 1962), reprinted in W.E. Minchinton, ed., *The Growth of Overseas Trade in the 17th and 18th Centuries* (London, Methuen, 1969), 106.
65. *Selected Letters of Josiah Wedgwood*, 24, 29.
66. R.G. Wilson, op. cit. 19, 42.
67. Marglin, op. cit. 68.
68. Loc. cit.
69. Ibid. 98 n.
70. Letter of Matthew Boulton to James Watt, February 1769, in Dickinson, *Matthew Boulton*, 76.
71. 1770 letter of Boulton, ibid. 60.
72. Letter of Josiah Wedgwood to Thomas Bentley, November 1769, *Selected Letters of Josiah Wedgwood*, 84. See also "It is this sort of *time loseing* with Uniques which keeps ingenious Artists who are connected with Great Men of taste poor, and would make us so too if we did too much in that way" (ibid. 85).
73. Letter of Josiah Wedgwood to Thomas Bentley, May 19, 1770, ibid. 92.
74. Ibid., letter of May 23, 1770.
75. K.H.D. Haley, *The Dutch in the Seventeenth Century* (London, Thames and Hudson, 1972), 19.
76. Violet Barbour, "Dutch and English Merchant Shipping in the Seventeenth Century," *Economic History Review*, ii (1929–30), reprinted in E.M. Carus-Wilson, *Essays in Economic History* (London, Edward Arnold, 1954), 239, 242.
77. William H. McNeill, *Venice, The Hinge of Europe, 1081–1797* (Chicago, University of Chicago Press, 1974), 6 and note 9, p. 244.
78. Marglin, op. cit. 72.
79. Ibid. 74.

80. *Selected Letters of Josiah Wedgwood*, 76.
81. Letter of April 1769 to Thomas Bentley, ibid.
82. John Prest, *The Industrial Revolution of Coventry* (London, Oxford University Press, 1960), 104.
83. See my essay on "*The Great Transformation*, by Karl Polanyi," *Daedalus*, ciii, no. 1 (Winter 1974), 45–52.
84. Peter Lazlett, *The World We have Lost* (New York, Charles Scribner's Sons, 1965).
85. *WN*, 734–5; V. i, Part III, Art. 2nd (V. i. f. 50, 51).
86. Mary Wollstonecraft, *French Revolution*, 1795, the conclusion. This and the following reference were kindly communicated to me by Ellen Moers.
87. John Ruskin, *Stones of Venice*, ii (London, 1853), ch. vi.
88. Herman van der Wee, 'Structural Changes and Specialization in the Industry of Southern Netherlands, 1100–1600," *Economic History Review* (2nd series) xxviii, no. 2 (May 1975), 204.
89. R. Braun, *Industrialisierung und Volksleben, Die Veränderungen der Lebensform in einem ländlichen Industriegebiet vor 1800 Züricher Oberland*, (Erlenbach–Zurich and Stuttgart, Euger Rentsch Verlag, 1965), 241.
90. R. Braun, *Sozialer und kultureller Wandel in einem ländlichen Industriegebiet im 19. und 20. Jahrhundert* (Erlenbach-Zurich and Stuttgart, Eugen Rentsch Verlag, 1965), ch. 2.
91. *Selected Letters of Josiah Wedgwood*, 159.
92. Scott, op. cit. 46.

6

Commercial policy between the wars

War and postwar reconstruction

The First World War marked the end of an era in the history of commercial relations among countries. New boundaries set in the peace treaties, especially with Austria and Hungary, converted pre-1914 internal trade to international trade. Trade relations interrupted by war could not always be restored. Extended fighting and disruption of peacetime economic intercourse produced substantial changes in the economic capacities and interests of major trading nations. Monetary disturbance evoked responses in trade policy, especially increases in tariffs, to offset effects of exchange depreciation abroad. A loosely concerted attempt was made after the war to patch up the fabric of trade relationships, but with nothing like the fervour exhibited after the Second World War. There was virtually no planning of postwar trade policies, despite President Wilson's third of the fourteen points that called for "removal, as far as possible, of all economic barriers and the establishment of an equality of trade conditions among all nations consenting to the peace and associating themselves with its maintenance."

Exigencies of war led to changes in commercial policy. The McKenna

* Published as Chapter II of Peter Mathias and Sidney Pollard, eds, *The Cambridge Economic History of Europe*, vol. VIII, *The Industrial Economies: The Development of Economic and Social Policies*, Cambridge: Cambridge University Press, 1989. The absence of references to the literature of the last decade is owing to the fact that the essay was turned in, slightly ahead of the deadline, in February 1976. I am grateful for the comments on the original draft of Barry Eichengreen, Jonathan Hughes and Donald Moggridge.

budget in the United Kingdom in 1915 imposed duties of 33⅓ percent on motor cars and parts, musical instruments, clocks, watches, and cinematographic film in an effort to reduce imports of luxuries and to save shipping space – although the point has been made that the shipping space taken by watches is minimal (Kreider, 1943, p. 13). Unlike previous luxury taxes in the United Kingdom, these duties on imports were not matched by domestic excises to eliminate the protective effect. The tariffs, moreover, made it possible for the United Kingdom to discriminate in trade in favour of the British Empire, something it could not do under the regime of free trade which had prevailed since the 1850s. Canada had granted preferential tariff treatment to the United Kingdom on a unilateral and non-reciprocal basis since 1898 – the United Kingdom assenting to the extent that it denounced the trade treaties with Germany and Belgium going back to the 1860s under which those countries had the right to claim concessions made by one part of the Empire to another on a most-favoured-nation basis. The Finance Act of 1919 further reduced excise taxes on Empire tea, cocoa, coffee, chicory, currants, and certain dried fruits by one-sixth, and on Empire wines by one-third. The Key Industries Act of 1919, designed to strengthen defence industries, equally contained preferences for the Empire, as did the Safeguarding of Industries Act of 1921. If the McKenna duties were designed to economize shipping and foreign exchange, the Finance Act of 1919 to raise revenue, and the Key Industries Act of 1919 to serve national defence, the Safeguarding of Industries Act levying tariffs on imports of gloves, domestic glassware, and gas mantles – a list extended in 1925 to include leather, lace, cutlery, pottery, packing paper, and enameled hollow ware – represented straightforward protection of industries hurt by foreign competition.

A number of countries increased tariff coverage and raised rates to gain revenue. French minimum tariff rates had been raised by 1918 from 5 to 20 percent, and maximum rates from 10 to 40 percent. The use of import quotas in France dates from 1919, rather than the depression in 1930, although export and import prohibitions were a widespread feature of Colbert's mercantilism two and a half centuries earlier. In countries where the principal fiscal instrument was the tariff, such as Canada, tariff duties were increased early after the outbreak of war.

Fitful attention was given to commodity problems by Britain. Long concerned about the prospect of interruption of cotton supplies from the southern United States as a result either of boll weevil or black rebellion, Britain had contemplated an Empire scheme for producing cotton. The planting of Gezira in the Sudan was started in 1914 with the decision to irrigate 300,000 acres, but the Empire Cotton Growing Corporation was not chartered until November 1921, sometime after the acute shortage of cotton fibre during the war and early postwar period. An Empire Resources Development Committee proposed in 1915 a scheme for producing palm kernel in West Africa and processing it in the United Kingdom, foreshadowing the East African groundnut scheme after the Second World War. The technique envisaged was an export tax of £2 per ton to be continued for five years after the war, but that was to be rebated in favour of British processors. The scheme was started in October 1919 but met sharp Gold Coast resistance. When the price of palm kernel fell, the project became untenable and the duty was withdrawn in July 1922 (Hancock, 1940, pp. 113–18).

Limited as it was, postwar planning took place along lines of military alliance. France took the lead in an Allied economic conference in June 1916 that produced a resolution committing the Allies to take first temporary and then permanent steps to make themselves independent of enemy countries in matters of raw-material supply, essential manufactures, and the organization of trade, finance and shipping (Drummond, 1972, p. 56). Neutral reaction, including that of the United States, neutral at that time, was hostile. When the United States entered the war, the notion was dropped despite French efforts to revive it at Versailles (Viner, 1950, pp. 24–5). On the other side, Germany and Austria concluded a treaty before the Armistice in 1918, providing for customs union after the war; the arrangement was not for complete free trade within the union, but permitted Austria-Hungary to retain protection at a preferential level in certain weak industries (ibid., pp. 105–6). In defeat it proved academic, except perhaps as a precedent to the 1930 proposal for *Zollunion* (customs union) between Austria and Germany, and the 1937 anschluss.

Commercial-policy features of the treaties ending the First World War were minimal. Germany was required to agree to apply the tariff nomenclature worked out at The Hague in 1913 (as well as to accept the international conventions of 1904 and 1910 suppressing the white slave trade, the conventions of 16 and 19 November 1885 regarding the establishment of a concert pitch (the agreed wavelength of the musical note of A above middle C) and a host of others). The principal effect of these measures seems to have been to stiffen German resistance to subscribing to the agreements. More significantly, Germany was required by the treaty of Versailles to grant the Allies unilateral and unconditional most-favoured-nation treatment for five years. On January 10, 1925, when the five years elapsed and Germany was free to negotiate trade agreements on her own, the postwar period of reconstruction may be said to have come to an end – at least in the area of trade. The lapse of these provisions helped Germany but posed a problem for France which now had to negotiate to obtain outlets for

Alsatian textiles and Lorraine minette iron ore which earlier had been marketed in Germany without payment of duties (Schuker, 1976, pp. 219–27).

These five years, however, constituted a period of considerable disorder in fluctuations of business and of exchange rates, and, in consequence, in policies relating to international trade. Anti-dumping legislation was enacted in Japan in 1920, in Australia, the United Kingdom, New Zealand and the United States in 1921, when also earlier legislation dating from 1904 in Canada was amended; the anti-dumping provisions of the Fordney–McCumber tariff took effect in 1922 (Viner, 1966, pp. 192, 219, 227, 231, 246, 258). The United Kingdom further authorized 33⅓ percent duties against countries devaluing their currencies, although these were never imposed and were allowed to lapse in 1930. With the franc free to fluctuate, France initiated a system of tariff coefficients which could be adjusted to compensate for inflation at home or revaluations of the exchange rate. The Fordney–McCumber Act of 1922 in the United States not only extended anti-dumping provisions but raised tariffs on a variety of materials which had fallen in price in the sharp recession of 1920–1. Insult was added to injury from this and from the wartime enactment of Prohibition in the United States that cut off imports of wine, beer, and spirits, when the United States took sanitary measures against Spanish grapes and oranges to limit the danger of entry of fruit flies, without giving consideration to the possibility of refrigeration which kills the fruit fly (Jones, 1934, p. 35).

In Eastern Europe, new countries struggled with inflation, depreciation and inadequate sources of revenue, and were forced to levy heavy taxes on trade in a vain effort to restore financial balance. Export taxes were imposed along with import duties, despite a variety of international resolutions urging strongly against prohibitions of exports, and taxation, on the basis of equal access to materials (Bergsten, 1974, pp. 23–4). The finances of Austria and Hungary were supervised by experts under programmes of the Finance Committee of the League of Nations – Austria in 1922, Hungary in 1924 – which experts exerted strenuous efforts to liberalize trade.

As the world economy slowly settled down, the prewar system of trade treaties was resumed, with extension of the principle of high legislative tariffs – so-called "bargaining" or "fighting" tariffs – which would be reduced through mutual tariff concessions agreed in bilateral treaties, and extended through the most-favoured-nation clause. To a degree, the initial increases in tariff rates succeeded better than the subsequent reduction through negotiation, especially as not all countries were prepared to subscribe to the unconditional version of the most-favoured-nation clause (Page, 1927). The United States especially, with its high Fordney–McCumber tariff, stood aloof from the system. Except in the period from 1890 to 1909, the United States administration was not empowered to enter into tariff treaties; under the Dingley tariff from 1897 to 1919, no tariff treaties came into force since Senate approval was required but not forthcoming. The Fordney–McCumber tariff of 1922, however, changed United States policy from conditional most-favoured-nation to unconditional treatment. Under the conditional version, concessions offered to one country were made available to others only in exchange for a reciprocal concession. The provision of the Tariff Act of 1922 for retaliation by the United States against countries which discriminated against American exports was judged to require the more general form of the non-discrimination clause (US Department of State, *Foreign Relations of the United States*, 1923, I, pp. 131–3). Exceptions to the unconditional most-favoured-nation clause were recognized for specific countries, such as Cuba and the Philippines in so far as the United States was concerned, and regional arrangements, in which "propinquity" was a usual characteristic (Viner, 1950, p. 19). The British position, opposed by the United States, was that a further exception could be based on "historical associations, such as were generally recognized". This referred to Empire preference.

As a policy, Empire preference meant more the relations of the United Kingdom with the Dominions than those with the colonies, including India. "Tariff reformers" at the turn of the century would have welcomed an imperial *Zollverein*, eliminating all tariffs between the mother country and the rest of the Empire. This was opposed not only by British free traders, who viewed free-trade areas and preferences as disguises for protectionism, but also by the Dominions that regarded tariffs as a symbol of sovereignty and were unwilling to remove all vestiges of protection for their manufactures against British products. Preferences in the Dominions meant largely tariffs to be levied in the United Kingdom against non-Empire foodstuffs, and higher domestic tariffs on foreign manufactures, rather than reductions in existing duties on British goods. Resistance to Empire preference in United Kingdom came not only from free traders, but from those who wanted to hold down the price of food, on the one hand, and those who sought protection against Empire as well as against foreign food producers, on the other.

The slogan of Empire visionaries in the United Kingdom and the Dominions after the war was "men, money, and markets". "Men" meant assisted settlement of British workers in the Dominions; "money" help for Empire borrowers in various ways, ranging from preferences in the queue to guaranteed interest; "markets" referred to Empire preference, to a considerable degree in new products that especially Australia wished to have produced for export by immigrants settled on new farms – particularly dried fruit and frozen beef – rather than the traditional wheat, butter, wool, apples, bacon, and cheese.

The Imperial Economic Conference of 1923 made little progress toward tariff preferences: the election called by Stanley Baldwin in 1924 to provide tariffs that could be used for the purpose ended in a Labor victory and even repeal of the McKenna duties and the preferences granted under them. The return of Baldwin to power eleven months later restored the McKenna duties, with lorries added to motor cars, but the Conservatives stopped short of extending tariff discrimination. Feeble efforts were made to undertake non-tariff discrimination through an Empire Marketing Board which was to perform research and promotion. Empire settlement fizzled gently. Empire preference was postponed.

The reconstruction period to 1925 or so was characterized by instability. Rapidly changing exchange rates required rapidly changing tariffs through countervailing charges, or the application of coefficients. Trade agreements were frequently contracted for only three months. Where changes in tariff rates did not occur, administrative regulation was applied. The League of Nations Economic Committee worked to improve the position through such actions as the International Convention Relating to the Simplification of Custom Formalities of 1923, although this soon proved inadequate as far as worst practices were concerned (Winslow, 1936, p. 182).

Normalization of world trade

The end of the reconstruction period about the middle of the decade was marked by the opening up of capital markets, following the success of the Dawes Loan in 1924 that primed the resumption of German reparations after the hyperinflation of 1923, by the restoration of the pound sterling to par on the gold standard in 1925, or perhaps by the expiration of the Versailles restriction on Germany's right to conclude commercial treaties, and with it the rapid extension of trade agreements in Europe. Whatever the event, it marked the initiation of increased efforts for trade normalization. A minor effort was represented by the International Convention for the Protection of Industrial Property of 1925 (Brown, 1950, p. 34). Of greater weight were the Convention for the Abolition of Import and Export Prohibitions and Restrictions, with which was associated a special agreement on hides, skins and bones, and a World Economic Conference on trade expansion, all in 1927. In 1929 a special conference produced a convention calling for national treatment for foreign nationals and enterprises. A modernized tariff nomenclature to replace the 1913 Hague list was started in the 1920s; a first draft was produced in 1931, and a final one in 1937 (League of Nations, 1942, p. 45).

A number of these conventions failed to be ratified. That on the treatment of foreign nationals fell through because some states were unwilling to liberalize, and the liberal states were unwilling to sign an agreement which would have weakened the force of the principle of national treatment (League of Nations, 1942, p. 27). The Convention for the Abolition of Import and Export Prohibitions and Restrictions finally lapsed when the Poles refused to sign, because of an exception made for Germany, which reduced the value of the treaty in their eyes. Agreement on a tariff truce and subsequent reductions in rates was reached at the 1927 World Economic Conference, but this meeting was attended by delegations in their individual capacities and did not bind governments. Governments agreed on the necessity of reducing tariffs but did nothing about it. The League of Nations review of commercial policies in the interwar period called it a striking paradox that conferences unanimously adopted recommendations, and governments proclaimed their intentions to lower tariffs, but did nothing (League of Nations, 1942, p. 101), asking why governments made such recommendations if they did not propose to carry them out (ibid., p. 109). The answer furnished by one economist who had served on the economic secretariat of the League was that "the pseudo-internationalism of the nineteenth century was clearly an outgrowth of British financial leadership and trading enterprise, backed by the economic supremacy of London and by the British Navy" (Condliffe 1940, p. 118). With British hegemony lost and nothing to take its place, international relations lapsed into anarchy. The United Kingdom lost the will and lacked the power to enforce international cooperation as she had done in the nineteenth century (ibid., p. 145).

Discouragement over the failure of tariffs to come down despite agreement to lower them led to an attempt at a commodity-by-commodity approach, foreshadowing the free trade for iron and steel undertaken in the European Coal and Steel Community on Robert Schuman's initiative in May 1950. The Economic Committee of the League of Nations reported in March 1928 that there was no prospect of a general tariff reduction by means of standard cuts or the setting of a maximum scale of duties. Cement and aluminium were chosen for a case-by-case approach. A year of negotiation, however, produced no result. The League's account of the attempt cites as reasons, first, that reductions in duties in single products would upset national industrial structures; second, that it would increase the protection of finished goods – implying the so-called effective-rate-of-protection argument which was more fully developed in the 1960s; and third, that among the limited groups of commodities and countries concerned, compensatory reductions were hard to find (League of Nations, 1942, p. 128–9).

While governments were agreeing to the necessity to lower tariffs but doing nothing about it, action was taken directly on a number of commodity fronts. Most conspicuous was the Stevenson rubber plan of 1923–4 which raised the price of rubber by 1926 to almost four times its 1923 level. To American protests, the British replied that it was

> impossible to argue that the present high price is attributable solely or even mainly to the operation of the rubber restriction scheme. It is due to the great expansion of the demand for rubber. Only one half of the supply comes from the restricted area. (US Department of State, *Foreign Relations of the United States*, 1926, II, p. 359)

The fact that the other half – the Netherlands East Indies – had been left out of the scheme contributed to its early breakdown (Knorr, 1946).

More cartels were formed in a variety of commodities, that Mason divides into three groups: industrial raw materials and foodstuffs, like tin, oil, wheat, sugar, etc.; standardized processed and semi-fabricated goods such as steel rails, cement, tinplate, plate glass, dyes, etc.; and highly fabricated, specialized, and frequently patented items such as electrical equipment, pharmaceuticals, glass, etc. (1946, p. 16). Mason notes that the Soviet Union was a party to at least three international control schemes and eight cartel arrangements, despite its hostility to capitalism (ibid., p. 14 n.). Most of the commodity agreements begun in the 1920s broke down in the depression of the 1930s. The rubber scheme collapsed in 1928. Prices of agricultural commodities leveled off in 1925 and declined thereafter, faster after 1928, as European reconstruction crowded the extra-European supplies expanded to fill the gap left by war and postwar shortages, and demand shrank with such changes as the replacement of oats for horses by gasoline for motor cars.

Two of the most durable agreements were in oil: the As Is Agreement concluded at Achnacarry, Scotland, in 1928 between Sir Henry Detering of the Shell Oil Company and Walter Teagle of the Standard Oil Company of New Jersey, that provided that no oil company would seek to penetrate into markets where it was not already distributing, so that everything would stay "as is"; and in the same year the Red Line Agreement, among members of the Turkish Petroleum Company, that drew a line across the Middle East (through what is now Kuwait) and limited exploration by partners below that line, thereby ultimately making it possible for the Standard Oil Company of California, which was not a partner, to discover oil in Saudi Arabia (Federal Trade Commission 1952, pp. 199ff., 63).

National programmes further affected world markets in wheat and sugar. The Italian "battle for grain" begun by Mussolini in 1925 was of limited economic significance, since Italy could not escape dependence on foreign supplies, but provided a disturbing symptom of the troubles of the 1930s. The United Kingdom expanded production of beet sugar through a bounty; Japan undertook sugar production in Formosa (Taiwan) and ceased to buy from Java. As the price of wheat declined, Germany raised tariffs in 1928 to slow down the movement of labour off the farm. From 1927 to 1931, German tariffs on foodstuffs were broadly doubled. France raised tariffs in 1928 and 1929 before resorting to quotas. Mixing provisions, under which foreign grain had to be mixed with domestic, were undertaken from 1929 on, patterned after the practice in motion pictures which allowed exhibitors to show foreign films only in fixed proportions to those domestically produced. In the United States, help for agriculture took the form of proposals for export subsidies, but President Coolidge's veto of the McNary–Haugen bill in 1928 led presidential candidate Herbert Hoover to seek other means of agricultural relief, and to promise help for farmers in his campaign speeches in the summer and autumn of that year. The League of Nations commented in 1942 that "before the end of 1928 it was evident that the United States tariff was going to be raised above the formidable level of 1922" (League of Nations, 1942, p. 126).

Grain exporters of Eastern Europe were especially affected by the world decline in price and sought solutions in meetings at Warsaw in August 1930, Bucharest in October 1930, Belgrade in November 1930, and Warsaw again in the same month. They tried, on the one hand, to limit exports of grain to improve the terms of trade, and, on the other, to obtain preferences in the import markets of Western Europe. The first proposal was never adopted. After the 1932 Stresa meeting, some reciprocal preferences were worked out between Austria and Hungary, on one side, and Italy, on the other, but with poor results.

A strenuous effort was made to halt tariff increases. The World Economic Conference of 1927 recognized that general demobilization of tariffs would be slow, and the Economic Committee of the League of Nations in March 1928 saw no prospect of general reduction. The September 1929 General Assembly of the League moved from attempts at reduction to an effort to halt increases. It called for a conference to stabilize rates for two or three years and then to lower them. The Preliminary Conference with a View to Concerted Action met in February 1930, but too late. It proposed extending existing agreements to April 1, 1931 and to provide opportunities for negotiation before tariffs were raised. By this time, however, retaliation against the forthcoming Hawley–Smoot tariff bill was far along. A second Conference with a View to Concerted Economic Action in November 1930 failed equally. The Netherlands, which, along with the United Kingdom, had pressed for the tariff truce, turned to a smaller group and organized the Oslo group. On 22 December, Norway, Sweden, the Netherlands, and Belgium signed an agreement undertaking not to raise tariffs without giving notice to other members. It was a brave example without much impact.

Quite unrelated to the fortunes of world incomes, prices, or trade, a highly original argument for tariffs emerged in Australia at the end of the prosperity of the 1920s. It bore resemblance to an earlier argument put forward by Alvin S. Johnson in 1908 that tariffs could add to capital formation by reallocating income from spenders to savers – an argument which went unnoticed until Harvey Leibenstein introduced similar notions into the discussion of economic growth in the 1960s. J.B. Brigden published an article in the *Economic Record* of November 1925 on "The Australian Tariff and the Standard of Living". He concluded that whereas the tariff on wheat in the United Kingdom favoured the landed classes, that on manufactured goods in Australia would redound to the standard of living of wage-earners, and increase the population of the country. Subsequently the Australian government appointed a committee of experts, including Brigden, D.B. Copland, E.C. Dyason, L.F. Giblin, and Wickens, which in 1929 produced *The Australian Tariff: An Economic Enquiry* (Australia 1929) that supported Brigden's conclusion. The analysis remained to be worked out by W.F. Stolper and P.A. Samuelson in their classic article of 1941. "Protection and Real Wages", and was to be rediscovered for Canada in the postwar period by C.L. Barber. It was heatedly debated during the 1930s both in Australia and in Anglo-Saxon economic literature. What was clear, however, was that Australia chose not to be guided by the neo-classical static maximizing calculus of foreign-trade theory, but to introduce into the discussion dynamic considerations of economic growth, migration, as well as income redistribution.

The disintegration of world trade

The Hawley–Smoot tariff

The origins of the Hawley–Smoot tariff, as already noted, reach back to the autumn of 1928 when Herbert Hoover, campaigning for the presidency, promised to do something to help farmers suffering under the weight of declining agricultural prices. A special session of Congress was called in January 1929, long in advance of the stock-market crash of

October of that year, and began to prepare a tariff bill. Its scope was widened from agriculture to include industry; Democrats joined Republicans in their support for tariffs for all who sought them; and both Republicans and Democrats were ultimately pushed from the committee room as lobbyists took over the task of setting the rates (Schattschneider, 1935). A groundswell of resentment spread around the world and quickly led to retaliation. Italy objected to duties on hats and bonnets of straw, wool-felt hats, and olive oil; Spain reacted sharply to increases on cork and onions; Canada took umbrage at increases on maple sugar and syrup, potatoes, cream, butter, buttermilk, and skimmed milk. Switzerland was moved to boycott American typewriters, fountain pens, motor cars, and films because of increased duties on watches, clocks, embroidery, cheese, and shoes (Jones, 1934). Retaliation was begun long before the bill was enacted into law in June 1930. As it passed the House of Representatives in May 1929, boycotts broke out and foreign governments moved to raise rates against United States products, even though rates could be moved up or down in the Senate or by the conference committee. In all, 34 formal protests were lodged with the Department of State from foreign countries. One thousand and twenty-eight economists in the United States, organized by Paul Douglas, Irving Fisher, Frank Graham, Ernest Patterson, Henry Seager, Frank Taussig, and Clair Wilcox, and representing the "Who's Who" of the profession, asked President Hoover to veto the legislation (*New York Times*, 5 May 1930). A weak defence was offered contemporaneously by President Hoover as he signed the bill, saying "No tariff act is perfect" (Hoover, 1952, p. 291), and another 45 years later by Joseph S. Davis, who claimed that the Senate got out of hand, but that Hoover had won two key points: inclusion of the flexible provisions permitting the Tariff Commission to consider complaints and recommend to the president higher or lower rates, and exclusion of an export-debenture plan along the lines of the McNary–Haugen bill (Davis, 1975, p. 239). Both views were in the minority.

The high tariffs of 1921, 1922, and *a fortiori* 1930 were generally attacked on the grounds that the United States was a creditor nation, and that creditor nations were required to maintain low tariffs or free trade in order that their debtors might earn the foreign exchange to pay their debt service. This view is now regarded as fallacious since the macroeconomic impacts effects of tariffs on the balance of payments are typically reversed, wholly or in large part, by the income changes which they generate. Under the post-Second World War General Agreement on Tariffs and Trade, balance-of-payments considerations are ignored in settling on tariff reductions in bilateral or multilateral bargaining. In addition, a careful study for the Department of Commerce by Hal. B. Lary states that the effect of the tariff increases of 1922 and 1930, and those of the reductions after 1930, cannot be detected in the import statistics. This was partly perhaps because tariffs were already close to prohibitive and early reductions were minimal, but mainly for the reason that wide fluctuations in world economic activity and prices overwhelmed any lasting impact of tariffs on trade (Lary, 1943, pp. 53–4).

The significance of the Hawley–Smoot tariff goes far beyond its effect on American imports and the balance of payments to the core of the question of the stability of the world economy. President Hoover let Congress get out of hand and failed to govern (Schattschneider, 1935, p. 293); by taking national action and continuing on its own course through the early stages of the depression, the United States served notice on the world that it was unwilling to take responsibility for world economic stability. Sir Arthur Salter's (1932, pp. 172–3) view that Hawley–Smoot marked a turning point in world history is excessive if it was meant in causal terms, apposite if taken symbolically.

Retaliation and business decline wound down the volume and value of world trade. The earliest retaliations were taken by France and Italy in 1929. In Canada the Liberal government kept parliament in session during the final days when the conference committee was completing the bill, and then put through increases in tariff rates affecting one-quarter of Canadian imports from the United States. Despite this resistance to its neighbour, the government lost the August 1930 election to the Conservatives, who then raised tariffs in September 1930, June 1931, and again in connection with the 1932 Ottawa agreements (McDiarmid, 1946, p. 273). The action in May under the Liberal, W.L. Mackenzie King, involved both increases and decreases in duties, with Empire preference extended through raising and lowering about one-half each of general and intermediate rates, but lowering the bulk of those applicable to Empire goods. Subsequent measures typically raised Empire rates, but general and intermediate rates more. In September 1930, anti-dumping rates were increased from 15 to 50 percent.

Deepening depression

The Hawley–Smoot tariff began as a response to the decline in agricultural prices and was signed into law as the decline in business picked up speed. For a time during the second quarter of 1930, it looked as though the world economy might recover from the deflationary shock of the New York stock-market crash in October 1929, which had come on the heels of the failure in London of the Clarence Hatry conglomerate after the discovery of fraudulent collateral used to support bank loans in September and the failure of the Frankfurt Insurance Company in Germany in August. This is not the place to set forth the causes of the depression in agricultural overproduction, the halt to foreign lending by the United States in 1928, the end of the housing boom, the stock-market crash, frightened short-term capital movements, United States monetary policy and the like. It is sufficient to observe that the chance of recovery was seen to fade at the end of June 1930 with the signing of the Hawley–Smoot tariff, the outbreak of retaliatory cuts in international trade, and the near-failure of the Young loan (to reprime German reparations) in international capital markets. Events thereafter were uniformly depressing, from Nazi gains in German elections in September 1930, the collapse of the Creditanstalt in Vienna in May 1931, the run on German banks in June and July, until the Standstill Agreement that blocked repayment of all German bank credits shifted the attack to sterling, which went off the gold standard in September 1931, followed by the yen in December.

One item of commercial policy contributed to the spreading deflation. In the autumn of 1930, Austria and Germany announced the intention to form a customs union. The proposal had its proximate origin in a working paper prepared by the German Foreign Ministry for the World Economic Conference in 1927. It was discussed on the side by Austrian and German Foreign Ministers at the August 1929 meeting on the Young Plan at The Hague. Germany took it up seriously, however, only after the September 1930 elections which recorded alarming gains for the National Socialists, and Chancellor Brüning felt a strong need for a foreign-policy success. The French immediately objected on the grounds that customs union between Austria and Germany violated the provision of the treaty of Trianon which required Austria to uphold her political independence. France took the case to the International Court of Justice at The Hague for an interpretation of the treaty. Other French and British and Czechoslovak objections on the grounds of violation of the most-favoured-nation clause were laid before the League of Nations Council (Viner, 1950, p. 10). The International Court ultimately ruled in favour of the French position in the summer of 1931. By this time, however, the Austrian Creditanstalt had collapsed – barely possibly because of French action in pulling credits out of Austria, though the evidence is scanty – the Austrian government responsible for the proposal of customs union had long since fallen, and the run against banks and currencies had moved on from Austria to Germany and Britain.

In the autumn of 1931, appreciation of the mark, the dollar and the gold-bloc currencies as a consequence of the depreciation of sterling and the currencies associated with it, applied strenuous deflation to Germany, the United States and to Western Europe from September 1931 to June 1932. Depreciation of the yen in December 1931 marked the start of a drive of Japanese exports into British and Dutch colonies in Asia and Africa, and of colonial and metropolitan steps to hold them down. June 1932 was the bottom of the depression for most of the world. The United States economy registered a double bottom, in June 1932 and again in March 1933, when spreading collapse of the system of many small separate banks climaxed in the closing of all banks for a time, and recovery thereafter. German recovery started in 1932 after the resignation of Brüning, who had hoped to throw off reparations by deflation to demonstrate the impossibility of paying them, the succession of von Papen as chancellor, the finally the takeover of the chancellorship by Hitler in February 1933. The gold-bloc countries remained depressed until they abandoned the gold parities of the 1920s – first Belgium in 1935, and the remaining countries in September 1936.

In these circumstances, there was little if any room for expansive commercial policy. Virtually every step taken was restrictive.

Ottawa

The Hawley–Smoot Tariff Act occupied most of the time of Congress for a year and a half (Smith, 1936, p. 177). Empire preference was the major issue in Canadian politics for more than half a century (Drummond, 1975, p. 378). The Imperial Economic Policy Cabinet worried more about tariffs than about any other issue (ibid., p. 426), though much of it dealt with objectively insignificant goods (Drummond, 1972, p. 25). Drummond several times expresses the opinion that the Ottawa discussions in the summer of 1932 should have abandoned the question of tariff preferences and focused on monetary policy, and especially exchange-rate policy. In fact Prime Minister Bennett of Canada sought to raise the issue of the sterling exchange rate prior to Ottawa only to be rebuffed by Neville Chamberlain with the statement that the Treasury could not admit the Dominions to the management of sterling. Canada did succeed in getting exchange rates put on the Ottawa agenda, but the Treasury insisted that the question was minor and nothing came of it (Drummond, 1975, pp. 214–16).

Monetary policy and tariff policy were occasionally complements, occasionally substitutes. The Macmillan Committee report contained an addendum, no. 1, by Ernest Bevin, J.M. Keynes, R. McKenna and three others recommending import duties, and, in so far as existing treaties permitted, a bounty on exports, the combination being put forward as a substitute for devaluation of sterling (Committee on Finance and Industry, 1931). In the event, the United Kingdom undertook both depreciation of sterling and the imposition of import duties.

Sterling left the gold standard on September 21, 1931 and depreciated rapidly from $4.86 to a low of $3.25 in December, a depreciation of 30 percent. Canada and South Africa adopted anti-dumping duties against British goods. On its side, the United Kingdom enacted an Abnormal Importations Act on November 20, 1931 that gave the Board of Trade the right to impose duties of up to 100 percent as a means of stopping a short-run scramble to ship goods to the United Kingdom before the exchange rate depreciated further. While 100 percent tariffs were authorized, tariffs of only 50 percent were imposed. This Act was followed in a few weeks by a similar Horticultural Products Act. Both the Abnormal Importations Act and the Horticultural Products Act exempted the Empire from their provisions (Kreider, 1943, p. 20).

In the Christmas recess of Parliament, Lord Runciman, President of the Board of Trade, persuaded Chamberlain to take up protection as a long-run policy, as had been recommended by Keynes and the Macmillan Committee, prior to the September depreciation, and opposed by Beveridge (1931), since without tariffs, the United Kingdom had nothing to exchange with the Dominions for preferences in their markets. The resultant Import Duties Act of February 1932 established a 10 percent duty on a wide number of imported products – but not copper, wheat, or meat – and created an Import Duties Advisory board, charged with recommending increases in particular duties above the flat 10 percent level. At the last minute a concession was made to the Dominions and colonies. The latter were entirely exempted from the increase, and the former were granted exemption until November 1932, by which time it was expected that mutually satisfactory arrangements for preferences would have been reached. Eighteen countries responded to the Import Duties Act by asking the United Kingdom to undertake negotiations for mutual reductions. The reply was universally negative on the grounds that it was first necessary to arrive at understandings with the Empire (Condliffe, 1940, pp. 300–8). In the spring of 1932, the Import Duties Advisory Board was hard at work raising duties above the 10 percent level, with the notable increase in iron and steel products to 33⅓ percent. Three years later in March 1935 the iron and steel duties were increased to 50 percent in order to assist the British industry in negotiating a satisfactory basis with the European iron and steel cartel (Hexner, 1946, p. 118).

Imperial economic conferences held in 1923, 1926, and 1930 had all broken down on the failure of the United Kingdom to raise tariffs which would have put her in a position to extend preferences to the Empire. Substitute assistance in the form of arrangements for Empire settlement or Empire marketing boards failed to produce significant effects on either migration or trade. British bulk-purchase schemes sought especially by Australia had been halted as early as 1922 and had not been resumed. Hopes were high for the Imperial Economic Conference of 1932 in Ottawa which now had British tariffs to work with.

Canada cared about wheat, butter, cheese, bacon, lamb, and apples; Australia about wheat, chilled meat, butter, cheese, currants, dried fruits, and canned fruits; South Africa about wine and dried and canned fruits; New Zealand about butter and mutton. The position differed in those commodities that the Dominions produced in greater amounts than the United Kingdom could absorb, like wheat, in which diversion of Dominion supplies to the United Kingdom from third markets would produce an offsetting increase in non-Dominion sales in non-British markets and leave Dominion export prices overall unchanged, from those in which the United Kingdom depended upon both Dominion and foreign sources of supply, among the latter notably Argentina in meat, Denmark in butter, Greece in dried currants and raisins, and, it would like to think, the United States in apples. Trade diversion from foreign to Dominion sources was possible in this latter group, but only at some cost in British goodwill in the indicated import markets. On this score, the United Kingdom was obliged to negotiate at Ottawa with an uneasy glance over its shoulder.

A significant Dominion manufacture, as opposed to agricultural product, which had earlier received preference in the British market, in 1919 under the McKenna duties, was motor cars. This preference had led to the establishment of tariff factories in Canada, owned and operated by United States manufacturers. Its extension in the Ottawa agreement led to the unhappy necessity of defining more precisely what a Canadian manufactured motor car consisted of, and whether United States-made motor parts merely assembled in Canada qualified as Canadian motor cars.

In exchange for concessions in primary products in the British market, the United Kingdom expected to get reductions in Dominion duties on her manufactures. But it proved impossible at Ottawa to fix levels of Dominion tariffs on British goods. Instead, the Dominions undertook to instruct their respective tariff boards to adjust the British preference tariff to that level which would make British producers competitive with domestic industry. Resting on the notion of horizontal supply curves, rather than the more usually hypothesized and far more realistic upward-sloping curves, the concept was clearly unworkable and gave rise to unending contention. It was abandoned in 1936.

Argentina, Denmark, Greece, Norway, and Sweden were not content to yield their positions in the British market without a struggle. Even before the Import Duties Act had taken effect, Denmark in January 1932 legislated preferences favouring Britain, and on raw materials used in manufactured exports. By June 1932, total imports had been reduced 30 to 40 percent, but import permits issued for British goods allowed for a 15 percent increase (Gordon, 1941, p.80). In similar fashion, Uruguay undertook to discriminate in the allocation of import licences in favour of countries that bought from her. The threat to discriminate against the United Kingdom was clear. Quickly after Ottawa, British customers pressed to take up negotiations postponed from early 1932 and to settle the extent to which Ottawa would be allowed to squeeze them out of the British market.

In the Roca–Runciman Agreement of May 1, 1933, the United Kingdom agreed not to cut back imports of chilled beef from Argentina by more than 10 percent of the volume imported in the year ended June 30, 1932, unless at the same time it reduced imports from the Dominions below 90 percent of the same base year. This was disagreeable to Australia, which was seeking through the Ottawa agreements to break into the chilled-beef market in the United Kingdom, in which it had previously not been strong (Drummond, 1975, p. 310). Three-year agreements with Denmark, Norway, and Sweden, running from various dates of ratification about mid-1933, provided minimum butter quotas to Denmark and (much smaller) to Sweden, a minimum bacon quota to Denmark amounting to 62 percent of the market, and agreement not to regulate the small and irregular shipments of bacon, ham, butter, and cheese by Norway. But guarantees to these producers left it necessary, if domestic British producers of, say, butter were to be protected, to go back on the Ottawa agreements which guaranteed unlimited free entry into the British market. The position was complicated by New Zealand's backward-bending supply curve which increased butter production and shipments as the price declined, and Australian policy, which evoked the most profound distrust from New Zealand, of subsidizing the export of butter to solve a domestic disposal problem (Drummond, 1975, pp. 320ff., 475). The problems of the Dominions and of the major foreign suppliers of the British markets for foodstuffs compounded the difficulties of British agriculture. In defence of the lost interest, the British agricultural authorities developed a levy-subsidy scheme under which tariffs imposed on imports were segregated to create a fund to be used to provide subsidies to domestic producers. The levy-subsidy scheme was first applied in the United Kingdom on wheat in 1932; strong voices inside the British cabinet urged its application to beef, dairy products, and bacon and ham. Wrangling over these proposals went on between

British and Commonwealth negotiators for the next several years as the United Kingdom tried to modify the Ottawa agreements, with Dominion and foreign-supplier consent, in order to limit imports. In the background, dispute deepened within the British cabinet between the agriculture minister, Walter Elliott, who wanted subsidies, and the chancellor of the exchequer, Neville Chamberlain, who feared their effect on the budget and consistently favoured raising prices and farm incomes, in the United Kingdom and abroad, by cutting production and limiting imports.

In its agreements in Scandinavia, the United Kingdom sought to bind its trading partners to give preferences to British exports, and especially to guarantee a percentage share of the market to British suppliers in that sorely afflicted export industry, coal. In eight trade agreements, British coal exporters were guaranteed generally the major share of import volume, with quotas as follows: Denmark, 90 percent; Estonia, 85 percent; Lithuania, 80 percent; Iceland, 77 percent; Finland, 75 percent; Norway, 70 percent; Sweden, 47 percent. In addition, Denmark agreed that all bacon and ham exported to the United Kingdom should be wrapped in jute cloth woven in the United Kingdom from jute yarn spun in the United Kingdom (Kreider, 1943, pp. 61–2). The Danish government gave British firms a 10 percent preference for government purchases, and undertook to urge private Danish firms to buy their iron and steel in the United Kingdom wherever possible. Kreider notes that these agreements constrained British trade into a bilateral mode: British agreements with Finland lifted the unfavourable import balance from 1 to 5 against the United Kingdom in 1931 to 1 to 2 in 1935. The agreement with the Soviet Union called for the import/export ratio to go from 1 to 1.7 against the United Kingdom in 1934 to 1 to 1.5 in 1935, 1 to 1.4 in 1936 and 1 to 1.2 in 1937 and thereafter. Argentina agreed to allocate the sterling earned by its exports to the United Kingdom to purchases from the United Kingdom.

The Ottawa agreement dominated British commercial policy from 1932 to the Anglo-American Commercial Agreement of 1938, and to a lesser extent thereafter. It was continuously under attack from foreign suppliers other than the United States that entered into trade and financial agreements with the United Kingdom, and from the United States which undertook to attack it as early as the World Economic Conference of 1933. But at no time could the agreement have been regarded as a great success for the Empire. It produced endless discussion, frequently bitter in character, and dissatisfaction on both sides that each felt they had given too much and gained too little. By 1936 and 1937, there was a general disposition to give up the attempt, or at least to downgrade its priority.

The Netherlands

The United Kingdom embraced free trade, broadly speaking, with the repeal of the Corn Laws in 1846, and gave it up with the McKenna duties in 1916. The Netherlands' support goes back at least to the sixteenth century, and lasted until 1931. A faithful supporter of attempts to spread freer trade throughout the world from the World Economic Conference in 1927 until the Convention for the Abolition of Import and Export Prohibitions and Restrictions and the Conference with a View to Concerted Economic Action, the Netherlands ultimately turned to the smaller arena of the Oslo agreement of Scandinavia and the Low Countries. The pressure from declining wheat prices, however, proved too severe. In 1931 the Netherlands undertook to regulate farm prices and marketing. The Wheat Act of 1931 set the domestic price at 12 florins per 100 kilograms at a time when the world price had fallen to 5 florins, necessitating the first major break with the policy of free trade in nearly three centuries. There followed in 1932 as a response to the depreciation of sterling, first an emergency fiscal measure establishing 25 percent duties generally, and then in agriculture the Dairy Crisis Act and the Hog Crisis Act, which were generalized in the following year as the Agricultural Crisis Act of 1933 (Gordon, 1941, p. 307). The freer-trade tradition of the Oslo group continued, however. At the depth of the depression in June 1932, the Oslo group concluded an agreement to reduce tariffs among themselves on a mutual basis by 10 percent per annum for five years. Though it was already blocking out the discrimination to be achieved at Ottawa two months later,the United Kingdom objected on the grounds that the arrangement would violate the most-favoured-nation clause. After dissolution of the gold bloc in 1936, the Oslo group resumed its example-setting work in reducing trade barriers, agreeing first to impose no new tariffs and then to eliminate quotas applied to one another's trade on a mutual basis. Since the most-favoured-nation clause applied only to tariffs and not to quotas, there was no basis for an objection or to claim extension of the concession.

During the period of restricted trade, the Netherlands licensed not only imports, but in some cases exports. The latter practice was followed where quotas in foreign import markets left open the question whether the difference between the domestic price and the world price would go to importers or exporters. A law of December 24, 1931 established a system of licensing exports in instances of foreign import quotas, with permits distributed among exporters in accordance with the volumes of some historical base period. Licence fees were then imposed, in the amount of 70–100 percent of the difference between the world price and the domestic price in the import market, with the collected proceeds distributed to Dutch producers. The purpose of the fees was to divert the scarcity rents available from import restriction, first to the exporting country as a whole, and then, within the exporting country, from exporting firms to agricultural producers (Gordon, 1941, p. 356).

France

The French are often given the credit in commercial policy between the wars for the invention of the quota, a protective device which was to flourish until well into the 1950s, and even then to experience revival in various forms in the 1970s. While its origins go well back in time, the proximate causes of the quota in 1930 were the limitation on France's freedom of action imposed by the network of trade treaties it had fashioned, beginning with that with Germany in 1927, and the difficulty of ensuring a restriction of imports sufficient to raise domestic prices – the object of the exercise – in the face of inelastic excess supplies abroad. Like the Hawley–Smoot tariff increases in committee, quotas spread from agricultural produce to goods in general.

Under an old law of December 1897 – the so-called *loi de cadenas* – the French government had authority in emergency to change the rate of duty on any one of 46 agricultural items. The emergency of falling agricultural prices after 1928 caused the laws of 1929 and 1931 which extended the list. With especially wheat in excess supply overseas in regions of recent settlement like Australia and Canada, the French decided that raising the tariff under their authority would not only pose questions about their obligations under trade treaties, but might well not limit imports, serving only to reduce world prices and improve the terms of trade. Australia, in particular, lacked adequate storage capacity for its wheat and had no choice but to sell, no matter how high the price obstacles erected abroad. The decision was accordingly taken to restrict quantity rather than to levy a customs duty (Haight, 1941, p. 145). The device was effective. As the depression deepened, and as imports grew with the overvaluation of the franc, it was extended to industrial goods. Other countries followed suit, especially Germany with its foreign-exchange control. In 1931, Brüning and Pierre Laval, the then French premier, reached an agreement establishing industrial understandings to coordinate production and trade between German and French industries. One such understanding in electrical materials developed into a cartel. The rest were concerned primarily with restricting German exports to France. When they failed to do so, they were replaced by French quotas (Hexner, 1946, pp. 119, 136). After a while, the French undertook bilateral bargaining over quotas, which led in time to reducing quotas below desired limits in order to have room to make concessions during negotiations.

Germany

Less by design than by a series of evolutionary steps, Germany developed the most elaborate and thoroughgoing system of control of foreign trade and payments. Foreign claims on Germany were blocked on July 15, 1931, when Germany could no longer pay out gold and foreign exchange to meet the demands of foreign lenders withdrawing funds. This default was followed by a negotiated Standstill Agreement between creditors and Germany, involving a six-month moratorium on withdrawals, subsequently renewed. The decision not to adjust the value of the Reichsmark after the depreciation of sterling in September 1931 made it necessary to establish foreign-exchange control, and to prevent the free purchase and sale of foreign currencies in the private market. The proceeds of exports were collected and allocated to claimants of foreign exchange seeking to purchase imports. Clearing agreements developed under which German importers paid Reichsmarks into special accounts at the Reichsbank in favour of foreign central banks, which then allocated them to their national importers of German goods. The foreign central bank faced a particular problem whether or not to pay out local currency to the exporter in advance of its receipts of local currency from national importers of German goods. Some central banks did pay off local exporters against claims on the German clearing, following what was later called the "payments principle," and experienced inflation through the resultant credit expansion. Other central banks made their exporters wait for payment which both avoided monetary expansion and held down the incentive to export to Germany (Andersen, 1946).

A number of countries with large financial claims on Germany, such as Switzerland, insisted that the proceeds of German exports be used in part to pay off creditors abroad, thus converting "clearing" into "payments" agreements. These payments agreements were also used in a few cases to require Germany to continue spending on non-essential imports of importance to the exporter, such as tourism in Austria.

Germany set limits on the use of foreign-owned Reichsmarks within Germany as well as against their conversion into foreign exchange. They were not permitted to be used for many classes of exports, capable of earning new foreign exchange, but only for incremental exports which could be sold only at implicit depreciated exchange rates, for travel within Germany – the so-called Reisemark – and under certain limitations for investment in Germany. Foreshadowing some postwar limitations on foreign direct investment, permission was granted for investment by foreigners in Germany with outstanding mark balances only when the investment was considered generally beneficial to the German economy, was made for at least five years, did not involve a foreign controlling interest in a German enterprise, and did not exceed a stipulated rate of interest (Gordon, 1941, pp. 92–3).

In August 1934, the New Plan was adopted under the leadership of the German minister for economics, Hjalmar Schacht. In the words of Emil Puhl, an associate of Dr Schacht's at the Reichsbank, it provided totalitarian control over commodities and foreign exchange, with stringent controls on imports and on foreign travel, administered through supervisory boards for a long list of commodities and foreign exchange boards in the Reichsbank (Office of the Chief Counsel for Prosecution of Nazi Criminality, 1946, VII, p. 496). Along with trade and clearing agreements, designed especially to ensure German access to food and raw materials, and to promote exports, the Reichsbank developed a series of special marks for particular purposes. In addition to the Reisemarks for travel, there were special-account (*Auslands-Sonder-Konto*, or "Aski") marks which came into existence through imports of raw materials, especially from Latin America, and which were sold by the recipients at a discount and used by the buyers on a bilateral basis for purchases of incremental German goods. The incremental aspect of the exports was, of course, difficult to police. Because Aski-marks would be sold only at a discount, the raw-material supplies against them tended to raise their prices in the bilateral trade (Gordon, 1941, p. 180). On the German side, Schacht established a price-control agency in 1935 in each export group – amounting to 25 in all – to prevent German exporters from competing with one another for export orders and to assure that all exporters sold at the highest possible price (Office of the Chief Counsel, 1946, VII, p. 383).

Beginning in 1934, German foreign-trade plans were intended particularly to ensure access to imported food and raw materials. The New Plan, and especially the Four Year Plan which succeeded it in the fall of 1936, were designed to produce synthetic materials, especially Buna-S (synthetic rubber) and gasoline from coal, where foreign supplies for wartime needs could not be assured. Particular problems were encountered in non-ferrous metals, in iron ore, for which the low-grade Salzgitter project was developed in the Four Year Plan, and in synthetic fertilizer required for self-sufficiency in food. Schacht at the Reichsbank, Goering as Schacht's successor in the Economics Ministry and as the head of the Four Year Plan, and the War and Food Ministries wrangled among themselves over policies, including especially whether to export wheat against foreign exchange following the bumper crops of 1933 and 1934 or to conserve it as a war reserve; whether to hoard Germany's meagre free foreign-exchange reserves or to spend them for crucially short raw materials; the mobilization of privately owned foreign securities and their conversion to cash for buying materials; the pricing of exports; the purchase of unnecessary imports like frozen meat from Argentina, for lack of which Schacht was unable to conclude a favourable trade treaty, etc. (Office of the Chief Counsel, 1946, vol. VII). The documents published by the prosecution at the Nuremberg postwar trials reveal considerable internal dissension, especially in the exchanges between Schacht and Goering that lasted through 1937 and ended in Schacht's defeat and resignation.

German sentiment had continuously decried the loss of the country's African colonies in the Versailles treaty. Schacht continuously referred to the loss in Young Plan discussions of the late 1920s and was still harping on the issue in an article in *Foreign Affairs* in 1937. In a conversation with the American ambassador, Bullitt, in the fall of 1937, Goering noted that Germany's demand for a return of the German colonies which had been taken away by the Versailles treaty was just, adding immediately that Germany had no right to demand anything but these colonies. Particularly sought were the Cameroons which could be developed by German energy (Office of the Chief Counsel, 1946, vol. VII, pp. 890, 898). Three weeks earlier, however, in a private conference, Hitler had stated that it made more sense for Germany to seek material-producing territory adjoining the Reich and not overseas (ibid., vol. I, p. 380). And at a final war-preparatory briefing in May 1939, he went further to explain the need for living space in the East to secure Germany's food supplies. It was necessary to beware of gifts of colonial territory which did not solve the food problem: "Remember blockade" (ibid., vol. I, p. 392). The directive to the Economic Staff Group on May 23, 1941 just before the attack on the Soviet Union stated that the offensive was designed to produce food in the East on a permanent basis.

It was widely claimed that Germany squeezed the countries of southeast Europe through charging high prices for non-essential exports, while not permitting them to purchase the goods they needed, at the same time delaying payment for imports through piling up large debit balances in clearing arrangements. In a speech at Königsberg in August 1935, Schacht expressed regret that Germany had defaulted on debts to numerous pro-German peoples abroad, indicated confidence that Germany could obtain the raw materials it needed, acknowledged that the trade relations of Germany with different countries had changed a great deal, but insisted that these new relations had created for a number of countries new possibilities of exporting to Germany which had helped relieve them from the rigours of the world depression (Office of the Chief Counsel, 1946, vol. VII, p. 486). In a polemical exchange in 1941, Einzig insisted that Benham was in error in holding that southeast European countries had improved their terms of trade in dealing with Germany, which paid higher prices than Western Europe was able to pay, and sold German goods competitively in the area. A postwar analysis of the matter tended to show that Benham and Schacht had been right (Kindleberger, 1956, pp. 120ff.).

An intellectual defence of the Benham–Schacht position had been offered in a somewhat different context as early as 1931 by Manoilesco, who expressed the view that the theory of comparative advantage had to be qualified if the alternative to tariff protection for an industry were either unemployment, or employment at a wage below the going rate. His statement of this position in *The Theory of Protection and International Trade* (1931) was strongly attacked on analytical grounds by the leading international-trade theorists of the day – Haberler, Ohlin, and Viner, each in extended treatment – but was resurrected after the war by Hagen, and then generalized into a second-best argument for interference with free trade, e.g. by tariffs. When the conditions for a first-best solution under free trade do not exist, protection may be superior in welfare for a country to free trade. By the same token, export sales at less than optimal terms of trade may be superior to no exports and unemployment.

The Union of Soviet Socialist Republics

During the 1920s, commercial policy in the Soviet Union had been the subject of a great debate under the New Economic Plan, between the Right that advocated expansion of agriculture, and of other traditional exports, plus domestic production of manufactured consumer goods to provide incentives for farmers, and the Left that favoured development of domestic heavy industry and the relative neglect of agriculture. Under the proposals of the Right, exports of agricultural products would be expanded to obtain imports of machinery, metals, raw materials, and exotic foodstuffs such as coffee and tea. This was the trade-dependent strategy. The Left, on the other hand, sought to increase trade in order to achieve autarky as rapidly as possible, as it feared dependence on a hostile capitalist world. With Stalin's achievement of power, the Left strategy was adopted in the First and subsequent Five Year Plans.

Strong efforts were made to reduce dependence on imports to a minimum. Territorial losses during the First World War, land reform which divided large estates, and the inherent bias of planning which favoured domestic users over foreign markets helped reduce the ratio of exports to national income, which fell from a figure variously estimated within the range of 7–12 percent in 1913 to 3.5 at the interwar low in 1931. Estimates of the volume of Soviet exports vary, depending upon the weights chosen, but on the basis of 1927–8 weights, exports fell from 242 in 1913 to 53 in 1924–5 before recovering to 100 in 1929. Thereafter they rose sharply to 150 in 1930 and 164 in 1931 with disastrous consequences for the Soviet peoples (Dohan and Hewett, 1973, p. 24).

In 1930 and 1931, Soviet exports conformed to the model of the backward-bending supply curve in which volume increases, rather than decreases, as price falls. Declines in the prices of grain, timber and oil, starting as early as 1925, had threatened the Soviet Union's capacity to pay for the machinery and materials necessary to complete its Five Year Plans, and threatened as well its capacity to service a small amount of foreign debt contracted in the 1920s. To counter this threat, the Soviet authorities diverted supplies of foodgrains from domestic consumption to export markets, shipping it from grain-surplus areas to export ports and leaving internal grain-deficit areas unsupplied. The result was starvation and death for an unknown number of the Soviet people numbering in millions. The world price of wheat fell by half between June 1929 and December 1930, and more than half again by December 1932. So hard did the Soviet Union push exports that supplies of pulp wood, woodpulp, timber, lumber, and even coal, asbestos, and furs threatened to enter the Canadian market, a notable exporter of these products in ordinary times, and led the Canadian government in February 1932 to prohibit the import of these commodities from the Soviet Union (Drummond, 1975, p. 205). Similar discriminatory restrictions were taken in many other markets. The dysfunctional character of forcing exports on the world market became clear and the volume of Soviet exports levelled off and started downward in 1932. As primary-product prices rose after 1936, moreover, the export volume declined sharply below the 1929 level.

Japan

Japan had not participated fully in the boom of the 1920s, but the fact that it had restored the yen to par after the First World War as late as January 1930 made it highly vulnerable to the liquidity crisis of 1930 and 1931. It was vulnerable, too, because of heavy dependence on silk, a luxury product, about to experience both a sharp decline in its income-elastic demand and severe competition from rayon and later from nylon. In 1929 silk was responsible for 36 percent of Japanese exports by value, and produced 20 percent of Japanese farm income. The price of silk fell by about half from September 1929 to December 1930. With the help of the depreciation of the yen after December 1931, it reached a level of $1.25 a pound in March 1933, compared with $5.20 in September 1929.

The combination of sharp exchange depreciation and the collapse of the American market in silk produced a drastic reorientation in Japanese export trade, away from North America and Europe and toward Asia, Africa, and Latin America. Export drives were especially intense in British and Dutch colonies, and in the so-called "yen bloc" of Korea, Formosa, Kwantung, and Manchuria. The Japanese share of the Netherlands East Indies market, for example, rose from 10 percent in the 1920s to 32 percent in 1934 before restrictive measures were applied under the Crisis Act of 1933 (Furnival, 1939, p. 431; Van Gelderen, 1939, p. 24). Japanese exports to the yen bloc rose from 24 percent in 1929 to 55 percent in 1938, with imports rising from 20 to 41 percent over the same period (Gordon, 1941, p. 473). Within Asia, Japan developed sugar production in Formosa and stopped buying it in Java in the Netherlands East Indies. The British and Dutch Empires imposed quantitative restrictions on Japanese imports, especially in textiles. Foreshadowing a technique extensively used by the United States after the war, at one stage the British asked the Japanese to impose export controls on shipments to India or face abrogation of the Indo-Japanese Commercial Convention of 1904 (Drummond, 1972, p. 133). By 1938 Netherlands East Indies imports from Japan were down to 14 percent of the total from a high of 30 percent in 1935 (Van Gelderen, 1939, p. 17). Japanese fear of reprisals led them to amend the Export Association Act of 1925, which had been enacted to promote exports, so as to control exports in accordance with restrictions imposed by importing countries (Gordon, 1941, p. 360).

The World Economic Conference of 1933

Sir Arthur Salter termed the Hawley–Smoot tariff a turning-point in world history. Lewis Douglas thought the Thomas amendment under which the dollar was devalued in March 1933 marked "the end of Western civilization as we know it" (Kindleberger, 1986, p. 200). W. Arthur Lewis regarded the failure of the World Economic Conference of 1933 as "the end of an era" (Lewis, 1950, p. 68). Each characterization contained an element of hyperbole. The World Economic Conference offered only the slightest of chances to reverse the avalanche of restrictions on world trade and to stabilize exchange rates. The reversal in tariffs came the next year with the June 1934 Reciprocal Trade Agreements Act in the United States. More stability in exchange rates took root with the Tripartite Monetary Agreement of September 1936 among, initially, the United Kingdom, France, and the United States.

The inspiration for a new world economic conference after 1927 went back to the early years of deflation and to a suggestion of Chancellor Brüning of Germany to treat disarmament, reparations, war debts and loans as a single package to be settled on a political basis, rather than separately in each case by economic experts. A preparatory commission of economic experts under the auspices of the League of Nations fashioned a package of somewhat different ingredients, in which the United States would lower the Hawley–Smoot tariff, France would reduce quota restrictions, Germany relax foreign-exchange control and the United Kingdom would stabilize the pound. War debts were excluded from the agenda by the United States, and consequently reparations by France and the United Kingdom. Pending the convening of the conference, delayed first by the November 1932 elections in the United States and then by domestic preoccupations of the newly elected President Roosevelt, Secretary of State Cordell Hull tried to work out a new tariff truce, but ran into blocks. The United States desired new tariffs on farm products subject to processing taxes under the new Agricultural Adjustment Act; the United Kingdom had some pending obligations under the Ottawa agreements; France reserved her position until she could see what would happen to US prices as a response to the depreciation of the dollar initiated in April 1933. Only eight countries in all finally agreed to a truce on May 12, 1933, many with explicit reservations. In the final preparations for the conference, commercial-policy measures seemed secondary to all but Cordell Hull, as contrasted with the problem of raising international commodity prices and international public-works schemes, for neither of which could general solutions be found. In the end the United States broke up the conference by refusing to stabilize the exchange rate of the dollar (only to reverse its position seven months later in February 1934), the British felt moderately comfortable with their Empire solution in trade with the vast volume of wrangles still to come, and the gold bloc battened down to ride out the storm. The only positive results were an agreement on silver negotiated by Senator Key Pitman of the US delegation, and bases laid for subsequent international agreements in sugar and wheat. Perhaps a negative result was the *de facto* constitution of the sterling bloc with most of the Commonwealth, save Canada and the subsequent withdrawal of the Union of South Africa, plus foreign adherents such as Sweden, Argentina, and a number of countries in the Middle East.

Commodity agreements

From the decline in commodity prices in the mid-1920s, one after another attempt had been made to devise schemes for raising prices. Some were private, like aluminum, copper, mercury, diamonds, nickel, iron and steel; some were governmental. Of the governmental, some were under the control of a single government – Brazil in coffee, Chile in nitrates, the United States in cotton, the Netherlands East Indies in cinchona bark; others, especially in sugar and wheat, were world-wide. Some of the private/government agreements in iron and steel, petroleum, and aluminum were regional, especially European (Gordon, 1941, pp. 430ff.).

The Chadbourne Plan in sugar was reached in May 1931 among leading export countries – Belgium, Cuba, Czechoslovakia, Germany, Hungary, Java, Peru, and Poland – later joined by Yugoslavia. But British India, France, the United Kingdom, and the United States – important consumers that also maintained substantial production – remained outside the agreement. The United States formulated its own legislation, the Jones–Costigan Act of 1934, which assigned rigid quotas to imports from abroad and discriminated in favour of Cuba. Under the Chadbourne Plan, production declined among the signatories but rose almost as much outside. Particularly hard hit was Java, which lost both the Japanese and the Indian markets, the former to Formosan production, the latter to domestic production. Unsold stocks in Java reached 2½ million tons in 1932, and the government took over in January 1933 as the single seller. The failure of the Chadbourne scheme led the World Economic Conference to push for a new agreement, which was finally reached under League of Nations auspices only in May 1937 at the height of the recovery of primary-product prices.

The World Economic Conference was the twentieth international meeting on the subject of wheat after 1928 when the price of wheat started to plummet – two of the meetings dealt with imperial preference, seven were limited to Eastern Europe as already mentioned, and eleven were general. The agreement that emerged after the World Economic Conference achieved a system of export quotas for major producers, but no agreement on acreage controls to limit production (Malenbaum, 1953).

Tea was regulated in this period by an international committee which met in London. In March 1931 the four leading producers of tin– Malaya, Bolivia, Nigeria, and the Netherlands East Indies–cooperated in the Joint Tin Committee. In May 1934 nine countries in Southeast Asia producing 95 percent of the world's rubber supply undertook to impose export quotas to reconstitute the Stevenson rubber plan which had broken down in 1928 (Van Gelderen, 1939, pp. 51ff.). Their problem was complicated by sharply differing supply elasticities in the plantation and the native sectors, the latter characterized in many countries by backward-bending responses. As rubber prices rose in the 1936–7 inventory boom, a number of governments sought to tax away the price increase from the producers, but until the price collapse of September 1937 succeeded mainly in raising the price to buyers in a sellers' market. With the eventual decline in prices, the incidence of the export taxes shifted back from the foreign consumer to the domestic producer and in most instances they were quickly removed.

Sanctions

In December 1934 a border incident occurred between Italian Somalia and Ethiopia. Italy demand an apology; Ethiopia refused. With tension rising, the League of Nations sought to arbitrate but received no help from Italy. After further border clashes, Italian troops invaded Ethiopia on October 3, 1935 without a declaration of war. Later in the month, the League of Nations declared Italy the aggressor and voted sanctions to be applied to her in arms supply, finance, and export-import restrictions. The League did not, however, decree sanctions in the critical item, oil. Germany refused to comply with the League vote; the United States, though not a member of the League of Nations, was strongly sympathetic. Oil sanctions were discussed again in March 1936. At this time an attempt was made to apply them informally through major world oil companies. These companies stopped selling to Italy, but the increase in oil prices thereby brought about encouraged a vast number of small shippers to enter the business for the first time and to deliver oil to Italian troops at Red Sea ports in the full quantities required. With the fall of Addis Ababa, the Italians proclaimed empire over Ethiopia and withdrew from the League. League members continued to apply sanctions with increasing resolution until July 15, 1936, when sanctions were abandoned (Feis, 1946, vol. III).

The disintegration of the world economy

In a few countries – notably France and the United States – foreign trade fell by the same proportion as national income from 1929 to 1938. In others trade fell more than output. Thus the ratio of imports to industrial production declined by 10 percent in the United Kingdom, nearly 20 percent in Canada, 30 percent in Germany, and 40 percent in Italy. Crop failures in the United States in 1934 and 1936, and in Germany in 1937 and 1938, prevented the decline in the proportion of imports from being wider (Meade, 1939, pp. 107–8). Buy-British and Buy-American campaigns, involving government discrimination against foreign as against domestic suppliers with margins of initially 10 percent, increased to 25 percent, in the United States, and 100 percent for items under $100, were often supported by programs affecting state governments, and campaigns to persuade the general public to discriminate as well (Bidwell, 1939, pp. 70–1 and Appendix A). The major influences, to be sure, were higher tariffs, quotas, clearing and payments agreements, and preferential trade agreements.

What trade remained was distorted, as compared with the freer market system of the 1920s, both in commodity and in country terms. The index of German imports for 1937, with a base of 100 in 1929, strongly reflected *Wehrwirtschaft*, and especially rearmament: "other ores" 153, manganese ore 142, iron ore 122, iron and steel 121, copper 100, cotton 73, wool 62, coal 59, oil seeds 57, timber 28 (Meade, 1938, p. 128). The share of Germany in Turkish, Greek, and Italian imports rose between 1928 and 1939 respectively from 13 to 43 percent, 8 to 29 percent, and 10 to 24 percent; the same percentages of national exports to Germany rose from 13 to 43 percent, 27 to 39 percent and 13 to 17 percent for the same countries in the same order (Thorbecke, 1960, p. 100). By 1937, bilateral clearings amounted to 12 percent of total world trade and 50 percent of the trade of Bulgaria, Germany, Greece, Hungary, Romania, Turkey, and Yugoslavia (League of Nations, 1942, p. 70). Pioneering estimates of the shrinkage of multilaterally as opposed to bilaterally balanced trade were made for the League of Nations Economic and Financial Department by Folke Hilgerdt. In 1928, bilateral balancing of export and import values between pairs of countries on the average covered 70 percent of merchandise trade, with about 5 percent more covered by exports or imports of services or capital movements, and 25 percent balanced multilaterally (Hilgerdt, 1941). Hilgerdt's two studies emphasized the shrinkage of the proportion of the trade balanced multilaterally during the depression years, without furnishing a precise estimate for the end of the 1930s (Hilgerdt, 1941; 1942). A postwar study on a somewhat different basis furnished a comparison for 1938 with 1928, shown in Table 6.1.

Major changes occurred both world-wide and within Europe. On a world basis, the largest change shown in the Hilgerdt analysis derived from the fact that the developing countries of the tropics no longer earned large surpluses in merchandise trade with the United States to pay their interest on debts owed to Europe, and especially to the United Kingdom. Regionally, within Europe, the most important change was the failure of Germany to earn an export surplus in Europe, largely the United Kingdom, to enable her to pay for her net imports of raw materials from overseas. Another striking feature was the shift by the

Table 6.1 Proportions of world trade balanced bilaterally and multilaterally, 1928 and 1938 (as percentage of total)

	By non-merchandise	Multilaterally	Bilaterally
1928	11.1	21.2	67.7
1938	14.3	16.9	68.8

Source: Thorbecke (1960, p. 82).

United Kingdom of procurement from Europe to the sterling area. France, the Netherlands, and especially the United Kingdom diverted trade from the rest of Europe to their colonial empires, a trend which would be reversed after the Second World War, and especially after the formation of the European Economic Community in 1957 and the United Kingdom's accession to it in 1973. In 1913 22 percent of British exports went to the Empire. By 1938 the figure had more than doubled to 47 percent. In imports, the proportion rose over the same period from 22.3 to close to 40 percent. As noted earlier, the figures might have risen further had it not been for what has been called "Imperial Insufficiency" (Hancock, 1940, p. 232; see also Drummond, 1972).

World trading systems

Recovery of raw-material prices from 1933 to 1937 was followed by some considerable reduction in tariffs, and relaxation of quota restrictions. The renewed, though less far-reaching, decline of these prices in September 1937, outside the fields dominated by European rearmament, set back the movement towards freer trade. The last five years of the interwar period were most clearly characterized by what have been called disparate "world trading systems" (Tasca, 1938). At the limits were the system of German trade, locked into a network of bilateral clearing and payments agreements, and practising autarky for the sake of war economy (Petzina, 1968), and at the other extreme, the United States, which stood aloof from all payments and clearing agreements, with few quota restrictions, largely in agriculture, some subsidies to export in agricultural commodities, plus government credit through the Export-Import Bank for export promotion. Within Europe, the Balkan countries were nearer to the German model, the Oslo group to the American. Midway between was the Empire preference scheme of the United Kingdom, the Dominions, India, and the dependent colonies. Latin America had been hard hit by declines in raw-material prices and the decline in foreign lending, but was hopeful of trade expansion under the Roosevelt "good neighbor" policy. The Soviet Union went its own way. Anxious to join a system, but largely orphaned outside them, were the Middle East and Japan, the latter of which carved out its own Greater East Asia Co-Prosperity Sphere.

There were limited attempts at achieving a single unified world trading system. The League of Nations Committee for the Study of the Problem of Raw Materials reported in September 1937 at a time when payments difficulties had eased but the position was on the point of reversal (Meade, 1938, p. 162). It found few problems of supply or access to materials, and argued in favour of valorization schemes to raise prices provided that consumers' interests were safeguarded. The report went to the League of Nations Assembly where it was pigeonholed as a consequence of the sharp check to commodity prices and deterioration in payment balances.

Before that time, the British and French governments had asked Paul Van Zeeland, a former Belgian prime minister, to prepare a program for world action in the commercial-policy field. In January 1938, the Van Zeeland report was presented to the public, equally an inopportune time. It called for reciprocal reductions of tariffs, generalized by the most-favoured-nation clause, replacement of industrial quotas by tariffs or by tariff quotas, removal of foreign-exchange control, clearing agreements, and the ban on new lending in London; and, as a final step when all else was in operation, six-month agreements on foreign-exchange rates leading ultimately to the establishment of fixed rates under the gold standard (Meade, 1938, p. 159). The report was received with universal agreement that the restoration of trade was needed, but equally universal reluctance on the part of all governments to take any decisive initiative in the matter (Condliffe, 1940, p. 47).

The 1937–9 recession in fact led to increases in tariffs in Belgium, France, Greece, Italy, the Netherlands East Indies, Norway, Sweden, Switzerland, and Yugoslavia in 1938, and in that stronghold of free-trade sentiment, the Netherlands, in March 1939. Rubber and copper quotas, which had been freed in 1937 under their commodity schemes, were tightened down again. Brazil, Colombia, and Japan extended their foreign-exchange restrictions. Germany and Italy introduced the death penalty for violations of foreign-exchange regulations in December 1936 and June 1939, respectively. Italy also constituted a Supreme Autarky Commission in October 1937 (Meade, 1939, p. 197). In all, the number of clearing and payments agreements rose from 131 on June 1, 1936 to 171 by January 1, 1939 (Gordon, 1941, p. 131).

Meanwhile some considerable relaxation of commercial policy was underway in the United States, led by Cordell Hull, whom Herbert Feis, his economic adviser in the Department of State, called a monomaniac on the subject of tariff reductions (Feis, 1966, p. 262). Hull had long been a Congressman from eastern Tennessee, which specialized in tobacco for export, before becoming Secretary of State, and had been in opposition to the Fordney–McCumber and Hawley–Smoot tariff increases in 1922 and 1930 as a member of the House of Representatives Committee on Ways and Means. As early as the World Economic Conference of 1927, as a Congressman, he had been thought to believe that the tariff of the United States was the key to the entire world situation (US Department of State, *Foreign Relations of the United States*, 1928, vol. I, p. 239). As Secretary of State and leader of the United States delegation to the World Economic Conference of 1933, he had been frustrated in his attempts to get world tariffs reduced by the repudiation of President Roosevelt which prevented him from encountering the profound disinterest of the other countries. The tariff truce of May 1933 lapsed when the conference failed, but Secretary Hull persevered. At the Seventh Conference of American States at Montevideo in November 1933 – the first having been held in 1889 – he had tariffs put on the agenda for the first time and induced President Roosevelt to offer the Latin American republics tariff reductions (Gordon, 1941, p. 464). The main business accomplished at Montevideo was the strengthening of the most-favoured-nation clause, as Hull had tried to do at London, by government agreement not to invoke the clause in order to prevent the consummation of multilateral tariff reductions in agreements to which a government was not a party. The full agreement provided for no tariff reductions, and was signed by eight countries, though ratified only by the United States and Cuba (Viner, 1950, p. 37).

Upon his return from Montevideo, Secretary Hull found that the President had established an Executive Committee on Commercial Policy under the chairmanship of George Peek, agricultural expert and opponent of trade liberalization, and that the committee had already drafted a bill providing for trade treaties to be subject to Senate ratification. This was unsatisfactory to Hull. The Department of State had already been negotiating with Argentina, Brazil, Colombia, Portugal, and Sweden in the summer of 1933, had signed an agreement only with Colombia, but had not submitted it to the Senate for ratification. In early 1934 new legislation was drawn up that delegated authority from Congress to the Executive branch of government to conclude reciprocal trade agreements on its own authority. The draft legislation was completed on February 24, approved by President Roosevelt on February 28, passed the House of Representatives on March 20, the Senate on June 4, and was signed into law on June 13, 1934 as the Reciprocal Trade Agreements Act. The initial delegation of authority was for a period of three years. The legislation was renewed in 1937 and 1940. It provided for mutual bilateral reductions in tariff duties, generalized by the most-favoured-nation clause, limited to 50 percent of the existing (largely Hawley–Smoot) tariff levels.

Even before the legislation had been drafted, further talks were going forward to reduce tariffs, with Belgium and Denmark in January 1934, and with Canada. Canada and the United States each made official public statements on the subject in February 1934, emphasizing the importance of their mutual trade relations. A request for negotiations was made by the Canadian government in November 1934 and an agreement was achieved a year later to the effect on January 1, 1936. Canada received concessions on 88 items, largely primary products, including, along with Hawley–Smoot items, the lumber and copper affected by the US Revenue Act of 1932. United States concessions obtained from Canada were largely in manufactured goods.

The first agreement under the Reciprocal Trade Agreements Act, however, was that concluded with Cuba in August 1934. By November 1939, agreements had been reached with 20 countries, 11 of them in Latin America. A second agreement was concluded with Canada in November 1938, but the most important was the British agreement concluded simultaneously with the revision of the Canadian agreement.

In the British and Canadian agreements, the United States hoped to break down Empire preference. This was beginning to happen of its own accord. In a British–Canadian trade agreement of 1937, five years after the Ottawa agreements of 1932, the British persuaded the Canadians to abolish the doctrine of equalizing competition and to substitute fixed tariff rates and fixed preferential margins in the agreements (McDiarmid, 1946, p. 295). New Zealand was ready to abandon the Ottawa agreements, and started to conclude agreements outside them with Sweden (1935), Greece (1936), and Germany (1937), and was negotiating a dozen others (Hancock, 1940, p. 278). Britain, meanwhile, was highly critical of Australian performance under Ottawa, on the ground that Australia had persistently violated its commitments. Australian Tariff Board studies were limited, and even when the Tariff Board recommended reductions on British goods, the government often failed to introduce them in Parliament (Drummond, 1975, pp. 392ff.). British and Australian interests were only partly complementary. Accordingly the United Kingdom, Canada, and the other Dominions as well were ready in their agreements with the United States to sacrifice advantages in each other's markets in return for significant compensation in the market in the United States (Hancock, 1940, p. 265).

To an extent, the Anglo-American trade agreement was more symbolic than effective. Two years of hard bargaining went into it, and it lasted only eight months, from January 1, 1939 until British wartime controls were imposed on the outbreak of war with Germany in September 1939. Reductions were agreed on nine items in which trade amounted to no more than $350 per annum. Important concessions, as in cotton textiles, were prevented from being generalized to Japan and other competitors through reclassification. Full 50 percent reductions in the United States were made on 96 items but the total trade involved was worth only $14 million. Under all 20 agreements, the unweighted (equal weights) United States *ad valorem* duties were reduced from 57 percent on products subject to the tariff to 35 percent, a reduction of 39 percent, whereas the reduction under the British agreement, from 42 to 30 percent on the same basis, amounted only to a reduction of 29 percent. The 35 percent level achieved on January 1, 1939 was somewhat lower than the Fordney–McCumber average of 38.5 percent and the Payne–Aldrich tariff (1909) of 40.8 percent, and well below the Hawley–Smoot average of 51.5 percent. It was nevertheless still well above the 1913 Underwood level of 27 percent (Kreider, 1943, pp. 170ff.).

Moreover, the trade agreements applied largely to industrial products and materials. United States opposition to Empire preference had export concerns in view, especially in competition with Canada in pork and apples. The reductions in tariffs under the agreements, however, went side by side with continued US protection against agricultural imports and subsidies on agricultural exports. Protection was required under those domestic programs which raised prices in the United States and would, without new restrictions, have attracted further supplies from abroad; and subsidies were deemed necessary to offset the price disadvantage this imposed on American producers in their traditional markets. The trade agreements reduced tariffs on a few items, such as maple sugar from Canada, which had been a particular irritant under the Hawley–Smoot Act, and altered the arbitrary valuations on fresh fruits and vegetables early in the season that had hitherto been kept out of Canada by this device. A sanitary agreement between the United States and Argentina on the regulation of foot-and-mouth disease was not ratified by Congress (Bidwell, 1939, pp. 217–18); and independence for the Philippines was accelerated to push its sugar production outside the tariff borders of the United States. On the whole, the trade agreements marked the beginning of regarding liberal commercial policies as appropriate only for manufactures, and their inputs, and leaving agricultural trade largely to special arrangements.

A small beginning was made by the United States on what was to be a major postwar issue, East–West trade. The United States was unwilling to recognize the government of the Soviet Union all through the

1920s. With President Roosevelt's New Deal, this was changed and recognition was accorded in 1933. In the mid-1930s, the United States and the Soviet Union undertook a series of trade agreements. In 1935, the Soviet Union contracted to purchase at least $30 million worth of US goods in the following year; in return, the United States accorded the Soviet Union most-favoured-nation treatment. In August 1937, under a new pact, the Soviet Union agreed to step up its purchases from the United States to $40 million (Gordon, 1941, p. 407).

British adherence to the more liberal trade policies pursued by Cordell Hull was highly ambiguous. Kreider claims that the British concessions were not spectacular but represented a reversal of policy (1943, p. 240). At the same time, the British government was unwilling to repudiate the principle of Ottawa, despite its effects, as Mackenzie King claimed, in destroying the principle of imperial harmony (Drummond, 1975, p. 316).

Moreover, British ministers were experimenting with a new technique quite at variance with the American professed principle of increased reliance on the international market. Mention was made above of the special tariff assistance given to the iron and steel industry to assist in its negotiations with the International Steel Cartel. At the depth of the depression, in October 1933, the British had encouraged negotiations between Lancashire and Indian cotton textile mill owners. The resultant Lees–Mody pact of October 1933 provided that India would lower her tariffs on British textiles to 20 percent while holding those against other (i.e. Japanese) goods at 75, to which they had been raised from 31½ percent in August 1932 in several steps. As part of the negotiation, involving governments and business groups on both sides, the British agreed to take 1½ million bales of cotton that had piled up as a result of a Japanese retaliatory boycott. At the time Lord Runciman stated: "The work of the Delegation has gone some way in justifying the Government in their belief that the best approach to the problem of international industrial cooperation is by the method of discussion between industrialists" (Drummond, 1972, p. 316).

In early 1939, immediately after signing the Anglo-American Reciprocal Trade Agreement in November 1938, and as part of an export drive, the British Board of Trade encouraged the visit to Düsseldorf of a delegation of the Federation of British Industry to meet with the Reichsgruppe Industrie, its institutional counterpart, and to fix quantitative relationships between the exports of the two countries in each commodity and market. In prospect, *The Economist*, after some qualifications, expressed itself as approving (CXXXIV, no. 4585 (February 25, 1939), p. 383). The agreement was concluded on March 16, 1939, one day after the German invasion of Czechoslovakia (text in Hexner, 1946,

Appendix III, pp. 402–4). The British government repudiated the agreement on political grounds, but not before *The Economist* had denounced it on the grounds that it involved cartelization of domestic industry as well as of trade, that it would extend Anglo-German subsidies to exports, and that it might involve joint action against competitors who refused to join the arrangement, including possible American firms (CXXXIV, no. 4589 (March 25, 1939), p. 607).

In Eastern Europe the German bloc was strengthened in ways to guarantee German access to raw materials and foodstuffs in short supply. An agreement with Hungary in 1934 provided for a shift of Hungarian agriculture from wheat to oilseeds with an assured outlet in Germany. German treaties with Romania in March 1935 and again four years later fostered the expansion of Romanian agriculture in oilseeds, feedgrains, and vegetable fibers, as well as industrial and financial cooperation, including the development of Romanian transport and petroleum under German–Romanian companies supervised by joint government commissions (Gordon, 1941, pp. 425–6). In 1937, the proportion of German exports sold through clearing agreements amounted to 57 percent, while 53 percent of her imports came through clearings. The comparable figures for Turkey were 74 and 72 percent respectively, for Romania 67 and 75 percent, for Switzerland 28 and 36 percent, for Sweden 17 and 24 percent, and for the United Kingdom 2 and 2 percent (Gordon, 1941, Table 7, p. 133).

The disintegration of world trade thus proceeded, despite the attempts of the United States, the Oslo group, Premier Van Zeeland under Anglo-French auspices and the economists of the Economic and Financial Department of the League of Nations. With some prescience Condliffe (1940, p. 394) concluded his book written at the outbreak of the Second World War: "If an international system is to be restored, it must be an American-dominated system, based on *Pax Americana.*"

Bibliography and references

Andersen, F. Nyboe (1946), *Bilateral Exchange Clearing Policy*, Copenhagen.

Arndt, H.W. (1944), *The Economic Lessons of the Nineteen-Thirties*, London.

Australia: Committee on Economics (Brigden, J.B.) (1929), *The Australian Tariff, An Economic Enquiry*, Melbourne, Melbourne University Press.

Benham, Frederic C. (1941), *Great Britain under Protection*, New York.

Bergsten, C. Fred (1974), *Completing the GATT: Toward New International Rules to Govern Export Controls*, British–North-American Committee.

Beveridge, William H. (1931), *Tariffs, The Case Examined by a Committee of Economists under the Chairmanship of Sir William Beveridge*, New York.

Bidwell, Percy W. (1939), *The Invisible Tariff. A Study of Control of Imports*

into the United States, New York.
Bidwell, Percy W. (1958), *Raw Materials: A Study of American Policy*, New York.
Brigden, J.L. (1925), "The Australian Tariff and the Standard of Living," *Economic Record*, vol. 1, no. 1 (November), pp. 29–46.
Brown, William Adams, Jr. (1950), *The United States and the Restoration of World Trade*. Washington, DC.
Childs, Frank C. (1958), *The Theory and Practice of Exchange Control in Germany*, The Hague.
Committee on Finance and Industry (1931), (United Kingdom, Macmillan Report, Cmd 3897), London.
Condliffe, J.B. (1940), *The Reconstruction of World Trade: A Survey of International Economic Relations*, New York.
Copland, Douglas B. and James, C.V. (1937), *Australian Tariff Policy: A Book of Documents, 1932–1937*, Melbourne.
Davis, Joseph S. (1975), *The World Between the Wars, 1919–1939: An Economist's View*, Baltimore, Md.
Dohan, Michael and Hewett, Edward (1973), *Two Studies in Soviet Terms of Trade, 1918–1970*, Bloomington, Ind.
Drummond, Ian M. (1972), *British Economic Policy and the Empire, 1919–1939*, London.
Drummond, Ian M. (1974), *Imperial Economic Policy, 1917–1939: Studies in Expansion and Protection*, Toronto.
Einzig, Paul J. (1938), *Bloodless Invasion: German Penetration into the Danube States and the Balkans*, London.
Elliott, William Y., May, Elizabeth S., Rowe, J.F.W., Skelton, Alex and Wallace, Donald H. (1937), *International Control in Non-ferrous Metals*, New York.
Federal Trade Commission (1952), *The International Petroleum Cartel*, US Senate Select Committee on Small Business, 82nd Congress, Committee Print no. 6, Washington, DC, August.
Feis, Herbert (1946), *Three International Episodes seen from E.A.*, New York.
Feis, Herbert (1966), *1933, Characters in Crisis*, Boston.
Friedman, Philip. (1974), *The Impact of Trade Destruction on National Income: A Study of Europe, 1924–38*, Gainesville, Fla.
Furnivall, J.S. (1939), *Netherlands India: A Study of Plural Economy*, Cambridge.
Gordon, Margaret S. (1941), *Barriers to World Trade: A Study of Recent Commercial Policy*, New York.
Haight, Frank Arnold (1941), *A History of French Commercial Policies*, New York.
Hancock, W. Keith (1940), *Survey of British Commonwealth Affairs*, vol. II: *Problems of Economic Policy*, London.
Hexner, Erwin (1946), *International Cartels*, Durham, NC.
Hilgerdt, Folke (1941), *Europe's Trade. A Study of the Trade of European Countries with Each Other and with the Rest of the World*, Geneva.
Hilgerdt, Folke (1942), *The Network of World Trade*, Geneva.
Hoover, Herbert (1952), *The Memoirs of Herbert Hoover*, vol. III, *The Great Depression, 1929–1941*, New York.
Hull, Cordell (1948), *The Memoirs of Cordell Hull*, New York.
Johnson, Alvin S. (1908), "Protection and the Formation of Capital," *Political Science Quarterly*, vol. XXIII (June), pp. 220–41.

Johnson, D. Gale (1950), *Trade and Agriculture; A Study of Inconsistent Policies*, New York.
Jones, Joseph M., Jr. (1934), *Tariff Retaliation, Repercussions of the Hawley–Smoot Bill*, Philadelphia.
Kindleberger, Charles P. (1956), *The Terms of Trade: A European Case Study*, New York.
Kindleberger, Charles P. (1986), *The World in Depression, 1929–1939*, revised edn, Berkeley, Calif.
Knorr, Klaus E. (1946), *World Rubber and its Regulation*, Stanford.
Kreider, Carl (1943), *The Anglo-American Trade Agreement: A Study of British and American Commercial Policies, 1934–39*, Princeton.
Lary, Hal B. (1943), *The United States in the World Economy*, Economic Series, no. 23, Washington, DC.
League of Nations (1935), *Enquiry into Clearing Agreements*, Geneva.
League of Nations (1942), *Commercial Policy in the Interwar Period: International Proposals and National Policies*, Geneva.
League of Nations Economic Committee (1935), *Considerations on the Present Evolution of Agricultural Tariffs*, Geneva.
Lewis, Cleona (1941), *Nazi Europe and World Trade*, Washington, DC.
Lewis, W. Arthur (1950), *Economic Survey, 1919–1939*, Philadelphia.
Liepmann, H. (1938), *Tariff Levels and the Economic Unity of Europe*, London.
McDiarmid, Orville J. (1946), *Commercial Policy in the Canadian Economy*, Cambridge, Mass.
Malenbaum, Wilfrid (1953), *The World Wheat Economy, 1895–1939*, Cambridge, Mass.
Manoilesco, Mihail (1931), *The Theory of Protection and International Trade*, London.
Mason, Edward S. (1946), *Controlling World Trade, Cartels and Commodity Agreements*, New York.
Meade, James E. (1938), *World Economic Survey, 1937/38*, Geneva.
Meade, James E. (1939), *World Economic Survey, 1938/39*, Geneva.
Office of the Chief Counsel for Prosecution of Nazi Criminality (1946), *Nazi Conspiracy and Aggression*, Washington, DC.
Page, W.T. (1927), *Memorandum on European Bargaining Tariffs*, Geneva.
Petzina, Dieter (1968), *Autarkiepolitik im dritten Reich, Der national-sozialistiche Vierjahresplan*, Stuttgart.
Reitsama, A.J. (1958), "Trade and Redistribution of Income: Is There Still an Australian Case?," *Economic Record*, vol. XXIV, no. 68 (August), pp. 172–88.
Richardson, J.H. (1936), *British Economic Foreign Policy*, London.
Roepke, Wilhelm (1934), *German Commercial Policy*, London.
Roepke, Wilhelm (1942), *International Economic Disintegration*, London.
Rowe, J.W.F. (1936), *Markets and Men: A Study of Artificial Control Schemes*, New York.
Salter, Sir Arthur (1932), *Recovery, the Second Effort*, London and New York.
Schacht, Hjalmar (1937), "Germany's Colonial Demand," *Foreign Affairs*, vol. XIV (January), pp. 223–34.
Schattschneider, E.E. (1935), *Politics, Pressures and Tariffs: A Study of Free Private Enterprise in Pressure Politics as Shown by the 1929–30 Revision of the Tariff*, New York.
Schuker, Stephen A. (1976), *The End of French Predominance in Europe: The Financial Crisis of 1924 and the Adoption of the Dawes Plan*, Chapel Hill, NC.

Smith, Mark A. (1936), "The United States Flexible Tariff," in *Explorations in Economics, Notes and Essays Contributed in Honor of F.W. Taussig*, New York.

Stolper, W.F. and Samuelson, P.A., (1941), "Protection and Real Wages," *Review of Economic Studies*, vol. 9 (November), pp. 58–73.

Suetens, M. (1955), *Histoire de la politique commerciale de la Belgique jusqu'à nos jours*, Brussels.

Tasca, Henry J. (1938), *The Reciprocal Trade Agreement Policy of the United States: A Study in Trade Philosophy*, Philadelphia.

Thorbecke, Erik (1960), *The Tendency toward Regionalization in International Trade, 1928–1956*, The Hague.

United Nations, Department of Economic Affairs (1947), *Customs Union: A League of Nations Contribution to the Study of Custom Union Problems*, Lake Success, NY.

United States Department of State Tariff Commission (1942), *Foreign Trade and Exchange Controls*, Report no. 150, Washington, DC.

Van Gelderen, J. (1939), *The Recent Development of Economic Foreign Policy in the Netherlands East Indies*, London.

Viner, Jacob (1943), *Trade Relations between Free-market and Controlled Economies*, Geneva.

Viner, Jacob (1950), *The Customs Union Issue*, New York.

Viner, Jacob (1966), *Dumping: A Problem in International Trade*, New York; first published 1923.

Winslow, E.M. (1936), "Administrative Protection: A Problem in Commercial Policy" in *Explorations in Economics: Notes and Essays in Honor of F.W. Taussig*, New York.

7

The postwar resurgence of the French economy

The postwar economic revival of France has perhaps been slighted in economic literature. It is easy to see why this might be so. The recovery of neighboring Germany seems more remarkable in the light of wartime destruction and postwar settlement; and attention in France has focused primarily on political problems. But the recovery of France is no mean feat: French industrial production rose about as much as German from before the war, though from a lower level in relation to capacity. And though France suffered less destruction and escaped the problem of refugees, its peculiar handicaps of war abroad and political crisis at home were severe enough.

The postwar economic vitality of France after about 1952 contrasts sharply with its miserable performance in the 1930s and the hesitant start in the early postwar period. Those delays produced a substantial literature on French economic backwardness, attempting to explain the country's incapacity to develop at rates equal to those of its neighbors. Some of this literature in fact appeared after the tide of recovery had definitely turned.

Even without the evidence of the present economic vitality, however, it is a mistake to regard France as a perennially backward developer. This essay, which will review the changes in the French economy,

---

*Published in Stanley Hoffmann, Charles P. Kindleberger, Laurence Wylie, Jesse R. Pitts, Jean-Baptiste Duroselle and François Goguel, *In Search of France*, Cambridge, Mass.: Harvard University Press, 1963. The book was the product of a seminar over two years at the Center for International Studies at Harvard University, directed by Robert R. Bowie. I am deeply indebted to the regular and occasional members of the seminar for ideas and criticism.

polity, and society accounting for the postwar resurgence, starts from a catalogue of explanations of French backwardness. But it should not be forgotten, despite the authors of these explanations, that French growth was rapid in at least three other extended periods in the last century or so – under the Second Empire from 1851 to about 1870; then from 1896 to 1913; and again in the 1920s. Some explanations for retardation imply that the French economy can never grow, others only that the growth will be sporadic and interrupted by the necessity to find new strengths. And it may be that the present period is due for interruption on similar grounds. In any case, interest in the current French recovery is heightened by past or current change in many of the alleged causes of retardation. French postwar experience commands attention on a more general basis than the history of the particular country, important as it is, in so far as that experience can illuminate the interrelations between a country's underlying characteristics and its economic growth.

The alleged causes of French economic backwardness must be analyzed with attention to what, if any, changes in underlying circumstances have supervened. One wants to know particularly whether the significant obstacles to growth have been removed – how, and when. I present the list of alleged causes first in brief summary, and then at greater length. The order is arbitrary.

The major explanations for French economic backwardness since about 1850 have been as follows.

On the side of production:

1. Lack of natural resources, especially of coking coal in an age of steel (Jean Chardonnet, Alexander Gerschenkron).
2. Lack of plentiful labor, not alone from the low rate of population growth but mainly from the slow release of manpower to the city by the agricultural sector with its love of the land and system of equal inheritance (W.A. Lewis, H.J. Habakkuk).
3. Diversion of savings from domestic capital formation to foreign political loans which "starved French industry of capital" (Maurice Lévy, Jean Weiller, A.K. Cairncross).
4. The organization of enterprise into family firms which resisted market competition (David S. Landes) and followed inefficient practices in financing, recruitment, and promotion of technical change (Jesse R. Pitts).

On the side of demand:

5. The slow rate of population growth, depriving France of an outlet for savings and a regular margin of expansion within which to effect technological change (Alfred Sauvy, Joseph J. Spengler).
6. The French national character, which favored high-quality rather

than mass consumption (Bert F. Hoselitz, Rondo E. Cameron).
7. Deep fissures in French society, preventing adjustment from traditional to modern patterns of social organization, exacerbating divisions among classes and sectors of society, promoting inflation, and diverting attention from growth to stability (John E. Sawyer).

On institutions:

8. "Malthusian" market organization with firms too small and markets highly cartellized (Charles Bettelheim, Herbert Luethy);
9. Governmental intervention, whether to maintain social stability, to direct resource allocation, or to carry out unduly ambitious national designs, and entailing contradictory policies, overcentralization, and economic incompetence (Warren C. Baum, Jean Gravier).

Though differing in emphasis, these explanations overlap and are not mutually exclusive. The importance which attaches to each factor will differ among observers, depending on one's view of the process of economic growth, the relative weight of economic and noneconomic factors, and the tolerable limits of governmental economic activity. Thus if one adheres to a Harrod–Domar view of economic growth in which capital formation by the process of compound interest is the central engine of expansion, the major foci of attention become the export of capital, the weakness of the family firm as a device for investing in industry, and the slow rate of population growth. But one who believes that the prime force for growth is technological advance, raising output per unit of factor inputs, will attach greater significance to the resistance to change of family firm, family farm, and government, and the organization of markets to limit competition.

What has happened since World War II to produce rapid economic growth in France can be seen in perspective, if at all, only after an examination of the separate factors which had supposedly held it back and the extent of the change in them.

On the side of production

Natural resources

The complaint that France has been handicapped by lack of natural resources, and particularly of coal, has been recurrent almost since the invention of the steam engine. From at least J.A. Chaptal in 1819 to Jean Chardonnet in 1960, French economists, occasionally supported by foreign observers, have singled out the limited amounts and poor quality of French coal as a major obstacle to industrialization as rapid as in Britain or Germany. More subtle commentators have suggested that the difficulty lay elsewhere – for example, that French natural resources, including iron ore, were too distant from industrial centers and ports; that the internally "balanced" nature of the separate regions of France limited the gains from specialization once the country had been joined by railroad interconnection; that France, unlike Britain and Germany, had difficulties in achieving cheap natural transportation because of the scarcity of navigable rivers and the rough terrain; or that France never developed the widespread trade in coal which, as an indirect consequence, would have thickened the transport network and, as a by-product, would have cheapened freight rates for other commodities, thus stimulating their interchange and their use as inputs by industry.

But examination of the case against natural resources raises doubts. Coal production grew substantially in the first two periods of rapid growth, during the Second Empire in the Nord, and in 1896–1913 in Lorraine. The latter period also saw a great expansion in coal imports. During most of this time there was a tariff, which could have been reduced to cheapen coal for industry. A canal from the Nord to Lorraine, which would have increased the availability of iron ore to the Nord and coal to Lorraine, was declared a public utility in 1881 but never constructed. Only after World War II was its purpose carried out by the double-tracking and electrification of the railroad from Valenciennes to Thionville. And even without the canal, French steel production grew at a rate of 8 percent per annum from 1880 to 1913, very close to the 10 percent rate of Germany and Belgium, and much in advance of the British performance.

Albert Hirschman holds that economic growth produces resources, rather than resources growth. This view seems to be borne out by the economic history of France prior to 1945, especially if one believes that the availability of resources is largely a problem of transport facilities, which are man-made. It is clearly borne out since the war. The nationalized coal industry, Charbonnages de France, has performed with technical brilliance, consolidating small pits into efficient units, mechanizing mines above and below ground, raising output per man-shift faster than Germany or Britain. (There may be more of a question about its economic performance – for example, whether it invested too many resources in coal, and whether its pricing policies did not unduly penalize efficient and subsidize inefficient mines.) French hydroelectric sites on the Rhône, in the Alps, and in the Pyrenees have been exploited on a rapidly widening scale. The discovery of oil in Algiers, and of natural gas at Lacq (made usable by the development of new techniques to separate the sulfur from the gas, which incidentally create new competition for the United States sulfur industry) also testify in Hirschman's behalf. A long-run question has been raised whether Algerian oil is cheap or dear, compared to the resources which France would have had to give up to get an equal amount of oil from other areas through trade. If the Algerian War was justified in part by the riches of the Sahara, the calculation must be altered to include an allowance for an appropriate portion of the cost of the war. It is said to be a close question even without war costs.

Finally, note that at no time has there been any complaint about lack of resources in agriculture. On the contrary, the emphasis in all discussion is on France's varied and rich endowment of land. Blame for backwardness in agriculture is ascribed, instead, to lack of social-overhead capital such as roads, lack of education and technological instruction, the system of inheritance, inordinate love of land, and other flaws in administration or social values.

It seems clear that the alteration of France's resource base since the war has been a result rather than a cause of economic growth. As earlier in French history, resources have responded to the stimulus of industrial expansion. In this, as in much that follows, there is an inescapable element of interaction; growth begets resources and resources permit further growth. But the main point is that natural resources are not the controlling factor. In France it was not a lack of resources that held down the economy in its stagnant periods, nor an abundance of resources that prodded it forward in the 1950s.

Labor supply

Chaptal in 1819 believed that France suffered compared to Britain from dear coal and cheap labor. The analysis evidently differed as between the two factors. Dear coal inhibited the plentiful use of an efficient fuel in static terms. The handicap of cheap labor was dynamic: it encouraged the abundant use of this input, maintaining the country in antiquated labor-intensive practices, and depriving entrepreneurs of an incentive to substitute machinery for labor.

There are traces of this view of labor through the nineteenth-century discussion. The present prevailing view, however, is diametrically opposite. It is believed that French industrial growth has been handicapped by stagnation in agriculture. This stagnation, arising from lack of education, French traditional love of the soil, and the Napoleonic system of equal inheritance, has limited the supply of savings for industry and the supply of agricultural raw materials used in industry, and has held down the demand for industrial products. Its major effect, however, is thought to have been its failure to release labor to industry rapidly enough. Industrial expansion has been frustrated not by too cheap labor, but by too expensive. Expansions have been brought to a halt by rising wages. Space does not permit a thorough treatment of this problem in these pages, but a few conclusions may be in order.

French agriculture has been less technologically frozen than is generally believed. In the Paris basin, and in the North especially, but to a lesser degree everywhere, French agricultural practice advanced during the nineteenth century. The advances in agricultural rationalization were particularly rapid during the periods of industrial expansion under the Second Empire and before World War I. The agricultural advances were forced by the movement of labor into industry. But this movement was largely local in character. In France, as in Britain, agricultural workers did not move long distances to urban employment, except to the metropolis. There was this difference: redundant farm hands in southern England who did not go to London emigrated abroad. In France, the rural surplus from the Southwest was recruited by Paris into the national services as gendarmes, railroad workers, postmen and employees of the tobacco monopoly. Those from Brittany, however, would move neither to Paris nor abroad. And elsewhere in France, while the industrial economic historians were complaining of lack of labor supply, agricultural observers bewailed the rural exodus.

There is little evidence that the halting of French industrial expansion in 1870, 1913, or 1929 was due to inadequate labor supply. It is true that wages rose sharply in the 1850s and 1860s, and that prior to World War I the labor requirements of the North and East had to be met by immigration because of the unwillingness of French labor (which in most cases had already been drawn off local farms) to move the requisite long distances. It is also true that in some areas – Clermont-Ferrand, Sochaux in the Franche-Comté, and Bas-Rhin – industry and agriculture inhibited one another through the operation of isolated rural factories which used workers who continued part-time farming; here the recruiting of industrial laborers was hampered by the lack of small part-time farms available to them and farming continued by archaic methods because it remained a marginal contributor to family income, rather than a main support. But these factories were exceptional; they were not found in Paris or the North nor even in every part of Lorraine. Moreover, the pressure of industrial expansion around 1910 was beginning to result in rapid agricultural reorganization when war intervened. Industry would have benefited from a willingness of French agricultural labor to move longer distances into industrial employment, rather than insist on limited local moves (frequently into the independence of *petit bourgeois* occupations). But, on the other hand, more persistent industrial expansion would have favored greater mobility.

Since World War II, there has been a rapid movement of labor off the farm and a rapid increase in French agricultural productivity. In the five years from 1949 to 1954, the active population engaged in agriculture, fishing and forestry – largely agriculture – fell by 30 percent, from 7.5 million to 5.2 million, or from 36.6 percent of the active population to 27.4 percent. The decline in men was only 19 percent, from 4.2 to 3.4 million, while the number of women dropped by 44 percent from 3.3 to 1.8 million. Productivity increased per worker and per acre, since the output rose while land tilled declined along with manpower.

This movement was partly motivated from the supply side. Mobility of the farm worker increased, with the spread of the motorbike, scooter, and automobile. Young women refused to continue to bury themselves in the village. But the major change came from the demand for workers in industry, the pull of jobs rather than the push of labor off the farm. If there had been a great demand for unskilled workers in industry, or greater education and skill among the agricultural population, the movement would have been still larger.

The backwardness of French agriculture at the beginning of the postwar period actually provided a force which sustained the subsequent growth, and in two ways. In the first place, it provided a reservoir of manpower for industry, just as German industry was helped by the influx of refugees which kept down wage rates, and Italian industry by the 2 million unemployed. Secondly, the movement off the farm led in turn to the necessity to rationalize agriculture, which contributed to the higher overall rate of growth in a way which is not possible in a country which already has an efficient agricultural sector.

There are some independent sources of improvement in farming in France. Some returning Tunisian settlers have taken over deserted farms in Aquitaine, built up the land with modern techniques, and farmed it by machine on a substantial scale with the liberal use of capital. The local peasants – those who had not abandoned the region – were at first skeptical but then became interested and sought to follow the pattern. This proved difficult because of their lack of access to capital.

The improvement of agricultural efficiency created new problems at the same time as it helped solve old ones. Efficiency, improving faster than labor moved out of the sector, gave rise to surpluses in grain, meat, milk, butter, and vegetables, to add to the traditional burdens of excess supplies in sugar and wine. The new surpluses have helped to color French attitudes toward the European Common Market, and especially toward British entry into it and toward the access to European markets of traditional overseas suppliers.

On the whole, it is difficult to maintain the case that the family farm held back French industrial growth before 1939, or that its breakdown after 1946 has been responsible for the recent economic expansion. By and large, and though there is interaction, agricultural rationalization, like the discovery of natural resources, is a dependent not an independent variable in the equation of economic growth.

Capital formation

In many formulations, economic growth is a result primarily of capital accumulation. According to them, the retardation in both the 1880s and the 1930s was due to lack of the capital which would have raised capacity and output. In the 1880s the lack is ascribed to capital exports – loans to the Balkans and tsarist Russia funneled through a financial community in Paris which corrupted the press and misled the public to earn its commissions on bond flotations. In the 1930s some capital, escaping Laval deflation and the Blum Popular Front, sought refuge in Switzerland and New York as hot money, while domestic business capital, on strike against the government of the Left, refused to undertake productive investment.

Like any unitary-valued explanation, this is too simple. Capital exports took place not only during the 1880s but also during periods of growth – in the 1850s and 1860s, between 1896 and 1913, and again in the 1920s. That Harry D. White's book on French capital exports contains the dates 1881–1913 in the title does not mean that capital exports began then, as Cameron has shown in great detail.[1] The notion that French industry was starved for capital in the period before World War I is clearly exaggerated; and though the rate of expansion in the 1920s was greater after 1926 when capital was returning than during the period of flight, it was still possible for capital exports and expansion to take place simultaneously. In the 1930s, French business had little reason to invest at home, either under Laval deflation or Popular Front inflation. Capital export was an induced rather than an independent and causal phenomenon.

One could make a case, perhaps, that it was not the overall amount of saving which determined the rate of French industrial expansion, but only those funds available for industry. Under the Second Empire, capital for industry was furnished by the industrial banks, associated with the names of the Pereire brothers and the Crédit Mobilier. When these were destroyed or tamed, stagnation set in. In the period before World War I, there was lending by regional banks in Lorraine and Haute-Savoie, plus liberal rediscounting of industrial credits by the Bank of France, despite its rules and traditions limiting the rediscount facility to commercial acceptances. In the 1920s, government credit for reconstruction was the source of capital formation. After World War II there was a variety of methods: self-financing by companies to the extent of nearly 50 percent of all industrial investment; government deficits; special governmental funds derived partly from the counterpart of foreign aid; inflationary finance through Bank of France rediscounting. In these operations the traditional Paris capital market continued to play a minimal role. On this showing, the critical variable for economic growth was not the overall supply of capital, but the mechanism for channeling savings into domestic investment. Capital exports were less a subtraction from the supply of capital available to industry than a means of mopping up the pool of savings which industry could not or would not use.

Blaming the barriers to capital flow into industry makes more historical sense than concentrating on the factors making for capital exports. But here, too, there is a problem of identifying cause and effect. Was it the barriers that restrained the demand, or the low demand that permitted the barriers to stand? Where demand for industrial capital is insistent enough, it can be said, institutional arrangements will adapt themselves to it and continue to channel savings into industry.

In any case, whether capital formation was deficient because of lack of demand or because of institutional blocks to industrial and governmental investment, it seems reasonable to exonerate the *supply* of capital. True, it is difficult to separate the demand and supply curves over time, because of their interdependence. On almost any showing, however, the supply of capital has moved in the wrong direction to explain France's postwar economic revival. Abundant during the period up to World War I, it was extremely scarce after World War II; yet this later period saw a larger expansion of domestic investment than the earlier. Postwar developments affecting the supply of savings – the discouragement to savers from inflation, the slight redistribution of real income to lower-income groups, and the growth of appetite for real income in the lower middle and working classes – have reduced rather than expanded the supply. It is perhaps fair to say that foreign-exchange control after World War II prevented the diversion of capital to hoarding in Geneva, London, and New York on the scale that had taken place in the interwar period. But this is a small difference compared with the postwar change in demand. The Monnet, Hirsch, and Massé plans, the renewal of construction, the need for roads, schools and other social-overhead capital, and, above all, the expansion of investment by nationalized industry, private enterprise, and even artisans, shopkeepers, and farmers, have put perhaps the severest strain on the capital supply that France has known since 1856. Bank credit has been tight;

dividends have been limited; capital markets and Plan authorizations have served to ration the tight supply of savings.

The *supply* of capital is an economic concept which is clear in itself. There is the behavior of domestic savers – corporate, private and governmental – and of foreign investors, and the competition of foreign borrowers for savings. But the domestic demand for capital is a less coherent aggregate. Back of it stand other factors with more basic explanatory force. It is to these factors – the character of entrepreneurship, the growth of population, functions assumed by the government, and so on – that we must turn.

The family firm

An important body of thought holds that French economic retardation has been due to the dominance of industry by the family firm. On this theory, family enterprises have slowed France's growth relative to other countries by various forms of behavior. Landes emphasizes their support of monopolistic or imperfectly competitive forms of market organization.[2] The wider-ranging Jesse Pitts version of the theory contains a multiple indictment.[3] For one thing, family enterprises refuse to grow beyond the size at which they can be dominated by the family; in particular, they refuse to dilute the family ownership by selling equity shares on the securities market. They minimize risks rather than maximize profits, and hence save in liquid form as insurance against adversity rather than invest in product or process innovation. They produce to fill orders rather than for stock. They are characterized by secrecy and mistrust; they fear banks, government, and even the consuming public. They hold prices high. Turnover is permitted to languish as the larger firms refrain from expanding output and sales in ways which would embarrass the small-scale inefficient producers at the margin.

The narrower Landes and wider Pitts theses are not universally accepted. Some scholars who do research on the origins of large-scale French industry insist that the theses overlook vast and significant fields of French entrepreneurial endeavor such as railroads, mines, iron and steel, automobiles, banks, and department stores. Some hold that family enterprise can function efficiently, as it has done in Britain. Some regard the family firm as a transitional form of enterprise in every country which happens to have lasted a little longer in France than in some other countries. It is generally agreed that family enterprise has characterized the French textile industry; but, even here, in various localities there have been examples of speculator firms which were interested in making money rapidly and selling out, rather than founding a conservative industrial dynasty as an extension of the bourgeois family. Family firms of a progressive nature can be found in iron and steel, tires, automobiles, locomotives, department stores, and so on. And when technological considerations require it, the pattern of many small-scale family-size units is replaced by concentration – despite the reluctance to dilute – by means of mergers, bankruptcy, or voluntary withdrawal after the sale of assets. Finally the French economic expansions of the 1850s and 1860s, of the period 1896–1913, and of the 1920s add to the doubts as the responsibility of the family firm for French economic stagnation.

But whatever its responsibility for stagnation, one would be hard pressed indeed to attribute the current French dynamism to changes in the structure of the family firm. A certain number of private mergers have taken place, especially in steel, and including some urged by the Planning Commission – though in Sollac, the new firm merely joins elements of the DeWendel family empire which had worked together earlier as an entente. Nationalization of coal, electricity, gas, and the Renault automobile firm has consolidated some small-scale family units into large organizations, or replaced family organizations by those recruited on universal rather than particularist lines. These changes are much less significant, however, than the change in attitudes of the family firms themselves. Landes was bold enough to say in 1957 that three years of expansion did not make an industrial revolution. Presumably he believed that the institutional bonds of the family firm would bring the recovery to a halt. What appears to have happened, on the contrary, is that the expansion in the economy altered the attitude, outlook, and hence the behavior of the family firm.

This result can be seen nowhere more sharply than in the automobile industry, where it is difficult and maybe impossible to judge from the behavior of the four major firms the nature of their ownership and direction.[4] The two family firms (Peugeot and Citroën, which is owned by the Michelin family) are respectively the most and the least profitable, respectively the most efficient producer and the most daring product innovator. The limited liability company – Simca – has perhaps the least distinguished manufacturing record, though it has participated in the growth of output of the industry by means of aggressive domestic marketing. The nationalized concern, Renault, has innovated brilliantly in production and in foreign sales. But all have been helped by a demand which grew at the rate of 25 to 35 percent a year and provided a margin within which risks of innovation could be undertaken.

I am not, then, disposed to attribute any great responsibility for the periods of slow growth to the family firm, nor to attribute the present resurgence to changes in this institution. There is, of course, some interaction between growth and the family firm in the postwar period of rapid technological change and increasing domestic investment. Inhibitions on the dilution of ownership through issuance of equity securities may slow down capital formation, just as the competition of public companies may have forced family firms to alter their policies on technical change. But basic causes of change cannot be found in the nature of the family enterprise.

On the side of demand

Population

It is a paradox that too little population growth is thought to have slowed economic growth in France – and in the 1930s in the United States – whereas too much population growth is inhibiting development in underdeveloped countries. But the reconciliation of the apparent conflict is fairly straightforward. When a country starts on the road to development, increases in income stimulate the net birth rate, generally by reducing disease through improvement of sanitation and medical care. The survival of additional young and old people lowers output per capita, reduces income available for investment, and slows the rate of growth on a Harrod–Domar model (compound interest based on increased savings). But in countries beyond the early stages of development, population growth may have a different effect. A static population may mean an excess of intended savings over intended investment, with unemployment, a reduced level of capital formation, and slower growth of capacity. Limiting children to a boy and a girl per family lessens pressure for mobility because children can follow parental occupations. Restricting investment to the level which will maintain the ratio of capital stock to a fixed population narrows the opportunity to incorporate technological improvements in the economy's assets. It is principally for these reasons, largely concerned with demand, that economic activity in a developed country is stimulated by expanding population – especially if the expansion results from the immigration of able-bodied workers or from the maturing of a new crop of babies to 15 years of age and more, rather than from an increase in the numbers of old people.

Since World War II both the economy and the population have grown at rapid rates. It is conceivable that the economic growth led to the population expansion, as occurs in underdeveloped countries, where development is accompanied by a reduction in infant mortality and improvements in public health which reduce the death rate. But in

Table 7.1 Net reproduction rate in France, 1911–59 (100 means population is reproducing itself)

1911	87	1921	98	1931	93	1941	77	1951	126
1912	94	1922	97	1932	92	1942	85	1952	125
1913	92	1923	94	1933	88	1943	90	1953	124
1914	88	1924	93	1934	90	1944	94	1954	125
1915	57	1925	94	1935	87	1945	93	1955	124
1916	45	1926	92	1936	88	1946	126	1956	125
1917	48	1927	93	1937	89	1947	131	1957	126
1918	46	1928	92	1938	91	1948	133	1958	126
1919	58	1929	89	1939	93	1949	133	1959	128
1920	98	1930	93	1940	82	1950	132		

Illustration: The rate of 128 for 1959 means that under the conditions of mortality observed for all females in that year and under the conditions of fecundity observed for all child-bearing women in that year, 100 women of child-bearing age would be replaced by 128 females. This corresponds to a 28 percent increase from one generation to the next.

Source: Annuaire Statistique de la France, *Rétrospectif* (Paris, 1961), p. 51, Table VIII.

France the causation almost certainly did not run in this direction. The net reproduction rate, which indicates the extent to which a population is reproducing itself, turned sharply upward from 1945 to 1946, well in advance of the rise in output. Table 7.1 shows the net reproduction rate over a period of nearly fifty years. A rate of less than 100 means that, under the conditions of female mortality and fecundity of the year given, the current generation will be replaced by a generation less numerous, and a rate higher than 100 means it will be replaced by a generation more numerous. The rate rose suddenly after both world wars, but in the second case it shot above 100 and stayed there, reaching the highest ground in at least a century and a half.

The question follows as to what *was* the cause of the population upturn – whether a simple (or complex) independent change of taste or a result of efforts of French demographers (especially Adolphe Landry) translated into the Code de la Famille of July 1939. The answer must be sought in timing, and, to the limited extent possible, in the differences in fecundity in different groups as affected by the family allowances.

On the first point – timing – it is generally believed that French interest in larger families took hold during the war.[5] In the bourgeois quarter of Vienne, baptisms had been rising since 1936;[6] and this would square with the very slight rise in the net reproduction rate from 1935 to 1939. But those observers, like Sauvy, who see the origin of the change as the adoption of family allowances at the insistence of the demographers can hardly be refuted by the fact that the upturn did not coincide exactly with the Code de la Famille. The Code itself had its forerunners, and significant effects were, of course, overwhelmed by the war and postponed until its end.

There is, however, a limited amount of evidence – and considerable opinion – to suggest that the change in attitude toward family size was not contingent upon subsidy. It would be desirable to have data by income group on the size of families formed since 1945. If such data showed that the lower income groups, to which the allowances provided a more substantial proportionate increase in over-all income, had experienced a larger increase in family size than higher income groups, we would be entitled to say that the family allowances stimulated the increase in fecundity. The available census data are of little use because they relate to existing families formed almost entirely before 1946.[7] Data on net birth rates by French departments are misleading because of interdepartmental migration. More young people migrate than old, and this results in higher birth rates in departments of immigration and lower in those of emigration, without regard to birth rates by income groups.[8] But there is evidence to suggest that the pre-World War II demographic pattern has changed drastically. In Vienne in the postwar period, bourgeois couples have had the largest families; the number of children per household was: bourgeois 1.46; workers 1.06; lower middle class (employees and small shopkeepers) 0.98.[9] In a small sample of independent businessmen Pitts found that the number of children per family was well above the French average.[10] And it is reported that in the poorest agricultural part of France the third child is always a mistake for which the "family allowances and premiums are never more than a consolation."[11]

One can conclude, then, that the claim of Sauvy and the other French demographers that the family allowances produced the dramatic change in birth rates is not established. These allowances have doubtless had other significant effects in promoting child welfare and health. But the change in birth rate must be regarded as an independent change in taste. The question remains whether the change in birth rate has produced the French recovery.

It is certainly possible to regard it as an important remote cause, if not the proximate cause. The rising tide of youth has impressed on the French – government and public alike – the necessity to bestir themselves to achieve growth. This was by no means the only such stimulus; the humiliation of France in 1940 after the sorry record of the 1930s could equally produce a resolve for more effective economic performance. Nor did the birth rate provide the mechanism for growth. But the wave of children has modified French attitudes toward family life and toward social, regional, and occupational mobility; has led to an insistence on more housing and schools; and has reduced the resistance to economic growth of static elements in the society. The change in population growth rates contributed to economic growth but was not the sole basis for it.

Social changes

The discontinuous change in population growth calls attention to the possibility that the change in the rate of economic growth may be attributable to wider social changes of which the step-up in the net reproduction rate is only one aspect. The economist is in no position to evaluate the quantitative importance of this sort of change. The purpose here is only to show how social attitudes and circumstances may have inhibited economic growth in the past, and, having undergone change, how they contribute to it at the present. Only two aspects will be discussed: values and social tension among classes.

It has long been observed that demand for mass products has been held back in France by French interest in elegance in consumption. Handwork was preferred to the output of machinery. The intense interest in individuality in consumption has kept Sèvres porcelain and Gobelin tapestries going today. In less durable goods the Paris dress industry provides the classic example, unless it be the French interest in good food and wine, which not only diverts demand to labor-intensive output but also slows production for several hours in the middle of the day.

Pitts attributes the French interest in quality to the long survival of aristocratic values, in particular the concern for prowess – the unreproducible act, whether of art, valor, sport, or craftsmanship. To these values were added the dynastic interests of the bourgeois classes, anxious to perpetuate the "extended family" and hence to amass savings; and the coexistence of quality consumption and a high propensity to save left little room for broad markets for consumers' goods. It is significant that in 1913, when France was the leading automobile producer in Europe, with a production of 45,000 cars, most of them were built to customer specifications and half the output was sold abroad, mainly in the United Kingdom. The country which originated the department store failed to adopt it as widely as did the United States, United Kingdom, and Germany, or to accompany it with the chain store or multiple shop.

The lack of demand for large-scale production is also partly explicable in class terms. With wide social barriers, one saved if one were ambitious to become a bourgeois, but the great mass of workers and peasants had little interest in owning durable goods, beautifying their houses, educating their children. Peasants saved to buy more land. The rise in workers' incomes went into meat and wine to give France the highest per capita consumption of these products in Europe.

Postwar recovery has been caused – or at least accompanied – by widespread interest in consumption of durable goods. The phenomenon is by no means restricted to France; it affects all of Western Europe. But it is perhaps most striking in France, where it is intimately linked to the change in the family from the "extended" to the "nuclear," and the change in the reproductive pattern. Instead of living for the future of the dynasty, French people today seek enjoyment, including enjoyment in children. Rudimentary facilities for consumer credit have developed to assist in these gratifications. In bourgeois circles, there is probably less personal saving than before.

Along with the revaluation of mass consumption, France has undergone a change in attitude toward work. Partly this involved an abandonment of the aristocratic value system which disdained work in general, and particularly accorded an inferior status to selling, which would involve submitting one's worth to the whim of a customer. More generally perhaps it may have grown out of changed attitudes inside and outside the family. To refer again to the views of Pitts, the tensions of the extended family induced a polar change in behavior when men escaped from the family scene into business. There they constituted a "delinquent peer group," defiant not only toward home but also toward customers, potential competitors, and especially toward government. (By contrast, in the United States the tensions of school and business produce – in the home – the immoderate behavior of children and the relaxed attitude of breadwinners.) But with a change in the family structure to the nuclear unit created for enjoyment rather than dynastic continuity, there is said to have been room for converting the business enterprise from a delinquent community into an outlet for creative energy and accomplishment.

As for social tensions, the uneven economic development of France in the past has been explained by a number of observers in terms of the inability of the French to resolve deep divisions which extend beyond the politics of, say, the Dreyfus affair and embroil important economic interests. "The history of the Second Empire is in good part illustrated by the struggles of rival financiers."[12] France had two capitalisms, one producer-oriented, family-oriented, Catholic; the other financial, speculative, Jewish or Protestant. The speculative group appeared to oppose the family-oriented group's values and structure, but used them for its own ends.[13] The economic history of France from 1830 to 1880 can be written as a struggle between the *grande* and the *petite bourgeoisie*.[14] Or the period from 1850 to 1939 was characterized by successive wars between the traditional economy and industrial society, with the petty bourgeoisie first on one side, then on the other. In this combat there was insufficient pressure from population, from foreign trade, from the new national market, and from spectacular and sudden rates of growth, permanently to alter the patterns of traditional and petty bourgeois resistance.[15]

These views tend to be rather vague on the mechanism by which growth is held back. Some observers point to the family firm, which we have discussed. In a few cases the mechanism is said to be inflation, caused by distributional difficulties coupled with economic and political power. It is therefore appropriate to examine the theory that social divisions have caused inflation and that inflation has had a decisive effect on growth.

It is true that a small burden laid upon a society can cause inflation and inhibit investment and growth if there is difficulty in agreeing on how the burden should be shared among income groups and if each income group has some power to resist an undue portion of the burden being imposed upon it. If labor has power to raise wages and industry to increase prices, and if agriculture is prepared to withhold supplies when its prices rise slower than the prices at which it is buying, inflation is inevitable. This inflation will continue until the whole burden has been imposed on the pensioners, civil servants, rentiers, and other classes with fixed incomes. The power to resist burdens need not be narrowly economic. If police and civil servants go on 24-hour strikes when the cost of living rises precipitously in advance of their pay scales, or wine growers blockade Route Nationale 117 as a response to higher costs, higher taxes, or lower subsidies, the spiral mounts. Monetary theorists insist that a condition of inflation is that the money supply expand, and that inflation could be stopped if the central bank willed it. But this assumes away the problem created by the fact that the separate classes have enough power to prevent the burden from falling on them; industrial loans expand when wages rise as a result of strikes which in turn stem from the increase in the cost of living. To say that loans should not expand is to change the condition of the problem which arises from the capacity of industry, through its social and political power, to overcome any tendency to restraint which would force the weight of the burden on it, just as the threat or actuality of strikes prevents it from falling on industrial labor. On occasion the social struggle to fend off a share of the burden will take the form of a budget deficit as laboring and agricultural classes insist on governmental spending and all classes refuse to vote taxes, and industrial owners and professional classes refuse to pay those direct taxes which are levied on them.

But the main vehicle of inflation is the market, and inflation came to an end not so much through a change in monetary or fiscal policy as from a change in market power. When a good harvest and foreign aid destroy the capacity of farmers to raise prices by withholding supplies, the inflation comes to an end with a part of the burdens saddled on the farm sector. Thus the bumper crop of 1950 and the subsequent agricultural expansion broke the back of French inflation and reduced agriculture's share of national income from 25 percent in 1949 to 14 percent in 1952.

But although inflation in France has been a symptom of social disharmony, revealed in persistent deficits and monetary expansion, it has not been harmful to growth. Nor, probably, has it helped. The growth of the 1850s and that of the 1920s were both accompanied by inflation, just as that of the late 1940s and early 1950s up to 1953.

Some of the deep social fissures in the nineteenth century are thought to have slowed growth in specific ways other than inflation; the *hautes banques* pulled down the Crédit Mobilier in 1868 and the Union Générale in 1882, and killed the Freycinet Plan of 1879 for investment in feeder railroads, canals, and roads. In the 1930s, the economy was crippled by the clash between the extremes of Left and Right, culminating in the Stavisky riots, the sitdown strikes, and Matignon agreement which humiliated industry. But there was also little social cohesion in the postwar period; yet growth began anyhow. Business groups emerged from the Vichy period in national disgrace.[16] Small businessmen and tradesmen fought against the collectivity in the Poujade movement. Peasants' dissatisfaction with their economic lot, expressed especially in the demonstrations and riots of 1961, has been continuous since 1952. The Algerian question has divided the country as nothing has since Dreyfus. All this without halting expansion. For in the postwar period the concern for expansion – stimulated by technocrats in government – has been dominant.

There is some evidence that economic growth has helped to narrow social divisions, but not much. The Frenchman is said to feel himself still disfavored, despite a 43 percent increase in per capita income between 1949 and 1958; and people are not happy.[17] The working classes have more material comfort, but their condition of life remains sharply differentiated from that of the bourgeois – except perhaps in the size of their automobiles. Tradesmen, farmers, and to some degree the petty bureaucrats have not done as well as the bourgeoisie and the industrial worker. They do not oppose the rise in the standard of living but are disgruntled that they do not fully share it. Particularly disaffected is the progressive farmer, who has changed his way of life as a producer, only to find, with falling agricultural prices on a saturated market, that he has taken on fixed service charges for his machinery which his enlarged output cannot help him to discharge because of the inelastic demand.

On the whole, then, France has adopted new attitudes toward the family and toward production and consumption, but without fundamentally altering class divisions and the mistrust felt by the individual for other classes, for other individuals, and for government as the embodiment of others. That the change in values was important in producing economic growth is likely but impossible rigorously to demonstrate. The unimportance of class antagonism as a general inhibition on growth – so long as all classes agree on the desirability of expansion – would appear to be established.

On institutions

When one turns from factors of supply and demand to the institutional arrangements governing the organization of production, he must acknowledge that the distinction is trivial. Institutions are outgrowths of underlying facts. The view that French economic growth has been held back by monopoly and monopolistic behavior is closely related to the view that it has been held back by the family firm.

The institutions that need close examination here are, first, the organization of the market, and second, the government.

Market organization

Two schools of thought may be distinguished in the field of market organization. The first is an outgrowth of the argument about the family firm: it holds that industry was small-scale and non-competitive, or that such large-scale industry as existed held back from competing with small firms in the interest of high profits and social stability. The other school holds that industry was dominated by large-scale monopolies which restricted production and held up prices. In both cases the emphasis is on the structure of the market rather than on that of the firm. The first version, however, would expect an improvement in competition and productivity from bigger units. The second would not.

The version that better fits the facts is the one that rests primarily on the existence of inefficient small units protected by the unwillingness of the large to compete. Industries dominated by large firms have done better on the whole than those in which the average size was smaller.[18] Much of the French economic literature falsely identifies large firms with concentration and small with competition, whereas it is possible for big firms to compete, as the automobile industry reveals, and for small-scale industry to maintain prices or standard markups, with resultant overcapacity and waste where entry is free. But even where this identification is correct, as it may sometimes be, the monopoly embodied in large-scale industry has not held back growth since 1945, whatever its prewar record.

Price maintenance by agreement (open or tacit), refusal to compete through innovation, insistence on protection in the home market – these are the earmarks of what the French call "Malthusianism."

> Malthusianism is the principal cause of the lag of the French economy. Industrialists and agriculturalists have always been haunted by the specter of overproduction and have feared a collapse of prices. To protect their interests they are organized into coalitions. These have as their purpose to maintain production at a relatively low level and to assure high prices for sales. They thus assure survival of the least profitable units . . . and occasionally even require the state to finance activities which have no interest for the national community . . . Mechanization and rationalization are held back; investment is limited . . . Prices are no longer competitive with foreign prices . . . Since the national market is limited, the forecasts of overproduction become justified along with the Malthusian measures which the industrialists and the agriculturalists demand.[19]

There has been an increase in the readiness of French industry to compete. This new attitude has appeared primarily in large-scale industry and reflects partly a change in attitude toward small French business. Rather than restrict production and hold a price umbrella over the heads of small firms in the interest of social stability, large-scale business now believes that its interests lie in lower prices, expanded output, and wider markets. Reduced profits per unit of sales will be more than made up, it is thought, by enlarged sales. And the Common Market provides a convenient cover for this change in attitude by large firms toward their inefficient compatriots. If small business succumbs to competition when tariffs are eliminated within the European Economic Community, it will look as though foreign enterprise, not French, wielded the weapons that destroyed it.

But the change in attitude goes wider. French business has lost its inferiority complex *vis-à-vis* foreign competition. Experience in steel in the European Coal and Steel Community, and in the metal, automobile, chemical, electrical and even the textile industry has persuaded efficient French firms that they can hold their own in competition with the best that the rest of the Common Market has to offer. It is sometimes suggested that the acceptance of the Common Market by French industry is no indication of self-confidence, because tariff barriers are going to be replaced with cartel agreements. There have indeed been numerous business agreements, mainly with a view to settling on different specialties for large-scale production by long factory runs. But European business is too well versed in the history of these agreements to depend on the forbearance of foreign rivals; such agreements are not respected unless they are between equals. Despite the industrial agreements, therefore, French entry into the Common Market signifies willingness to compete at home, and capacity to compete abroad.

Malthusianism has gone, or been very much reduced. But what has produced this result? Not an independent change in the size of firm, not capital investment, not an increase in domestic and foreign competition, though these changes are associated and related to one another and in sum represent the end of Malthusianism. A major change occurred in technology, including innovations in both process and product. And this technological change, latent in French technical capacities, was the outcome of deep-seated social and value changes.

Government

Intimately related to social cohesion and division, on the one hand, and to market organization, on the other, has been government, the focus of myriad French forces and ambivalent attitudes. Although government has occasionally taken a positive role, as under the Second Empire, its normal function has been to operate to maintain social stability in the face of divisive forces. Individuals, firms, and social groups curse the government for its favoritism to others and appeal to it for assistance to themselves.

Warren C. Baum has studied the postwar record of government and found it poor.[20] He particularly attacks the inconsistencies and contradictions in policy. Government tried to improve efficiency and yet to maintain inefficient small firms and small farms. In providing security it discouraged output. In taxing sales on the *forfait* system, it encouraged high markups on low turnover with bad effects on the price level and efficient distribution. Rent controls inhibited building and limited labor mobility. The regressive system of social security taxes both raised manufacturing costs and had the effect of making the laboring classes pay for their own security.

An effective case can be made that French tax reforms have consistently been in the direction of encouraging private modernization, expansion, concentration, and adaptation.[21] Much of this occurred after the period covered by Baum, and during or after the strong upsurge of recovery from 1953 to 1958. Baum's book, suggesting that the state has made it impossible for France to grow (most of it written in 1953), appeared in 1958 when the rate of growth was very high. Its more important weakness, however, is that government seems to be viewed as an independent organization outside the economy, whereas government is really a reflection, direct or distorted, of the contradictions embedded in the social fabric. French tariff history in recent years has reflected the same unresolved conflicts in that there have been tariffs for all – on foodstuffs and home-grown raw materials, for farmers, and on industrial products, for manufacturers. As already indicated, inflation is an escape from the dilemmas implicit in sharing a burden, not a result of ignorance of monetary or fiscal policy.

Not only does government intervene internally. It is the instrument of foreign policy. Government and the country may make a success or failure abroad through ineptitude or excessive ambition. Here the postwar record is not distinguished, whether in Indochina or Algeria, or in France's share of NATO's defense of Europe. Large sacrifices have been imposed on the country and French allies alike, without substantial achievement, as concern for French greatness has outstripped capacity. But these failures have not had disastrous consequences for economic growth.

Two important discontinuities have occurred in government policy, one a decision to resist further centralization of control and activity in Paris, and the other a return to an ancient practice of government planning and investment.

All the French literature – produced partly by economists but mainly by geographers – has denounced the centripetal pull of Paris. Because of Louis XIV, or Napoleon I, or the layout of the railroads, or whatever factors, Paris is thought to have drained the rest of the country of vigor, capital, and opportunity. The Bank of France is stated to have taken steps as late as 1930 to centralize bank credit in Paris.

During the last quarter of a century this centralizing tendency has altered. In the late 1930s, the program of dispersal of aircraft manufacture helped; the transfer of more than one plant to the provinces (for example that of a Renault parts plant to Le Mans) may have been due to an urge to escape the Popular Front. But the real discontinuity occurred during the war. The division of France into the Occupied and Unoccupied Zones required initiative outside Paris. Moreover, a series of studies by geographers[22] formed the basis, after their publication in 1945, for a vigorous program of government support for investment outside Paris, especially after 1953. The attraction of Paris for economic vitality and brains has by no means been destroyed; local talent is still being seduced to the capital, and certain regions of France remain unattractive for private investment. Nevertheless, expansion is most rapid in a few towns of great tourist attraction, like Annécy; and Lorraine, the Nord, and the Dauphiné are leading French economic growth.

There remains, however, a large question how much of the growth of economic vitality outside Paris is the result of government policies, and how much of it is spontaneous. Separate influences are, of course, impossible to disentangle. Policy changed, and the facts changed, but whether the policy change was responsible for the alteration of the facts is impossible to say with any finality. Both may have depended upon the rise in economic energy throughout France. In the 1920s, it was easy to identify the expansion of the North with the governmental policies of reconstruction in that devastated area. After World War II, the most that can be said is that the conscious decision of government to reverse the concentration of economic decision-making and vitality in Paris either produced the geographic decentralization or was the product, along with that decentralization, of the revival of economic energy in France.

Government planning and investment were a new departure, at least since the defeat of the Freycinet plan in 1882. Their roots, however, lay deep in French culture in Saint-Simonism, the technocratic view which found favor with Napoleon III. In the emperor's view, government was not an ulcer, but a motor, and his early support for the construction of railroads, canals, telegraph facilities, ports, and roads, and for the rebuilding of Paris, Marseilles, and Le Havre set the stage for the period of rapid growth from 1851 to 1857 and even to 1870. His letter to the Minister of Commerce published in the *Moniteur Industriel* of January 15, 1860, outlined a plan for the economic development of France eight days prior to the unpopular Anglo-French treaty for tariff reduction, imposed by decree in opposition to the majority of the French Parliament. The Freycinet plan represented similar Saint-Simonian tendencies under the Third Republic, though it was defeated by the bankers; and Michel Augé-Laribé insists that "everyone knew what needed to be done for agriculture in 1880 – better methods, fertilizer, seed selection, irrigation, drains, roads, cheaper transport and education – but it did not get done, even slowly."[23]

Although the Monnet Plan thus represented an ancient tradition, the vigor with which it was carried out and followed up by the Hirsch Plan and subsequent ones was new in French governmental annals. I shall explore presently the forces that gave rise to this burst of energy, which was felt earliest in the nationalized coal, electricity, gas and railroad industries, in the nationalized Renault automobile firm, and also in steel. The Monnet Plan, with its variety of controls and financing techniques, has been said to have raised the level of investment without overexpanding basic capacity. But the level of investment which France could maintain was much higher than it would have been in the absence of the Marshall Plan and other aid from the United States, such as the Export-Import Bank loan of 1946. Of course the possibility exists that this aid supported France's overseas wars rather than recovery, and that without it defense expenditure would have been cut back rather than investment.

Government, apart from its intervention in investment, may have made some contribution to economic recovery after the war by means of economic policies in other lines – but this is more questionable. The monetary theorist may contrast the Laval deflation with the Rueff stabilization plan of December 1958, or the 40 hour week under Blum with the policy of forced mergers under the Monnet Plan. It is dangerous to push the contrast too far. The French economy began to pick up after Munich when the Reynaud government took office. This was partly attributable to defense spending, though mainly to the removal of unwise policies which held back production. On the other hand, it is hard to find sound governmental policies in the early postwar recovery period, except on investment. Monetary flaccidity, along with the policy of a prize for every group, permitted inflation. The devaluation of 1946 was unsuccessful. Inflation was halted more by foreign aid and a bumper harvest that by Pinay's policies. And with all respect to the Rueff Plan, which was a model of its kind, the devaluation and stabilization of 1958 were successful because of the recovery that had taken place rather than responsible for it. There is no justification for attributing great significance for French recovery to these monetary policies, which tidied up but did not build.

In brief, governmental policy is an expression of social and political consensus or its absence. It is naive to blame contradictory, muddled, or inept policies on the intelligence of members of the government rather than the political matrix in which the government operates. With his superior vision, Paul Reynaud may have advocated policies which hindsight rates as far superior to those adopted. But it is almost as much of an error to be in advance of the times as behind them. And few are the Churchills with the luck and leadership to have the bankruptcy of other views demonstrated in time.

French recovery

This recital of alleged causes of economic backwardness has dismissed lack of resources, labor, and capital as causes of French economic backwardness, and has found no profound independent change in the French family firm which would account for the postwar revival (or for the earlier periods of rapid expansion). More interest attaches to the demand side – to the independent change in rates of population growth which occurred during the Second World War and to the change in French attitude toward levels of living. Market organization was found to be a dependent rather than an autonomously changing variable, and government too was largely dependent since it and its policies reflected the national consensus in the economic field or, as under the Second Empire, reflected the seizing of power by a strain of French thought normally in the minority. It remains to examine how French attitudes toward growth changed, whose hands carried out the new consensus, and what modalities were used. But before we get to these topics it is important to address one significant ingredient of growth which has not been blamed for French economic backwardness – technical capacity. Economists are increasingly persuaded that economic growth is a process less of accretions of capital, labor, and new resources in a given state of the arts than of technological change.

Technological change

It was the insight of Joseph Schumpeter that focused attention on the role of the entrepreneur as the introducer of new techniques. But after the Schumpeterian view of development had given way to the Harrod–Domar view that growth was the result of substituting capital for labor, a number of statistical investigations found much more growth than could be accounted for by the expansion of capital, and attributed it once more to technical advance.

As Schumpeter pointed out, technical change requires invention and innovation, the latter consisting of transforming new processes or new products from ideas to economic realities. Frenchmen claim that they are more effective at invention than at innovation. William N. Parker goes further and suggests that French intellectuality in the Cartesian tradition produced inventions of wide adaptability whereas British empiricism and especially German method yielded industrial secrets of immediate *local* usefulness.[24]

This is evidently too complex a subject to the dealt with summarily. It is fair to say, however, that France was technologically very backward at the beginning of the nineteenth century. At this time French technical progress was clearly differentiated from British, being inspired by government rather than spontaneous and private, and it was in response to the British example and the competition it provided. After the Napoleonic wars, French businessmen flocked to England and undertook a mass imitation of British methods, assisted after 1828 by the removal of the British embargo on machinery exports.

The British technological lead over the world was at its biggest at the time of London's Great Exhibition of 1851, and was especially pronounced in textiles, iron, and railroading. It did not exist in all fields, however, nor was it maintained long. The major competition came from Germany and the United States; but even in France, by the 1880s, successes in industrial technology were being achieved in locomotives, glass, jute, shipbuilding, chemicals, and, of greatest importance, steel.

Even so, French technology was not distinguished on the whole, either prior to 1914 or in the interwar period. Believers in the family firm as the cause of economic retardation are persuaded that this institution is notoriously slow to take the risks involved in innovation. French business was riddled with secrecy, which provides exactly the wrong atmosphere for technical progress. Innovating firms must exhibit a willingness to absorb a large quantity of technical information, survey potential ideas, be willing to share knowledge, to look outside the firm, and so on.[25] The distrustful family firm hardly fits this picture. Pitts has gone further: "To change the industrial secrets of the firm which have been taught to a few is like withdrawing the sacraments from a communicant."[26]

The period since the war has brought significant change in the French technological performance. The success in solving the desulfurization problem at Lacq has been mentioned, as have the innovations in the automobile field from the DS19 and the 2CV to the Dauphine and 404. Renault developed its own machine-tool production in an effort to acquire modern automatic machinery for automobile production, and in so doing created a new machine-tool industry in France. The Caravelle is well known in aircraft, as is the Mystère. A brand new firm, Bull, has risen to international prominence in computers. French railroads have set new technical standards for the world, including the feeding of electric current into locomotives at 20,000 volts, so as to eliminate the need for stationary transformers. Electricité de France, in placing orders for power-generating equipment, has continuously raised the technological standards until by 1958 it was generating power and transmitting it to Paris from Genissiat at 380,000 volts.

Cameron exaggerates when he claims that French industry played a large role in spreading economic development to the rest of Europe in the nineteenth century.[27] The technical contribution was almost entirely limited to civil engineering and mining, two fields in which French education at the Ecole Polytechnique and the Ecole des Mines was particularly distinguished. Today, however, French engineers are spread all over the globe on a variety of technical tasks. In the short space of 15 years, French engineering has risen from a European substandard to the equivalent of the world's best.

French technical virtuosity in the postwar period has been largely overlooked. British economists, for example, were disposed to attribute the fact that France's economic growth was faster than Britain's to the forced-draft investment by the "secret government" represented by the permanent civil service, which investment could be undertaken because all mistakes were underwritten by United States aid. German monetary theorists, and their sympathizers, considered that French economic recovery was achieved by the Pinay and Rueff policies of deflation. But technical change is to a considerable degree independent of the level of investment, as demonstrated by British experience of investment without technical flair, and expanding in technically advanced lines may be said to have made deflation possible, rather than the other way round. The discontinuity in French technical performance is an important causal factor which, like the changes in population growth and in social values, can be traced back to the war.

War and economic change

One economic theorem holds that war on a considerable scale reinforces economic trends already under way. A growing country will grow faster, as the United States did during and after World War I. And a stagnant economy will continue to stagnate, as Britain's did in the 1920s. But the postwar French recovery on top of the spreading collapse of the economy in the 1930s provides a contrary case where the direction of economic change was reversed.

There are also other cases. German interest in nationalism, and indirectly in national economic development, dates from the defeats inflicted on Prussia by Napoleon. In turn the German victory over Denmark assisted that country in transforming itself from a grain producer to a major exporter of animal products. Even the French economic expansion after 1896 is linked to the defeat at Sedan and the 1871 Treaty of Frankfurt – for one leading industry, woolens, was developed at Elbeuf by refugees from Alsace;[28] the discovery of new iron deposits was the result of exploration undertaken to compensate for war losses; and the growth of Lorraine, and the steel industry there, was stimulated by the pressure of refugees and the need to make up national losses. The time lag was long, until the Gilchrist Thomas process was developed and the technological difficulties at Briey were overcome. But the association of this expansion with defeat in 1870 is not altogether farfetched. The classic example, however, is Germany's economic revival after World War II. More ambiguous cases are furnished by Italy, which was and was not a defeated country, and by France, whose war was even more anomalous.

On this showing, defeat may be a greater stimulant to economic expansion than victory. The case is not clear-cut, as the example of the United States after World War I demonstrates. Nor is the stimulant of defeat a simple phenomenon. Part of the explanation is the purging effect of war's destruction, which assists development by making it possible to build new plants embodying the most modern techniques.[29]

But this is not all; the humiliation of defeat – and in the French case, defeat without the satisfaction of having made an effective stand – may destroy old values and induce a country to sublimate in ways which are conducive to economic growth. Refugees who have lost their possessions are particularly ambitious in these respects, as suggested by the Alsatian migration and the more recent influx of East Germans into West Germany. But even without a particular class which seeks to compensate for its losses through economic success, a country may undergo in defeat a change of values which releases its energies for economic advance.

There were, of course, contributing factors which turned French interest after 1940 to economic expansion. Ideas were contributed by the success of the Russian experiment, the New Deal in the United States, and even Swedish Socialism. Pierre Lalumière believes that the most important intellectual change was the discovery of Keynes by the Inspection des Finances.[30] It is necessary to point out that Keynes was concerned not with growth but with stability. On the other hand, the "discovery of Keynes" can be taken to mean the change of attention from problems of monetary stabilization – which had occupied Aftalion, Rist, and Rueff – to concern for real output. The point is well made.

The ancient formula of social stability made no sense in a world of French defeat and possible nuclear holocaust. Living for the future led nowhere. It was time that France turned from balancing social forces to expansion which would hopefully spill over to all groups.

The new men

Who were the new men called for by the Schumpeterian system to lead the expansion? A number of different answers have been hazarded. In one view they had existed all along, buried in the business staffs of 1935–40. Or they emerged from the experience of Vichy, which developed efficient business administrators like Pucheu, or from German occupation. The difficulty here is that business finished the war thoroughly discredited in French public opinion from its opposition to the Popular Front, its support of Vichy, and its failure to participate fully in the Resistance. Or they thrust themselves forward from government, not from the ranks of politicians but from the civil service.

One thesis is that the Inspection des Finances was the focus of change. Great numbers of the men in the Inspection left government for industry. These civil servants, who are said to have admired businessmen but not politicians, went largely into finance – either into banking and insurance, where their financial training was particularly useful, or into the financial side of large industry like automobiles and chemicals. Moreover, most of the members of the Inspection who remained in government had long since given up the narrow auditing function for general administration, and operated not in the Inspection but throughout the government. By 1955, approximately 170 members remained in the agency, and 109 of them were on detached service: 26 in the nationalized banks, 11 in other nationalized industry, 26 in international organizations, 30 in the regular ministries, and 16 in other governmental jobs.[31] (Those in non-economic international organizations were able to contribute only marginally to French economic development, and many of those in the ministries were concerned with non-economic problems of foreign policy or defense.) Lalumière regards the Inspection des Finances as "alone or almost alone" as an active group, in the middle of general French inertia.[32]

But this view attributes too much credit to the Inspection des Finances and underestimates the change which occurred elsewhere in the economy. Assume that there were 50 or 60 inspectors inside the government and concerned neither with auditing nor with noneconomic administration, plus an equal number of alumni outside. To ascribe the vigor of the French postwar recovery to these men alone is excessive. The French civil service as a whole, or at least that portion of it which had not followed de Gaulle abroad, emerged from the war rested, fresh, ready for a fast start, in contrast to British governmental employees, who reached VE day fairly exhausted from almost six years of overtime. The entire French civil service, and not only the Inspection des Finances, had time and opportunity to reflect on the deficiencies of French economic and social life prior to 1940.

But more than the civil service was involved. The change in attitude toward economic expansion was universal in France. The proof is that the net reproduction rate moved in a big jump in violation of normal causation as recognized in social science. There was vigor in many sections of society: in the Resistance leaders themselves; in the Communist Party which organized the revival of coal production; in the neo-Catholic Centre des Jeunes Patrons; and among geographers. Economists organized the Institut Scientifique d'Economie Appliquée with its focus on national-income accounting. The Confédération National de Patrons Français gradually abandoned its protective attitude toward little business. The family firm looked for outside help. One significant index: the demand for youth in business expanded rapidly. The Ministry of Labor stated in 1951 that the top hiring age for middle-rank executives (*cadres*) declined from 60 in 1898 to 50 in 1945, 45 in 1950, and 40 in 1951.[33]

Nationalized industry and planning

It remains to evaluate the role in French economic recovery of the "planning" carried on by the Planning Commission under the initial direction of Jean Monnet and later under Messrs Hirsch and Massé. A certain mystique has collected about this effort; in particular the British, conscious of the wide gap in postwar expansion between their country and France, have sought to find in planning the force responsible for French success.

There can be no doubt that the French government has controlled a large proportion of the French economy. Approximately 30 percent of national income has gone through government hands in the form of taxes. Nationalized industry was responsible for half of total investment. But the scope with which government operated to direct the economy was much wider than that implied by its tax receipts and the income of nationalized enterprises. The Planning Commission affected the operations of private enterprise in ways which were almost as pervasive as those of nationalized industry, and in some cases equally so.

Nationalization may have been necessary to French postwar economic recovery, though this is dubious in the light of the general public interest in expansion. Alone it certainly was insufficient to bring the recovery about. The British experience is relevant as a touchstone. Productivity increased much more in the nationalized French coal, electricity, and railroad industries than in the similar nationalized industries in the United Kingdom. Nationalization need not spark technological change.

Moreover, the extent of control over industry deriving from governmental ownership is debatable. The first five-year plan called for expansion in six key sectors: coal, electricity, transport, steel, cement, and agricultural machinery. Only the first three were nationalized. And the government contributed finance to private industry through the various funds for modernization and equipment, as well as underwriting the large deficits of the railway system and providing huge capital sums for electrical construction. Ultimately, to be sure, Electricité de France sold its obligations in the capital market much like a private company, although it had a state guarantee. And Pierre Lefaucheux, the dynamic leader of the Régie Renault, "recalled unceasingly as much by his action as by his intervention and speeches that if the Régie belongs to the state, it is in fact administered in the same fashion as a private enterprise."[34] The quality of leaders – Massé in electricity and Armoud in railroads, along with Lefaucheux – was more important than state ownership.

If not nationalization, then what about planning? In 1961 the British suddenly awakened to an interest in French planning, hoping to find in the techniques a secret of growth that could be applied to the sluggish British economy.[35] The hope, unfortunately, is doomed to frustration. French planning is in some important respects the opposite of planning. Knowledge of income and industry projections and faith in the inevitability of expansion are communicated to firms at intra- and inter-industry meetings. This is perhaps the most powerful effect, and one which has a faint resemblance to a revivalist prayer meeting. In addition, and importantly, the Planning Commission uses a series of controls – powers to fix prices, adjust taxes, control credit, lend governmental capital, and authorize construction – to encourage firms to expand.[36] There is far more stimulation than restraint. But levels of output are decided by the individual entrepreneur, not by planners; and profit anticipations have ultimate power of decision. Industry projections are fitted into national-income accounts as a check against their logical consistency, and even measured against input–output tables. These operations, however, have exhortatory rather than regulatory results, unless they imply an absence of stimulation.

The fact is that French planning is empiricism. The total polity is bent on expansion. This fact is communicated to all corners of the economy, expressed, so far as possible, in terms of numbers. Given the underlying faith in expansion, the numbers tend to confirm themselves, within limits. Where a sector or industry falls short, one weapon or another may be employed to help. The French insist that their *planification* is flexible (*souple*). This comes close to a contradiction in terms. There is little *dirigisme* in the system, and much readiness to proceed by whatever paths lie open. The roles have been reversed from the nineteenth century when the British were the pragmatists and the French were doctrinaire.

Much is made in the recent French literature of the "technocratic" character of the expansion. In some quarters this spirit is identified with James Burnham's "managerial revolution" in which the bureaucratic employees have interests different from those of the owners, the workers, and the consumers.[37] This hardly fits today in France. To the extent, however, that the term can be taken to refer to a society in which all groups are interested in expansion, partly by capital investment but primarily through technological change and increased total productivity, the characterization is apt.

The technological character of French expansion is one further proof of the unimportance of planning as such in French postwar expansion. Immediately after the war, planning referred primarily to investment planning, with implicit Harrod–Domar models of capital output ratios and the like. The growth of output was estimated from the growth of investment. The strong element of technological change in the expansion was unplanned. It emerged, unexpectedly, from the French intellectual tradition and the nation-wide consensus on the need for economic expansion.

Conclusion

The economic recovery of France after the war is due to the restaffing of the economy with new men and to new French attitudes.

The opportunity for hiring new staff came from the discrediting of many of the existing leaders of the economy (whether in the prewar government or in Vichy), the passage of time with little constructive work taking place, and the upthrust of new energetic people in the Resistance and in the invading French army. Unlike World War I, the 1940s brought no widespread loss of youth which made it necessary to retain the prewar generation in economic command. The new men were found in private as well as nationalized industry, in family firms as well as corporate enterprises, in administrative positions as well as technical ones. Some of them had a "passion for innovation," some for expansion, all for efficiency of one sort or another, whether economic, engineering, administrative, or in terms of profit maximization. Dissatisfaction with the past led them to substitute change for stability as the operating guide.

New attitudes followed from the change in leading economic personnel. But the new attitudes went far wider. Not only did firms want to expand, but workers and consumers became willing that they should. The movement from the extended to the nuclear family, and to increased numbers of children, has been referred to. The causal connections between these sociological phenomena and the new staffing are not easily comprehended, but doubtless exist. And these new attitudes on the part of the public – at least in the social field though perhaps not in the political – seem to have had their origin in the frustration of the 1930s and the war and the occupation. Workers have become less revolutionary, more practical. The individual, or his parents on his behalf, has begun to be seized with more ambition for education and opportunities, and less for holding on to place, position, acquired rights.

To conclude that the basic change in the French economy is one of people and attitudes is frustrating to the economist. *Natura non facit saltum* (Nature does not make a jump) was Alfred Marshall's motto in the *Principles of Economics*. Marginal analysis, compound interest, growth as a function of fixed resources, evolving technology, and growing capital are more compatible with the economist's modes of reasoning. It is true that capital has grown, and technical progress has been made, but these are accompaniments of a more far-reaching process, rather than exogenous variables.

Nor have the sociologists and economic historians furnished much in the way of explanation. The family firm and deep-seated fissures in the social structure fail to explain the rate of progress of the past, and exist even today when growth is again rapid.

The interest in progress is not new in France. Saint-Simon was a technocrat, and Napoleon III, Michel Chevalier, Eugène Rouher, and Charles de Freycinet continued in the tradition. When there was a clear view of the need to expand, whether responding to the destruction of World War I or taking advantage of the railroad, the Thomas process in steel, or the discovery of Briey iron mines, expansion followed. The present demand for economic growth at all levels in French society is different only in the extent to which various groups in society share in it. It has not been accompanied by a similar consensus in political matters. Whether its continuance into the future for a decade or a score of years will be self-perpetuating, as it has not been in the past, remains to be seen.

Notes

1. See Harry D. White, *The French International Accounts, 1881–1913* (Cambridge, Mass.: Harvard University Press, 1933); and Rondo E. Cameron, *France and the Economic Development of Europe, 1800–1914* (Princeton, NJ: Princeton University Press, 1961).
2. David S. Landes, "French Entrepreneurship and Industrial Growth in the XIXth Century," *Journal of Economic History*, May 1949, pp. 49–61; Landes, "French Business and the Business Man: A Social and Cultural Analysis," in *Modern France*, ed. E.M. Earle (Princeton, NJ: Princeton University Press, 1951), pp. 334–53; and Landes, "Observation on France: Economy, Society and Polity," *World Politics*, April 1957, pp. 329–50.
3. Jesse R. Pitts, "The Bourgeois Family and French Economic Retardation," unpublished thesis, Harvard University, 1957.
4. John Sheahan, "Government Competition and the Performance of the French Automobile Industry," *Journal of Industrial Economics*, July 1960, pp. 197–215.
5. See, for example, the discussion by M.L. Henry in Colloques Internationaux du Centre National de la Recherche Scientifique, *Sociologie comparée de la famille contemporaine* (Paris: Editions du Centre National de la Recherche Scientifique, 1955), p. 67. He asserted that a brusque change in fecundity was manifest in couples married in 1943, and perhaps in those married in 1941 and 1942.
6. Pierre Clément and Nelly Xydias, *Vienne sur le Rhône* (Paris: Colin, 1955), p. 28.
7. For what they are worth as an indication of the fertility characteristics of various occupational groups, however, I offer the following 1946 census data as given in Alain Girard's paper in *Sociologie comparée de la famille*

contemporaine (cited in note 5), p. 56. These are the numbers of children surviving per 100 married men aged 45–54.

Miners and terracers	272
Farmers	253
Common labor, workers, foremen	189
Shopkeepers, artisans	181
Salaried staff, liberal professions, and employers of more than five persons	170
Storeowners, employers	165
Office workers	162
Sales clerks	139

8. For their limited value, the data are suggested by listing below the departments with the highest rates of excesses of births over deaths (ten or above), and the lowest (two or below) in 1954. The national average was 6.8. It will be noted that the highest birth rates were in departments of high (and rising) income as well as high immigration, and the low birth rates were in the poor agricultural regions of the Southwest. The data are from *Annuaire Statistique de la France, 1956*, pp. 17, 18:

Ten or above		*Two or below*	
Moselle	13.6	Lozère	2.0
Orne	12.9	Allier	1.8
Calvados	12.3	Basses Alpes	1.5
Meurthe-et-Moselle	11.9	Corrèze	1.5
Seine-Maritime	11.5	Nièvre	1.4
Doubs	11.1	Pyrénées-Orientales	1.4
Ardennes	11.0	Haute-Vienne	1.2
Manche	10.7	Haute-Loire	1.1
Meuse	10.4	Lot	0.7
Aisne	10.2	Alpes-Maritimes	−0.9
Haute-Marne	10.2	Creuse	−3.0
Sarthe	10.0		

9. Clément and Xydias, p. 27. A more detailed table on total size of household is presented in ibid., p. 25, but is impaired by the fact that the bourgeois and farmers maintain the "extended family" rather more than workers, employees, and small employers (36 percent and 40 percent as against 12, 16, and 20 percent respectively). Both tables presumably relate to 1950. From the table in ibid., p. 25, come the following data on the average number of persons per household in Vienne by occupational groups:

Higher technical staff	3.90
Liberal professions and large-scale employers	3.77
Foremen	3.27
Small traders	3.11
Artisans	2.97
Workers	2.95
Employees	2.87
Retired	1.75
Farmers (only 3 percent of total sample)	3.85
Others	2.25
Average	2.80

10. Pitts (cited in note 3 above), p. 260.
11. Robert Mendras, *Etudes de sociologie rurale*, *Novis et Virgin*, Cahiers de la Fondation Nationale des Sciences Politiques, no. 40 (Paris: Colin, 1953), p. 69.
12. G. Lefèvre, *Politique intérieure du Second Empire* (Paris: Centre de Documentation Universitaire, n.d., *c.*1953), p. 56.
13. François Perroux, "Prise de vues sur la croissance de l'économie française, 1780–1950" in International Association for Research in Income and Wealth, *Income and Wealth*, series V (London: Bowes & Bowes, 1955), pp. 59ff.
14. Jean Lhomme, *La Grande Bourgeoisie au pouvoir*, *1830–1880* (Paris: Presses Universitaires de France, 1960), *passim*.
15. John E. Sawyer, "Strains in the Social Structure of Modern France," in *Modern France*, ed. E.M. Earle (Princeton, NJ: Princeton University Press, 1951), pp. 301–5. See also, in the same volume, John Christopher, "The Dessication of the Bourgeois Spirit," pp. 55ff.; and Jacques Fauvet, *La France déchirée* (Paris: Arthème Fayard, 1957), esp. pp. 90ff.
16. See Henry W. Ehrmann, *Organized Business in France* (Princeton, NJ: Princeton University Press, 1957), pp. 104, 107.
17. L.A. Vincent (1959), "Niveau de vie: évolution économique et mécontentment," *Etudes et conjecture*, vol. 14, no. 2 (February), pp. 143–50.
18. See Institut National de Statistiques et Etudes Economiques (INSEE), *Mouvements économiques en France de 1944 à 1957* (Paris, 1957), p. 42, where it is noted that output grew much faster in the industries with large-scale units. With 1938 as 100, petroleum products in 1957 had an index of 199, mechanical and electrical industries 168 each, chemicals and rubber 149, metals 141, and glass, tiles, and building materials 141, compared with 101 for textiles and 104 for leather.
19. Pierre Lalumière, *L'Inspection des finances* (Paris: Presses Universitaires de France, 1959), p. 194 (translation mine). This is set out as the analysis made by the Inspection.
20. W.C. Baum, *The French Economy and the State* (Princeton, NJ: Princeton University Press, 1958), *passim*.
21. For a discussion of the changes in depreciation rules governing corporate income taxes, see Martin Norr, "Depreciation Reform in France," *The Tax Magazine*, May 1961, pp. 391–401. These changes started out as a series of *ad hoc* measures but were generalized in the 1959 tax reform.
22. See *Rapports et travaux sur la décongestion des centres industriels* (Paris: Ministère de l'Economie Nationale, 1945), vols. I–VI.
23. Michel Augé-Laribé, *La Politique agricole de la France de 1880 à 1940* (Paris: Presses Universitaires de France, 1950), p. 80.
24. See William N. Parker, "Comment" on C.P. Kindleberger, "International Trade and Investment and Resource Use in Economic Growth," in *Natural Resources and Economic Growth*, ed. J.J. Spengler (Washington, DC: Resources for the Future, Inc., 1961), pp. 187–90.
25. C.F. Carter and B.R. Williams, *Industry and Technical Progress* (London: Oxford University Press, 1957), pp. 179ff.
26. Pitts (note 3 above), p. 353.
27. Cameron (note 1 above), *passim*.
28. René Sédillot notes in *Peugeot* (Paris: Plon, 1960), p. 53, that the Franche-Comté was economically stimulated after 1871 by refugees from Alsace.
29. For a discussion of how destruction can help, as opposed to the econ-

omic argument which holds that any asset which survives the war can be abandoned if it is not useful, see my "Obsolesence and Technical Change," *Oxford Institute of Statistics Bulletin*, August 1961.

30. Lalumière (note 19 above), p. 179.
31. Ibid., p. 85.
32. Ibid., p. 126.
33. François Jacquin, *Les Cadres de l'industrie et du commerce en France* (Paris: Colin, 1955), p. 19.
34. Bernard Vernier-Palliez, "La Régie Nationale des Usines Renault devant la concurrance" in Travaux du 3e Colloque des Facultés de Droit, *Le Fonctionnement des entreprises nationalisées en France* (Paris: Dalloz, 1956), p. 95.
35. Political and Economic Planning, "Economic Planning in France," *Planning*, August 14, 1961.
36. For a full-length description of the French government's controls and their effectiveness in promoting recovery, see John Sheahan, *Promotion and Control of Industry in Postwar France* (Cambridge, Mass.: Harvard University Press, 1963).
37. See Jean Meynaud, "Qu'est-ce que la technocratie?", *Revue Economique*, July 1960, p. 520. See also Meynaud's book, *Technocratie et politique* (Lausanne, 1960), for references to the current French discussion of efficiency as an end in itself.

PART 3

The United States

8

US Foreign economic policy, 1776–1976

I

It is tempting to view the evolution of US foreign economic policy from 1776 to 1976 as one from isolationism to participation to leadership of the world economic system, a process now starting to show signs of reversal. In terms of the theory of private and public goods, the United States for some 170 years looked after its private national interest, then spent a quarter of a century playing a leadership role, pursuing at the same time what it conceived as the public international interest, before exhausting itself and perhaps turning back exclusively to its own affairs.[1] Or, in Albert Hirschman's brilliant model of relations within social groupings, the country has moved from "exit" to "loyalty" to "voice" – first a participatory voice and then the voice of command – and may be again heading for the exit.[2]

But such themes would be too simple. The country is not a unified actor with a single set of purposes, but an amalgam of shifting interests which engage customarily in ambiguous compromises. Economic foreign policy may be global or may make distinctions among regions (North America, Europe, Latin America, Asia, Australasia, and most recently Africa); among functions (trade, money, capital and aid trans-

---

*Commissioned as part of the Council of Foreign Relations celebration of the Bicentennial of the Declaration of Independence, and published both in *Foreign Affairs*, vol. 55, no. 2 (January 1977) and in William P. Bundy, ed., *Two Hundred Years of American Foreign Policy*, A Council of Foreign Relations Book, New York: New York University Press, 1977.

fers, migration, not to mention foreign growth and integration). At any one time there are complex trade-offs among various national and international interests rather than any one dominating the others. There is likely to be a high positive correlation among policies regarding different aspects of the country's economic relations with the rest of the world; none the less, there is no escape from detailed description and analysis.

Our interest attaches principally to the recent past. I propose first to sketch the period to World War I rapidly. Thereafter follow sections dealing separately with the 1920s, the Depression, the years following World War II through the 1960s, and then from about 1968 to the present. A brief section concludes with reflections on the prospects now facing both the United States and the world.

II

The American Revolution represented not so much a withdrawal from European and especially British life as an insistence on relating to Europe on different terms from those decreed by British decision. The Navigation Acts which determined where and how colonial shipping could be used, taxation from Whitehall, impressment of colonials as sailors in the British Navy – all were economic as well as political issues in which colonial interests were threatened by imperious decisions at a distance. The isolationism of Washington's Farewell Address (1796) and the Monroe Doctrine (1823) came later, with a revulsion against the Napoleonic wars over more than 20 years – wars that incidentally enabled the struggling nation first to win its military independence and second to conduct its economic affairs independently.

But the nation had little in the way of a unified national interest. The Constitution of 1789 prohibited export taxation, deliberately foreclosing the possibility that central government could hurt the interests of an exporting state through taxing its output sold abroad. The idea originated not from the free trade of Adam Smith's *Wealth of Nations* of 1776 but in earlier Physiocratic doctrine, which Smith also embraced. "*Laissez-faire, laissez-passer*" was a French agricultural doctrine to free food for exports, as opposed to the doctrine of supply which would keep it at home for domestic consumption. The latter echoes today in embargoes on steel scrap, peeler logs, soybeans, wheat and the like.

In the absence of export taxes, federal revenues came largely from duties on imports. The Continental Congress levied a tariff of 5 percent "for revenue only" across the board. Debate followed almost immediately. Madison and Jefferson, from Virginia, wanted low tariffs to expand export trade through buying imports freely. Massachusetts and Pennsylvania sought protection for manufacturing. The tariff of 1789 was a moderate compromise, with 5 percent duties in general except for rates ranging up to 15 percent on a limited list of manufactures. Alexander Hamilton's well-known "Report on Manufactures" of 1792 did not affect the course of events.[3]

More significant was the embargo of December 1807, precipitated by British impressment of American seamen. That embargo, the Non-Intercourse Act of 1809, and war with England in 1812 produced substantial change in the course of economic development. War is the ultimate protective tariff. Embargo and war stimulated the cotton and woolen textile mills of New England and the iron foundries of Pennsylvania. With the restoration of peace, the tariff question became acute. It was a matter not of procreating infant industries, but of preventing infanticide. Agriculture was preoccupied with supplying Europe with grain, cotton and tobacco after the Congress of Vienna, and did not immediately resist; it began to do so after the fall of European agricultural prices, and the passage of the Corn Laws in Britain in 1819. Tariffs were raised further in 1824, but after the "tariff of abominations" of 1828 reaction set in. Early in the 1830s some duties were lowered, and in 1833 the Compromise Tariff produced a more general reduction. That this was followed by the depression of 1837 – a result of the expansion of the bank credit by the Second Bank of the United States – led to the Whig, later Republican, view that tariff reductions spell depression.

In this period – and indeed until the last 40 years – the tariff was a domestic issue only. Higher duties in 1842 and reductions in 1846 and 1857 were unrelated to the free-trade movement under way in Europe. Led by Britain, which rationalized tariffs in the 1820s and 1830s before dismantling the Corn Laws and the Navigation Acts in the 1840s and freeing the export of machinery, the Continent moved to tariff reduction on a reciprocal basis during the boom of the 1850s, but especially after the Anglo-French (Cobden–Chevalier) Treaty of 1860. British leadership in the movement was important, as was the ideological character of certain free-trade forces under the influence of the economic doctrines of Smith, Ricardo and Mill.

Canada was sharply affected by the repeal of the Corn Laws and the Navigation Acts, and some Montrealers contemplated annexation to the United States. A less far-reaching remedy was found in reciprocal trade in natural products in a treaty of 1854. The special economic status of Canada, between the United States and Britain and having particular relations with each, remained an issue for the rest of the period.

While the United States was largely absorbed in its own affairs, many of those affairs, or those of constituent parts of the country, involved foreign economic questions. The Louisiana Purchase of 1803 – financed by a loan issued in Amsterdam – riveted the attention of the Middle West briefly on Europe, from which it turned again on a heightened basis to exploration, Indians, land settlement. New York merchants and financiers, New England shipbuilders and traders, Southern planters, canal-builders and railroaders all had eyes on European markets. In transportation, the United States pioneered in fitting steam engines to ships: in the liner, or scheduled vessel that sailed each Saturday whether it had a full cargo or not, and in clipper ships. Cotton-growing in the South exploded in the 1820s and 1830s, and moved rapidly inward from the sea islands and the coastal belt to the Gulf states and across the Mississippi. New York bankers established branches in Liverpool (later moved to London) to finance the movement of staples eastward and of a wide variety of goods westward. The First Bank of the United States sold shares abroad, and the Second Bank borrowed in London on bullion.

With the rise of shipping came an upsurge of immigration, initially from Britain and Scandinavia, and, after the disastrous crop failure of 1846, in a flood from Ireland and Germany. (An American myth holds that the Germans who flowed to these shores after 1848 were moved by conscience in revolt against monarchical repression and military conscription. The Carl Schurzes among the migrants, however, numbered several hundred out of hundreds of thousands.) Industrialization in Britain, Germany and Scandinavia after mid-century slowed down the flow of overcrowded peasants from these sources.

In the 1880s, however, there developed an entirely new economic interaction between the United States and Europe. Up to that time the farms of the New World had furnished largely exotic foods and materials not produced on a large scale in Europe – cotton, tobacco and sugar. But after the Civil War, the opening up of the Northwest Territories, with 40 acres and a mule for war veterans, made possible dramatic increases in grain production, while newly constructed railroads and iron-clad, steam-powered, screw-propeller ships became available to move the grain to Europe. Along with similarly stimulated supplies from Canada, Australia, Argentina and the Ukraine, the new flow led to a drastic fall in the price of wheat in Europe, and uprooted a vast army of peasants and landless workers in southern and southeastern Europe – who poured into the steerage holds of ships bound for Ellis Island and New York.

Limitation of immigration of "undesirables," including the ill, convicts, and Oriental "slave labor," had been undertaken in the United States in 1862 and 1875. In 1885 an attempt was made to stem the flow from Europe through a ban on contract labor. There was, however, no stopping the flood of workers who came individually and without work, looking for a new chance. The strong tradition of the United States as a place of asylum for the oppressed of Europe prevented the passage of any effective legislation to limit immigration, such as by a requirement of ability to read and write English.

Moreover, immigration from Europe met a critical need in the American growth process. In Europe, economic growth to a considerable extent was achieved through what is called the (Sir Arthur) Lewis model of "growth with unlimited supplies of labor," hardly distinguishable from the Marxian "reserve army of the unemployed." Unlimited supplies of labor off the farm held down wages, raised profits, led to reinvestment of profits and sustained growth. In the United States, early growth came from unlimited supplies of land which furnished a good livelihood to independent farmers. When manufacturing began to flourish – mainly because of the spillover of demand from affluent agriculture and only partly as a response to protectionist tariff policies – the massive infusion of labor sustained the process.

A high land–labor ratio from the beginning meant high wages, and high wages in turn predisposed American manufacturers to labor-saving invention. Eli Whitney responded with the cotton gin, which made possible the expansion of the cotton crop and of British and New England cotton textile industries. He further perfected interchangeable parts. The Colt revolver, the McCormick reaper, the Singer sewing machine, and the typewriter were among the labor-saving devices which poured forth from Yankee ingenuity. They quickly led to manufactured exports and subsequently to subsidiary factories abroad. The roots of the multinational corporation in manufacturing, usually thought of as a product of the jet aircraft and transatlantic telephone 100 years later, stretch back virtually to the middle of the nineteenth century. The Colt revolver and the McCormick reaper scored successes at the Crystal Palace Exhibition of 1851 and the Paris Exposition of 1855.

Finance had gone abroad as a handmaiden of trade long before manufacturing. Industry and the states of the Republic had borrowed in foreign financial centers since the 1820s, and had chalked up a substantial record of default and failure. The role of the federal government in these matters was small until the 1840s, when the first borrowing of consequence since the Revolution was undertaken to finance war with Mexico. Peabody, Seligman, Morgan, Drexel, and other less illustrious names gradually shifted their overseas operations from trade to investment banking more generally.

In monetary affairs, the United States sought to adhere to bimetallism, and then to the gold standard, although its finances seemed chaotic in the view from European centers, as speculative excess led to boom and bust, mania and panic, especially in 1836, 1857, 1872, 1893 and 1907, which sent shock waves reverberating back to Liverpool, London, Paris, Amsterdam and Hamburg. It was necessary to suspend specie payments and to issue greenbacks during the Civil War, resulting in depreciation of the Union dollar – though to nothing like the extent of Confederate money or the Continental currencies. After the war, the question was merely one of when to resume specie payments, and how. Resumption was achieved in 1879. An important change had been made in 1873, when the flood of silver from Nevada after 1869 depressed its price. A continuous preoccupation since the Coinage Act of 1792 had been to get the ratio of silver to gold right, so as to thwart Gresham's law that overvalued money drives undervalued out of circulation. Up to the 1830s, when the United States ratio was 15 of silver to 1 of gold to the general European ratio of 15.5 to 1, the country gained silver and lost gold. In 1834 and 1837 the ratio was changed to 16 to 1. By 1872, however, 16 to 1 was too high a value for silver, and bimetallism was then abandoned in favor of gold, to the distress of populists for the rest of the century.

Tariff policy at this time was dominated by fiscal considerations. When the Treasury was pinched, as in 1862 during the Civil War, tariffs were raised; when revenue was ample, as in 1872, tariffs were lowered. But by 1890, as a result of depression, the McKinley tariff raised rates, especially on wool and sugar, only to have the act of 1894 under President Cleveland partly reverse the result, largely on the basis of the charge that it had been produced by "trusts." The 1890s were a period of trust-busting and opposition to monopoly. Action against trusts, however, stopped at the water's edge. No action was taken against the collaboration of large American firms with one another or with foreign firms in foreign markets, except in so far as they conspired to restrain competition in the US market.

By the turn of the century, the United States was beginning to move away from an isolationist parochialism to a role in world society. As early as 1853–4, Commodore Perry had opened up Japan to American and European shipping and trade. When the Berlin Conference of 1885 among the European powers accelerated the pace of imperialistic acquisition, the United States became restive. In 1898 the explosion of the *Maine* in Havana harbor provided an excuse for a war against Spain in which Cuba, among others, obtained its independence, but Puerto Rico and the Philippines became United States protectorates. In the chaos which followed liberation, American investors (trusts?) acquired major properties in Cuba, especially the Isle of Pines, in an episode which recalls the carpetbagging in the South during the Reconstruction after the Civil War.[4] Fearful of being left behind by European powers, the United States sought an open door in China. The beginnings of foreign aid may be found in US use of its share of the indemnity required of China after the Boxer uprising of 1900 for charitable work in China.

The sharp depression of 1907 raised questions about the efficacy of the national banking system established in 1863. No longer completely self-sufficient, the country established the Aldrich Commission which reviewed banking legislation in other countries to study how to improve banking organization. Senator Aldrich also gave his name to the Payne–Aldrich Tariff of 1909 which raised tariffs to their highest point in the history of the country before World War I. Democratic victory in 1912 with the election of President Wilson brought the passage of both the Federal Reserve Act and the sharply reduced Underwood Tariff of 1913. The Payne–Aldrich Act was said to favor trusts, and to have produced depression in 1910.

Up to 1914, dominant economic issues were argued in terms of domestic interests in a world taken as given, which US action did little to affect, rather than in terms of economic theory or foreign relations. The British-dominated international economic system served American interests well. The country could afford to be loyal to that system, despite the claims of Southwestern farmers and Western miners that it depressed prices. Gold in California in 1848, silver in Nevada in 1869, the expansion of wheat acreage in the 1870s, and the bubbles followed by bursts throughout the century from 1815 to 1914 affected the system in ways we chose to ignore. That was the business of someone else – perhaps in London. The United States did what it did. Feedback to other nations was ignored.

III

World War I changed the entire position of the United States in the world economy. According to economic analysis, a country progresses through a series of stages: young debtor, mature debtor, young creditor and mature creditor. The United States went from the first to the fourth in three years, from 1914 to 1917. Assembly-line methods devised by Henry Ford just before the war were expanded to produce equipment and munitions for the Allied powers of Europe and for the United States itself. Based on the Federal Reserve System, the financial apparatus of the country grew in parallel. J.P. Morgan & Co. financed British and French private borrowing in the United States, and served as fiscal agent in supporting the pound and franc in foreign-exchange markets. In the end, the US government itself undertook to finance

Allied borrowing in dollars, especially those for consumption and reconstruction in 1918 and 1919.

Revisionist historians maintain that the entry of the United States into World War I was a continuation of the imperialist policies of the turn of the century, and of the expansion of American trusts into overseas markets needed to sustain the rate of profit at home. These policies are thought to have been motivated by the Eastern establishment's desire, conscious or unconscious, to take over world economic domination from the City of London and other European economic power centers. The US government is said early to have sought the expansion of overseas banking in order to push the use of the dollar in world trade and finance.[5] The theory suffers a logical flaw. Aggressive economic designs would have been more readily achieved by staying aloof from the battle, remaining "too proud to fight." The simpler and naive purpose of "saving the world for democracy" – a non-economic motive – better fits the facts and the logic.

Saving the world was one thing; keeping it saved was something else. President Wilson had plans for remaining involved in European and world affairs. They were not widely shared. The United States refused to ratify the Treaty of Versailles, to accept reparations, or to join the League of Nations with its Economic and Financial Department to worry about world economic questions. It did, however, join the International Labour Organization, established at Geneva in response to a proposal of the British trade unionist, Albert Thomas, and did cooperate with the League on a wide number of issues. General commitment to participate in the world political and economic system was withheld.

The war interrupted a wave of immigration which had reached, on a gross basis, 1 million persons in 1913. In 1917 an Immigration Act was passed after long debate, and over the veto of President Wilson, providing that immigration be based on quotas conforming to national origins of the existing population. This restricted immigration from southern and southeastern Europe in favor of the northern and western sections. In 1921 and 1924, overall quotas were reduced. The action is generally ascribed to trade-union desire to limit the workforce and preserve wage gains achieved during the war. More fundamentally, the motivation was socio-political rather than economic, reflecting widespread concern that it would be difficult socially to absorb the vast numbers of would-be immigrants backed up in the countries of supply.

The most serious economic issues arising from the war dealt with reparations and war debts. Having been strengthened economically rather than hurt by war, the country refused to accept reparations, but insisted on being repaid by its Allies for war and postwar loans. It further maintained that war debts and reparations were unrelated, contrary to French and British positions, the latter expressed in the Balfour Note of August 1922. Not until the Hoover moratorium of June 1931 was the connection acknowledged; and even after reparations had been buried at Lausanne in July 1932, Hoover in 1932 and Roosevelt in 1933 continued to try to collect war debts.

The United States played a role in reparations, however, through private individuals. When the Versailles arrangements broke down after the German inflation and after the occupation of the Ruhr by Belgian and French troops, Charles G. Dawes served in 1923–4 as chairman of a commission to write a new plan. The conventional wisdom has held that Dawes was simply American window-dressing for a staff plan drawn up by British civil servants, but this is now known to be an oversimplification.One British aim in the Dawes Plan was that the revised Reichsbank should hold foreign exchange, that is, pounds sterling, among its reserves. On US insistence the Dawes Plan specified that Reichsbank reserves be held in gold – an echo of a controversy between France and the United States over 40 years later but with the US role reversed.[6]

By 1930, when Owen D. Young served in a similar capacity on a revised reparation scheme, US involvement in European financial questions was complete. While much of the attention of government was focused on domestic problems – the Florida land boom, the rise of the automobile industry, and the decline in agriculture – Eastern finance was being drawn into world affairs. The Dawes Plan provided for issuance of a loan for Germany. The New York tranche (or slice) was oversubscribed 11 times and gave a sharp stimulus to foreign lending generally. The Agent-General for Reparations, established under the Plan, was S. Parker Gilbert, formerly of J.P. Morgan & Co.

During the 1920s, moreover, Benjamin Strong, the president of the Federal Reserve Bank of New York, was often called upon to arbitrate the central-bank quarrels of Europe, largely between Montagu Norman of the Bank of England and Emile Moreau of the Bank of France. Strong had a leading role of urging the return of the pound to par in April 1925. Then, within two years, he faced a dilemma, whether to lower interest rates in New York to assist the British with outflows of capital, or to raise them to slow down the boom in business and in security prices. He chose the former, and from March 1928 the stock market soared.

Economists call it a "dilemma position" when monetary policy is pulled in one direction by external and in another by internal requirements. For a long time, Strong's choice of aid to Britain's maintenance of the gold standard over curbing the speculative excesses of the stock market was regarded as a bad one. More recently, "monetarist" economic historians such as the Nobel laureate Milton Friedman have shifted the debate, arguing that, while Strong was wrong in favoring foreign over domestic considerations, he should have ignored the stock market and focused on a steady expansion of the money supply.[7] I am no more moved by this revisionism than by the political brand. Money supply was growing, and in fact declined very little up to March 1931. To the economic revisionists, it was not growing fast enough, a subtle argument but unconvincing.[8]

In Wilson's Fourteen Points, only the third had dealt with economic questions, and called for "removal, so far as possible, of all economic barriers and the establishment of an equality of trade conditions among all nations consenting to the peace and associating with its maintenance." It evoked little response, either at home or abroad. The United States in Harding's administration took action in the Fordney–McCumber tariff of 1922 to nurture its new crop of wartime infant industries. Tariffs were similarly raised all over the world.

The League of Nations undertook to reverse the trend in a series of conventions, many of them technical, for lifting trade from the chaos into which it had fallen during the war and the period of postwar monetary disturbance. In 1927 a World Economic Conference, with the United States as observer, met in Geneva and adopted a series of resolutions for lowering tariffs and opening up trade channels. No action was taken under it. Instead, Herbert Hoover, campaigning for the presidency in 1928, promised to do something for agriculture to alleviate its plight under the pressure of falling prices, which had begun in 1925. That something was to be what Josef Schumpeter called "the Republican household remedy": increased tariffs. In due course, this commitment ended up as the Hawley–Smoot tariff of June 1930.

On tariff matters, disaggregated economic interests and recommended policies diverged for ideological reasons, or what is perhaps better explained as cultural lag. The North and Middle West, interested in manufacturing, favored Republican high tariffs; the South, with a traditional stake in the export of cotton, was Democratic and opposed to protection. (Middle Western agriculture was ambivalent: interested in exports of grain and lard, but worried about farm imports from Canada and Australia.) But the economic base underlying these positions was changing. In the Middle West, manufacturing had risen through mass production to an export position, which would benefit from freer trade; in the South, especially North and South Carolina and Georgia, the cotton textile industry, moving in from New England in the 1920s and 1930s, gave many states a greater interest in cotton textiles than in cotton production. Not until after World War II did the South begin to qualify its doctrinaire espousal of free trade; and a Senator such as

Robert Taft from Cincinnati, a city exporting machine-tools to the world, never altered his inherited protectionist views in the economic interests of his constituents. Detroit in the 1920s was rising to a position like Manchester in Britain during the first half of the nineteenth century. It was slow in drawing policy consequences.

IV

To Herbert Hoover, the Depression which started in 1929 was the fault of Europe, and there was little that the United States could or should do internationally to remedy it. The Hawley–Smoot tariff of 1930 was a domestic measure, undertaken to relieve agriculture. If the movement to raise tariffs spread beyond farm products to manufactures, and if tariff rates were raised to unconscionable levels, as 34 protesting nations abroad contended, Hoover nevertheless regarded it as a private US matter. He did not answer widespread criticism that creditor nations should not raise tariffs on the ground that this prevents debtors from paying interest and amortization – an oversimplified and dubious doctrine, as it happens. (Tariffs under stable conditions raise income which spills over into further imports, to change for the most part the structure rather than the total quantity of imports.) Mostly, however, he failed to see the Hawley–Smoot tariff as the major action in setting off a retaliatory tariff war of the beggar-thy-neighbor sort. World trade shrank in a declining spiral, as the quantities and prices of traded commodities continuously fell.

The impact of the depression in the United States ricocheted abroad in other ways. The United States stopped buying as much abroad and also stopped lending, thus cutting down on available foreign exchange in two ways. In British lending of the nineteenth century, foreign and domestic investment alternated: when the periphery lost receipts from exports, it was able to borrow. This was not a matter of policy, but of the action of market forces. In the United States lending policy was minimal. The Department of State had asked Wall Street to notify it of impending bond issues so that it could indicate if there were foreign-policy objections to particular loans. And the Johnson Act of 1930 stipulated that borrowers in countries in default on war debts could not have access to American capital markets, but this manifestation of Congressional irritation on war debts should not have had any effect on major borrowers in Germany, the Dominions and Latin America that owed no war debts. Nevertheless, there was nothing that President Hoover could do to stimulate lending. It picked up in the second quarter of 1930 and then mysteriously collapsed.

In 1931, Hoover acceded belatedly to the suggestion for a moratorium on war debts and reparations; failed to take vigorous action to stop the financial runs on Austria, Germany and Britain, partly because of the necessity of agreeing with France; and ignored the strongly deflationary impact of the appreciation of the dollar – flowing from the depreciation of the pound sterling – on US farm prices, banks in agricultural areas, and ultimately on banks more generally. Hoover had an enviable record in international affairs as mining engineer and as administrator of food relief for Belgium immediately after the war. His vision of interrelations among world economies under stress, however, was a limited one, and contrasted sharply with the broader view espoused by such Eastern establishment spirits as Dwight Morrow, a Morgan partner.[9]

Foreign economic policy suffered in 1932–3, when Hoover was unable to govern and Roosevelt refused – after the election but before his inauguration – to make decisions before he bore responsibility. With the inauguration and the Bank Holiday, the "Hundred Days" involved a hectic series of decisions, largely on domestic programs – the Agricultural Adjustment Act, National Recovery Act, Thomas Amendment, and the like. Within the Roosevelt administration an intense struggle took place between the Middle Western views of advisers like Moley and Tugwell, and the Eastern–Southern retinue of Norman Davis, James Warburg and Cordell Hull. The former dominated, and problems like the clash between agricultural imports and measures to raise domestic prices, or the World Economic Conference (scheduled for 1932 and postponed to 1933), were put to one side.

The dollar was allowed to depreciate, and when the World Economic Conference finally met in June 1933, President Roosevelt torpedoed it by refusing to accept an agreement worked out by the experts in which Britain would stabilize the pound, Germany would renounce foreign-exchange control adopted in the summer of 1931, France would give up import quotas undertaken because of the ineffectuality of tariffs in keeping out foreign grain, and the United States would stabilize the dollar. The conference broke up in early July after concluding only a small agreement sought by Senator Pitman of Nevada for the silver interests. Its consequence was to divide the world economy further. The gold bloc of continental Europe – France, Belgium, the Netherlands and Switzerland – drew together, as did the sterling area of most of the British Commonwealth and a few countries closely allied to Britain in trade. At the center of the sterling area was the preferential trade system of the Commonwealth worked out at Ottawa in August 1932.

Under Roosevelt, however, the inward-looking phase of American policy did not last long. At the end of 1933 he and Secretary of the Treasury Morgenthau had lost interest in daily changes in the gold price and were exploring a stabilization agreement with the British. Failing this, in February 1934 they fixed the dollar in terms of gold anyhow, at $35 an ounce.

In the same month Roosevelt gave Cordell Hull – the Secretary of State with a fanatical preoccupation with free trade – the green light to introduce a bill to lower tariffs on a bilateral basis. (Under the unconditional most-favored-nation clause the country had adopted in the 1920s, reductions negotiated with one country would be extended to others.) This was signed into law in June 1934. Within the half-decade to 1939, 20 agreements were concluded, the first with Cuba in August 1934, the most important with Britain in November 1938 and two with Canada, in November 1934 and November 1938.

An awakening interest in foreign policies, both political and economic, also led the United States to normalize relationships with the Soviet Union, from which recognition had been withheld since the Revolution of 1917 on the ground that successor governments are required to assume the debts of their predecessors, which the Soviet government had been unwilling to do. Trade relations with the Soviet Union, which had been minimal to this time, expanded somewhat with the establishment of Soviet official buying agencies in the United States, but the development was not substantial.

To the south, Roosevelt initiated a good neighbor policy, without, at this time, much in the way of specific content. It was, however, a significant change both from the Monroe Doctrine, which had been directed mainly against European intervention, and from the imperialism of the turn of the century – the imperious use of the marines to collect debt service from Nicaragua and Haiti, and unquestioning support for such companies as United Fruit and Mexican Eagle in their operations in the area.

Of multilateral and more general import was the Tripartite Monetary Agreement entered into on September 26, 1936. The occasion was the collapse of the gold bloc, and especially of the French franc. The agreement provided a convenient cover under which the franc rate would be adjusted as part of an international exercise to provide exchange-rate stability. The engagement was limited: each country undertook to hold currency of the others without conversion to gold only for 24 hours. Symbolically, however, it marked an initiative by the United States in stabilizing the world economy. A separate similar exercise was undertaken in the spring of 1937, when the country refrained from changing the price of gold under pressure of the "gold scare" in which foreign private citizens and even a few central banks sold gold for dollars against the prospect of a reduction in the gold price. At some inconvenience, but no real cost, the US Treasury held to the $35-an-ounce price, buying all gold that was offered to it and sterilizing it by raising reserve requirements and open-market operations.

Exactly what forces produced the change in US economic policy in 1933 and 1934 from isolation to involvement is not self-evident. Elements contributing to the shift included recovery from the depths of the depression that had focused attention on domestic concerns, perhaps a shift of the president's interests from the populist position adopted during the campaign and especially during the first exciting days in office to his more comfortable views as an Eastern establishment figure; growing preoccupation with the threat to world peace posed by dictators in Europe and the Far East, with a natural extension of interest from foreign policy to foreign economic policy; and, as already noted, familiarity and boredom with the esoteric games of changing the gold price to alter the exchange rate to raise US commodity and share prices – especially after July 1933, when the technique ceased working. The circumstances and the personality of the president played a large part. More fundamental reasons would argue that the inward-turning of 1928 to 1933 was a deviation from trend, to which 1934 marked a return.

A European effort to regularize the international economy through agreement was initiated in 1937, leading to the preparation of a report under the direction of Paul Van Zeeland, former prime minister of Belgium. Appearing in 1938, the report was ignored under the stress of recession in the United States, which had struck in September 1937, and of rapidly expanding rearmament in a Europe threatened with war.

Foreign economic policy records two episodes associated with the rising threat of war. In 1935 Italy launched an unprovoked attack on Ethiopia, and the League of Nations somewhat diffidently called for sanctions on the delivery of oil to Italy. Though not a member of the League, the United States none the less supported the campaign and urged US oil companies to stop selling oil to Italy. The large companies complied with the request; unfortunately a rapid increase in Italian oil prices induced the entry of a host of single-ship operators who escaped control and delivered to Italy at Eritrean ports more gasoline than it had previously imported.

And, in 1938, the United States took another economic-warfare action of its own in cutting off the export of scrap iron and steel to Japan, foreshadowing a cutoff of oil in the summer of 1941, which helped precipitate the decision of Japanese military leaders to make war on the United States.

As war began in Europe in 1939, President Roosevelt honored more in the breach than in the observance the Neutrality Act of 1939, passed by Congress in an effort to keep the United States uninvolved; got around the Johnson Act of 1930 by interpreting it to apply only to private lending in the United States, and not to government advances to foreign borrowers; and finally, after the tide of battle had turned against Britain in 1940, and well before the United States had entered the war, enacted Lend-Lease in February 1941 as a way to transfer resources to its Allies without piling up the kind of recount of war debts that had occurred after World War I. A special feature of Lend-Lease was the Hyde Park Agreement of December 1941 with Canada, under which supplies and components needed by Canada for incorporation in *matériel* produced for Britain would be lend-leased to Britain, but delivered to Canada. This had the effect of keeping Canada off the books as a recipient of US assistance. Before US entry into the war, the United States and Canada established a Joint Economic Committee to expedite cooperation in mobilization and in planning postwar reconstruction. When the United States did enter, joint boards were established with Britain in a number of economic areas, parallel to the military arrangements, and especially in procurement, shipping and food.

As one condition of qualifying to receive assistance, the Lend-Lease agreement required that the recipient promise to cooperate with the United States in the design and construction of a liberal postwar world economic system. In the summer of 1941, President Roosevelt and Prime Minister Churchill met aboard a warship off Newfoundland. In addition to strategic planning of military operations, they drafted an Atlantic Charter that laid down broad principles for the establishment of a liberal economic system after the war.

V

In the Department of State, Leo Pasvolsky was assigned the task of preparing postwar plans for US policy for the world economy. No government agency waited for such plans to emerge. The Treasury moved ahead with monetary reconstruction. In 1943 the Agriculture Department organized a Hot Springs meeting on food. From the Department of State came a design for world trade. The United Nations was to be assigned a watching brief over world economic policies generally, but with operating responsibilities assigned to specialized agencies.

These responsibilities are indicated by the substantives used in the titles of the major world organizations. First in functional order was the United Nations *Relief* and *Rehabilitation* Agency (UNRRA). Relief was the provision of foodstuffs to hungry allies after the war. Rehabilitation consisted of restocking. The Bretton Woods bank was the International Bank for *Reconstruction* and *Development* (IBRD), beginning with the reconstruction of war damage, and going on to the development of countries which had not begun industrialization. The International *Monetary* Fund (IMF) would deal with exchange rates, balances of payments and the financial side. An International *Trade* Organization (ITO) was to lower restrictions and set rules for commerce. The world order would be pieced out with lesser specialized agencies in health, meteorology, aviation and the like. While these institutions were being brought into being, the United States enlarged by $3 billion the lending capacity of the Export-Import Bank, established in 1934 primarily to assist exports and employment. Of this, $1 billion was initially set aside for a loan to the Soviet Union, pending settlement of Lend-Lease and other wartime financial arrangements. The loan failed to materialize for reasons that have never been made clear but that undoubtedly reflected the influence in that first Truman year of such men as James Byrnes and Leo Crowley.

As the country least hurt by war, the United States took a major role in contributing to UNRRA, stocking it in large part with surplus army provisions. A first tranche of $2.75 billion was to be followed by a second equal amount in August 1945. A number of countries raised objections. Canada chose to give its aid directly to Britain. Britain refused to join unless the feeding of Austria and Italy were shifted from military aid (in which its share was 50 percent) to UNRRA (in which it was 8 percent). The USSR insisted that while it was a donor, to the extent of 2 percent, and hence not entitled to receive aid, the Ukraine and Byelorussia should be recipients. With one vote in 17, in the United States reluctantly agreed to take over the Canadian 6 percent, thereby increasing the US total from 72 to 78 percent, and to add recipients, thus diluting the aid provided for others. It resolved thenceforward to render aid bilaterally, rather than through multilateral organizations that lacked objective principles of aid-giving and were subject to logrolling.

The need for relief, rehabilitation and reconstruction had been seriously underestimated in the postwar period, on several scores beyond the dilution mentioned. In August 1945, on the surrender of the Japanese, Lend-Lease was stopped precipitously – a decision made by President Truman and Secretary of State Byrnes *en route* to the Potsdam negotiations without consulting their economic advisers. The decision was based on commitments made to Congress in the Lend-Lease legislation process, commitments which they both, as former senators, felt bound to honor. In his *Memoirs*, Truman recognized this as a serious mistake and put most of the blame on Byrnes. In addition to this blow, price control was removed in June 1946, so that a given amount of dollars went less far. Military destruction had been overestimated, but a serious underestimation of greater significance was made of the under-maintenance of capital, using up of stocks, and wearing out of consumers' inventories of clothing and household goods. Post-UNRRA direct assistance by the United States was undertaken in the strenuous conditions of 1946, along with the use of IMF and IBRD loans for emergency consumption rather than the reconstruction and balance-of-payments purposes for which they had been established.

The British position had been alleviated temporarily by an Anglo-American Financial Agreement which provided for a $3.75 billion loan to enable Britain to resume convertibility of the pound. During the early debates on postwar policy, John H. Williams of the Federal Reserve Bank of New York and Harvard University had opposed the IMF as a universal device for restoring world monetary health, and argued an opposing "key-currency" principle in which certain major moneys, around which pivoted large currency areas, would be restored to health separately and in sequence. As often happens when alternative courses are debated, both the IMF and the British key-currency loans were adopted. The initial amount of the loan was cut from $5 billion, perhaps a political necessity since the measure ultimately passed the Senate by only one vote. (The vote ratifying the agreement in Parliament was also close, as the Opposition contended that the conditions of the United States in granting the loan were too onerous.) As it worked out, the British were unwilling or unable to negotiate the write-down or funding of accumulated sterling balances or to institute effective controls on the export of capital. In consequence, the convertibility of sterling instituted in July 1947 lasted only six weeks before the bulk of the loan was gone.

Relief for the defeated countries of Germany and Japan was a low priority for the Allied governments but not altogether ignored. US policy toward Germany was complicated by joint occupation with Britain, France, and especially the Soviet Union; in Japan, where the United States was the sole occupation power, decision-making was easier. US policies called for avoiding the connections between reparations, war debts and foreign lending which had held after World War I. At Potsdam the United States insisted that the four zones of occupation be treated as a single economic unit, and that the first charge on current German production from all zones be commercial exports necessary to pay for imports, rather than reparations. The point was to prevent some occupation powers from taking out reparations from current production while others were obliged to feed the population in their zones. Reparations, it was agreed, should be paid through removal of capital equipment from Germany that was in excess of the peacetime requirements of the German people.

Strong forces in the United States pushed for restrictive and repressive policies in Germany. Under a Joint Chiefs of Staff directive (JCS 1067), drawing its inspiration from the so-called Morgenthau Plan, the US commander was instructed to take no steps to revive the German economy beyond those necessary to prevent such disease and unrest as might endanger the occupation forces. In July 1945, however, French, Belgian and Dutch need for coal made it necessary to try to restore German coal production for export. By fall, Poland was asking for spare parts for German machinery in Silesian coal mines. It proved impossible to reach sustainable agreements with the Soviet Union on what the latter could remove from Germany as war booty, restitution and reparations, and in particular the Soviet Union did acquire foodstuffs from the eastern zone of occupation while Britain and the United States were feeding their zones in the west. Gradually the zonal arrangements broke down, and so did arrangements for reparation removals. The economic importance of Germany in the revival of Europe became clear. By September 1946, the Secretary of State made a speech at Stuttgart outlining a more positive policy of German economic recovery in a European setting.

Governing and feeding Germany were further complicated in the fall of 1946 by a British government approach to the United States, stating that the country was unable to continue to pay the import bill for its populous zone of occupation including the Ruhr. A Bizonal Agreement in December 1946 provided that the two zones would be treated as a unit and that the United States would advance the bulk of the sums needed for imports. Later the French joined, with her smaller, self-sufficient zone.

Continued British economic weakness led in February 1947 to that country preparing to give up its support of Greek resistance to domestic and foreign infiltrating communist forces, and to another substitution of American for British responsibility, in the Truman Doctrine, for military aid to Greece and Turkey. Much of the assistance, especially in roads in Turkey, served a double economic and military purpose and could be said to be the beginnings of US aid to economic development. Its main purpose was military.

A harsh winter in Europe in early 1947, which burst pipes, blocked transport, flooded fields and rotted seed, threatened economic breakdown throughout Western Europe. Funds made available from the United States under the British loan, UNRRA relief and post-UNRRA aid were nearing exhaustion. Political stalemate with the Soviet Union over German questions, plus economic disintegration which overwhelmed the stopgap measures applied to separate countries, produced in Washington a strong desire for a new, cooperative, enlarged effort to achieve recovery in Europe. On June 6, 1947, Secretary of State George C. Marshall gave a speech outlining a European recovery program. He proposed that Europe should prepare a program of recovery which would involve the cooperation of all the countries participating, including Germany, and that with it as a basis the United States would undertake a new coordinated program of aid.

The invitation was extended to all the countries of Europe, including the Eastern bloc and the Soviet Union. Foreign Minister Molotov met with Foreign Ministers Bevin and Bidault in Paris but refused to participate unless the United States handed over a fixed sum first and let the countries of Europe use it in their own way. Following this refusal, Czechoslovakia and Poland, which had previously accepted the invitation to participate, reversed their decisions. When the three western zones of occupation of Germany went ahead with monetary reform in their own zones and in their districts of Berlin, in June 1948 as the Marshall Plan got under way, Soviet military forces blockaded land access to Berlin, effectively dividing the country. Western links to Berlin and the Berlin economy were maintained only by airlift.

Considerable ambiguity attached to US views as to what was meant by a European recovery plan. In the eyes of many, it meant the extension to Europe as a whole of French techniques of *planification* begun with the Monnet Plan of 1946. To William L. Clayton, Under Secretary of State for Economic Affairs, and Lewis W. Douglas, Ambassador to the Court of St James, it implied return to liberal principles of free markets. The preamble to the European Recovery Act of April 1948, and Paul G. Hoffman's speech of October 31, 1949, emphasized the reproduction in Europe of a vast continental market like that of the United States. The United States applauded when in May 1950 French Foreign Minister Robert Schuman proposed a measure of functional integration in the European Coal and Steel Community. It supported a European Payments Union. At the same time, it maintained pressure for the elimination of quota restrictions, which largely discriminated against US exports in the interest of economizing on dollars, and worked more broadly for the adoption of generalized rules for trading in the draft Charter of the ITO signed at Havana in 1948.

As indicated earlier, the ITO was to be a cornerstone of a world-wide system of liberal trading, setting down procedures for lowering tariffs on a multilateral basis, providing for freedom of investment, limiting restrictive business practices, and establishing machinery for handling necessary exceptions and adjustments. Countries emerging from the difficulties of war, and those embarking on programs of development, insisted on so many exceptions to the general rules, against quantitative restrictions and in favor of low, non-discriminatory tariffs, that the Congress of the United States judged the document worthless. The United States would be held to the general rule; other countries would claim avoidance under saving clauses.

The Department of State ultimately did not submit the treaty to the

Senate for ratification. Instead, it concluded an executive agreement, not requiring Congressional assent, the so-called General Agreement on Tariffs and Trade (GATT) that embodied the principal clauses of the ITO, and provided for a small staff to supervise operation of the agreement in Geneva. Under its aegis, a series of multilateral reductions of tariffs was negotiated in the postwar period, from the Geneva Round in 1949 to the Dillon, Kennedy and Tokyo Rounds. The Kennedy Round negotiated after 1962 was particularly salient.

Help to developing countries was initially limited to the "development" aspect of the IBRD and Greek and Turkish aid. In his inaugural speech of January 1949, however, President Truman included a Point IV aimed at this group of countries. This program initially consisted of technical assistance, especially in agriculture, education, and the planning of public works. As the 1950s wore on, it became increasingly evident that much more was needed, especially capital assistance. A euphoric mood developed that poor countries could all follow the development path of Britain, the rest of Western Europe, North America, and most recently Japan, and succeed in raising their standards of living. Needed were resolve on the part of local government and foreign aid in the form of goods, modern technology and effective management. Under the Republican regime of President Eisenhower, and later under Nixon, emphasis shifted from official aid to the role of American corporate investment in countries initially called "underdeveloped," then "less developed," and finally "developing." Both political parties put faith in the beneficent role of American food aid, under Public Law 480, designed to help developing countries and the American farmer, the latter by disposing of surplus stocks. Other groups were not slow in taking advantage of the opportunities afforded by foreign aid, shipping lines insisting on transporting it in American bottoms, suppliers that it be spent on or tied to American goods only. Even Congress benefited through a provision that 5 percent of the local-currency counterpart derived from the sale of aid goods be set aside for American use, largely the building of embassies and the entertainment of junketing Congressmen.

Assistance was furnished through multilateral agencies and bilaterally. Under the former, there were UN programs: those of the IBRD and its subsidiaries – the International Development Association (IDA) for non-bankable projects, and the International Finance Corporation (IFC) to invest in private enterprise in developing countries. In time special regional banks were established, largely with American capital, in Latin America, Asia and Africa. In due course, aid to development was extended by other industrial countries after their recovery from the war. Development became an international concern of the Organization for Economic Cooperation and Development (OECD), which emerged under the Marshall Plan from the original Organization for European Economic Cooperation (OEEC) – enlarged to include the United States, Canada, Australia and Japan. Its Development Assistance Committee (DAC) gathered statistics, compared national efforts, and urged increased aid.

Foreign aid was assisted in the early stages by the Cold War. South Korea, Taiwan and Israel were especially favored by US aid because of their strategic importance. Cuba got no aid from the United States, a great deal from the Soviet Union. At the last minute Secretary of State John Foster Dulles backed away from building the Aswan Dam in Egypt and let the Soviet Union take on the project. Bilateral aid was divided into military and economic, and the latter was often not that much different from the military aid in its implications for political alignment and support.

Discouragement with foreign aid set in during the 1960s. Economic development was stubbornly slow. Aid achieved little growth, less gratitude, few political objectives. The Hickenlooper Amendment, which required withholding aid when American property was nationalized without prompt, adequate and effective compensation, proved ineffective. Internationalists deduced from these circumstances that foreign aid should be multilateral, not bilateral. Those not so internationally minded thought there were better things to do with the money at home. Detente with the Soviet Union lessened the urgency of helping the developing countries. Aid still could be used in particular political impasses to grease a solution – help for both Egypt and Israel, or support for Rhodesia. But the moral commitment eroded.

Last in this catalog of areas of foreign economic policy was the monetary field. The IMF went into hibernation after the start of the Marshall Plan, except for a series of small operations, largely the furnishing of advice to developing countries, since the major financial needs of developed countries were covered by the Marshall Plan and by the substantial volume of dollars earned by Japan as a staging area for US troops in Asia.

As recovery progressed, however, the countries of Europe and Japan began to accumulate foreign-exchange reserves, a process which continued after Marshall aid ceased. Some insignificant amounts of dollars were converted into gold in the 1950s. The greatest part was held in deposits in US banks and in US Treasury bills. The country became banker for the world, spending abroad, investing, lending, furnishing assistance in amounts which exceeded the dollars earned through exports of goods and services. Accumulation of dollars by foreign countries began to be regarded as a deficit in the balance of payments of the

United States, and was a matter of concern to President Eisenhower in the closing days of his term of office, and to presidents Kennedy and Johnson from 1960 to 1968. Gradually the country's economic preoccupations shifted from the rest of the world to the international position of the United States.

VI

Immediately after the war, the French economist François Perroux wrote of the United States as a dominant economy; i.e. its every action affected the rest of the world, but it was not in turn called upon to react to events outside.[10] A recent English observer, seeking to make an elusive distinction between "hegemony" and "leadership," characterized the role of the United States in international economic affairs in the 1950s and up to the middle of the 1960s as "hegemonic."[11] The decline in dominance was visible about 1960.

One view holds with hindsight that the shift from pre-eminent concern in foreign economic policy for the public international good began with the permanent exception sought by the United States in 1955 to the rule against quantitative restrictions in GATT for its agricultural products.[12] US support for freer trade in agricultural products is highly selective: it favors freer trade in export products such as grain, oilseeds and meal, citrus fruit, poultry and tobacco; and opposes it in dairy products, meat, rice, sugar, cotton and wool, which are on its import list.[13] Farm groups have long had power in legislatures well beyond their economic significance, as a result of Engel's law and cultural or perhaps political lag. Engel's law – that food consumption as a proportion of expenditure declines as income rises – means that farm groups are in continuous decline in the proportion of national income produced, of persons employed, and in votes. Political lag – until the Supreme Court one-man, one-vote decision in 1962 required state legislatures to be reapportioned on a regular basis – meant that the states retained control of the decennial reapportionment process and that farmers dominated it. This fact and the seniority system kept them in effective control of key legislation far out of proportion to their numbers or economic importance. Where farm groups led the way in insisting on domestic special interests over the interest of the economic system on a world basis, other groups – trade unions, industries, shipping, large corporations and the like – did not tarry in asserting their own interests. The executive branch often fought a rearguard action, yielding slowly in watering down the successive trade legislation, for example, with escape clauses, peril point provisions, the application of export quotas abroad, anti-dumping provisions, and exceptions to freer imports in the interest of national defense.

The primary unraveling of the American dominance, hegemony or leadership in the world economic system, however, came in the monetary field, and had its roots in technical and political difficulties. The technical difficulties were those of understanding. The Bretton Woods system had strongly opposed flexible exchange rates on the basis of the 1930s experience of competitive depreciation. It permitted or encouraged control of international capital movements in the defense of a fixed exchange rate. At the end of the 1950s, members of the economics profession – prominent among them Yale Professor Robert Triffin – began to fear that the world money supply would prove inadequate. Gold production furnished only about $1.5 billion of additional reserves annually to the world, and much of this – ultimately all of it – went into private hands for industrial use and hoarding. Liquidity was furnished to the world by the US balance-of-payments deficit, measured by the increase in dollar reserves by countries abroad. When the United States succeeded in correcting this deficit there would be insufficient liquidity to finance world production and trade. Observers like Jacques Rueff of France and Roy Harrod of Britain wanted to raise the price of gold; Robert Triffin recommended issuance of a new international money. Meanwhile, the United States sought unsuccessfully to correct its balance-of-payments "deficit" by halting capital exports through taxes on security issues, controls over bank lending, and restrictions on taking capital abroad by firms investing overseas – all to no or little avail. And countries like the United States and Germany conducted their monetary policies independently, without recognition that their money markets had been joined through the joining of each with the Eurocurrency market which had grown up outside the United States.

In retrospect it is clear that there were a number of errors of economic analysis in these views. First, it proved impossible to halt capital movements in most societies. Money is fungible and flows through many channels. To cut off one or two channels at a time will only increase the pressure on others and maintain the flow which, so long as there are enough conduits open, is impervious to the closing off of any one. Other temporizing devices worked out by the ingenious Under Secretary of the Treasury, Robert V. Roosa, such as issuing special bonds which guaranteed the buyer against exchange risk, or negotiating special offsets by Germany against American expenditure for the maintenance of its forces in Europe, were of little help, based as they were on the reasoning that the deficit in the US balance of payments was a passing disturbance. Second, most of the deficit was a function of the fact that the United States was acting as banker to the world. Liquidity needs determined the deficit, rather than the deficit accidentally filling liquidity needs. This became less true in the final years of the Vietnam War after about 1968, and especially in 1970 and 1971, when the merchandise trade balance in the United States balance of payments turned adverse on an annual basis for the first time since 1894. The meaning of surplus and deficit in the balance of payments is different for a bank and for a bank customer. The United States was acting as a bank. The rest of the world represented customers. Third, when money markets are joined, as European markets were with those of the United States and Canada, monetary policies cannot be independently determined. In 1966 and 1969–70, US attempts to tighten interest rates pulled a flood of money from Europe. The system ultimately collapsed in 1971 when the United States tried to achieve cheap money while Germany was seeking to raise interest rates. Dollars poured abroad and drowned the Bretton Woods system.

The Bretton Woods misconception about the possibilities of control of capital movements had another consequence. The IMF had been designed to fund cyclical – not persistent – balance-of-payments deficits on current accounts, not to handle capital flows. The amounts available were too small, even before postwar inflation, and provision of assistance was stretched out over time. The IMF was no help in a crisis on this score, and also because its decision-making procedures were time-consuming. A few steps were taken to modify IMF procedures to correct these disabilities. With convertibility in 1958, however, it proved necessary to provide a special fund for countries under speculative attack, called the General Arrangements to Borrow (GAB), organized by leading financial countries (the Group of Ten). A run on the pound sterling in March 1961 occurred while this machinery was being completed, and was met by an informal emergency loan to Britain on the part of a number of countries. This so-called Basel Agreement, led by the United States, was regularized in arrangements to swap claims on foreign central banks for foreign claims on domestic central banks, which were activated in subsequent foreign-exchange crises in Canada in 1962, Italy in 1963, and Britain again in 1964 and 1967. As the largest supporter of the agreement, the United States found it of little help when the crisis affected the dollar.

In 1965, under President Johnson and Secretary of the Treasury Henry H. Fowler, the United States decided that it would be useful to adopt Triffin's suggestion of a new international reserve asset, but to do so in addition to gold and dollars, not as a substitute for them. The reason was that gold was going into hoarding and was not available for adding to world liquidity. The world had accumulated $25 billion or so of dollars and was wary of taking more. To increase world liquidity at some appropriate rate, therefore, it was believed necessary to add a third asset. Subconsciously, perhaps, the American authorities were more interested in restoring the US ratio of reserve assets to foreign liabilities than they were in global liquidity. They failed to recognize that special drawing rights for the United States meant SDRs for all.

An asymmetric or hierarchical system in which the United States acted as banker for the world; the ultimate provider, along with military security, of a market for distress goods; a source of goods in short supply, and of capital requirements; a monitor of the system of international money including the pattern of exchange rates; and a lender of last resort in crisis – such a system may be possible to contemplate in economic terms. By the 1970s it was no longer on the cards politically. Attacks on the system came from many sources: from within the United States, where some industries, and most labor unions, joined farmers in asserting the primacy of their parochial interests over the international interest of the system; from radicals who insisted that US professed action in the international interest was in fact a selfish imperialist one; from a stronger Europe, led by France and followed somewhat reluctantly by West Germany, Britain and Italy, claiming an enlarged share of decision-making; and from the developing countries. It was largely the domestic interests in the United States that led Secretary of the Treasury John Connally in August 1971 to insist on devaluation of the dollar, to break the pressure on import-competing industries, and which led President Nixon in August 1973 to embargo the foreign sales of soybeans, thus administering a second shock to Japanese economic interests and sensibilities. The French voice in international economic matters was larger than their economic specific gravity for a number of reasons: because they mobilized the European Economic Community (EEC) in support on occasion; because they were willing to exit – converting dollars to gold ostentatiously in 1965, withdrawing from NATO, refusing to vote in the EEC until they got their way over agricultural prices.

The developing countries had organized themselves as the Nonaligned Nations at Bandung in 1955 and as the Group of 77 in the United Nations Conference on Trade and Development (UNCTAD) in 1964, and began gradually offering an alternative view of how the international economic system should be managed. In the United Nations, making effective use of a large majority because of the numbers of newly independent states, the developing countries gradually fashioned a position which differed from the free-market one professed by the United States in a long list of economic functions, from trade to commodity prices, assistance for balances of payments, foreign aid, the multinational corporation, and the issuance of international liquidity. They denounced the conception of a liberal system as neo-colonialist, continuing economic subjection after political independence had been granted, and opposed it with a list of demands packaged as the New International Economic Order. The success of the Organization of Petroleum Exporting Countries (OPEC) in converting a political embargo into a drastic price rise in oil in December 1973 in the wake of the Yom Kippur War raised expectations of the developing countries in their demand for a share of SDRs, and their demand for generalized preferences for manufactured exports of developing countries in industrialized nations. Secretary of State Henry Kissinger initially reacted to this importunism by ignoring it. Gradually, however, he began to take a hand, seeking a way to find an accommodation with the developing countries. At the Seventh Special Session of the General Assembly in September 1975, he went along with a proposal for a Committee of Twenty, to meet at Paris, with four committees, to prepare detailed plans. And during 1976 a genuine bargaining process seems to have been under way, in Paris, at the Jamaica meeting on monetary matters, at the UNCTAD Conference in Nairobi in May, as well as in the related area of the Law of the Sea Conference, where a deadlock between developed and developing countries persists on the issue of how to exploit and distribute the proceeds of the mineral resources of the ocean seabeds.

VII

Public goods are those the consumption of which by any one person or consuming unit does not diminish the amount available for the consumption of others. Short of some level of congestion, roads and parks furnish an example. Other types of public good are law and order, clean streets, economic stability.

Public goods are difficult to get produced on a voluntary basis because it is in no one person's interest to undertake the expenditure of time, effort or money to do so. And, if they are going to be produced, the individual can enjoy them without payment, as a free rider. Hence, public goods are notoriously underproduced. They must be furnished by government, and even then sectional or group interests may politick against their production on the ground that *their* costs exceed *their* benefits.

In the international economy, there is no government to produce public goods. Certain international agencies are endowed with powers to discharge certain functions. For the most part, however, international public goods are underproduced unless some countries take on a leadership role, cajoling, persuading, arm-twisting other countries to take their appropriate shares of the cost. There can be stalemate: at the 1927 World Economic Conference under the auspices of the League of Nations, all countries, including the United States which attended as an observer, agreed to lower tariffs, but no country took action. All waited for a lead which was not forthcoming. At the World Economic Conference of 1933, no country was willing to abandon its national plans for recovery for the possibly illusory hope of a joint recovery effort.

Without leadership, international public goods are underproduced. With leadership there is the opposite danger that some country starts out believing that it is acting in the public or general interest and slips knowingly or unwittingly into serving its own ends exclusively.

The international economic system flourished, more or less, from 1870 to 1913 when Britain served as world economic leader. The public goods that it provided were a market for surplus or distress goods, a countercyclical source of capital, management of the gold standard that maintained a coherent set of exchange rates and coordinated macroeconomic policies, and the lender of last resort in crises. After 1913 Britain was unable to discharge these functions, and the United States was unwilling to. The great depression is largely ascribable to this gap.

Beginning about 1936 and with assurance during and immediately following World War II, the United States undertook to provide the public goods needed for world economic stability. Instead of the gold standard as cover, it had the United Nations and its specialized agencies. From the early 1960s, however, and increasingly from 1965 as the Vietnam War deepened, the United States became less willing to act as a leader and the world became less ready to accept it in that role. Some of the UN agencies can go on without strong national initiatives, notably the IBRD. Most cannot. France is prepared to assert a claim to leadership, with the help of its EEC partners. It receives limited support. One or two voices have been raised in favor of a duumvirate or a triumvirate of the United States and Germany, or the United States, Germany and Japan. Quite apart from grave doubt as to whether the interests of such a pair or trio of countries could be harmonized sufficiently, there are questions first whether either Germany or Japan would be willing – up to now they prefer "loyalty" to "voice" – and whether the rest of the world would accede in such an arrangement. On all three counts, the prospects appear slim.

The New International Economic Order, calling for developed countries to accede to developing countries' demands on the ground of historical equity, seems to this observer utopian. Equally so is the possibility of negotiating on a long-run basis a giant "package deal" covering aid, preferences in trade, rights and duties of multinational corporations, international commodity stabilization, the "link" for the issuance of SDRs and the like. When principles are rejected, *ad hoc* arrangements may take their place but are unlikely to have much staying power. The universal historical record of failure in commodity agreements originates in the fact that while buyers and sellers may be content at any one time, at a later date when the agreement comes up for renewal, the price in the open market has changed and one or the other is dissatisfied. Complex package deals appeal to the diplomats, and the historical record contains a number – like the Congress of Vienna – that have demonstrated survival value. Most have not, nor have such deals in the economic field.

What, then, is ahead? Since 1971, despite inability to agree on the international economic system, the world has managed to avoid the beggar-thy-neighbor policies to competitive tariffs and competitive exchange depreciation which gave us the 1930s. Instability has been avoided though stability has not been assured. The nationalistic response to the oil embargo of November 1973 – Operation Independence and end-runs to Tehran to assure national supplies of Iranian oil – has subsided without doing particular damage. But the world is far from agreement on a system, accepting it as legitimate, and responding to the cajoling or armtwisting of a leader-enforcer. Moreover, the United States is the only candidate for the role visible on the horizon, and whether she would be willing or acceptable – absent the charisma of a Roosevelt or a Kennedy – is very much in qestion.

What might such a system consist of? To a conventional liberal economist, the answer is relatively straightforward. It should be a market system on the whole, but with market solutions modified when they become intolerable, i.e. when goods are very scarce or so abundant as to threaten livelihoods. This does not mean commodity agreements so much as some provision for stocking grain against a repetition of 1974, some industrial materials stockpiling, but primarily international action to maintain world income in depression. Tariffs or quotas would be acceptable only on a disappearing basis, to moderate but not to forestall adjustment. A multilateral agency would be established on the multinational corporation, not to handle compensation for nationalization problems, on which no meeting of minds is likely, but to cope with questions of antitrust, trading with the enemy (whether the policies of one country in this area may intrude into another through foreign subsidiaries of domestic corporations), double taxation, tax evasion, corruption and the like. The OECD is the obvious locus of such an agency today, but it should be open to other countries, as they perceive it in their interest. The OECD should also be the setting for coordination of macroeconomic policies, once discussed by Working Party No. 3, but lately fallen into desuetude. The DAC should continue to preside over aid, though the function needs a greater stimulus than the example-setting efforts of Sweden, Norway and Canada seem to provide.

The most sensitive area is that of money. At the moment, fixed exchange rates have been rejected in favor of flexible exchange rates, but sentiment seems to favor such management of flexibility as approaches fixity. A return to the dollar standard, a return to the gold standard, or the development of a full-blown SDR standard each seems unlikely. The Eurocurrency and the Eurobond markets are private organizations, escaping national and international restraint. Darwinian evolution seems inescapable in this field, and is perhaps superior to Bretton Woods planning. It is possible, and even probable, that *ad hoc* international management of the Eurodollar and Eurocapital markets through combined open-market operations, led perhaps by the Bank of International Settlements, will provide the stability needed. In any event, the evolution is toward the internationalization of monetary policy. Monetary autonomy, like national military security, is a will-o'-the-wisp in an interdependent world.

In all these matters, it is useful to think of normal management of the system, and crisis management. Those in trouble will think the system always in crisis. This view must be resisted. Yet the rules applicable to market forces, discrimination, exchange control, foreign aid and the like which hold in normal times may have to be set aside in a true crisis. This poses a dilemma. Readiness of the system to cope with crises reduces discipline in normal times and increases the frequency of trouble. The knife-edge must be negotiated.

The United States must be prepared to contribute to the public good of management of the international economic system in the long run, and to respond to crises, applying different rules and standards to each, striving not to let the one corrupt the other. That is difficult enough. She must at the same time associate the other nations of the world in this task in ways that are not subject to entropy and decay. It is a tall order.

Notes

1. Mancur Olson, *The Logic of Collective Action*: *Public Goods and the Theory of Groups*, Cambridge: Harvard University Press, 1965.
2. See Albert O. Hirschman, *Exit*, *Voice and Loyalty*; *Responses to Decline*

in Firms, Organizations and States, Cambridge, Mass.: Harvard University Press, 1970.

3. Frank W. Taussig, *Tariff History of the United States*, 8th edn, New York: G.P. Putnam's Sons, 1931, p. 15.
4. See Carlos F. Diaz Alejandro, "Direct Foreign Investment in Latin America," in *The International Corporation*, ed. C.P. Kindleberger, Cambridge, Mass.: MIT Press, 1970, p. 321.
5. Paul P. Abrahams, "The Foreign Expansion of American Finance and its Relation to the Foreign Economic Policies of the United States, 1907–1921," Ph.D. dissertation, University of Wisconsin, 1967, p. 84. A somewhat premature expression of financial aggression is contained in a statement of the *New York Herald* in an 1857 issue:

   > Each panic has resulted in making the city of New York the centre of finance and trade for this continent. In 1837 it stood on a sort of struggling emulation with Philadelphia and Boston . . . The rivalry between New York and other cities has ceased. The late struggle of 1857 was in great degree between New York and London, and has terminated in the advantage of the former city. And the time must not ere long arrive, when New York, not London, will become the financial centre, not only of the New World, but also to a great extent, of the Old World.

   See D. Morier Evans, *The History of the Commercial Crisis, 1857–58 and the Stock Exchange Panic of 1859* (1859), reprinted New York: Kelley, 1969, pp. 113–14.
6. Stephen V.O. Clarke, *Central Bank Cooperation, 1924–31*, New York: Federal Reserve Bank of New York, 1967, pp. 60–7.
7. Milton Friedman and Anna Jacobson Schwartz, *A Monetary History of the United States, 1867–1960*, Princeton, NJ: Princeton University Press, 1969, pp. 298–9.
8. C.P. Kindleberger, *The World in Depression, 1929–39*, Berkeley: University of California Press, 1973, pp. 136–8.
9. See Joseph S. Davis, *The World between the Wars, 1919–1939: an Economist's View*, Baltimore, Md: Johns Hopkins University Press, 1975, p. 421: "Personalities counted heavily and clashes of strong personalities were recurrent sources of intranational and international friction. There were never enough harmonizers (such as Morrow, Salter, D'Abernon, Stamp. Monnet and Stresemann) to help divergent minds meet."
10. François Perroux, "Esquisse d'une theorie de l'économie dominante," *Economie Appliquée*, nos. 2–3, 1948.
11. Andrew Shonfield, "Introduction: Past Trends and New Factors," in *International Economic Relations of the Western World, 1959–71*, vol. 1, *Politics and Trade*, ed. Andrew Shonfield, London: Oxford University Press, 1976, p. 33.
12. T.K. Warley, "Western Trade in Agricultural Products," in Shonfield, op. cit., pp. 345–7.
13. Ibid., p. 322.

9

The aging economy

I am enormously honored by the Institut für Weltwirtschaft which I persist in thinking of as the Institut für Seeverkehr and Weltwirtschaft, a name that had to be changed, I suspect, when aviation became general. I first learned of the Institute when I read some of the inordinately long Enquêteausschuss, produced in the 1920s by, among others, Gerhard Colm, the first winner of the Bernhard Harms Prize, and a man much loved and honored in the United States. I later had the good fortune to spend four months in 1971 in Kiel, living at the Haus Welt-Club, and using the Institute's magnificent library to read German economic history. Those were golden months, and I feel very much at home.

The Harms Prize is given in international economics, which makes me feel a bit of an impostor as for years I have been beating a retreat out of international economics as such, and into economic history, or, as I prefer to call it, historical economics. It is sometimes possible to combine international economics and economic history, as I hope to demonstrate. But the aging professor, like the aging economy, may have lost an old comparative advantage in a field now full of innovations such as distortions, effective rates of protection, growth theory, macro-economic policies under flexible exchange rates, econometric testing and the like, and find a need to transform along the production-possibilities curve to find a new good (or rather service) that he is capable of exporting in competitive markets.

---

*Lecture given by the author when he was awarded the Bernhard Harms Prize at the Institut für Weltwirtschaft, Kiel, July 5, 1978, and published in *Weltwirtschaftliches Archiv*, vol. 114, no. 3 (1978).

My choice of a topic for this occasion was only partly stimulated by these narcissistic reflections on the passage of time. I have for some years been interested in economic maturity, as contrasted with the economic adolescence associated with development economics. At the Institut für Weltwirtschaft in 1971, studying Germany's rise to economic maturity, I chose to contrast it with the British "Climacteric," or falling back. In a paper in a popular periodical, I compared the position of the United States today with that of Britain in 1890 or 1900, although this has been called "Spenglerian nonsense." But most of all, I suspect, I was moved at the time of Professor Giersch's invitation, by the advice of Lord Kaldor, contained in an interview in *Le Figaro* (February 18–19, 1978) under the headline "Only Protection Can Save England." Kaldor argued that there should be tariffs for aging economies, comparable to the infant-industry tariff for young countries. The ordinary response of the international-trade economist is to transform along the production-possibilities curve, i.e. to adjust, perhaps with adjustment assistance. If you can no longer do international economics in the fast company of dynamic growing economists, find something else worthwhile to do, by which I mean something with a positive price, even economic history. Kaldor suggests instead that the country ought to keep on doing what it is doing, in the old way, cutting off the competition of the market by tariff or other barriers.

Observe first that this advice applies best to import-competing activities and means cutting down on access to new and cheaper goods and services from abroad. We shall address somewhat later the question of demonstration effect that may arise in this connection. But protection does not help with export activities unless the country can find one or more other countries to join with it in a bloc that discriminates against the outside world. Such a suggestion has been made, that the developed countries trade mainly among themselves, retaining the production of textiles, shoes, electronic apparatus, shipbuilding, automobiles and the like, while the developing countries compete with each other, but not with the developed world, in products that they have normally purchased in Europe, North America and Japan. I return to this suggestion below. Note now, however, the difficulties that were faced by Britain in trying to forge an Empire or Commonwealth preference scheme to assure outlets for its exports. As Drummond's brilliant study shows, the customers of the aging economy were not prepared to continue to buy its high-priced and dated-quality brand of products when there were cheaper and up-to-date alternatives available, and when the young partners themselves wanted to take over lines of production that their aging partner sought to reserve for herself (Drummond, 1974). The aging professor of international economics may retain with protection

1950 theory and statistical testing for the economics he buys from the outside – thus turning rapidly away from most of the articles in today's leading journals. To whom does he sell if he wants to export? Happily universities have a friendly tolerance for and loyalty to their old staffs, a tolerance and a loyalty that would have undergone change, I suspect, if the mandatory retirement age for tenured staff had been raised in the United States from 65 to 70.

Apart from the difficulty about exporting, Kaldor's advice may apply better to individuals than to entire economies. Individuals, like old dogs, are often incapable of learning new tricks. With a limited time horizon, however, and terminal conditions under which their intellectual capital can safely be consumed in its entirety, they had perhaps in some cases better do what they know how to do, even though the price for it be declining, and repulse the efforts of those who would urge that they maintain productivity by transforming into better-paid lines, peopled by the young with higher productivity. But individuals and dogs are mortal. Aging economies have no choice but to carry on, without contemplation of any terminal stage. A society is not an organism that dies at the end of its reproductive cycle, but rather a branch in the evolutionary tree. Such branches survive only by adaptation, and by giving up the old specialization and returning to a simple undifferentiated form to specialize in new ways.

Perhaps before I get much further I should define a little more precisely what I mean by "aging." There is here a grave danger of circular reasoning, defining aging in terms of certain characteristics, and then deriving the characteristics from the "fact" of aging. I shall ask you to accept the hypothesis that growing economies, like many other structures, proceed along a path described by the Gompertz or S-curve, starting slowly, picking up speed in growth, gradually slowing down, and then levelling off or declining. The process is often repeated, with new Gompertz curves at some stage growing out of the old. I shall not identify the early stages with Rostow's (1960) preconditions, take-off, drive to maturity; you are free to do so if you choose. But at the last stage I definitely part company with Rostow, who postulates a stage of high-level mass consumption of durable goods, that presumably lasts forever as the economy lives happily ever after, whereas I am more interested in the capacity of the economy to respond to changes in economic conditions. It is this that seems to me to slow down with aging.

In the writing of economic history, a fundamental choice is when to use a static, and when a dynamic economic model. The infant-industry model is on the whole dynamic. A tariff increases profits in the industry, expands scale, and through learning-by-doing or economies of scale, the industry shifts its supply curve downward and to the right. Until

Arrow discovered learning-by-doing, something which international-trade economists understood by intuition, theory told us that there could be no declining-cost curve since it was incompatible with perfect competition (Arrow, 1962). In all competitive static models, supply curves slope upward.

The difference between static and dynamic models is illustrated by the contrast, suggested some years ago by Henry Wallich (1960) in his *Monetary Problems of an Export Economy*, between Keynesian and Schumpeterian models. In a Keynesian model, increased demand raises income, decreased demand reduces it. In a Schumpeterian economy, on the other hand, reduced demand stimulates the entrepreneur to innovate and reduce costs. The shift of the demand curve to the left and down often kicks off a displacement of the supply curve to the right and down, which may maintain or even increase income (Wallich, 1960). On the basis of these two types of analysis, I concluded some years ago (1961) that increased exports, decreased exports, increased imports (perhaps through lower tariffs), decreased imports (perhaps through higher tariffs) – all or any can either stimulate growth or slow it down. For example, increased exports may stimulate growth through the Keynesian multiplier/accelerator, or reduce it by diverting attention from the necessity of the economy to adapt to new technological conditions, as, in Britain at the end of the nineteenth century, increased exports of iron and steel rails, galvanized iron roofing, cotton textiles, etc. to poorer markets, undermined the evident necessity to face effectively the new industries of electricity and chemicals, or to adopt new processes in old industries, like Gilchrist Thomas in steelmaking. Economic historians using econometric models have had no difficulty in showing that Britain at the turn of the century was not well suited to undertake certain changes (McCloskey 1971). Prices of some needed inputs were too high; in other cases demands were too low. The reasoning implied static models. What remains unanswered is why the historians chose static instead of dynamic models in which disproportions and other adversity lead to innovation and cost reduction. The lowering of the tariff on silk by William Huskisson in the 1820s forced the British industry to improve productivity the better to reduce French imports, and it did so, a fact widely noted by the Saint-Simonists in France who favored tariff reductions, and by Cavour in Italy. Cavour in fact used the dynamic argument that tariff reductions stimulate growth as a basis for his low-tariff policies in Piedmont in the 1840s and 1850s, and for Italy in 1860, with unhappy results in the latter instance. As a British civil servant told a friend of mine asking about the stimulation of industry anticipated from British entry into the Common Market: "Not every kick in the pants galvanizes; some merely hurt."

The foreign-trade aspects of aging permit a return to an old interest of mine, the terms of trade, and venturing the thought that aging economies are like adolescent ones in another respect, their preoccupation with the terms of trade. To equate changes in the terms of trade with changes in welfare, of course, is another instance of partial-equilibrium analysis, taking other things as equal when they may have changed, or perhaps should have changed. In the *Terms of Trade* (1956), I concluded that it was true that developing countries experienced declining terms of trade, but not for the reasons advanced by Prebisch, based on the differential market behavior of primary products and manufactured goods. LDCs were typically unable or unwilling to transform in response to price changes. When prices fell, they were left stranded in unrewarding industries and occupations; when prices rose – at least until the advent of OPEC – easy entry for mature competitors brought them down again. Easy entry and difficult exit constitute a formula for declining terms of trade that may apply to aging economies as well as to those starting up the Gompertz curve. But it is not the terms of trade that count. Most economies in the full vigor of health have no idea what their terms of trade are. Preoccupation with the terms of trade is a form of economic hypochondria, like the frequent taking of one's temperature. To the healthy economy, price changes are a signal to adjust; to the economy that finds adjustment difficult, they appear to be changes in welfare, or the balance of payments, or both (Kindleberger, 1956).

The question of static and dynamic models has a macro- as well as a micro-economic component. All economists agree that micro- and macro-economic questions should be separated as far as possible, and that tariffs, for example, should be used to improve the balance of payments only with the greatest reluctance, as a second- or more nearly fifth- or sixth-best policy, since tariffs are a micro-economic tool, and the balance of payments a macro-economic target. None the less, I remain impressed by how rapidly young growing countries respond to tariff reductions in overcoming transitional balance-of-payments deficits, and how slowly do aging countries. From history take the response of Britain to the repeal of the Corn Laws in 1846 or of France to the reduction in tariffs under the Anglo-French (Cobden–Chevalier) treaty of 1860. The latter, to be sure, was a reciprocal agreement, so that exports were stimulated along with imports. As a young country in the 1840s, however, Britain scorned the necessity to have tariff reductions reciprocal. Economic theory taught that the balance of payments embodied an adjustment mechanism; an increase in imports would lead to an increase in exports. And so it proved. The balance of payments righted itself very quickly. There were, to be sure, many factors at work; discoveries of gold in California and Australia, the boom in foreign lending to India, rapid growth after 1848 on the Continent. If you need a purer case, closer to our time, recall that Germany in 1956 sought to correct its strong balance-of-payments surplus with a unilateral reduction in tariffs. The current-account surplus barely took notice. You may regard this as a proof of low elasticities, or, like me, as part proof of the absorption theory of balance-of-payments adjustment, while dismissing the income effect of the tariff change which would tend to lower income and savings. It follows, in either case, that raising tariffs – unless to prohibitive levels – is not likely to improve the balance of payments much in an aging economy, nor are reductions likely to worsen them in a young and dynamic one.

This brings me to the savings question, which is a complex one with many dimensions. First, it makes an enormous difference to savings whether an old or aging country, or individual, is poor or rich. I start with individuals. Most people have to reduce their consumption as they get old, and at the same time run balance-of-payments deficits, i.e. consume their capital, because productivity falls off more than consumption, and they lack a substantial flow of income from investments. Luckily in most cases the appetite for consumption declines to some extent as well. For those without much in the way of savings, or lacking transfers from the state, consumption may have to fall a great deal. Not so the rich; they may run balance-of-payments deficits and draw on wealth, unless they have their hearts set on leaving a big estate, but in a very few cases, income from property is so substantial that while savings decline they remain positive to the end.

In countries, as in individuals – though generalization is fraught with danger – it makes a considerable difference whether a country has accumulated substantial claims on other countries through foreign investment, and has not dissipated them, for example by drawing them down to fight a war, and how substantial its demonstration effect is.

Rapid growth in leading countries is often associated with the acquisition of foreign claims, although interest in international finance may itself be an early sign of aging, like the first lock of gray hair. Venice, Genoa, Antwerp, Amsterdam, London and New York were first mercantile and then financial centers. The transition from trade to finance, first at home and then abroad, was usually made smoothly, and finance flourished as commerce began to wilt under intense competition from younger economies. Amsterdam in the latter half of the eighteenth century, Britain in the second half or perhaps the last third of the nineteenth century, and the United States thus far in the last third of the twentieth century were in various degrees slipping in industry and trade, but going strong in international banking. It is worth noting that in the last quarter of the nineteenth century Germany had ambitions in international finance, and sought to rival Britain in this field, as well as in commerce. But the domestic boom was so intense that from time to time it proved desirable to sell off foreign investments – Argentine bonds to Britain, and Russian bonds to France, for example – to stoke the fires of investment at home. Dynamic early middle age, that is, does not accumulate foreign claims but builds capital at home; successful late middle age makes the transition from home to foreign investment.

It is hard to say what would happen if a country aged with its foreign capital intact since Amsterdam and Britain, at least, spent large portions of their foreign wealth in the Napoleonic and two world wars, respectively. Even without war, however, there is likely to be serious capital consumption from the aging process because of demonstration effect. I suggested that the passion of individuals for consumption may cool with age. The generalization is dangerous, since the propensity to consume may shift upward in at least two items of consumption: tourism and medical expense, as opposed to such items as household goods and other durables, especially books, where the problem becomes one of decumulation rather than the accumulation of youth. For countries, however, the demonstration effect that Nurkse detected in developing countries that seek to consume and invest in excess of income may play a role. A few with long memories may remember the economic writings of Lord (then Sir Geoffrey) Crowther in dollar shortage. His explanation ran in terms of goods produced by the United States that the rest of the world had to have "no matter what they cost." Crowther pioneered in the sort of comparison between individuals and economies that I am indulging in today, even reciting Shakespeare's seven stages of man from the infant "mewling, and puking in the Nurse's arms," to the old man "sans teeth, sans eyes, sans taste, sans every thing." He surely exaggerated the price inelasticity of British import demand for trucks, airplanes, earth-moving equipment, computers and the like, but the point is a relevant one (Crowther, 1957). The fact that a country loses its capacity to innovate and to transform smoothly and effectively from one industry in which it is losing comparative advantage to another does not mean that it will not want to continue to share in the consumption of the new goods of the world. Or the point may be put in terms of the Duesenberry effect. Loss of capacity in countries to produce effectively does not necessarily go hand in hand with loss of appetite for continued high consumption. The best illustration of this generalization, I suspect, and one which is fateful in many respects, is the unwillingness, or inability, of the United States to adopt an effective program of conserving energy.

Let us return to the saving functions. Aging seems to me to be critical to the question of personal savings at the national level, although again the discussion runs the risk of circular reasoning. The fact that saving out of disposal income is close to 25 percent in Japan, 15 percent in Germany, 7 percent in the United States and 5 percent in Britain is doubtless a function of such institutions as the thirteenth monthly paycheck and the rudimentary state of social security in Japan, flourishing instalment credit in Britain and the United States, as opposed to Germany and Japan, and the like, but the institutions themselves reflect the fact that Germany and Japan are future-oriented, interested in accumulation, social advancement, building for later generations, whereas in the United States and Britain there is more attention to the present. In an interesting paper on modern Germany, Karl Hardach (1977) has tried to dispell the "myth" of German interest in hard work and saving, pointing to the strong propensity for tourism. But the travel is paid for in advance, out of savings, whereas in the United States and Britain, vacations are more likely to be requited with credit cards. In the steady state, with no growth, it makes no difference whether one pays now or later, since equal numbers are saving and dissaving equal amounts. With continuous growth in income and consumption, however, the use of credit to finance consumption leads to continuously mounting consumer credit, and dissaving net, whereas saving in advance of consumption piles up savings.

I should perhaps insert a paragraph here on the aging of population, and the ratios of working to total population in young, middle-aged and aging countries, but I lack the requisite demographic capacity. I suspect that in very young and very old countries, the ratio is low for different reasons – because of large numbers of children under 15 years of age in young countries, and large numbers over 64 in the old. Between the two, in countries that have finished their Malthusian revolution, but have not yet accumulated a thick layer of gray-haireds over 64, the ratio is at its highest, with important effects on productivity, creativity, savings, etc. But I am incompetent to do more than to pose the issue.

As always in discussing economic history, I am reminded of my friend Alexander Gerschenkron, with his debatable and debated theory of backwardness. You will remember his generalization that the more backward a country is as it starts the process of economic development, the more it relies on banks and government instead of leaving the direction of economic activity to the private market and its entrepreneurs. Other aspects of the theory are that backward countries are more likely to start with heavy instead of light industry, with large firms instead of small (Gerschenkron, 1962).

One need not here settle the validity of these views on backward developing countries. The question is how they apply to aging ones. I have a hard time in discerning a particular role for banks. For young countries banks may be, in the Saint-Simonist phrase, a stimulus and a regulator, a motor and a brake, with the emphasis on the first of the two effects in each instance (Vergeot, 1918). In growing economies of early middle age, banks may shift to a more regulatory role, although the statement runs the risk of implicit theorizing. For aging and old economies, it is hard to find a useful generalization about banks.

More can be said about government, however. I am partial to a vacuum-filling theory of government. I refer not simply to public goods, such as lighthouses, roads, parks, etc., where the consumption of each individual, short of a level of congestion, leaves the consumption of others unaffected, nor to natural monopolies like public utilities where the choice between government regulation and government ownership and operation is often a close one. Even in what are normally thought of as private goods, with competition possible, government may enter because the private market is not discharging the function well. The failure of the market may produce private diseconomies – uneducated, sick and slumdwellers – which public action is designed to eliminate. Wagner's law that the role of government increases with time may apply to all countries. The portion of national income passing through government hands is substantial in Germany and Japan. But one cannot help but be struck how more and more functions are being turned over to government in Britain and the United States because of dissatisfaction with the performance of the market. The forms taken are more nearly nationalization in Britain, regulation in the United States. It may be that Germany and Japan started along the Wagner path at higher levels of government intervention than did Britain and the United States, partly because of backwardness, and are therefore now, at different stages of aging, at roughly the same government-to-private-activity ratio. In any event, I suspect that aging economies find the private market less and less able to discharge particular functions effectively and call on government to take them over. The evidence is incomplete, but one is well advised to be sceptical, whether government can successfully fill the vacuum in housing, health care, education, steel, coal, shipbuilding, etc.

It is perhaps injudicious of me to disclose that Gerschenkron has been working on time preference in relation to backwardness, with the hypothesis that the more backward the country, the more it thinks of the present, and the less willing it is to take heed for the morrow. Again in my opinion, age resembles extreme youth, with the addition that it is interested in the past (as well as the present) more than the future. Vigorous middle age is, as indicated earlier, future-oriented, which supports the propensity to save, lowers the rate of interest, spurs investment, stimulates growth. There may be cultural dimensions to living in the past, such as preoccupation with history, literature, the performing arts and the like. I doubt that there is an economic equivalent to such dimensions, overall, but surely the focus is relevant for technical change and for income distribution. Aging economies are dominated by *positions acquises*, a French expression not well rendered in English as "vested interests." It means the Duesenberry effect in consumption, maintaining expenditure at the expense of saving when income falters. It is especially relevant to a decline in risk-taking, clinging to old techniques even when new and more economical are available, resistance to rationalization, a propensity for featherbedding, maintaining old wage differentials that have become technologically obsolete. A problem in Western Europe and the United States is whether it will be possible to change the wage structure so as to attract sufficient numbers of workers to the menial and dirty jobs of street-cleaning, rubbish disposal, hospital orderlies, dishwashing in hotels and the like, without letting loose more inflation as traditionally-skilled workers agitate to maintain differentials. The world of the future is surely going to have to alter the wage structure. In aging economies, the attempt is likely to be inflationary.

But I have gone on perhaps too long with diagnosis. If I reject the Kaldor remedy of bundling up the aging economy in blankets and rolling it in its wheelchair into the sunshine, what do I have in mind for therapy and prognosis, particularly if it should turn out that there is no fountain of youth to be found by an economic Ponce de León?

The world economy is facing a serious crisis. In the last few years I have been studying financial crises, and there are some financial aspects to the present position. I refer today, however, to the more intractable problems of structural adjustment, the need to adapt to the diffusion of world technology not only in textiles, shoes, synthetic fibers, electronic components, but also in steel, shipbuilding, oil refining, petrochemicals, precision instruments, and a host of other industries. In 1954, Sir Donald MacDougall made the startling statement that automobiles would be the textiles of tomorrow (MacDougall, 1954). He was perhaps a little ahead of his time, but he was surely right, as we see Brazil making Volkswagens, and even sending parts to Germany, Ford bodies being stamped out in South Korea, and countries everywhere gearing up to reproduce the successful Japanese drive into the world automobile market. Labor-intensive manufacturing is going abroad. Where technological change is still advancing in developed countries, it runs along capital-intensive lines. As such it may bring certain processes back from developing to developed countries but without providing much in the way of employment. At the OECD Meeting on Technology in Paris in 1977, Christopher Freeman put the point dramatically that the advanced countries now face the necessity to slim down their manufacturing sectors in terms of employment, as they once slimmed down the agricultural.

I mentioned earlier the proposal by André Grjebine (1978) for a division of world trade primarily into that within two blocs, the developed countries on the one hand, and the developing on the other. Some few products would be traded between the blocs – oil and a few metals from the developing countries, plus coffee, tea and cocoa, against wheat, cotton, wool and advanced manufactures like computers and aircraft from the developed. For the most part, however, the developing world would produce its own high-cost manufactures, and the developed world retain its high-cost labor-intensive sectors. This is customs union, with trade diversion instead of trade creation, on a global scale, and I find the picture appalling. It is fair to say that Grjebine recommends the policy as an improvement on what he anticipates will be the probable course of events: high national protection. Protection by blocs in his judgment preserves more competition and lower costs than seems to him otherwise likely. The problems posed by this solution are too many to explore: where to put intermediate countries, the necessity to redistribute resources within rather than between blocs, the choice of what commodities to trade between blocs and how, the intensification of the possibility of global economic warfare. Grjebine has surely made a contribution in illuminating the problem. I hope his solution will appeal to few.

The alternative to Kaldor's protection for the single country and Grjebine's new order based on two world customs unions is evidently adaptation, what Carl Major Wright (1939) called *Economic Adaptation to a Changing World Market*. Where individuals cannot adapt, their contracts can be bought up, and they can be pensioned off early. There are no pension schemes available to national economies, so this choice is not open. Moreover, adjustment assistance below the level of the nation, while the subject of some talk, thus far has failed to demonstrate successful action.

The process of reducing sectors is difficult in democracies because the old large sectors relinquish political power more slowly than they are forced by the market to give up economic rewards. Engel's law and economic growth produce the result that agriculture is overrepresented in legislative assemblies. Obsolete retailing (and manufacturing) industries can muster political support as the Robinson–Patman Act in behalf of retail-price maintenance, the similar movement in Germany, Poujadism in France, etc., amply testify. Railroad unions in the United States spent substantial amounts of money to demonstrate that the presence of the extra "fireman" in the locomotive, retained long after there was a fire to be tended, increases the chances of avoiding accident by some small but finite amount, but without mentioning featherbedding, and without a reasonable calculation of cost and benefit.

Adaptation is difficult, and it is possible that some fashions are not worth adapting to. It is discouraging for people of my generation to be told in stores when we ask for a certain item: "We haven't stocked that for 20 years." A stopped clock is right twice a day. If some of us refuse to adapt to the latest fashion and maintain the same styles with respect to haircuts and face-hair that were *à la mode* in the 1930s, we shall be back in style before too long. It is not self-evident that following the fashions in dress and comportment is vital to happiness in all cases.

Some may think I am making too heavy weather of the aging problem and that it can be handled by some simple rule, in the case of the aging economy, such as a fixed money supply, or one growing at a constant rate, or clean floating of the exchange rate, or leaving resource allocation entirely to the market, or turning it over entirely to indicative planners. I do not deny that optimal monetary, exchange, competitive, and even interventionist policies will help, but contend that the achievement of optimal policies becomes more difficult with aging. It is tempting to suggest that the adaptability of the economy that is a function of age is more important that the content of policies within a wide margin of variation, but I stop short of that. It is important to recognize that the success of policies is a function of things other than age.

In discussing economic development, my colleague Everett Hagen (1962) has focused on "the will to achieve." It is presumably stronger in the younger person than in the aging or old. But it is affected in other ways as well. McClelland (1961), from whom Hagen has derived some of his inspiration, relates the need for achievement (or N-achievement) in the individual to the family situation from which he or she springs. A man with a strong mother and a weak father tends to have a stronger N-achievement than one with parents in the converse situation. For nations much may depend upon the degree of social cohesion or purpose, in turn affected by victory or defeat in war. Denmark responded to the fall of the price of wheat in the 1880s, I have asserted (1978), in a dynamic way – rather than the static liquidation of the agricultural sector that took place in Britain – switching from exports to imports of grain as an input in new industries of dairy products and meat production, partly as a result of its defeat by Germany in 1864, and of loss of territory, falling back on a more densely settled country. The experience of Germany and Japan with their economic miracles after World War II is not wholly dissimilar. Victory in both world wars made Britain, and to a lesser degree France, feel that they had earned a higher standard of living, and compounded, I would think, the problems of simple aging. I suspect that defeat is a solvent that melts old ideas and old resistances, whereas victory strengthens the pressure groups and vested interests that make adaptation difficult.

The consolidation of individuals into groups that fight to protect their interests has gone far in democracies and threatens stability, as is widely recognized, but also threatens adaptability. It is often necessary for groups to take what Walker has called "extra-market action" to protect themselves against exploitation, but such action can quickly turn into exploitation of others. It would be idle to multiply examples, but John Lindsay's retreat before the vested interests of New York may serve. When all groups demand 110 percent of the national income, and government is unable to resist them, 10 percent inflation is inevitable. The shift of responsibility from the individual to the group has a strong tendency to run wild through logrolling and the fallacy of composition, with the action of each to protect itself assuring the hurt of all. But to ask individual groups to sacrifice their possible class advantage in the interest of the total is interpreted as yielding to the interests of other groups, and becomes a counsel of perfection. Leading with one's chin is a game-theoretic recipe for disaster.

Some years ago there was an intense debate in Britain over the disadvantages of the headstart. Those who thought the headstart entailed disadvantages argued interrelatedness of capital structures, which meant that to change equipment at one stage of a process you had to change all (Frankel, 1955), or the failure of markets always to articulate linked investments in different states of a vertically integrated process where the stages were owned by different capitalists and the division of costs and benefits was uncertain, as in joint costs, joint products and the like (Kindleberger, 1964, ch. 7). Much more could have been said of the burden of an economy's historical memory, which inhibits it on occasion from sensible action: the burden of the German memory of inflation of 1923, still flourishing today, or of the British unemployment after the 1925 return of sterling to par. John Jewkes insisted that if an existing obsolete capital structure was in the way it could be torn down. Bygones are bygones. Sunk costs are to be forgotten. For him there was no disadvantages in the headstart. New starts could be undertaken at any time (Jewkes, 1946).

This gets to the heart of the matter. I doubt that the past is so easily discarded, and especially not the collective memories that inhibit, or the groups with *positions acquises* that fight to resist loss of income and especially of status. The physical past is not so important, as Europe discovered after the destruction of World War II. But how to wipe out collective memories and how, especially, to devise means to move from class responsibility to the responsibility of the individual? Defeat in war seems to have done it in the past, if my hunch is correct, but the price is an impossible one.

One may well say that the problem is one for political science, but politicians more and more address their promises to pressure groups rather than to the good sense of the individual; or for sociology, although that science seems better at description than at shaping society and can tell us mostly, for example, that we have moved in selecting individuals for economic roles from status to achievement and back to status again. Or perhaps we could derive inspiration from evangelical religion and contemplate how entire societies can be "born again," and return to a state of innocence in which the individual was responsible for his behavior and his achievement. At the moment we seem to be in the unhappy position where progress is made by class action, rather than individual effort and it is permissible to think that all developing nations become rich, all blacks and women equal to white men, all students learned, by a stroke of the pen, rather than by unremitting effort. I hear myself sounding querulous and shrill the way my father sounded in the days of the New Deal. These may be the maunderings of galloping senility, but I think we need a fountain of youth to dissolve the social arteriosclerotic structures in the body politic. William James sought a "Moral Equivalent of War" the better to focus society on single objectives. Perhaps we need rather to find a "Sociological Equivalent of Defeat."

References

Arrow, Kenneth J. (1962), "The Economic Implications of Learning by Doing," *Review of Economic Studies*, vol. 29, pp. 155–73.

Crowther, Sir Geoffrey (1957), *Balances and Imbalances of Payments*, The George H. Leatherbee Lectures, Boston.

Drummond, Ian M. (1974), *Imperial Economic Policy, 1917–1939. Studies in Expansion and Protection*, London.

Frankel, Marvin (1955), "Obsolescence and Technological Change in a Maturing Economy," *American Economic Review*, vol. 45, pp. 296–319.

Gerschenkron, Alexander (1962), *Economic Backwardness in Historical Perspective. A Book of Essays*, Cambridge, Mass.

Grjebine, André (1978), "Vers une autonomie concertée des régions du monde," *Revue d'Economie Politique*, vol. 88, pp. 250–68.

Hagen, Everett E. (1962), *On the Theory of Social Change: How Economic Growth Begins*. The Dorsey Series in Anthropology and Sociology, Homewood, Ill.

Hardach, Karl (1977), "Germany, 1914–1970," in Carlo M. Cipolla ed., *Contemporary Economies*. The Fontana Economic History of Europe, vol. 6, Hassocks, New York, part I.

Jewkes, John (1946), "Is British Industry Inefficient?", *The Manchester School*

of Economic and Social Studies, vol. 14, pp. 1–16.
Kindleberger, Charles P. (1956), with the Assistance of Herman G. van der Tak and Jaroslav Vanek, *The Terms of Trade: A European Case Study*, Technology Press Books in the Social Sciences, New York, London.
Kindleberger, Charles P. (1961), "Foreign Trade and Economic Growth, Lessons from Britain and France, 1850 to 1913," *Economic History Review*, vol. 14, pp. 289–305.
Kindleberger, Charles P. (1964), *Economic Growth in France and Britain, 1851–1950*, Cambridge, Mass.
Kindleberger, Charles P. (1978), "Group Behavior and International Trade," in Kindleberger, *Economic Response*, *Comparative Studies in Trade*, *Finance*, *and Growth*, Cambridge, Mass.; first published in 1951.
MacDougall, Donald (1954), "A Lecture on the Dollar Problem," *Economica* (new series) vol. 21, pp. 185–200.
McClelland, David C. (1961), *The Achieving Society*, Princeton, NJ.
McCloskey, Donald N., ed. (1971), *Essays on a Mature Economy*: *Britain after 1840*, Papers and Proceedings of the Mathematical Social Science Board Conference on the New Economic History of Britain, 1840–1930, held at Harvard University, 1–3 September 1970 London.
Rostow, W.W. (1960), *The Stages of Economic Growth*, Cambridge.
Vergeot, J.B. (1918), *Le Crédit comme stimulant et régulateur de l'industrie. La conception saint-simonienne, ses réalisations, son application au problème bancaire d'après-guerre*, Paris.
Wallich, Henry C. (1960), *Monetary Problems of an Export Economy*, *The Cuban Experience*, *1914–1947*, Harvard Economic Studies, vol. 88, Cambridge, Mass.
Wright, Carl Major (1939), *Economic Adaptation to a Changing World Market*, Copenhagen.

10

America in decline? Possible parallels and consequences

In a recent magazine article, George P. Shultz (1989, p. 26), the retiring Secretary of State, a good economist and an experienced government official, wrote: "In this environment, anyone who claims America is in decline had better see a doctor." As the issue appeared, the *New York Times* wrote a series of three outsized editorials on successive days, asserting that "U.S. Prosperity is Eroding" (January 8, 1989, p. E23), that Japan is outstripping the United States in innovation and productivity, (January 9, 1989, p. A16), and that the country faces enormous tasks to compete, save and stimulate output (January 10, 1989, p. A22). The debate is a salient one, and the issues have been raised by many past and current observers. Rather than visit my doctor, however, I thought it might be of interest to explore the record of decline in other nations over the last half millennium, including especially Venice, Spain, Holland and Britain. This is economic history which may or may not afford us insights into our present condition. I am encouraged to address the question in this manner by a passage in an article by Peter G. Peterson (1987):

> To find the proper historical parallel for the United States in the 1980s, we should not look to Japan in the 1950s . . . The lumbering deficit-hobbled, low-growth economies that come most easily to mind are Spain's in the late sixteenth century, France's in the 1780s and Britain's in the 1920s.

I have no interest in nitpicking but think that the French Revolution was the consequence of bursting energy rather than economic arterio-

*A lecture given at Georgetown University on April 6, 1989 on the occasion of the receipt of the Georgetown Bicentennial Medal. Unpublished.

sclerosis. Moreover, when the British economy began to age is a subject of some dispute – perhaps as early as the 1870s, or the 1890s, or in the Edwardian period rather than the 1920s. The Spanish analogy is telling, however, and so is the Dutch, whose Golden Age petered out toward the end of the seventeenth century.

Reasons for economic decline vary widely among observers, from the broad analogy to the specific. A review of Oswald Spengler's *Decline of the West* observes:

> Everything that is alive shows an organic rhythm, moving through stages of birth, growth, maturity, decline and eventual death. If this happens to all men without exception, there is surely no inherent improbability supposing that the same organic rhythm extends to larger human units of life. (Frye, 1974, p. 2).

Frye goes on to discuss Spengler's hypothesis that applies to cultures rather than nations in terms of spring, summer, autumn and winter. Parenthetically, I am moved to remark that when I once discussed economic decline some years ago, a fellow economist attacked me for "Spenglerian nonsense."

Less broadly, Paul Kennedy (1987), the Yale historian, has lately attributed Spain's decline to excessive military expenditure, and a strong case can be made that war gives rise to large deficits and high taxes without producing earning assets. An earlier study not addressed to the United States even implicitly, is *The Economic Decline of Empires*, edited by Carlo Cipolla, a distinguished economic historian, that emphasized consumption:

> Improvements in standards of living brought about by a rising economy lead to more and more people demanding to share the benefits. Incomes increase and extravagances develop as new needs begin to replace those that have been satisfied . . . Public consumption in mature empires has a tendency to rise sharply and outstrip production . . . In general empires seem to resist change. (1970, back jacket)

Still other explanations run in terms of a shift from trade and industry to finance, as entrepreneurs become rentiers (Burke, 1974, pp. 101–12); gridlock among "distributional coalitions" or organized interests, each working for its own agenda, and particularly seeking to evade a share of the economic burdens of the time, and thus leading to deficits, inflation and stagnation (Olson, 1982); and a loss of economic adaptability to new conditions – the resistance to change noted by Cipolla – whereas growth requires innovation, new institutions, and resource reallocation.

First let me stipulate that the word "decline" may be poorly chosen. In case after case, the analyst notes that the economy continues to grow but is outpaced. The decline is relative, not absolute. In the twentieth century Britain has continued to grow in income per capita, despite the impression of decline, as its income has been surpassed by Scandinavia, Switzerland, the Federal Republic of Germany, by France, and, most recently, Italy. Some relative decline of leaders is inevitable when new and burgeoning economies come along.

Second, before getting down to cases, permit me an apparent digression that I deem essential. There is very little in most discussions of what a country can and cannot afford. As wartime expenditure shows, a country can "afford" to spend half its national income on shot and shell that produce no income and no direct utility, provided that it has the resolve to do so. Senator Robert Taft argued against the Marshall Plan legislation on the ground that the United States could not afford it. What he meant was that there were other expenditures he valued higher. If others willed the ends of the Marshall Plan, he opposed willing the means. To be sure, it may take great effort in mobilizing an economy, for example, for France in 1871 and 1872 to pay the indemnity to Prussia after its defeat, or the reparations that Finland paid to the Soviet Union between 1944 and 1952, an amount far higher as a percentage of national income than Germany found itself unable to pay after World War I. The Finns were resolved to wipe the slate clean; the Germans were not. Various German groups especially – labor, farmers, industry, civil servants, pensioners – were each resolved to resist payment. Military expenditure represents the demand side; accepting heavy taxation and reduction in consumption is the supply. Both must be taken into account. When Louis XIV on his deathbed said "Too many palaces, too many wars," he should have added "relative to my capacity to squeeze resources out of the country."

As a third preliminary, I assert that the importance of the issue transcends questions of the good life for Americans in this generation and whether our descendents will be able to live as well as we do. It transcends even the vital question whether we successfully tackle the obdurate problems of poverty, ignorance, homelessness, substance abuse and the like. I refer to world economic stability. In a book on the 1929 depression I suggested (1986) that it was so wide, so deep and so long because the United Kingdom had reached the point in decline where it no longer could act as the stabilizer of the world economy in crisis, and France and the United States were unwilling to do so. Involved was a sort of domino or tenpin model, that if the Austrian economy had been propped up in May 1931 when the Creditanstalt failed, the collapse that spread successively to Germany, Britain, Japan, the United States and ultimately the gold bloc might have been prevented. Admittedly, the depression was fairly far advanced by May 1931, and there are highly intelligent observers who say that something more fundamental was required than a lender of last resort in financial crisis – something more of the order of the Marshall Plan. That world stability requires a stabilizer seems as an idea to have appealed more to political scientists than to my fellow economists. Political science puts it in terms of hegemony and the need for a hegemon, whereas I had used the term "leadership." In the absence of a hegemon, some political scientists maintain that stability in the world economy, or peace in the polity, can be managed by a "regime" – principles, norms, rules and decision-making procedures, perhaps developed in a period of hegemony, but extended into a pluralistic world. Such institutions as the International Monetary Fund, the World Bank, the General Agreement on Tariffs and Trade may or may not function effectively in the absence or the resignation of a hegemon. Whether peace and stability depended on a *Pax Romana*, *Pax Belgica* (Schama, 1988, p. 236, discussing the world paramountcy of the United Provinces of the Netherlands), *Pax Britannica* or *Pax Americana* is an open question. It is, moreover, a crucial question today when and if the United States' will or capacity to furnish the leadership in world peace and economic stability is going into relapse.

Shifts in world leadership take place, as I shall show, and the transitions from one to another may be fraught with danger, as the 1930s amply demonstrate. I share the view of Ortega y Gasset (1930, pp. 147, 149, 156), regarding the loss of "command," as he put it, of Europe:

> The European commandments have lost their force, though there is no sign of any other on the horizon. Europe – we are told – is ceasing to rule, and no one sees who is going to take her place . . . It would not matter if Europe ceased to command, provided there was someone to take her place. But there is not the faintest sign of one. New York and Moscow represent nothing new . . . one does not know what they really are . . . Europe's loss of command would not worry me if there were in existence another group of countries capable of taking its place in power and in the direction of the planet.

I shall come back to Ortega y Gasset's view that Europe as a single nation, rising above "provincial England, Germany and France" that he saw in decay, would be able to fill the role.

Let me start with the Italian city-states, and especially Venice. The usual view accounting for its decline is the Age of Discovery under the Portuguese, Henry the Navigator. He, with the help of the rudder in place of the steering oar and the fore-and-aft sail – the two leading to larger ships that could sail closer to the wind – enabled first the Portuguese and then the East India Company of England and the United East India Company (VOC) of Holland to sail around the Cape of

Good Hope and get pepper, other spices and silk for sale in Europe more effectively and cheaply than the caravan trade and Venetian ships calling at Aleppo and Alexandria. This view has been challenged by an economic historian who claims that Venice and other Italian cities lost their economic eminence because of the forceful competition from English traders, who passed off their low-quality products as those of Venetian make – shoddy woolens often wrapped with a fine piece on the outside of the bale, or soap made with tallow stamped with the bas-relief of the Doge to make it look like fine Venetian soap of olive oil (Rapp, 1976; 1976). This sort of competition, it should be noted, has continued through the centuries, as the Germans stamped their Remscheid cutlery "Made in Sheffield," and the Japanese at one stage were said to have christened a town of Usa to be able to mark goods "Made in USA."

Venice maintained a large fleet of galleys to protect its shipping lanes to the Levant. Its naval victory at Lepanto in 1570 finished off the last threat from the Ottoman Empire. But the caravan trade dwindled slowly, lasting more than a century after the competition around the horn of Africa. Venetian decline, according to Cipolla, was rather the result of a loss of entrepreneurial energy, as rich merchants moved to large estates on *terra firma* and elevated agriculture to pride of place over industry and trade. Competition of northern European woolens and linens gradually wiped out Italian production of woolen cloth. The high cost of Italian cloth was the result of guild control, an awkward tax system, and high labor costs (Cipolla, 1970, pp. 203–10; 1974, p. 9). Italian exports suffered. Devaluations of the Genoese, Milanese and Venetian lire between 1620 and 1700 by amounts ranging from 15 to 30 percent helped in the short run but did little in the long to correct the decay in investment and productivity. Genoa suffered especially in the financial crisis of 1596 in Spain, to be discussed presently. With no hinterland for agricultural or industrial production, it was more specialized in trade than the other Italian city-states. Like them it made the transition from trade to finance, and when Philip II repudiated his obligations, the Genoese bankers were hurt.

Spain had the disability of getting too rich, too fast, with the discoveries first of America by the Genoese sailor, Columbus, and then of the silver mountain, Potosí, in Peru (modern Bolivia). Silver brought inflation and ruin. In 1650 one Saavedra Fajardo wrote:

> the possession and abundance of such wealth altered everything. Agriculture laid down the plough, clothed herself in silk and softened her work-calloused hands. Trade put on a noble air, and exchanging the work-bench for the saddle, went out to parade up and down the streets. The arts disdained mechanical tools . . . As men promised more from their incomes than in reality they had, ostentation and royal pomp grew, pensions, pay and other

forms of crown payment rose on the basis of foreign wealth, which was too badly administered and kept to meet so much expense, and this gave rise to debt. (Vilar, 1976, pp. 167–8)

Spain went into debt to finance its wars. It fought in the Mediterranean: in the Atlantic, where the Spanish Armada was defeated by Sir Francis Drake, the British navy and the weather; against France from time to time; but especially in the Netherlands, where Spanish kings fought to defend the Catholic faith and the territory of the Holy Roman Empire. The costs were heavy, especially as Spanish troops were few and most of the fighting was undertaken by mercenaries – primarily Germans and Italians – who mutinied if they were not paid, and sacked any handy town. Silver arriving in Seville and Cadiz had for the most part already been pledged to German and Genoese bankers – the Fuggers, Welsers, Spinolas, Bonvisi and the like – who had advanced funds in Flanders, or to Portuguese merchants who could produce money in Antwerp with pepper brought from Malacca. When fighting flared up and more troops were needed, or when the silver *flota* from Hispaniola was delayed by storms, or harried by British or Dutch privateers, the Spanish kings were unable to pay off their debts with reals, defaulted on their promises of silver and the proceeds of designated taxes, and issued *juros*, bonds payable only in Spain and of doubtful value. Such crises occurred at frequent intervals in the Eighty Years War – in 1576, 1596, 1607, 1627 and 1653. Spain brought from the New World to Europe something of the order of 43 tons of gold and 17,000 tons of silver, but ended up with a currency largely of *billon*, a compound mainly of copper (Parker, 1974, p. 528). There was a considerable amount of silver around. According to one source, the Duke of Alva, a Spanish captain-general in Flanders and a member of the Court in Madrid, died with 600 dozen silver plates and 800 silver platters (Braudel, 1981, p. 563).

About 1600 it was appropriate to call Spain a leading power only because of its precious metals and military efforts. Civilian production was limited. Along the French border net imports were substantial as Spanish prices and wages were far higher than French. Dutch, English, French and Portuguese ships brought to Seville and Cadiz the vast amounts of goods needed in the colonies, mostly drawn from northern Europe, as well as the grain needed to feed Spain herself, and the timber and naval stores required for shipbuilding. Foreign merchants and bankers dominated the Spanish in Seville and Cadiz. Within Spain, merchants dominated producers of goods, and financiers dominated merchants.

There were many contributing factors to Spain's decline – expulsion of the Moriscos who did the menial work in the cities, depopulation of the countryside, demands on the peasants of the Crown, the landlords, the Church, and the recruiting officer. Mainly, however, it was the continuous war. Parker (1972, p. 125) uses as an epigraph a quotation from one Mr Wylkes in 1567:

> The matter of the greatest difficulty in the . . . maintenance of this action is in the proportioning of the charges of the warres and the number of souldiers to be maynteyned with the contributions and means of the countreys.

Parker (1972, p. 145) then goes on to say about the Spanish attempt to repress the rebellion in the Netherlands:

> On the whole there were few in Spain prepared to admit that the war in the Netherlands could not go on indefinitely and that its cost would prove too great for the treasury. As Mr. Wylkes observed [above], the problem of 'proportioning' the expenses of a war with the resources available was one which challenged and defeated almost every government in the sixteenth century; politics in those days [was] seldom weighed in the 'Scale of a Tradesman.' So the Army in Flanders was under orders to maintain maximum military pressure on the Dutch until all resistance collapsed, whatever the cost . . . The cost of the exercise was ruinous, of course.

"Whatever the cost" conveys echoes of the aristocratic German general staff in World War I with its motto, *Geld spielt keine Rolle* (literally "Money plays no role," or, in more colloquial translation, "Hang the cost"). And the derisory mention of the "scale of a tradesman" evokes the sociologist, Jesse Pitts, on French aristocratic virtues. Aristocrats in this view are concerned primarily with unreproducible acts of virtuosity – in battle, sport, the salon or the boudoir, and live by such mottos as "Never take cover" and "Never count your change."

Spain led in wealth and the Habsburgs had a dominant political position in Europe in the sixteenth and first half of the seventeenth centuries. Apart from silver, however, the Spaniards' economic position was not one of leadership. They were importers, not exporters, borrowers who failed to meet their obligations, not lenders. They had no single challenger and they took on and challenged most of Europe. It would be difficult to say that they were the center of the world economy, with others representing the periphery, to use the metaphor of Braudel and Wallerstein.

The rise of Amsterdam was connected with fighting in Flanders, with a big upsurge when the Sea Beggars of the United Provinces invested the Scheldt and cut Antwerp off from the sea in 1585. Antwerp's loss was Amsterdam's gain not only in trade with the outside world but also with large numbers of merchants, bankers and industrialists among the 150,000 migrants from southern to northern Netherlands. Amsterdam became an entrepôt port, assembling goods from all over the world and sending goods all over the world. Shipbuilding at Zaandam with imported Baltic timber provided a more apposite example of economies of scale from specialization of labor and tools than the pinmaking illustration of Adam Smith's *Wealth of Nations* in 1776. The flyboat was a formidable innovation, small, maneuverable, with a smaller crew than those of English ships, light because of lack of guns, but capable of being escorted in conveys in time of war. The Dutch excelled at herring fisheries, making their catches along the British shore – a contributing cause of the three Anglo-Dutch wars of the seventeenth century. But their major success was trade, based on a quasi-monopoly of knowledge of what goods were available where, and what wanted where. The First Hand carried the goods in what Adam Smith called "distant trade"; the Second Hand sorted, broke bulk, repacked grain from the Baltic headed for the Mediterranean to forestall spontaneous combustion. The VOC, formed in 1601, outcompeted the Portuguese in trade around the Cape of Good Hope and held its own with the imitative East India Company of England. The Dutch responded to the currency disorders of the early seventeenth century by establishing the Bank of Amsterdam. Amsterdam became the leading market for precious metals in Europe, and the hub of the system of payment by bills of exchange throughout Europe.

Evocative of today's leveraged buy-outs, mergers and acquisitions activity, program trading, options, futures and the like, the Amsterdam bourse was the scene of great speculative manias in the seventeenth and early eighteenth centuries (Schama, 1988, p. 350). Trade in futures was called *Windhandel*, or buying and selling wind. Schama's brilliant book on the Dutch Golden Age, *The Embarrassment of Riches*, stresses the tension between Dutch wealth and conspicuous consumption, on the one hand, and piety, on the other. Like the United States two centuries later (Bell, 1988), the Dutch Republic considered itself the "Great Seventeenth Century Exception" (Schama, 1988, p. 244). By the eighteenth century it had reached fiscal exhaustion and experienced a *de facto* resignation as a great power (ibid., p. 598).

Dutch decline had many components. For one, direct trade superseded the entrepôt or relay function of Amsterdam, as knowledge of what was available where and wanted where became widely diffused. Merchants turned from trade to finance to reduce the risks and strains in commodity trade. As early as 1652 it was complained at Amsterdam "that the regents were not merchants, they did not take risks on the seas but derived their income from houses, land and securities, and so allowed the sea to be lost" (quoted in Burke, 1974, p. 104). Burke goes on to say that the shift was from sea to land, from work to play, from thrift to consumption, from entrepreneur to rentier, from bourgeois to aristocrat. Wages rose as the Dutch Republic levied the taxes needed to support its navy on houses (fireplaces and windows) and on imports for home consumption such as wine, spirits, salt and soap, while keeping export and import taxes low to encourage trade turnover (but discourage home industry). There was difficulty in maintaining ships' crews as other countries enticed away this mobile element of the labor force. From 1688 to 1713 the majority of the army was made up of mercenaries; the Dutch navy supplemented its sailors with Scandinavians, Scots and Germans (Schama, 1988, p. 284). The VOC was forced to rely on "uneducated louts from the heart of Germany" (Boxer, 1970, p. 246).

But especially the Dutch seemed to lose their energy and confidence, as the British gained. This was observed as early as 1670. By 1730, the Dutch had clearly peaked and were starting to decline. At the time of the Restoration (1660), the Duke of Albemarle in England said "What we want is more of the trade the Dutch now have" (Williams, 1970, p. 484). English antipathy to the Dutch, fostered by the three Anglo-Dutch wars of 1652–4, 1665–7 and 1672–4, produced such derogatory expressions as Dutch courage (drink), double Dutch (gibberish), Dutch treat (not a treat at all) and Dutch uncle (stern rather than avuncular). The Navigation Acts to take shipping out of Dutch and into British bottoms were passed in 1651 and strengthened in the 1660s.

The Dutch economy did not collapse, said Charles Wilson (1968), the leading English historian of the country and the period. Its golden age merely faded and withered. It was vulnerable to war, but emerged at the end of the eighteenth century wealthy and powerful with slow change eroding its foundations. The mercantile rivalry of Hamburg kept growing, and other nations, especially England, moved forward. Along with economic stagnation, Wilson asserts, historians have detected a stagnation of spirit (Wilson, 1968, p. 230).

The transition from trade to finance occurred in Venice and Amsterdam. Financial centers retain an entrepôt function longer than trade centers because of economies of scale in financial intermediation and because the cost of transporting money in space is exiguous compared with that of transporting goods, costs saved when intermediaries are replaced by direct dealing. Holland declined as a trading center in the early eighteenth century. It continued as a financial center until the occupation by French troops in 1794. But it was weakening relative to London earlier. The financial crises of 1763, at the end of the Seven Years War, and of 1772 a decade later led to losses in bill-brokering to London with the latter's superior organization under the leadership of the Bank of England (Buist, 1974, p. 22). The Fourth Anglo-Dutch War of 1780–4 produced a fateful switch of Dutch lending from England, to which Dutch investors had been lending for almost a century, to France, the foreign loans of which were repudiated a few years later in the French Revolution. The Bank of Amsterdam, which had been fully solvent with 100 percent reserves of specie from 1609 to the late eighteenth century, was persuaded by the government to lend to the VOC to cover its losses in competition and war with the British East India Company, and was bankrupted in the process.

Seventeenth-century Holland is held up as an example, along with Renaissance Italy, of a "failed transition to modern industrial society" (Kranz aud Hohenberg, 1975). Various reasons are given by various writers – high wages of labor because of the tax system (Mokyr, 1976), low tariffs to promote the import and export trades that exposed Dutch industry to intense foreign competition (Wright, 1955), lack of coal and iron deposits (Parker, 1984), the shift from entrepreneurship to rentier status (Burke, 1974, pp. 101ff.). These reasons are, of course, not mutually exclusive, and probably it would be impossible to assign separate weights that would be agreed. Holland finally managed to industrialize after the middle of the nineteenth century, but lost its distinction among the countries of Europe (Schama, 1988, p. 600). When it had commercial and financial leadership, however, it could hardly have been called a country with responsibility for world economic stability, despite the open markets it maintained for gold and silver (money) and for commodities. Nor was it a center with responsibilities beyond its borders. Its wealth went with irresponsibility to such an extent that Amsterdam merchants not only had no compunction about trading with the enemy, but also invested in privateers that preyed on Dutch shipping. The Dutch capitalist, it has been said, could not be characterized as a man without a city, but was, where business was concerned, a man without a country. And that country, moreover, had no interests in the world beyond its own (Barbour, 1966, pp. 130–1).

A rather scholastic debate among economic historians today concerns whether or not there was an industrial *re*volution in Britain, in contrast with industrial *e*volution. The issue is irrelevant to our interest in decline. It may be useful, however, to observe that despite Adam Smith's espousal of free trade (though he defended the Navigation Acts), the industrialization of England was assisted by tariffs and import prohibitions, particularly on printed calico (1700) to assist the printing industry, and then on muslins (1712, 1714, 1720). In the 1740s taxes on exports of manufactured goods were abolished, plus those on imported materials, to assist the infant cotton textile industry (see Chapter 5 of this volume, pp. 111–12). Once the industry was established, its home, Manchester, fought for free trade in wheat imports, to lower the price of food and wages and to discourage the shift of labor on the Continent out of agriculture into industry. For a long time, however, Manchester sought to prohibit the export of textile machinery and the emigration of skilled workers, so as to inhibit the development of textiles on the Continent that might erode its industrial lead. The period is sometimes referred to as free-trade imperialism to underline the fact that the repeal of the Corn Laws, the Navigation Acts and the timber duties by Great Britain in the middle of the nineteenth century was undertaken in the British, not the world, interest. At the end of the century, Empire preference was sought by groups led by Joseph Chamberlain of Birmingham to protect export markets in the Empire. So strong was the free-trade tradition, however, that protection was adopted only for a few defense industries in World War I. Geriatric tariffs were enacted at the depth of the depression, along with depreciation of sterling.

British attempts to prevent the loss of its technological monopoly proved futile. Machinery was smuggled abroad after the Napoleonic wars, sometimes in picnic hampers. The prohibitions on skilled workers emigrating backfired because the legislation made it awkward for workers who could easily get to the Continent to return if and when they became disaffected (Musson, 1972). Open and covert visits to British plants from the Continent in the interest of industrial espionage were continuous. In due course the British leads in cotton textiles, iron and steel and shipbuilding were threatened by competition, and Germany and the United States broke new ground in electrical machinery, chemicals and automobiles.

In Holland, there was trade without industry. In Britain, industry and trade worked in tandem through the first half or three-quarters of the nineteenth century before yielding supremacy to finance. A borrower in the eighteenth century, Britain used its efficient financial machinery, based on the City of London, to lend abroad, partly during the Napoleonic wars when loans and subsidies were difficult to disentangle, but especially after 1815. The unexpected success of the Baring indemnity loan to France to recycle Napoleonic reparations led to a wave of foreign lending that collapsed in 1825. There were subsequent spurts in the 1840s, 1850s, 1860s, the late 1880s, and especially from 1896 to 1913. In the last year of the lending boom, 1913, Britain lent abroad half its savings and 5 percent of its national income.

The leading institutions of British world leadership were the Bank of England and the British navy. They are occasionally linked. A recent observer produced the parallels of sterling and the British navy, on the one hand, and the American dollar and the atom bomb, on the other (Hogan, 1987, p. 213). In early September 1931, a disturbance in the British navy at its base in Invergordon over food was regarded on the Continent as mutiny, and contributed to the run on sterling as the other great British institution.

The Bank of England played a world role as it managed sterling, which was a world currency. The price of gold had been set at £3 17s. 10½d. an ounce in 1717 by Isaac Newton, then Master of the Mint, remaining at this level, with interruptions for the Napoleonic wars and World War I, for 200 years. There had been financial crises. The Bank of England learned in these how to protect the London money and capital markets by acting as a lender of last resort. It also learned to manage sterling by manipulation of the discount rate. On occasion, official banks on the Continent had to come to the rescue of the Bank of England itself. For the most part, however, the Bank of England went it alone and came to the assistance of others, such as the Bank of France. There is some dispute as to when London pulled ahead of Paris as the world's main financial market, but this was clearly the case after France gave up convertibility of the franc into gold during the Franco-Prussian War of 1870–1. In general, the Bank of England can be said to have provided the public good of an international money from 1821, when gold convertibility of sterling was resumed after the Congress of Vienna, to 1914. Britain tried to resume its leadership role by an ill-advised resumption of gold convertibility at the old price in 1925. The effort was conclusively demonstrated to have failed in 1931 when Britain proved unable to help in the currency troubles of central Europe, and finally had to abandon convertibility in September of that year.

The British navy and especially the merchant marine were the king-pin of an attempt by a distinguished economist, Ralph C. Hawtrey, to analyze international power politics. Let me quote a summary from my review of the second edition (Kindleberger, 1954, p. 508):

> The major concern of the state is prestige. The means to prestige is power. Power is economic productivity capable of being applied as force, and is represented primarily by output of movable goods and capacity to move them (British accent on marine transport). Centers of power come into inevitable conflict. These conflicts are mitigated by distance and the balance of power. But any balance of power is inherently unstable. Changes in relative power occur and are dangerous.

This is old-fashioned power politics, and fails to take into account the possibility, and even the likelihood, that a dominant power may not be able or willing over time to make the effort to maintain its economic productivity and its capacity to move its output.

The decline of Britain can be dated as early as 1870, and was already being discussed in the 1890s, when one E.E. Williams wrote a polemic entitled *Made in Germany* (2nd edn, 1896). Williams observed that goods of German origin and mark had been gimcrack and shoddy, but had evolved to such an extent that they had become of high quality. (The parallel with Japanese goods sold in the United States needs no underlining.) British industry was being abandoned by the rising generations, including the sons of successful entrepreneurs, in favor of the City of London, the professions, and especially country living, which might include service as a Justice of the Peace or member of Parliament. Investment turned abroad because of the absence of riskless outlets at home, the railroads having been completed and the national budget being balanced. Private companies went public and the funds received sought trustee investment outlets. There was persistent talk of the need for technical education, but little was done about it.

British foreign investment could have produced a substantial income, since there were few investment disasters such as that of the French investors who bought tsarist Russian bonds in large amounts after 1887, but much of it was consumed in World War I. Wartime casualties produced another loss of a vital productive asset – young males. The British attempt to resume its world economic and political leadership after World War I was a failure partly of mistaken policies, such as resumption of gold convertibility of the pound at par, but also, in my judgment, because of a dessication of entrepreneurial *élan* – what Keynes has called "animal spirits." An enormous literature on the subject includes the view that Britain was doing the best it could, given its resources – a view close to *ne tirez pas le pianiste*. The analysis rests on static reasoning, whereas economic growth is surely a dynamic process.

Ortega y Gasset (1930) generalizes the depressed state of England at the end of the 1920s to all of Europe, and ascribes it to the "suffocation" of the narrow boundaries of the separate countries that would be overcome by the creation of a United States of Europe. Two generations later this view, clearly wrong in 1930, has a new lease on life. It would appear, however, that the difficulties of achieving a unified European economy with no internal barriers, harmonized regulations of all sorts, a central bank, unified currency, and common policies, pose such a challenge to the countries of Europe that there will be, at least for an extended period, little energy available for stabilizing the world economy.

The great depression of the 1930s, as I have attempted to demonstrate, came about partly because of economic and financial imbalances – the restoration of European production without an adjustment in the extra-European output that had partly replaced it in wartime, together with inconsistent national policies on reparations and war debts, exchange rates and foreign lending, plus the New York stock-market boom and the halt of lending on bonds in 1928. It was extended and deepened, however, by the inability of the erstwhile world economic leader to act as an international lender of last resort, and the unwillingness of the United States and – with less ostensible obligation – France, to occupy the role. Gradually in the 1930s, and especially during and after World War II, the United States learned the lesson that a vacuum of power gives rise to economic and military disorder. First with the Reciprocal Trade Agreement Act of 1934, more surely with the Tripartite Monetary Agreement of 1936, the United States took the lead in ordering the world economy. Lend-Lease, the UN Relief and Rehabilitation Administration, Bretton Woods, the British loan, the Marshall Plan and economic assistance for development were undertaken by the United States, either alone or with others on US initiative, and can fairly be said to have helped to produce 40 years of the absence of world war. The country responded to aggression in Korea with success after setback, and less effectively in Vietnam. Since about 1970, however, the world economic position of the country has been slipping.

The slippage has been relative to a great extent, rather than absolute, because of the spectacular growth of Japan and the Federal Republic of Germany. Elimination of vested interests in these countries, dissolved during dictatorship and by defeat, made possible the adoption of effective measures for economic growth without the veto of adversely affected interests (Olson, 1982). The United States has suffered setbacks – in a loss of pre-eminence in the production of automobiles, electronics and in such an industry as steel which used to have the protection of substantial transoceanic shipping costs. Like the Boer War in Britain, the Vietnam War produced something like a loss of confidence, of belief in America's manifest destiny. Production and trade lost prestige relative to finance – at least until October 19, 1987 – and conspicuous consumption of so-called "Yuppies" – young, upwardly-mobile professionals from prestigious law and business schools – abounded. The rate of savings out of household income declined, sliding from 10 or 12 percent down to 3 or 4, primarily accounted for by institutionalized saving out of pension and life-insurance accumulations. Buying and selling companies took precedence over buying and selling goods. A misguided economic doctrine that lower tax rates would both increase revenue and lead to higher savings rates was a demonstrable failure. The resultant deficit in the US government budget led to a deficit in the balance of payments that dollar depreciation after February 1985 failed to correct, a deficit that drew imports of capital from Japan, Taiwan and West Germany and reduced the United States from the position of the world's greatest creditor to the world's greatest debtor. It is satisfactory to borrow to acquire productive assets, or even to pay for public goods such as health, education, housing and the maintenance of the national infrastructure, but less so when the moneys are used for consumption or to build military equipment, some of it of doubtful fighting quality. In the troubles of law firms, financial houses and advertising agencies, it is possible to detect a decline of team spirit as the more successful members of a firm or partnership demand a change in the agreed-upon division of income, failing which they will dissolve the association and strike out for themselves.

Notable in this situation is that as the United States becomes weaker economically and in its resolve to provide the public goods of peacekeeping and economic stability that the world requires, there is no other country in the wings, ambitious to take over the power, prestige and responsibilities of world leadership or hegemony. The dollar survives as a vehicle currency because the authorities of no strong currency are prepared to play the role. Japan lends to the United States because it is unwilling to reduce its saving habits, on the one hand, or to lend directly to other debtors, on the other. Germany and Japan have been loyal followers during the period of confident US leadership. Recoiling from the aggressive efforts of the 1930s, they hold back from challenging US proposals. Neither has been ready to take a prominent role in stabilizing political conditions in the Middle East, though both have high stakes in the continued availability of oil from the region. The world seems to be embarking on a transition of power and prestige from the United States to some other country, but it is far from clear which that other country might be. As Hawtrey commented in 1929, "changes in relative power occur and are dangerous."

Two alternative courses are regularly proposed, trilateralism and a regional solution. The suggestion of trilateralism among the United States, Japan and usually the Federal Republic of Germany, or sometimes, as Ortega y Gasset (1930) contemplated, the united wider European community, strongly resembles the attempt of Britain after World War II to cling to the appurtenances of its earlier leading position. As Hogan's (1987) book on Anglo-American diplomacy over the Marshall Plan makes clear, the British sought in 1947 and 1948 to preserve the special relationship with the United States, to keep intact the sterling bloc, and to proceed into Europe no further than the point of no return. In particular, Foreign Minister Ernest Bevin wanted Britain to intermediate between the United States and the countries of Europe. By drawing Japan and West Germany (or the EC) into a cartel of world economic leadership, the United States might be able to prolong its position of eminence in the world, only slightly diluted.

As an economist and economic historian rather than a political scientist, I am probably not entitled to have an opinion on this suggestion, but I am skeptical. Joint ventures in business generally break up sooner or later unless there is a complete takeover, as the interests of the partners almost never converge completely, and any divergence may widen and lead to stalemate. Soviet politicians under Brezhnev, I believe, talked of a *troika* with three leaders, on the analogy of a method of harnessing three horses to a sleigh or wheeled vehicle. In the pictures of such rigs that I have seen, however, I observe that the right-hand horse has his head turned rigidly to the right, the left-hand horse to the left, and only the center horse has any idea where the team is headed.

Proposals for organizing the world economy on a regional basis have been around for decades, but acquired salience from the European Recovery Program with the pressure exerted by the United States for European economic integration, starting with a free-trade area or customs union, moving to a monetary union and perhaps ultimately a United States of Europe. It is sometimes suggested that there should be an organized region in the Western Hemisphere, one for the Far East, perhaps another for the Middle East and Africa, as well as for Europe. The regional commissions of the United Nations and the regional development banks lean in this direction. The idea was put forward most forcefully three decades ago by William Yandell Elliott (1955), who had worked on the Herter Report of Congress on the Marshall Plan.

There is not much to be said in favor of this idea, despite the recent Canadian – US free-trade agreement and its possible ultimate extension to Mexico. Some contiguous countries, or countries in the same region, have economies that are complementary, but many have economies that are strongly competitive, with economic and political ties to countries in other regions. The case of New Zealand may be apposite and support the idea: it was closely associated with Britain, found these ties severed when the United Kingdom joined the EC, and is slowly entering into closer relations with Japan, ties with Australia always having been strong. Against the idea are the cases of the Middle East and sub-Saharan Africa, where close cooperation among all neighboring countries is an obvious non-starter as far ahead as one dare look. But even if the number of "orphaned" countries with stronger ties outside than inside regions were small, and the cases not serious, questions would still remain about interregional relations: is it anticipated that trade, capital movements, exchange rates and the like between regions would shrink to unimportance, and, if not, how would they be regulated? It seems evident that some considerable amount of world economic organization will be required, and that regionalism, for what it may be worth to Europe and possibly elsewhere, is not a universal solvent.

I share, then, the view of Ortega y Gasset that the world economy functions best when some country takes charge. Writing in 1930, he was wrong about the ultimate capacity of the United States to take "command," wrong or at least very premature about the likelihood of European unification, and excessive in his rhetoric about the perils of the lack of a hegemon. Permit me one last quotation:

> The world at the present day is behaving in a way that is the very model of childishness. In school, when someone gives the word that the master has left the room, the mob of youngsters breaks loose, kicks up its heels, and goes wild. Each of them experiences the delights of escaping the pressure imposed by the master's presence . . . Once the plan which directed their occupations and tasks is suspended, the youthful mob has no formal occupation of its own, no task with a meaning, a continuity, and a purpose. It follows that it can only do one thing – stand on its head. (p. 145)

This may have fit well at the end of the 1920s with its Mussolini, the emerging Hitler, and the prospective attack of Japan on Manchuria. It is, of course, a caricature of the position today. Germany and Japan have been faithful followers of US leadership for at least four decades since World War II. Doubtless distinction should be made between times of serenity, when the regime established by US hegemony keeps the system under control, and crisis, when leadership or hegemony or command is needed.

The state of the world today is on the whole serene, with confrontation moderating between the Soviet Union and the United States, and between Iraq and Iran, the Soviet Union withdrawn from Afghanistan, Cuban troops withdrawing from Angola, Central America working out its own agenda for Nicaragua. There is still great tension between Israel and Palestine, and some may view the world economy as in crisis – with the problems of Third World debt and the deflation it imposes, the US balance-of-payments deficit, European unemployment, and Japan and Taiwan piling up huge claims in dollars. None is an acute crisis, however, and the world seems to drift along in the mood of "If it ain't broke, don't fix it," rather than of the opposing doctrine of "A stitch in time saves nine."

Yet there may be "A Morning After," "a day of reckoning" (Friedman, 1988), a revulsion against declining US productivity and savings, and rising US borrowing from the rest of the world. Japan and West Germany are becoming more assertive, and West Germany in particular, may become preoccupied with its own interest in *Ostpolitik* as the military threat from the Soviet Union subsides. If acute crisis comes, it is possible that the United States can produce a heroic effort and reassert world leadership. It is also possible that deadlock, indecision, and divergence of effort will prevail. In that circumstance, it may be necessary to muddle along until a new leader emerges and restores order to the world economy and polity.

Bibliography and references

Barbour, Violet (1966), *Capitalism and Amsterdam in the 17th Century*, Ann Arbor: University of Michigan Press; first published 1950.

Bell, Daniel (1988), "The 'Hegelian Secret': Civil Society and American Exceptionalism", paper presented to Conference on American Exceptionalism, Nuffield College, April 14–16.

Boxer, C.R. (1970), "The Dutch Economic Decline," in C.M. Cipolla, ed., *The Economic Decline of Empires*, London: Methuen, pp. 235–63.

Braudel, Fernand (1981), *The Structures of Everyday Life*, vol. 1 of *Civilization and Capitalism, 15th–18th Century*, New York: Harper & Row.

Buist, Marten G. (1974), *At Spes Non Fracta: Hope & Co., 1700–1815, Merchant Bankers and Diplomats at Work*, The Hague: Martinus Nijhoff.

Burke, Peter (1974), *Venice and Amsterdam: A Study of Seventeenth-Century Elites*, London: Temple Smith.

Cipolla, C.M., ed. (1970), *The Economic Decline of Empires*, London: Methuen.

Cipolla, C.M., ed. (1974), *The Fontana Economic History of Europe: The Sixteenth and Seventeenth Centuries*, vol. 2, Glasgow: Collins/Fontana.

Elliott, William Yandell (1955), *Foreign Economic Policy for the United States*, New York: Holt.

Friedman, Benjamin M. (1988), *The Day of Reckoning*, New York: Norton.

Frye, Northrop (1974), "The Decline of the West by Oswald Spengler," *Daedalus*, vol. 103, no. 1 (Winter), pp. 1–13.

Hawtrey, Ralph C. (1952), *Economic Aspects of Sovereignty*, 2nd edn, London: Longmans, Green.

Hogan, Michael J. (1987), *The Marshall Plan: America, Britain and the Reconstruction of Western Europe, 1947–1952*, Cambridge: Cambridge University Press.

Kennedy, Paul (1987), *The Rise and Fall of Great Powers: Economic Change and Military Conflict from 1500 to 2000*, New York: Random House.

Keohane, Robert O. (1984), *After Hegemony: Cooperation and Discord in the World Political Economy*, Princeton, NJ: Princeton University Press.

Kindleberger, Charles P. (1954), "A Monetary Economist on Power Politics," *World Politics*, vol. 6, no. 4 (July), pp. 507–14.

Kindleberger, Charles P. (1986), *The World in Depression, 1929–1939*, 2nd edn, Berkeley: University of California Press.

Krantz, Frederick and Paul M. Hohenberg, eds. (1975), *Failed Transitions to Modern Industrial Society: Renaissance Italy and Seventeenth-Century Holland*, Montreal: Interuniversity Center for European Studies.

Krasner, Stephen D. (1983), "Structural Causes and Regime Consequences: Regimes as Intervening Variables," in S.D. Krasner, ed., *International Regimes*, Ithaca, NY: Cornell University Press, pp. 1–21.

Mokyr, Joel (1976), *Industrialization in the Low Countries, 1796–1850*, New Haven, Conn.: Yale University Press.

Musson, A.E. (1972), "The Manchester School and Exportation of Machinery," *Business History*, vol. 14, pp. 14–50.

Olson, Mancur (1982), *The Rise and Decline of Nations: Economic Growth, Stagflation and Social Rigidities*, New Haven, Conn.: Yale University Press.

Ortega y Gasset, José (1930), *The Revolt of the Masses*, New York: Norton.

Parker, Geoffrey (1972), *The Army of Flanders and the Spanish Road, 1567–1659: The Logistics of Spanish Victory and Defeat in the Low Countries' War*,

Cambridge: Cambridge University Press.

Parker, Geoffrey (1974), The Emergence of Modern Finance in Europe, 1560–1730," in C.M. Cipolla, ed., *The Fontana Economic History of Europe*: *The Sixteenth and Seventeenth Centuries*, vol. 2, Glasgow: Collins/Fontana, pp. 527–94.

Parker, William N. (1984), *Europe, America and the Wider World*: *Essays on the History of Western Capitalism*, vol. 1, *Europe and the World Economy*, Cambridge: Cambridge University Press.

Peterson, Peter G. (1987), " The Morning After," *The Atlantic* (October).

Rapp, Richard T. (1974), "The Unmaking of Mediterranean Trade Hegemony: International Trade Rivalry and the Commercial Revolution," *Journal of Economic History*, vol. 35, no. 3 (September), pp. 499–525.

Rapp, Richard T. (1976), *Industry and Economic Decline in Seventeenth Century Venice*, Cambridge, Mass.: Harvard University Press.

Schama, Simon (1988), *The Embarrassment of Riches*: *An Interpretation of Dutch Culture in the Golden Age*, Berkeley: University of California Press.

Shultz, George P. (1989) "My Final Word", *The International Economy*, vol. 3, no. 1 (January–February), pp. 26–30.

Vilar, Pierre (1976), *A History of Gold and Money*, *1450–1920*, London: New Left Books.

Williams, E.N. (1970), *The Ancien Regime in Europe*: *Government and Society in the Major States*, *1648–1789*, New York: Harper & Row.

Williams, Ernest E. (1896), *Made in Germany*, 2nd edn, London: Heinemann.

Wilson, Charles (1968), *The Dutch Republic and the Civilization of the Seventeenth Century*, London: Weidenfeld and Nicolson.

Wright, H.R.C. (1955), *Free Trade and Protection in the Netherlands*, *1816–1830*, *A Study of the First Benelux*, Cambridge: Cambridge University Press.

PART 4
Finance

11

Financial deregulation and economic performance
An attempt to relate European financial history to current LDC issues

This paper takes off from Diaz-Alejandro (1985). It takes way off. I am unable to comment on capital markets in developing countries, either on that of South Korea where McKinnon (1973) and Shaw (1973) first developed or expressed their criticism of repressed and shallow financial markets, or on those of Latin America in which Diaz-Alejandro (1985) observed that ending repression led to binges of lending that ended in crash. I have a nodding acquaintance with some of the literature, including Fry (1982) on models of repression, and McKinnon and Mathieson (1981) which blamed the disaster in Argentina on mistakes in correcting repression, pointing to the success in Chile. This was just before, as it happened, Chile itself experienced a disastrous boom and bust. I am impressed by the special issue of *World Development* (Corbo and de Melo, 1985), exploring in considerable depth the experience of Argentina, Chile and Uruguay, but lacking sufficient background am unable to judge the validity of the conclusion of either Vittorio Corbo and Jaime de Melo that the main reason for the eventual failure of the reforms was inconsistencies in policies (p. 864) or that of Michael Bruno that the most important problem for any successful reform is the paths followed in such areas as capital controls, trade controls, financial regulation and fiscal policy (to reduce the inflation tax) (p. 867). The order of reform steps is also judged as critical by McKinnon (1982) and Edwards (1984).

*Reprinted from the *Journal of Economic Development*, vol. 27, nos 1–2 (October 1987), Special Issue on "International Trade, Investment, Macro Policies and History: Essays in Memory of Carlos F. Diaz-Alejandro." The paper benefited from the comments of Rondo Cameron and from the Yale Economics Graduate Club to which it was presented on March 5, 1986.

Lacking sufficient background in financial markets in less developed countries, I choose to approach the problem tangentially, by way of the history of European national capital markets. First, however, I offer to scholars of Latin American and Korean experience the suggestion that what may affect the outcome of deregulation is less the order of various steps than the speed with which they are applied. Bruno makes the point that "the issue of credibility is clearly at the heart of the success or failure of any reform" (Corbo and de Melo, 1985, p. 878). When steps are long foreshadowed and separated by intervals in various fields, markets become stably adjusted to them.

When my *Manias, Panics and Crashes* (1978a) appeared, an Argentine friend wrote privately that the model beautifully explained the Argentine financial crisis of 1974. In that model an autonomous shock to economic markets opens up new investment opportunities, resulting in a reallocation of investment. It can happen that the first investors in this new set of opportunities are followed by others in a euphoric wave as the second tier sees the first reaping substantial profits. The new direction of investment grows. If an attempt is made to contain the boom by restrictive monetary policy, financial innovation that monetizes unutilized forms of credit may overcome the intended restraint. At some stage, with followers close on the heels of leaders, expectations of continued profitability give way, slowly or rapidly, and some of those who have been moving out of money or monetized credit into real or illiquid financial assets begin to move back into cash. Whether there is a financial crash or not depends partly on the extent of the leveraged speculation and partly on the speed of the reversal of expectations.

The displacement or autonomous shock that may lead to a wave of new and excited investment may be either real or financial. Real shocks come from the start of a war, the end of a war, a bumper crop, a short crop, discoveries as in gold or oil fields, development of a new and pervasive technology – e.g. canals and railroads – or the extension of old technology to a new location, a sudden jump in a pervasive price such as that of oil in late 1973. Financial shocks have included the unexpected success of a sizable loan flotation in a new direction – the Baring indemnity loan of 1817, the Thier *rentes* of 1871 and 1872, the Dawes loan of 1924, leading in the three cases to new waves of investment, conversion of interest rates on outstanding debt, forcing the holders of the old to look for new outlets to maintain income level, and hence to take greater risks. Such conversions led to investment booms in England and France in the 1820s, as did the Goschen conversion to England in 1888, foreshadowed much earlier. All three led to or were followed by financial crashes. Laws widening the avenues for incorporation can also lead to investment surges, and even the anticipation of laws that may narrow such avenues. In the 1880s a number of companies went public quickly before an anticipated restriction on converting private companies to public form, and the success of the Guinness public issue in October 1886 was said to act like the crack of the starter's pistol, leading to the issuance of public shares by 86 other breweries (Cottrell, 1980, pp. 169–70).

I am further persuaded that a salient feature of the boom in Third World lending in the 1970s was a sudden lowering of interest rates that took place well before the real shock of the OPEC price hike following the Yom Kippur war of November 1973. The Federal Reserve Board under the chairmanship of Arthur F. Burns undertook to lower interest rates in the United States to help ensure the re-election of Richard Nixon as president of the United States, this at a time when the Bundesbank was maintaining tight money in an effort to control inflation in the Federal Republic of Germany, Inconsistent monetary policies led to a flood of funds from the United States to the intermediating Eurocurrency market where they were borrowed by German business, trying to refund high-cost loans, sold to the Bundesbank and redeposited by the latter in the Eurocurrency market. From a level of $2 billion to $4 billion a year, the "deficit" in the balance of payments of the United States on the liquidity definition rose to $20 billion in 1971 and $30 billion in 1972. The Federal Reserve System overpowered the Bundesbank, world interest rates fell, and Eurocurrency banks set out to find new loan outlets. A bubble in Third World lending took place from what Bacha and Diaz-Alejandro (1982, p. 27) call "the most unregulated market in the world," this well before the first OPEC price rise.

Rather than explore more deeply the possibility that deregulation can of itself provide the autonomous shock that may lead to financial crisis in developing countries, where I lack adequate background, I choose to explore the financial history of some countries in Western Europe to see what light they throw upon the comparative merits of repressed and unrepressed financial markets. The thesis that emerges is that the McKinnon–Shaw contrast between regulated and unregulated markets, with its implication that repression or shallowness come from government intervention and that all *laissez-faire* markets behave in the same way, is too simple. Participants in unregulated markets can behave in different ways, shaped by their history, national character, and by differing horizons that may change discontinuously, and regulated and unregulated markets can behave in the same ways.

Interest in deregulation today is partly theoretical, rooted in the comeback of neo-classical economic theory, and comes partly from the increase in the speed and reduction in the cost of transport and communication that has enabled investors to scan wider horizons, move funds with less government hindrance, and more and more escape the writ of national governments with their fixed jurisdictions. The prime example of recent decades, of course, is the Eurocurrency market. The change from banking within nations to supranational banking did not come about through overt deregulation. While some regulation of foreign banking existed in foreign countries, the force limiting banking to national confines was largely custom and limited horizons. One can perhaps maintain that the reluctance of Britain to supervise dollar deposits of branches of American banks in London was a negative sort of deregulation. I argue, to the contrary, that the *laissez-faire* money and capital markets are not all alike, and that they are shaped by other forces as well as – perhaps more than – government intervention.

Theoretical interest in deregulation is largely based on the belief in the efficiency of free markets. At the limit, it is embodied in the Austrian school of today that would go so far as to shut down central banks, allow anyone or any business to issue money without governmental supervision, and to argue that such a system would approach Pareto-optimality. This extreme belief in *laissez-faire* rests on a denial that money is a public good, even in the unit-of-account or measuring function, on a conviction that transaction costs for establishing what is good money and what is not are low, and on a disbelief in Gresham's law, or perhaps on a belief in the antithesis of Gresham's law, i.e. that good money drives out bad. It can point in support to one historical episode, to a period from 1000 to 1125 AD when private mints in France and Catalonia competed in issuing good money that sellers would accept (Bisson, 1979). In strong sellers' markets, to be sure, sellers can insist on receiving good money for their wares. Gresham's law works in the normal direction, with bad money driving good money into hoarding or export, when buyers can choose what money they spend and what they keep. Roland Vaubel (1977) maintains in his support of completely deregulated currency that different moneys will have different prices that reflect their relative merits and maintain equilibrium among them. To my mind, however, this destroys their moneyness. Money is the one truly liquid asset which means that it is convertible from one form to another without delay and at a fixed price. Just as fluctuating exchange rates are the denial of international money, so changing prices of the demand liabilities of various money users would imply the absence of national money.

Other historical support for the Austrian school is said to be furnished by Scottish banking history from 1775 to 1845 when the banks were brought under the regulation of the Bank Act of 1845. White's (1984) study of those years claims that bank supervision was unnecessary at the time. Two points can be made. First, the study starts a few years after a major bank disaster in Scotland, the failure of the Ayr Bank in 1772, and stops short – by almost three decades – of that of the City of Glasgow Bank in 1878, though the latter can perhaps be blamed on the surveillance of London. Second, the Edinburgh banks supervised each other, and the smaller Scottish banks, by accumulations of the notes issued by other banks that were presented for conversion into specie when it was thought that a particular bank was lending too freely. This is the supervisory technique used by the Second Bank of the United States that so disturbed American populists. It is a spontaneous form of central banking. Nor am I disposed to accept White's view that free banking in the Middle West from 1840 to the National Bank Act of 1863, especially wildcat banking in Michigan, would have been successful and stable had it not been for government interference. Some discipline provided from some source seems to be necessary to restrain the inherent tendency of some issuers of money to go too far. A further illustration of self-selected banks as stabilizers in the absence of a central bank is furnished by Sprague's (1968) account of the money-market banks under the National Bank Act preparing to offset the destabilizing activities of country banks as they lend to New York in boom and withdraw funds in time of trouble.

In an insightful aside, in a comparison of financial markets in Argentina, Australia and Canada, Jones (1982) stated that monetary history falls into four classes: the orthodox, the heroic, the populist and the statist. The orthodox consists of the development of institutions to contain the exuberance of lenders, much as the history of the Bank of England from its founding in 1694 to the Bank Act of 1844 and beyond was directed to restraining the country banks, getting control of the note issue, developing techniques of managing interest rates and using open-market operations (Fetter, 1965). The heroic mode stressed break-throughs, like the establishment of the Société Général de la Belgique in the 1830s or the Crédit Mobilier that Cameron (1961) thought spear-headed the economic development of France and served as a model for developmental banking in Germany, Austria, Italy, Sweden and Spain, where, according to Gerschenkron (1962), banks were necessary to economic development because of the absence of indigenous entre-preneurs. Populist banking history is applicable to the Jackson period in the United States and the veto of the Second Bank of the United States that had tried to restrain wildcat expansion. Jones said that Argentina, Australia and Canada all fell into the statist category, with central banks starting to assist in financing public debt. Note additionally, however, that the Bank of England and the Bank of France were each established during wars to help finance the conflict, and that the National Bank Act of 1863 in the United States had the dual function of correcting the populism of free banking and helping to finance the Union during the Civil War. As these examples indicate, national financial history is not restricted to one mode but may shift from one to another.

It might be possible to use this taxonomy to categorize the history of money and capital markets. It happens, however, that a thesis dealing with the Italian capital market, and a paper related to it, are at hand (Pagano, 1985a; 1985b) and offer a different schema. Marco Pagano remarks that stock markets originated in different ways in different countries, and that these origins have had long-lasting and pervasive effects. He distinguishes two broad categories: one of stock exchanges founded by free associations of private individuals, as in the Netherlands, Great Britain and the United States, and those that came into existence as a result of government action. The latter class is further divided into two groups, the *bourses des banquiers*, in which stock-dealing is reserved for bankers and their representatives and trade is regulated by chambers of commerce (Germany, Austria and Switzerland), and the *bourses du roi* (France, Luxemburg and Spain) which are directly regulated by the central government. The Milan stock exchange, to which Dr Pagano's thesis is directed, is a mixture of the two governmental types, having been influenced by its founding under the Napoleonic occupation of Lombardy, and later affected by a return of the region to Austrian domination. Organized stock exchanges, to be sure, do not encompass the total of money and capital markets, and the Pagano taxonomy might have to be modified if the larger area were being categorized.

The Coase theorem that institutions do not matter except when transaction costs are particularly high might be said to be subject to testing in this financial history. If institutions do not matter, different origins of money and capital markets would presumably make no difference in outcomes, provided that national demands for capital ran roughly parallel. The latter condition cannot, of course, be assumed. Accordingly we proceed to a discussion of the development of money and capital markets in Europe over the last two centuries, up to the 1960s when a number of European international institutions – the Bank for International Settlements (1964), the European Economic Community (EEC) (1966), the Economic Research Group of a consortium of banks from four different countries (1966), and the Committee on Invisible Transactions of the Organization of Economic Cooperation and Development (OECD, 1967; 1968) produced a welter of research material on European capital markets that resulted, however, in virtually no action. The discussion is necessarily sketchy and, in the absence of information on the demand side, inconclusive. Enough is offered, it is hoped, on Amsterdam, England, France, Germany and Italy to suggest that the issue of regulation and deregulation is not critical to performance.

The Amsterdam capital market is said to have been completely unregulated. It was a relative pioneer in developing the public bank as an institution, with 100 percent bullion backing that lowered transaction costs by eliminating the necessity for each merchant to test the money he received (Van Dillen, 1934). Smith (1937, p. 453) asserted that the Bank of Amsterdam had a guilder of specie for every guilder of liability and Van Dillen (1934, p. 109) confirms that in 1760 this was more or less right. In 1780, however, following the troubles of the Dutch East India Company, the Bank loaned its specie to help out that company, at the persuasion of the city of Amsterdam, and went bankrupt in the process. This is a clear case of dysfunctional government intervention.

It was not just in money and banking that the Dutch pioneered. Their finance of trade was highly developed with specialized bill brokers, as was the stock exchange which invested in loans to governments at home and abroad, shares of trading and shipping companies, futures, options, and similar instruments for leveraged speculation called *windhandel* (trade in air). Dutch speculators gambled heavily in the South Sea and Mississippi bubbles but were shrewd enough to avoid the most obvious swindles of the former, and to sell out at the right moment in the latter, and lost little in the crashes (Wilson, 1941, pp. 72, 107–10). Substantial investments in British securities led to the settlement of a large number of Dutch capitalists in London. But Dutch skill in skating unregulated on the thin ice of the South Sea and Mississippi bubbles in 1720 was not proof against subsequent trouble. In 1763 the de Neufville bank failed after having expanded rapidly with a chain of discounted bills, as described by Smith (1937, pp. 292–300). Similar disaster occurred in 1772 with the failure of Cliffords. Worst of all, the Fourth Anglo-Dutch war in 1780–4 led Dutch investors to shift their foreign lending from Britain to France in time to be wiped out by the French Revolution. Three earlier Anglo-Dutch wars had not interrupted lending to British merchants (Barbour, 1966, p. 130). In the seventeenth century Dutch capitalists were men without a country, even though they had a city, Amsterdam.

Perhaps the most fateful aspect of Dutch money and capital markets, however, was the absence of loans to industry. Demand was doubtless limited. Capital went abroad because it was abundant and cheap. But the merchants and bankers who controlled trade, finance and government were interested in speculating in everything but industry. Tariff protection was kept down in the interest of trade turnover. Taxes were light on trade and incomes, heavy on the cost of living which kept wages high. Money and capital markets were highly unstable, despite the lack of government interference, and provided no stimulus to industry apart from that, like shipbuilding, closely associated with trade.

Britain had the example of the United Provinces to follow in the field of finance, but behaved otherwise. The Bank of England was founded to assist in funding government debt – a statist pattern – not like the Bank of Amsterdam to reduce transaction costs in trade. The financial revolution that took place after Parliament deposed the Stuarts in favor of the House of Orange in 1688 produced the beginnings of the capital market with trading in government stock, Bank of England shares, South Sea Company shares to add to the existing shares of the East India Company and the Sun Life Assurance (Dickson, 1967). An important feature of the revolution was a smooth and easy transition, as in the Netherlands, from the archaic and expensive system of tax farming and spending of governmental moneys by private bureaus, as contrasted with the traumatic change in France requiring the guillotining of 28 of the *financiers* and *officiers* who looked on their offices as private property, salable and inheritable.

From this statist start, the financial history of Britain follows an orthodox path from the middle of the eighteenth century. Local personalized markets for most industry and ships were integrated into the national market in London only slowly. London specialized in trade and insurance, and moved into industry gradually as breweries, railroads, iron and steel reached sizes beyond the capacity of provincial informal dealings. The financial and trading institutions in London – acceptance houses, discount houses, jobbers, brokers, merchant, private and joint-stock banks – divided functions in an evolutionary but highly discriminating way. Country and provincial joint-stock banks were gradually suppressed or merged into a few giant national banks. In the process, banks in areas with excess savings sought to merge with those in the industrial areas that needed funds. In the transition to an integrated national market, Lloyds Bank found that it could not hold its deposit rate steady while having the London interest rate follow Bank Rate, as depositors learned to move funds from London to the provinces, or the reverse, as the two rates diverged (Sayers, 1957, pp. 110, 165, 270).

Widespread local initiative in Britain, however, contravened the Coase theorem in two or possibly three particulars. The first is the Macmillan gap in finance for equity capital between the sum of £100,000, less than which could be raised fairly readily in the local port or industrial town, and the £1,500,000 required as a capital sum before one could count on selling an issue economically in London. This gap was discovered by the Macmillan Committee in 1931 – hence the name – but it is said to have been a blemish on English capital markets as early as the second half of the nineteenth century. The second was a temporal gap between short- and long-term foreign lending, both highly developed, the one for finance of commodity trade, running usually 90 or 180 days, and the other for long-term government or railroad borrowing of

10 to 20 years. Between were capital exports needed to finance equipment, with terms of five to ten years, for which no private lending agencies sprang into being. The third possible area of market failure was the institutional diversion of British savings to foreign borrowers from potential domestic users (e.g. Lewis, 1978). The debate over this issue cannot be resolved here. The alleged mechanism can be noted, however: the growth of fortunes disassociated from industry, giving rise to a need for trustee-approved bonds, when government finance produced no new borrowing, and the railroad building boom was coming to an end. As private companies sold out to public shareholders, trustees found a dearth of suitable investments at home and went abroad. In this circumstance it is claimed, not without controversy, that British capital markets discriminated against domestic industry in favor of foreign governments and railroads.

In due course, government sought to correct these "gaps." The Export Credit Guarantees Department was established in the 1930s to assist in financing the export of capital equipment. Other specialized agencies have been set up since 1945 to fill the Macmillan gap, including the Industrial and Commercial Finance Corporation, Ship Mortgage Finance, Charterhouse Industrial Development Corporation. Higher death dues gave rise to a new financing need not fully cared for by the private market, so that an Estate Duties Investment Trust was created to forestall unwanted business liquidation upon the death of the entrepreneur. Owing to the troubles of the balance of payments and to help finance priority needs, especially as war approached, new security issues were rationed by government, in the 1930s and after the war, with Commonwealth and foreign borrowers assigned to the end of the queue or stricken from it altogether.

Deregulation may be said to have begun with the establishment of the Eurocurrency market, largely in London and an institution that evolved in Darwinian fashion out of private initiatives rather than governmental intention. This consisted primarily of foreign banks dealing in foreign currencies that the British authorities decided to leave unregulated, or that were regulated, if at all, by the governments and institutions of their home countries. The Eurocurrency market served as the thin end of the wedge for further deregulation. The traditional division of function among London joint-stock banks, discount houses, brokers, jobbers, merchant banks and the few remaining private banks is being torn down, largely for the sake of improving trading in British debt and to finance the privatization of companies nationalized before the present Conservative government took office.

To summarize, money and capital markets in Britain grew up with gaps that the government tried to fill, and evolved in an ossified way that government, with the help of private financial houses, is now prepared to see changed.

French financial history is centripetal. Various efforts to decentralize the financial structure were initiated in the eighteenth century, largely by foreigners such as John Law of Scotland, and Isaac Panchaud and Jacques Necker of Switzerland, in all cases without success. Attempts to spread banking to the provinces by creating regional note-issuing banks or branches of the Bank of France were advocated by Napoleon I, by the Saint-Simonists, and by provincial bankers and businessmen, but were defeated by the Paris banking establishment of the Bank of France and the Haute Banque. Under Napoleon III, a crypto-Saint-Simonist when in exile and in office until converted to an establishment view, the Pereire brothers were permitted to start the Crédit Mobilier to stimulate public works in France. The government earlier detected gaps in the financial spectrum and created the Crédit Foncier to improve the market for mortgage credit, and in 1860 the Crédit Agricole to lend to farmers. This last found little demand for credit from the countryside and occupied itself, from 1873 to 1876, in lending money on speculative bonds to Egypt.

Large deposit banks were created in France, primarily in the early 1860s. The Comptoir d'Escompte (of 1847) and the Société Générale were founded in Paris. In due course the Crédit Lyonnais (of Lyons) moved its head office to Paris. After the success of the Thiers *rentes* all banks speculated in government bonds, and by the end of the 1870s, in foreign bonds. Rather than trying to balance the intake of domestic savings and outlet of domestic lending, as British banks had done in merging into national networks, the Crédit Lyonnais concentrated on establishing branches where deposits were abundant and avoiding communities with an urgent demand for loans, and it drew deposits to Paris for investment in speculative foreign issues (Bouvier, 1961, esp. ch. 2). The high-flying Union Générale of Lyons was allowed to collapse in 1882, while the equally or even more speculative Comptoir d'Escompte that had unsuccessfully backed an attempt to corner the world copper market (evocative of the American Bunker Hunt's attempt to corner the silver market nearly a century later) was rescued (Bouvier, 1960). In the twentieth century the Bank of France was accused with some plausibility of having suppressed regional banks in Haute Savoie and Lorraine (Charpenay, 1939).

A special class of *banques d'affaires* got going in the 1870s but spent the first years of existence speculating in bonds before settling down to lend to industry. This again was focused in Paris with governmental blessing. Among the earliest was the Banque de Paris et des Pays-Bas which grew out of a merger involving a bank started in Holland by the

German exile, Ludwig Bamberger, to lend to France from an offshore location, much as the Eurocurrency market later developed (Zucker, 1975, p. 77).

It is hard to see that there were wide differences between the instability of British and of French finance, despite the decentralization of the one and the centralization of the other. When it came to the allocation of savings, both are accused of favoring foreign borrowers at the expense of domestic, but the point is debatable. The 1960 studies of European capital markets singled out the French, especially, for collecting savings deposits throughout the country into a central Caisse des Dépôts et des Consignations that existed from the early nineteenth century and investing them, now in housing, now in government debt, now in para-statal nationalized bodies in various industries, or in government capital allocation to control investment under the various plans that had been adopted since 1946. In due course first planning and then the program of nationalization under Mitterrand were allowed to fade into obscurity. It is difficult to make a case that the nationalization of banks or centralized government control of credit made a major difference in the way that French credit was allocated from the center.

German money and capital institutions were originally widely diffused because of the country's division before 1870 into a large number of states, principalities, free cities and the like. A group of financiers in Cologne, in Prussia, wanted in the 1850s to start a bank along the lines of the Crédit Mobilier and was refused at locations in Cologne and in Frankfurt am Main. It was forced ultimately to go to Darmstadt in Hesse, across the state border. From an early period, however, German banks were closely tied to industry, not to trade, trade being much less developed than in Holland or England. With unification in 1870, a centripetal process started as banks moved head offices to Berlin. Even from Hamburg, a mercantile city with a Hanseatic tradition of openness to the world and a disdain of Prussian Junkers, the Commerzbank gradually shifted its head office to Berlin, but indirectly after an intermediary move to Frankfurt. The Deutsche Bank, established in 1872 to rival London in foreign-exchange trading, got caught up in the boom that followed the founding of the Reich and loaned predominantly to industry.

The close association of banks and industry in Germany had some gaps. One or two steel companies stayed aloof from intimacy with the leading D-banks (the Deutsche Bank, the Dresdener Bank, the Darmstädter und National Bank) as did the chemical industry as a whole (Riesser, 1911, pp. 721, 741). In the boom of 1870–3 a host of mortgage banks and brokers' banks were started in Germany and in Austria, but melted quickly thereafter. Gerschenkron (1962, pp. 87–9) makes much of the banks' action in aiding Italy in starting new banks along German lines in the 1890s at the behest of Bismarck. Two things seem to me wrong with this claim: first, that the German banks quickly sold back the shares they bought in the new banks in the first wave of enthusiasm, and the banks ended up by 1900 owned largely in Italy and France (Confalonieri, 1976, ch. i); second, as discussed below, Italian lending to industry after the spurt from 1895 to 1913 proved largely unsuccessful.

Of interest in comparing German and Italian banks, both intimately bound to industry through "mixed" or "industrial" banks that owned industrial shares on their own account, and in the German case voted the shares of their depositors left in their custody, was that when the system broke down in the 1930s, the Germans left it intact while the Italians changed it. Industrial finance under the Nazis was conducted by new instruments invented by government that produced economic recovery that slowly floated the clogged banks (Hardach, 1984). In Italy reform was undertaken, separating "ordinary" from investment banking, as in the Glass–Steagall Act of 1933 in the United States, and providing most finance for industry by a Reconstruction Finance Corporation – the Istituto per la Ricostruzione Italiana (IRI), as in the United States (Ciocca and Toniolo, 1984). In Italy, however, IRI became a permanent institution, whereas in the United States the RFC was metamorphosed into the Defense Plant Corporation during the war but liquidated afterwards.

The Italian capital market has been called "colonized" (Bonelli, 1971, p. 43) or an exercise in the second best (Kindleberger, 1984, p. 11). Prior to the unification of Italy that took place in stages in 1860, 1868 and 1870, the country consisted partly of independent states, but partly of states controlled by or having close relations with outside powers, notably France, Austria and Spain. With unification led by Piedmont, closely allied with France, foreign borrowing in the 1860s was largely in Paris, except for one issue that the French were unwilling to take in 1881 that was shifted to London. Pagano (1985b) notes that in 1854 Italian railway shares were regularly traded in Vienna but not in Milan. Collapse of the banks associated with France in the early 1890s and the creation of new, started from Germany, led to the boom that lasted to 1913, apart from the relapse in 1907. Wartime inflation destroyed any private market for bonds that might have existed, leading personal savers to hold mostly short-term government bonds and bank deposits, while banks accumulated industrial shares along with industrial loans. The interwar history of the capital market includes the failure of only one bank in 1923 when the postwar bubble burst, severe troubles for others in the stock market crash of 1926, following the appreciation of the lire from 150 to the pound to 90 (the so-called *quota novanta*), each forcing the Bank of Italy to take over industrial shares from the mixed banks to save the latter. When 1930 troubles were piled on top of the earlier accumulations, IRI was formed to relieve the Bank of Italy of its burden, and later other state financing funds, IMI and EMI. In today's "dual" Italian economy, multinational business finances itself in the Eurocurrency market, ordinary domestic industry turns to IRI, and small-scale business, especially in the black market that pays no social security or corporate income taxes, relies on internal and parochial informal finance.

It is difficult to claim that the Italian capital market troubles originate in governmental regulation. Rather regulation and the substitution of government for private credit through IRI, EMI and IMI come from a less than Pareto-optimal capital market with roots deep in Italian history. Government is often regarded as an ulcer that debilitates the body economic. It sometimes, however, is an instrument for filling vacuums left by private persons seeking their own interest (Kindleberger, 1978b). In the case of the Italian capital market, I judge that government has been less of a disturbance to private equilibrium and more of a correction of private disequilibria.

I conclude that the issue of financial regulation and deregulation implicit in the McKinnon view of repression is unduly simple. One cannot postulate repressed and unrepressed money and capital markets as if there were only two types. Financial history, national character, evolving institutions and relationships affect both how financial markets will respond to changes in the environment – real, financial, governmental regulation or deregulation – and how efficiently capital markets allocate resources among competing uses. Excitable Dutch, without regulation, will indulge in bubbles, their own or those of others, successfully on occasion, unsuccessfully at other times. In moving from regulation to deregulation – if it be assumed, as is most likely the case, that an economy will do well in an unregulated state most of the time – it is plausible that one should proceed slowly and cautiously, giving expectations, after each step, time to absorb the changes in a quiet way and steady down. There may be some merit in talking about capital markets at length, as was done by the EEC, OECD, BIS, etc., in the 1960s, and then doing nothing beyond letting the Eurocurrency and Eurobond markets move Europe some distance along the road to integration. The present positive steps of deregulation in response to technical change with satellite communication and computers bear careful, perhaps even prayerful, watching.

Bibliography and references

Ashton, T.S. (1953), "The bill of exchange and private banks in Lancashire, 1790–1830," in T.S. Ashton and R.S. Sayers, eds., *Papers in English monetary history*, Clarendon: Oxford, 37–49.

Bacha, Edmar Lisboa and Carlos F. Diaz-Alejandro (1982). "International financial intermediation: A long and tropical view," in *Essays in international finance*, no. 147, International Finance Section, Princeton University: Princeton, NJ.

Bank for International Settlements (1964), *Capital markets*, Basle, January.

Barbour, Violet (1966), *Capitalism and Amsterdam in the 17th Century*, University of Michigan Press: Ann Arbor; first published 1950.

Bisson, Thomas N. (1979), *Conservation of coinage, monetary exploitation, and restraint in France, Catalonia and Aragon c.1000–1125*, Clarendon: Oxford.

Bonelli, Franco (1971), *Le crisi del 1907: Una tappa dello sviluppo industriale in Italia*, Einaudi: Turin.

Bouvier, Jean (1960), *Le Krach de l'Union Générale, 1878–1885*, Presses Universitaires de France: Paris.

Bouvier, Jean (1961), *Le Crédit Lyonnais de 1863 à 1882: Les années de formation d'une banque de dépôts*, 2 vols, SEVPEN: Paris.

Cameron, Rondo (1961), *France and the economic development of Europe, 1800–1914*, Princeton University Press: Princeton, NJ.

Charpenay, George (1939), *Les banques régionalistes*, Nouvelle Revue Critique: Paris.

Ciocca, P. and C. Toniolo (1984), "Industry and finance in Italy, 1918–1940," in "Banking and industry in the interwar period," a special issue of *Journal of European Economic History*, 13, 2, 113–36.

Confalonieri, Antonio (1976), *Banca e industria in Italia*, vol. 3, *L'experienze della Banca Commerciale Italiana*, Banca Commerciale Italiana: Milan.

Corbo, Vittorio and Jaime de Melo, eds (1985), *Liberalization with stabilization in the Southern Cone of Latin America*, special issue of *World Development*, 13, 8.

Cottrell, P.L. (1980), *Industrial finance, 1830–1914: The finance and organization of English manufacturing history*, Methuen: London.

Diaz-Alejandro, Carlos F. (1985), "Goodbye financial repression, hello financial crash," *Journal of Development Economics*, 19, 1/2, 1–24.

Dickson, P.G.M. (1967), *The financial revolution in England: A study in the development of public credit, 1688–1756*, St. Martin's Press: New York.

Economic Research Group of Amsterdam-Rotterdam Bank, Deutsche Bank, Midland Bank, Société Générale de Banque/Generale Bankmaatschappij (1966), *Capital markets in Europe: A study of markets in Belgium, West Germany, the Netherlands and the United Kingdom.*

Edwards, Sebastian (1984), "The order of liberalization of the external sector of developing countries," in *Essays in international finance*, 156, International Finance Section, Princeton University: Princeton, NJ.

European Economic Community, Commission (1966), *The development of a European capital market: Report of a group of experts appointed by the EEC Commission*, Segré Report: Brussels.

Fetter, Frank Whitson (1965), *The development of British monetary orthodoxy, 1797–1875*, Harvard University Press: Cambridge, MA.

Fry, Maxwell, J. (1982), "Models of financially repressed developing countries,"

World Development, 10, 9, 731–3.

Gerschenkron, Alexander (1962), *Economic backwardness in historical perspective*, Harvard University Press: Cambridge, MA.

Hardach, G. (1984), "Banking and industry in Germany in the interwar period, 1919–1939," *Banking and industry in the interwar period*, a special issue of *Journal of European Economic History*, 13, 2, 203–34.

Hayek, F.A. (1972), *Choice in currency: A way to stop inflation*, Institute of Economic Affairs Occasional Papers no. 48, IEA: London.

Jones, Charles (1982), "The monetary politics of export economies before 1914: Argentina, Australia and Canada," paper presented to the Symposium on "Argentina, Australia and Canada: Some comparisons, 1870–1950," at the 44th International Congress of Americanists, Manchester, September 8.

Kindleberger, Charles P. (1978a), *Manias, panics and crashes: A history of financial crises*, Basic Books: New York.

Kindleberger, Charles P. (1978b), "Government and international trade," in *Essays in international finance*, 129, International Finance Section, Princeton University: Princeton, NJ.

Kindleberger, Charles P. (1984), "Banking and industry between the two World Wars: An international comparison," *Banking and industry in the interwar period*, a special issue of *Journal of European Economic History*, 13, 2, 7–28.

Lefebre, Georges (1967), *The coming of the French Revolution*, Princeton University Press: Princeton, NJ.

Lewis, W. Arthur (1978), *Growth and fluctuations, 1870–1913*, Allen & Unwin: London.

McKinnon, Ronald I. (1973), *Money and capital in economic development*, Brookings Institution: Washington, DC.

McKinnon, Ronald I. (1982), "The order of economic liberalization: Lessons from Chile and Argentina," in K.A. Brunner and A. Meltzer, eds., *Economic policy in a world of change*, vol. 17 in the Carnegie Mellon Series on Public Policy, North-Holland: Amsterdam, 59–86.

McKinnon, Ronald I. and Donald J. Mathieson (1981), "How to manage a repressed economy," in *Essays in international finance*, 145, International Finance Section, Princeton University: Princeton, NJ.

Organization for Economic Cooperation and Development, Committee on Invisible Transactions (1967; 1987), *Capital markets study*, 5 vols, OECD: Paris.

Pagano, Marco (1985a), "Market size and asset liquidity in stock exchange economies," dissertation, Department of Economics, MIT: Cambridge, MA.

Pagano, Marco (1985b), "The historical development of the Milan stock market," term paper, MIT: Cambridge, MA.

Riesser, Jacob (1911), *The great German banks and their concentration, in connection with economic development of Germany*, US Government Printing Office: Washington, DC, for the National Monetary Commission.

Sayers, R.S. (1957), *Lloyds Bank in the history of English banking*, Clarendon: Oxford.

Segré, Claudio (1966), *The development of a European capital market: Report of a group of experts appointed by the EEC Commission*, European Commission: Brussels.

Shaw, Edward S. (1973), *Financial deepening in economic development*, Oxford University Press: New York.

Smith, Adam, (1937), *An inquiry into the nature and the causes of the wealth of nations*, edited by E. Cannan, Modern Library: New York; first published 1776.

Sprague, O.M.W. (1968), *History of crises under the National Banking Act*, Kelley: New York.

Van Dillen, J.G. (1934), "The Bank of Amsterdam," in J.G. Van Dillen, ed., *History of the principal public banks*, Kelley: New York.

Vaubel, Roland (1977), "Free currency competition," *Weltwirtschaftsliches Archiv*, 113, 435–59.

White, Lawrence H. (1984), *Free banking in Britain: Theory, experience and debate, 1800–1845*, Cambridge University Press: New York.

Wilson, Charles (1941), *Anglo-Dutch commerce and finance in the eighteenth century*, Cambridge University Press: Cambridge.

Zucker, Stanley (1975), *Ludwig Bamberger, German liberal politician and social critic, 1823–1899*, University of Pittsburgh Press: Pittsburgh, PA.

12

Write-off or work-out? A historical analysis of creditor options

When loans go "bad" because debtors are encountering difficulties in meeting interest and paying back principal on schedule, the creditor faces a menu of policy options of which the polar ideal types are writing off the bad loans or working them out, that is, keeping the loans on the books at cost in the hope that circumstances will change and make the loans good. This paper discusses the polar extremes, analyzes some of the intermediate cases, and furnishes historical examples. I have confined myself mostly to examples drawn from US and European financial history, which is all that I know.

Write-offs are the classic medicine for bad loans. If the discussion is limited to bank assets, these should be "marked to market" at some regular period – daily, weekly, monthly, quarterly – that is, maintained on the books at cost or market whichever is lower. When the asset has fallen in price below cost, it must be written down on the asset side of the balance sheet, with a corresponding charge against the profit-and-loss statement, where the valuation takes place at intervals when income is calculated, or against capital surplus. Where there are assets for which the market is thin or non-existent, classic therapy calls for writing them down to realistic levels of their present discounted value (PDV), based on the prospects for payment of interest and principal.

When a debtor announces that it cannot or will not pay, there is of course no option, and the loan has to be written off under any conceivable accounting rule. On occasion, subsequent negotiations, perhaps

* Paper presented to a Conference on Financial Crises and Crisis-Containing Mechanisms sponsored by the National University of Mexico and Washington University of St Louis, March 9–11, 1987. Published in Spanish as "Cancelación o Revalidación: Un Análisis Histórico de la Opciones del Acreedor," in Carlos Tellos Macías and Clemente Ruiz Durán (eds) (1990), *Crisis financiera y mecanismos de contención*, Mexico DF: Universidad and Fondacion, pp. 211–31.

with a Council of Foreign Bondholders, will produce resumption of partial debt service and enable the holder of the obligation to get some value from it. In the case of bonds, the debtor may default and then buy up outstanding bonds in the market at derisory prices to clear its own books of debt. But where a debtor insists that it wants to pay, but is for a time unable to do so, or can only pay so much – as with the 10 percent of export proceeds offered by Peru – the choice of write-off or work-out is open – open perhaps to the creditor, or possibly in the case of bank loans, mainly to the bank examiner. Where a bank is subject to examination by several agencies – the Comptroller of the Currency, the Federal Deposit Insurance Corporation (FDIC) and/or the Federal Reserve System – and they disagree, the choice may require negotiation among the parties.

Working out a bad asset calls in the first place for not writing it off, maintaining it on the books at cost, and doing nothing in hopes that the conditions which caused the loan to turn bad will change, making resumption of debt service possible and the loan good again. For Latin American loans today, the hoped-for circumstances include effective policies of austerity in the debtor countries, cutting imports and releasing output for exports – policies undertaken in a determination to maintain debt service and credit standing so that later loans may be obtained to expedite economic growth. In the world beyond the debtor's control at least three conditions are critical to assure work-outs: low interest rates to hold down payments under floating-rate arrangements, sustained prosperity in the developed countries; and successful governmental resistance to demands for protection against debtor-country exports. Note parenthetically that if the probability of achieving each of these three conditions were ½, and the three were unrelated (which they are not), the probability of meeting all three would be ½ × ½ × ½, or ⅛. It happens, however, that low interest rates in the developed world would assist in maintaining prosperity, and that sustained prosperity would assist governments in resisting calls for protection, so that the probability of achieving all three is above ⅛, although probably considerably below ½.

A fourth condition on which creditors and debtors have difficulty agreeing, and especially different groups in the creditor countries, is more loans. Jacques de la Rosière, erstwhile managing director of the International Monetary Fund (IMF) and James A. Baker, US Secretary of the Treasury, have properly, in my judgment, insisted on more loans to keep the debtor countries growing economically. United States banks are skeptical and reluctant on the basis of the slogan that one should not throw good money after bad. But good money after bad on the right occasions is a highly desirable therapy, whether in poker, bank lending or lender-of-last-resort operations. World depressions started in 1873, 1896 and 1929 when foreign lending was suddenly cut off, shortly followed by declining imports by the developed world. Each bank, and especially the smaller regional banks which feel no responsibility for general economic conditions and are fully occupied minding their own balance sheets, views lending more when outstanding loans turn sour with acute distaste. This is one of those examples of the fallacy of composition where what is bad for the individual is good for society when all do it together.

Marking to market with write-off of the difference between market and cost is ostensibly called for by the standards of bank examiners, if the discussion is limited to banks as a single class of creditors. In practice, however, examiners typically allow banks to carry loans at book value or cost. Newspaper accounts of December 1986 (see, for example, the *New York Times* of December 15) mention that more than 400 thrift institutions in the United States are "essentially bankrupt," but are allowed to continue operating because the assets of the Federal Savings and Loan Insurance Corporation (FSLIC), needed to make good depositor losses in the event of failure, have declined to very low levels. One compromise on the part of authorities maintaining surveillance over banks is to allocate particular loans of questionable payout to special categories, such as "problem loans," even while carrying them on the books at book, sometimes limiting the amount of problem loans a bank may be permitted to carry without write-off, or possibly requiring a certain proportion of problem loans to be written off in each income period. Another technique is to impose a ratio of bank capital to total assets, such as 5, 6 or 6½ percent, leaving it up to the bank whether to charge off loans against earnings, obtain more capital, or something of both. If the bank has trouble selling shares to raise its equity capital, it may sell subordinated debentures that qualify as capital because they rank behind deposits and certificates of deposit in the event of liquidation, although ahead of equity.

The highest standard of banking, as noted, calls for writing off bad loans against earnings, or capital and surplus. An outstanding example of a bank following this practice today is the Deutsche Bank of the Federal Republic of Germany, which is known and applauded for having drastically written down its loans to Eastern Europe, perhaps to a point below their true value so that it has acquired hidden reserves in the process.

There is one argument against writing off dubious loans. If the debtor learns that its paper has been written off, its resolve to take strong action to meet debt service as fully as possible may be weakened. The classic example concerns a governmental obligation: German reparations after World War I. When Keynes (1919) asserted that Germany would be unable to pay the large amount of reparations that the Allies were trying to levy at Versailles, the Germans lost interest in trying to pay, if they ever had much. When President Hoover in June 1941 announced a compromise between write-off and work-out – the Hoover moratorium postponing any debt service on both reparations and war debts for one year – it effectively wrote off both sets of obligation entirely, as Germany stopped paying reparations altogether, and the Allies soon followed suit with war debts owed to the United States.

The contrast between write-off and work-out applies not only to bad loans, whether bank or intergovernmental, but also to other cases. After World War II, the United States and the United Kingdom handled an awkward military financial problem in entirely different ways. The problem arose because the military forces, whether through lack of understanding of the consequences of their action or concern that troop morale would otherwise be adversely affected, redeemed at par exchange rates large amounts of inflated German and Japanese currency presented to them for conversion by their own servicemen. These conversions resulted in what was euphemistically called "an excess of foreign currency" but what was more accurately a deficiency of dollars (or sterling) in the troop-pay account. The British brought their accounts into balance by a Parliamentary appropriation of over £100 million, writing off the worthless enemy currency; the United States, on the other hand, took years of taking in dollars from Congressional appropriations for service personnel and occupation civil servants in occupied Germany and Japan, paying out Reichsmarks (later Deutschemarks) and yen, plus renting quarters and buying goods for post exchanges in enemy currency, and renting and selling them to Allied servicemen and women in dollars. In total, five or six years went by before the enemy currency had been converted into dollars in the extended work-out. The troop-pay account was balanced in foreign exchange, but at the expense of German exports of goods and services, with the enlarged deficit in the German balance of payments made up, in those days, by US Congressional appropriations for non-military purposes such as relief and Marshall Plan aid.

Another extended work-out by United States officials took place in the 1930s when the Treasury stabilization fund bought £1 million sold by the Soviet Union on September 26, 1936 at the time of the Tripartite Monetary Agreement. The purchase took place on a Saturday when the New York exchange market lacked support from London and was thin. Secretary of the Treasury Henry Morgenthau took over the sterling at a price close to $5 per pound, accused the Soviet Union of trying to undermine the financial stability of the world, and insisted that the

Treasury would make a profit on the transaction. It happened that the pound opened at around $4.86 when trading was resumed on Monday and never went above that level in the weeks and months to come. The work-out was accomplished by adding the ¼ percent service charge on gold transactions, both purchases and sales, to the particular exchange account, making it possible after an extended period to close the account with a profit.

One of the more salient forms of work-out, not widely discussed, is the practice of central banks in keeping foreign-exchange reserves on the books at cost under regimes of flexible exchange rates, rather than marking them to market. Some of the richest central banks in the world, notably the Bundesbank and the Bank of Japan, must have had their capital impaired – a condition under which with strict banking rules they would have had to close their doors as bankrupt – when the dollar declined in 1973–5 and again in 1985–6. Having acquired large quantities of dollars in the course of vain efforts in support of that currency, the decline of the dollar would have occasioned them substantial losses if they had been required to write their exchange reserves down. (They doubtless had at the same time substantial hidden reserves from failing to write gold holdings up to market.) To the extent that economists take notice of the price at which foreign exchange is valued on central-bank books, they regard the issue as unimportant. While a large loss on foreign exchange will matter to a country, it is of minor importance to the central bank. Central banks cannot go bankrupt; losses on foreign exchange can be offset by a claim in local currency against the government, perhaps a notional one if the government does not explicitly agree. This would leave the liability side of the balance sheet unchanged. Central-bank profits go to the government, and so can central-bank losses. The question was regarded as important in the interwar period. The Bank of France in 1926 refused to buy foreign exchange for francs to hold down the currency as it rose until the Poincaré government agreed to make good any possible Bank loss (Moreau, 1954), and the National Bank of Belgium was surprised when the Minister of Finance blithely agreed to take over the Bank's loss in sterling following that currency's depreciation in September 1931 (Van der Wee and Tavernier, 1975).

Between write-offs and work-outs there is an almost infinite variety of compromises. One is to add unpaid interest to the loan, increasing its nominal value and including the interest, though not received, in income for the relevant period. The interest rate can be reduced or capped, with the unpaid portion at the original rate either written off or added to the loan. Interest and/or principal can be rescheduled, perhaps with a period of grace in which the payment on one score, the other, or both, is cancelled or added to the loan or to payments due later. All these leave the nominal amount of the debt unchanged (or increased), but most lower the PDV. The hurt is felt on the profit-and-loss statement, but not on the balance sheet. The strong propensity to avoid writing down the face value of such bad loans seems to me a form of "debt illusion" on the part of the creditor. I am not clear whether debtors would prefer to keep something like the old terms and write down the principal amount, or whether they are typically happy to participate in the self-deception of the creditor. The Paris Club and the World Bank both avoid writing down the face amount of debt on which service cannot be maintained on the original terms, even when the necessity for change is traceable to the wild extravagance of dictators who are later deposed, notably Sukarno in Indonesia and the assassinated Nkrumah in Ghana. The absence of tangible productive assets to service the loans would seem to justify the write-off of principal amounts, reducing the face amount as well as the PDV of debt service to amounts perhaps near zero, but that ultimate step seems to be regarded as anathema. I conjecture that creditors are fearful that if the book value of loans is written down in one case, other debtors will be more likely to demand negotiation than if debt service is only rescheduled. Such a belief, however, seems hardly rational.

In addition to economic conditions and policies in the debtor and in creditor countries, plus the world economy, the choice between write-off and work-out of bad loans is affected also by the use to which the loan has been put, as the examples of Sukarno and Nkrumah illustrate. To use ideal types again, consumption loans for people at the subsistence level should be written off – in fact assistance to such people or countries should take the form of grants, rather than loans in the first place, whereas funds borrowed for productive purposes presumably create assets and productivity out of which interest and principal can be paid under ordinary circumstances. The evil of usury in Mohammedanism and in Christianity in pre-Aquinas times was based on the ethical duty of those better off to help those in need in periods of adversity, such as famine. To charge interest was to take advantage of the troubles of others, especially of co-religionists. When starving Indian peasants borrowed from moneylenders, they typically had to continue to borrow the interest, adding to the loan, because there was no additional source of income from the loan. The same is often true of gambling debts.

Consumption loans are entirely normal today in rich countries, as households experiencing shortfalls in income or one-time increases in expenditure expect either to earn more or to compress expenditure in future to provide a margin for debt service. Buy now and pay later is the antithesis of the life-cycle consumption function in which one saves first and dissaves subsequently. The latter model accords with the Calvinist convictions of the Swiss (and the Japanese?), but borrowing for consumption is widely accepted in today's world when there is an expectation that it can be paid for by future austerity or increased earnings. In the subsistence economy of peasants at the margin, no such expectation was rational.

This distinction between consumption loans at the subsistence level and loans for productive projects calls into question a criticism of international lending that is frequently raised in Latin American discussion, i.e. that based on a comparison of new loans and investment with interest on old loans, dividends on direct investment, repayment of principal and depreciation and depletion, that the United States takes more money out of Latin America than it puts in. I have attempted unsuccessfully in the past to scotch this hoary fallacy (see under "Cumulative Lending" in the 1953 to 1973 editions of my *International Economics*). The analysis applies well to amortization, depreciation and depletion, but not to interest and dividends which have no connection whatsoever with new investment. If I buy a share of General Motors, the company may urge me to reinvest dividends automatically, but I am free to take them as income and spend them, without any implicit moral obligation to reinvest. It happened in the nineteenth century that Britain reinvested annually amounts more or less equal to its earnings on foreign investment, but except in the case of retained earnings used to expand a given direct investment, or depreciation and depletion used to maintain a given asset, the rough equality of the two flows was fortuitous: moneys earned abroad entered into the income stream in Britain where they were divided between consumption and savings, and savings out of foreign income joined those on domestic income to be divided again between foreign and domestic investment. To expect that an individual, household or country should reinvest the total of its foreign-earned income in the countries where it is earned calls for geometric growth of foreign investment. When famished peasants or losing gamblers fall behind in paying interest and principal on their debts, to be sure, the debt rapidly approaches astronomical amounts.

There is one type of loan on which one legitimately has to borrow the interest, arising in the case of construction projects of long gestation. Suppose a country borrows $100 million at 10 percent a year for a project that will have its first product in five years – the Egyptian High Dam at Aswan, for example. Interest begins the first year, but there is no output with which to pay it. The interest must be borrowed, and the same is the case in years 2, 3, 4 (and possibly 5). The project costs not $100 million but that amount plus compound interest for five years.

Waiting is necessary, and in the circumstances specified, the waiting is productive. The case is sharply different from borrowing for consumption at the subsistence level, when borrowing of the interest is inescapable, too, but unproductive.

Consumption and investment do not comprise the full range of purposes for which individuals, households, firms or countries may wish to borrow. For countries, in particular, borrowing may be undertaken to buy military equipment which is productive only in the sense implied by Adam Smith when be said that defense was greater than opulence. It is not productive of a stream of income that can be used in part to meet debt service. In and after World War I, the United States took a bankerish view of war loans. Calvin Coolidge said of the European allies "They hired the money, didn't they?" meaning that the loans should bear interest and be repaid. In the war-loan negotiations of 1923–6, however, interest rates were set below market rates for most debtors – though not for the United Kingdom – and in working out these rates, account was taken of ability to pay of the separate debtors. In World War II, the Lend-Lease Act left open the question whether advances would be made on the basis of loans or grants, and if loans, on what terms. In the Lend-Lease settlements after the war, the cost of military equipment used up in the war – consumed, so to speak – was written off entirely by the United States, as were supplies consumed by the military and the civilian populations. Goods that survived the war or that emerged from the pipeline after new inputs were halted, were valued in terms of their civilian worth – almost nil for military aircraft for example, but more for food, petroleum products, trucks, military clothing, tenting – and put on a loan basis. The terms were generous, 28 years with a period of grace and below-market rates of interest, the whole, that is, with a PDV well below the nominal amount of debt.

On Christmas Eve 1986, the US Treasury offered to defer interest payments on military loans to Israel, Egypt and 36 other countries, including Spain, Greece, Thailand, Turkey and Korea, citing the United States' interest in the military forces of these countries. The loss was estimated at $3.5 billion in uncollected revenue in the six following years (*New York Times*, December 25, 1986). It is not clear how much these write-offs were due to ability to pay and how much to the purposes for which the moneys were borrowed. The news account went on to state that the action postponed the need to come to grips with the accumulating American support for economically weak allies, and that it is easier to get loans through Congress than grants. Presumably the tactic is to make loans and reschedule them later should the need arise. It is clear, none the less, that military aid, like consumption loans, produces no direct income from which debt service can be subtracted in the normal manner.

Congressional preference for loans over grants goes back at least to the Marshall Plan experience of 1948–52. Most assistance was made in the form of grants, rather than loans, on the ground that it was needed for consumption and or restocking or reconstruction which would only restore previous levels of income, not raise output. In the event, a number of the receiving countries found themselves experiencing "economic miracles" of extraordinarily high rates of growth from which they would have been able to extract debt service. While it would have been possible to convert loans into grants if economic growth had fallen short of expectation, there was no possibility of replacing grants with loans when the outcome was the reverse. Germany did, to be sure, use some of the surpluses in its national budget and its balance of payments to prepay principal on much, if not all, of the loan portion of its Marshall Plan aid and other advances during the occupation and reconstruction well ahead of the agreed schedule. The PDV of these payments, of course, exceeded that of the original formula.

Apart from pure consumption, military aid and reconstruction assistance, there are difficult cases such as those presented by economic projects where the anticipated results are not realized, whether because of bad judgment to start with – overly ambitious plans that end up building unproductive "monuments," cases of unrelated bad policy that harms the project's prospects – or instances in which circumstances beyond the control and expectations of borrower or lender changed drastically. The collapse of the price of oil in 1982 may or may not be one of this last class, depending upon how euphoric or detached an observer was at the time.

Where the circumstances of the original loan or investment change in ways that cannot reasonably be foreseen, there is a presumption that work-out is a better option than write-off on the assumption that circumstances may change against in unanticipated ways, and for the better. They may, to be sure, continue changing for the worse. For the German loans behind the Iron Curtain, the chances of a massive improvement are perhaps so slight as to warrant write-off rather than work-out. In Third World loans, much depends upon the particular economic outlook, seriously and soberly judged. Commodity prices move with general business conditions, but are also subject to independent influences – coffee (Brazil) to the sizes of harvest and carryovers, oil (Mexico, Venezuela, Peru) to the strength of the OPEC cartel and the course of the Iran–Iraq war, copper (Chile) to the trend of substitution of optic fibers for copper wire.

Decisions by individual banks as to whether to write off or work out bad loans will again depend on particular circumstances. Regional banks may take one view, money-center banks another. Regional banks entered syndicated sovereign bank lending to Third World countries late, with little experience, relying on the wisdom of the lead banks. In a number of cases, they are disillusioned and anxious to turn their backs on the field. Where holdings are small, they are often prepared to sell off the loans for what little they can bring, write off the rest, and get clear of the field. As I understand it, however, they cannot sell just a portion of their holding and keep the remainder on the books at cost. Just as when a debtor announces it cannot and/or will not pay, writing off a portion of a loan calls to the attention of the lender the real facts of life. If this be true, the market for sovereign bank loans without recourse to the seller in case of default, and especially that provided by direct investors who are sometimes able to arrange to buy foreign debt at a deep discount and exchange it for pesos, cruzeiros or australs for which they promise to hold the investment counterpart for an extended period, is small. Money-center banks with large holdings are unable to take advantage of these quasi-write-off devices since they would have to take charges against income or surplus which would be very large in any one period. The nine leading money-center banks had syndicated sovereign bank loans of close to $60 billion on June 1986, amounting to 130 percent of their capital adjusted to market valuation. This is well down from the peak ratio of 300 percent in 1982 – the decline having been brought about partly through a reduction of the loan volume by almost 10 percent but primarily through a doubling of the banks' market-adjusted capital. The regional banks are especially anxious to work their way out from under Third World loans so as to avoid what the money-center banks have been forced to do by the IMF, and urged to do by the US Treasury – make new loans in the process of working out the old. The attitude of individual banks toward write-offs as opposed to work-outs depends additionally, of course, on their loans in other weak sectors – oil, real estate, farm property – not to mention the pressure of particular bank examiners. The smaller the bank in the United States, however, the more likely its option will be write-off rather than work-out. Since the big banks dominate the statistics, however, work-out is the dominant choice over write-off.

Thus far the discussion has been at the level of banks' loans, on the one hand, and intergovernmental loans (or grants), on the other. There is a third dimension to the problem that merits consideration: the choices made by governments, central banks, and other official bodies when they take over bad loans from commercial banks in acting as lenders of last resort. When a commercial bank gets into difficulty with bad loans, it may or may not be rescued, or, as the Italians say, salvaged. The doctrine of the lender of last resort grew in Britain where the Treasury, the Bank of England or the London money market as a whole, through guarantees of an institution's liabilities, came to the rescue of a bank in trouble, or perhaps did not. The basis of decision was typically whether the bank's assets were deemed sound in the longer run, once it had gotten past the liquidity crisis. Walter Bagehot rationalized the procedure and propounded the rule that in a crisis the Bank of England should lend freely, without limit, albeit at a penalty rate. The Bank's rule was to lend only on good assets, by which it meant bankers' acceptances with less than two months to run and on two good London names. In practice it was not always "overly nice," lending on mortgages, iron works, copper works, promissory notes, acquiring a West Indian plantation, etc. (Clapham, 1945). Rules do not stand up in crisis. In the Continental Illinois crisis of July 1982, the $100,000 limit on insured deposits of the FDIC had to be abandoned because not to rescue the holders of large deposits and certificates of deposit, many of them foreign, would have given rise to runs on other banks. The FDIC was established in 1934 to head off runs by small depositors who were thought not to have enough financial knowledge and experience to judge the soundness of banks, and should therefore be protected from their ignorance, as a public good. Runs today typically start – for commercial banks at least if not for the thrift institutions – among the knowledgeable, foreign-deposit holders, other commercial banks who will take the CDs of the troubled institution only at high discounts if at all, or who refuse to deal with it in the federal funds market. The public good is less concerned with safety for the little depositor and more with the preventions of runs, no matter how touched off.

When lenders of last resort take over bad loans from commercial banks in trouble, they also have a choice whether to write off or work out. As noted for the FSLIC, something depends upon whether the relevant body has liquid assets – a central bank can, of course, create money – and what its chances are of getting more. In the case of the FSLIC, the opening of the new Congress in January 1987 is expected to bring new funds to restore its capacity for normal operations, but the process involves introducing politics into lender-of-last-resort functions. With commercial banks failing because of foreign loans, the political element would be doubled, foreign policy on top of domestic fault-finding.

One contrast is between the Reconstruction Finance Corporation (RFC) in the United States and the Istituto per la Ricostruzione Industriale (IRI) in Italy, both started in the 1930s to take over bad loans from banks. The loans, to be sure, were domestic. The RFC worked its loans off for the most part during the 1935–7 boomlet, was converted into a Defense Plant Corporation at the time of the war to assist in financing factories and equipment built for defense purposes, and was wound up after World War II by selling off its assets in what would be known today as "privatization." IRI was started by taking over the bad assets of the Italian "mixed banks," accumulated by the Bank of Italy in the recessions of 1923, 1926 and the early 1930s. The original intention was to work them off, but so difficult did this become that IRI took over the assets, wrote off the debts of the banks, and operated a substantial portion of Italian industry as a major conglomerate or holding company (Toniolo, 1980).

The great depression in Germany saw the failure of one major bank, the Darmstädter und Nationalbank, generally called the Danat. A modern economist asserts that this would be unthinkable today (Irmler, 1976, p. 287). With the ensuing rearmament program under National Socialism, the banks were left alone, not called upon to make new loans for industrial rearmament, with their old bad loans gradually floated by the widespread recovery and the armament program financed by government paper (Hardach, 1984).

The point to be emphasized is the role of the lender of last resort is highly political. When it has to be played internationally, foreign-policy aspects are likely to be mixed with economics. The $1 billion bridging loan from the Federal Reserve System for Mexico in 1982 would probably not have been available for a country with which the United States felt less close. The swap network among the Group of Ten leading financial countries presumably rests on solid expectations of economic capacity to make good the undoing of swaps at the end of six months or the chosen period. It is uncertain, however, whether the United States would extend the swap arrangement to a country with which it was quarreling over foreign-policy matters. We further have the examples of France insisting on political conditions – the cancellation of the *Zollunion* (customs union proposed between Germany and Austria in the fall of 1930) before it would lend a second time to Austria in June 1931, and Germany scrapping construction of the *Panzerkreuzer* (pocket battleship) before it would come to its rescue the same month. In September 1965 France refused to join the other members of the swap network in assistance to Britain, ostensibly as a matter of foreign policy after saying "No" to the British request to join the Common Market (Strange, 1976, II, p. 136).

Debtor countries from time to time say they are incapable of following the austerity policies laid down by the IMF and creditor countries or institutions because of domestic political resistance. Balancing the budget or creating a surplus out of which to pay debt service involves levying taxes under circumstances, on occasion, when no group is willing to take its share of the burden. Depreciating the exchange rate to the level needed to produce an export surplus is likely to raise prices, producing, with nominal income unchanged, a cut in real income resisted by what Olson (1982) calls "distributional coalitions."

Domestic politics plays a role in creditor countries, too. When the lending of last resort is undertaken by a central bank which creates money, there may be an "inflation tax" with a particular incidence. The choices made of which banks are to be rescued and which allowed to fail are likely to evoke criticism. Even when the explicit criterion is the likelihood of further disintermediation or runs, it will be asserted that insiders are taken care of and outsiders are left to their unhappy fate. Rescue of banks gives rise to cries of "bail out," the widespread populist sentiment in the United States resenting the financial community as contrasted with the real economy of farmers and workers. Where institutions like the FDIC, FSLIC, Farm Loan Board and Federal Home Owners' Bank run out of money and it becomes necessary to approach Congress for more, who gets saved on what terms becomes squarely a political question. The issues are legion: how much should be raised by assessment on the banks, and how much provided out of the national budget; whether surpluses of one support institution can be transferred to others in need; whether insurance premiums should be uniform or can be graded in consonance with risks taken by the banks in question; the need for reserves against off-balance-sheet items; with deregulation, whether non-banking institutions trying to break into world finance are favored by regulations and fees levied on banks. The political problems of lenders of last resort in creditor countries are perhaps more complex than those of debtors in another dimension: rescue or bank salvage must be done quickly to halt financial disintermediation or unravelling, and political processes take time to reach consensus.

One close call in the United States was that experienced by the Overseas Private Investment Corporation (OPIC) which would have had to pay out in losses far more than its reserves and foreseeable premium income when the Allende government in Chile took over a number of US-owned direct investments that had been insured against nationalization. To settle the potential claims on it, OPIC would have had to ask Congress for an appropriation. This would have opened up a highly politicized and exquisitely embarrassing debate on direct investment, who benefited from it and the appropriateness of governmental support for risky private enterprise. As it happened, the Allende government was overthrown and the nationalization decrees rescinded before it became finally necessary to pay the claims.

The lender of last resort in the domestic arena typically writes off the bad loans as far as the liquidated or bailed-out bank is concerned but may seek to work out the acquired assets for itself. The Bank of England in 1837 took over the three American so-called "W" banks it had rescued in 1836, but did not get their assets off its books until 1852 (Clapham, 1945, II, p. 157). Where a regional bank today sells off a foreign loan to a manufacturer who invests the local-currency proceeds, there is a partial write-off by the bank and presumably an extended work-out by the direct investor.

When debtor countries overtly default, US banks with their loans on the books must write them off. If that should render the banks insolvent, they would be taken over by governmental authorities at some level – FDIC, a new RFC, or the Federal Reserve System. Under no circumstances would a major bank be allowed to fail today if it were thought that such failure would lead to a flight into hand-to-hand currency or foreign exchange. The result would be to inject US banking agencies into the process of trying to work out claims on foreign debtors. The political implications are not attractive.

In the circumstances, the US clear hope is that there will not be overt defaults, that US banks will continue to work out their foreign loans, lending more to keep debtor countries growing, writing off bad loans where inescapable, but not at a rate to render them bankrupt. The process looks trying. I suspect it is far more attractive than the alternatives.

References

Clapham, Sir John (1945), *The Bank of England: A History*, 2 vols, Cambridge: Cambridge University Press.

Hardach, G. (1984), "Banking and Industry in Germany in the Interwar Period, 1919–1939," *Journal of European Economic History*, vol. 13, no. 2 (special issue), pp. 203–34.

Irmler, Heinrich (1976), "Bankenkrise und Vollbeschäftigungspolitik (1931–1936)," in Bundesbank, ed., *Währung und Wirtschaft in Deutschland*, Frankfurt am Main: Fritz Knapp.

Keynes, John Maynard (1919), *The Economic Consequences of the Peace*, London: Macmillan.

Kindleberger, Charles P. (1953), *International Economics*, Homewood, Ill.: Richard D. Irwin.

Moreau, Emile (1954), *Souvenirs d'un gouveneur de la Banque de France: Histoire de la stabilization du franc (1926–1928)*, Paris: Editions Génin.

Olson, Mancur (1982), *The Rise and Decline of Nations: Economic Growth, Stagflation and Social Rigidities*, New Haven, Conn.: Yale University Press.

Strange, Susan (1976) *International Monetary Relations*, vol. 2 of Andrew Shonfield, ed., *International Economic Relations of the Western World*, New York: Oxford University Press.

Toniolo, Gianni (1980), *L'economia dell' Italia fascista*, Rome: Laterza.

Van der Wee, Herman and K. Tavernier (1975), *La Banque Nationale de Belgique et l'histoire monétaire entre les deux guerres mondiales*, Brussels.

13

Exchange-rate changes and ratchet effects: A historical perspective

I have long complained that discussion of the great depression in the United States typically assigns no role whatsoever to the large exchange-rate changes, or to some small ones for that matter, that took place in the period. Two episodes are worth attention: first, the depreciation of the currencies of Argentina, Australia, New Zealand and Uruguay in 1929 and 1930; and second, appreciation of the dollar in the fall of 1931, generally characterized as the depreciation of sterling. I argue that both were seriously deflationary, and that in depression, depreciation is largely neutral while appreciation is deflationary. On the other hand, in the 1970s, appreciation was neutral and depreciation inflationary. In short, it can happen that fluctuating exchange rates affect international prices through a ratchet that works to accentuate inflation in a period of boom, and deflation in periods of depression. It can happen, too, that a change in exchange rates can raise prices partway in the depreciating currency, and lower them partway in appreciating, with no ratchet operating. Economic analysis that supposes that exchange-rate changes always operate in the same fashion, must be modified in the light of historical experience.

The first depression episode perhaps should be classified as a group of small exchange-rate changes rather than large. Shortly after the stockmarket crash of October 1929, first Argentina, then Australia, New Zealand and Uruguay either floated their currencies or depreciated them substantially. There was no direct connection with the stock

*A paper presented to a conference held at Brandeis University, December 4–6, 1987, and published in Stephan Gerlach and Peter Petri, eds, *The Economics of the Dollar Cycle*, Cambridge, Mass.: MIT Press, 1989.

market. These countries normally borrowed capital in London and New York, but had been unable to do so since the spring of 1928 when the stock-market boom began, when investors turned from foreign bonds to equities, and when interest rates rose in response to speculator demands for call money to buy stocks on margin. In the usual case, such a cut-off of long-term borrowing induces a shift to short money, and this response took place in Germany. It happened, however, that the London capital market worked somewhat differently with respect to the dominions and such favored borrowers as Argentina. These countries typically ran substantial bank overdrafts which built up as the deficit on current account ran along and were paid down with the proceeds of long-term borrowing when the lending banks considered that the overdraft was reaching an appropriate limit. When long-term lending was cut off in 1928, the borrowing needed to reduce or wipe out the overdraft was impossible. Given the reluctance of the London banks to enlarge the overdrafts, the central banks of these "regions of recent settlement," as they were called in League of Nations publications, had no choice but to let their currencies depreciate. The fact that this occurred after the stock-market collapse in October 1929 is fortuitous, although if the central banks had been able to hold on a little longer, the recovery of interest rates in New York and London might have enabled long-term debt to be sold in the spring of 1930, when foreign-bond markets briefly recovered and in fact hit new highs. As it happened, Argentina let the peso go in December 1929 and the other three currencies began to depreciate in the first quarter of 1930.

The depreciations of the Argentinian and Uruguayan pesos, and of the Australian and New Zealand pounds are usually thought of in terms of the stated currencies, but can be regarded as a small appreciation of the US and Canadian dollars. They had the effect of softening world prices in dollars for wheat and wool, and the sterling price of butter in London. The price of wheat fell from $1.50 a bushel in June 1929 to $1.05 in June 1930 – and New Zealand butter from 157.0 shillings per hundredweight in London in February 1930 to 135.2 shillings in April of the same year. Both price declines were well in excess of the percentage of depreciation – close to 5 percent at this early stage – commodity prices were generally soft and the appreciation of the US and Canadian dollars and of sterling in terms of the currencies that dominated wheat, wool, and butter markets gave these commodities a push against which resistance was weak.

It should be noted that wheat had not been strikingly affected by the spreading deflation from the stock market to commodities imported into New York that was a serious cause of deflation early in the depression. Wholesale prices fell between August 1929 and September 1930 by 22 percent in Japan, 16 percent in Canada, 15 percent in Great Britain, 14 percent it Italy, and 12 percent in the United States and Germany. I ascribe much of this to the liquidity squeeze of New York banks as they struggled in the crash to meet the consequences of the decline in stock prices for brokers' loans and stopped lending elsewhere. At that time, commodities exported to the United States, and especially to New York, were for the large part shipped on consignment to be sold on arrival to brokers who operated with credit. If credit seized up, the brokers who could not get their usual loans could not undertake their normal buying. The prices of import commodities traded in this way fell between September and December 1929 by as much as 26 percent in rubber, 18 percent in hides, 17 percent in zinc, 15 percent in cocoa, 13 percent in coffee, 10 percent in tin and silk, and 9 percent in copper and lead. An import commodity normally financed by the processing corporation in the United States, sugar, fell only 7 percent, and the export commodity, wheat, only 4 percent over these months. Overall, to be sure, the liquidity squeeze emanating from the stock market was far more important in depressing commodity prices than the limited effective appreciation of the dollars of Canada and the United States, and of sterling. They none the less added a small push against an open door.

Of much greater importance was the appreciation of the dollar and the gold bloc (depreciation of sterling and the sterling bloc) in September 1931. The sterling rate went from $4.86 on September 20 to $3.25 in December at the high for the dollar, a decline for sterling of 30 percent, or an appreciation of the dollar (and gold) of close to 40 percent. Prices did not rise in sterling, but fell in dollars and French francs. Measured from September 1931 to March 1932, prices of internationally traded commodities expressed in dollars behaved as shown in Table 13.1.

Whether prices rise in the depreciating country or fall in the appreciating when substantial change occurs in exchange rates, or fall in between, with some rise in the depreciating and some fall in the

Table 13.1 Changes in average dollar prices of specified internationally-traded Commodities between September 1931 and March 1932 (percent)

Cocoa	–	Hides	−29	Tin	−11
Coffee	+12.5	Lead	−29	Wheat	–
Copper	−31	Rubber	−34	Wool	−10
Corn	−23	Silk	−33	Zinc	−25
Cotton	+10	Sugar	−19		

Source: Calculated from Kindleberger (1986, Table 16, p. 187).

appreciating currencies, depends, of course, on the elasticities. The normal classical assumption of elasticity optimism is that a country is a price-taker for imports and a price-maker in exports, so that the terms of trade go against it when its currency is depreciated. The ultra-classical assumption of such an economist an Frank Graham is that a country is a price-taker for both imports and exports and that an exchange-rate change will leave prices in foreign exchange, and the terms of trade, unchanged. In the British case, however, the terms of trade improved with depreciation – an anti-classical outcome – as Britain in world depression was more of a price-maker in imports, the world depending on its market for primary products more than it depended on world markets for its manufactured exports. It is noteworthy that the elasticities are partly associated with the nature of the commodities concerned, but also very much affected by the state of world markets, whether they are poised on the edge of deflation which makes elasticities of both demand and supply low for price decreases (and high for price increases which were not involved).

It can be argued that the spread between dollar and gold prices, on the one hand, and sterling prices, on the other, was achieved more or less by a part rise in sterling and part decline in dollars and gold. A chart of Australian export prices in Kindleberger (1986, p. 86) shows Australian export prices rising in sterling and Australian currency at the end of 1931, falling in dollars. But the Australian commodities, wheat and wool, behaved differently from the bulk of primary product prices in Table 13.1. The large number of prices falling 23 to 34 percent in dollars makes the case for the ratchet on the down side in depression.

There is something of a mystery why United States prices turned up with the depreciation of the dollar in the spring of 1933, with sterling and gold prices steady rather than pushed further down. In this instance the exogenous depreciation of the exchange rate lifted an index of internationally-traded commodities (Moody's) and of the Dow Jones industrial stock price index at a time when the world economy had not recovered very far from the lows of June 1932. Some commodities doubled in price from March 1933 to June – corn and rubber for example, one an export and the other an import commodity. Hides went from 5.2 cents a pound to 12.2 cents, a rise of 135 percent, as the dollar went from $3.40 to the pound sterling to $4.80. The depreciation was undertaken in response to the Warren and Pearson (1933) study of the relationship between commodity prices and the agio on gold in the greenback period from 1863 to 1879, when again US prices varied with the rate of depreciation and world prices held steady. At that time, however, the United States was much less of a dominant power in the world economy than in 1933.

I lack a satisfactory explanation why British prices held steady when sterling depreciated in 1931 while US prices rose and world prices remained unchanged when the dollar depreciated two years later. One could hypothesize that the world economy had hit bottom via the investment multiplier with gross investment close to zero and net investment strongly negative. It would be hard to claim that the United States was more a price-taker in internationally-traded goods than Britain, although this explanation is probably valid for the period after the Civil War.

Some part of the explanation may lie in the fact that the US exchange rate at par was strongly overvalued – certainly against sterling and the yen – and that letting the exchange rate go lifted a deflationary pressure. Ragnar Nurkse (1949) once wrote that the United States was wrong to depreciate the dollar when the US current account in the balance of payments was in surplus. In early Keynesian analysis it was thought that if a country had a surplus, it meant that its foreign trade was giving a positive stimulus to national income and that it would be a beggar-thy-neighbor type of policy to depreciate. These strictures clearly applied in the 1930s to Japan, which consciously adopted policies of depreciating to undervalued rates to export its unemployment. In the US case, however, it can be argued against Nurkse that the dollar rate had been overvalued, but that the declines in national income and in imports through the national income multiplier were so severe that imports fell more than exports and produced a residual export surplus, with no implication that the exchange rate was undervalued. Depreciation, in other words, relieved strong deflationary pressure on income and prices from the foreign-trade sector, and imparted an upward pressure to prices. But this and other explanations are very much *ad hoc*, and the divergent behavior in prices between Britain in 1931 and the United States in 1933 remains to be understood.

If we leave aside the 1933 case of the US dollar, it can be said that depreciation in the 1930s left domestic prices in the depreciating country relatively unchanged and put strong downward pressure on prices in those countries where the currency appreciated, producing a ratchet in which an exchange rate that went up and down could be expected to produce a net decline in prices. The ratchet in the 1970s, on the other hand, moved in the opposite direction. If depreciation raises domestic prices and appreciation leaves them unchanged, a currency moving sinusoidally down and up will find prices raised on balance. This is what happened during the 1970s, starting with the depreciation of the dollar in 1971 and the adoption of floating in 1973. Dollar prices rose when the dollar depreciated, and remained unchanged when the dollar recovered.

The ratchet worked in the 1970s on the whole as a market phenomenon, based on the circumstance that the world economy operated as a sellers' market, as contrasted with the 1930s when there was a buyers' market. The 1970s were poised on the edge of inflation, whereas the 1930s were strongly deflationary. But the model can be seen with conscious direction behind it if one looks at the Organization of Petroleum Exporting Countries (OPEC) and the price of oil.

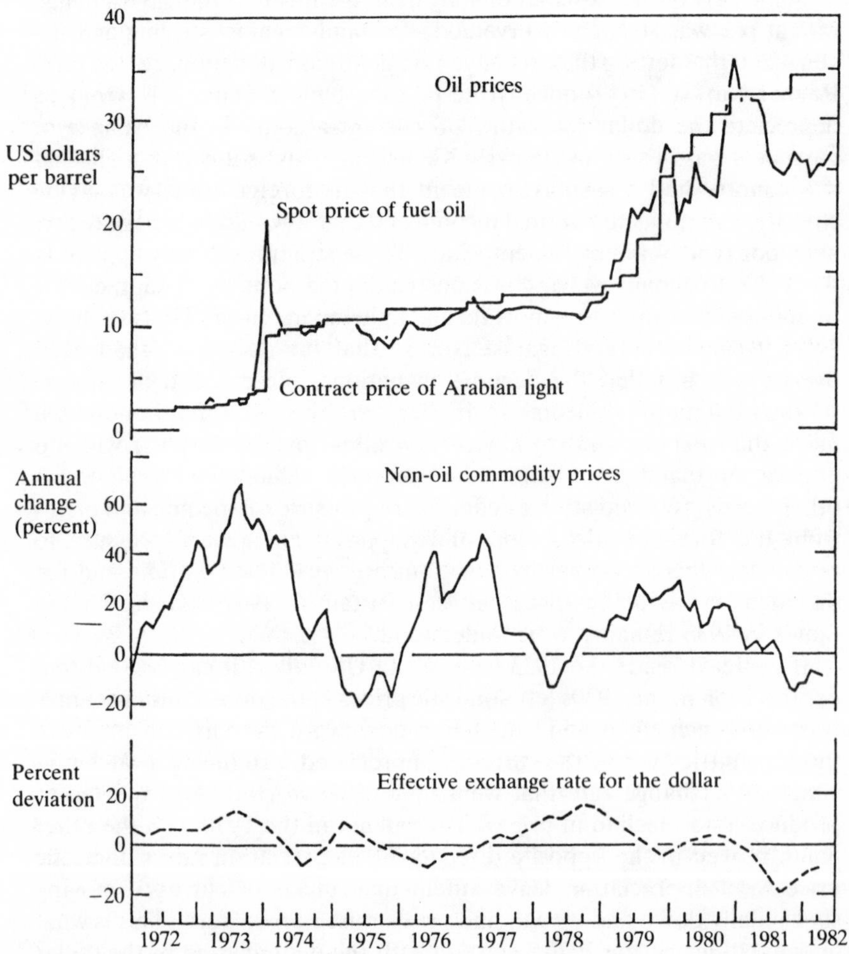

Figure 13.1 World-market commodity prices, oil and non-oil, compared with the effective exchange rate for the dollar, 1972–82. (Source: Bank of International Settlements (1982, pp. 40 and 42.)

In November 1973, at the time of the Yom Kippur War, the Arabian members of OPEC embargoed all oil exports to the United States and the Netherlands, which were deemed to be partial to Israel, and reduced all other exports by 25 percent. The price rose sharply to $20 per barrel before settling down at $10. Thereafter if the dollar depreciated, OPEC raised the price in dollars to maintain it in other currencies, such as the Deutschmark, sterling, and the yen. But if the dollar appreciated, the dollar price of Arabian crude was left unchanged, while prices in other currencies necessarily rose as these currencies depreciated against the dollar. The ratchet worked intermittently and with varying degrees of timing. Figure 13.1 shows the two oil shocks of 1973 and 1979 and the inching up of the dollar price of Arabian crude between those episodes when the effective exchange rate for the dollar rose in 1975 and 1978, with no decline in 1974 or 1976 when the dollar fell. The ratchet is much less clearly seen in non-oil prices during the decade: the effective exchange rate for the dollar, measured as a percentage change over four quarters, moves in a sine wave up and down, while world non-oil commodity prices exhibit for the most part price increases over 12 months, except in the recession of 1974 and in 1978.

The belief that prices in general, traded-goods prices and exchange rates behave differently in relation to one another, depending upon whether economic conditions are inflationary or deflationary, has an analogue in the operation of Gresham's law. Most economists summarize Gresham's law as bad money drives out good, i.e. that people spend bad or overvalued money and hoard, melt down or export good or undervalued money. Roland Vaubel's (1977) recommendation of parallel currencies rules out this possibility on the ground that good money may drive out bad. In his opinion, sellers will demand good money and refuse to take money that has been overissued or otherwise become overvalued. The possibility must be admitted. In a study of mints in Spain and France at the beginning of this millennium, Thomas Bisson (1979) cites a case of mints competing to have their coinage accepted and circulated and mints with full-weight coins succeeding over those which issued coins underweight. The usual formulation of Gresham's law as bad money drives out good rests on the belief that the choice of which money is spent rests with the buyer, not the seller, and implies a background of buyers' markets dominating over sellers'. The issue may be complicated in particular cases by laws governing legal tender, money which the law decrees has to be accepted in payment of debts. The general point, however, is that in the circulation of money, as in the relationship between domestic prices and exchange rates, outcomes may depend upon particular circumstances, in the instant cases whether buyers' or sellers' markets prevail.

This brings us to the present. The price of oil collapsed at the end of 1986 as the cartel proved to be unable to agree on sharing production cuts during stable phases of the Iran–Iraq war. The Federal Reserve undertook tight monetary policy from 1982, leading to high interest rates, capital inflow and an appreciation of the dollar that continued unexpectedly, in view of the fundamentals – a substantial budget deficit and a substantial trade deficit – to February 1985. The appreciation of the dollar may have held back inflation in the United States, but it did not lead to deflation. United States prices declined to the end of 1982, rose mildly through mid-1984 and then declined again. Prices in the Federal Republic of Germany rose substantially while the Deutschmark was depreciating in 1983, held steady during 1984, and came down again as the Deutschmark appreciated after February 1985. West German prices seem to have moved up during Deutschmark depreciation and down during appreciation, with US prices relatively steady. There was no ratchet such as took place on the upside during the 1970s or the downside in the 1930s. The historical analysis seems not to have applied, probably because world prices were slipping consistently during the 1980s until early 1987. Commodity schemes such as that for tin and coffee collapsed. The Green revolution and the policies of the European Community in agriculture depressed world food prices. Such a commodity as copper was hurt by the development of optic fibers. With Third World and other primary product prices falling, depreciation of the Deutschmark to 1985 and of the dollar thereafter did not produce the inflationary conditions of the 1970s.

Before the stock-market decline in October 1987, there were signs that this was changing. Raw material prices rose substantially in many commodities from the fall of 1986 or the early months of 1987 through September. There was fear that if the dollar depreciated still further, it would be highly inflationary, perhaps restoring the ratchet of the 1970s on the up side. The stock-market crash of October 1987 seems to have differed from that of 1929, as I write, in that the liquidity squeeze in the stock market has not been communicated to commodities. Not only has the ratchet model of the 1930s and the 1970s been suspended, but the connection between share prices and commodity prices that played a major role in the 1929 depression is out of action – thus far – as well.

This experience leads me once again to emphasize that in the real world it is necessary to change models frequently. As economists we are trained to look for models which are general, and to distrust *ad hoc* explanations. At the same time, it is vital to recognize that differences in the initial conditions may require changes of models from those that have functioned well on earlier occasions.

References

Bank for International Settlements (1982), *Fifty-second Annual Report, 1st April 1981 to 31st March 1982*, Basle.

Bisson, Thomas N. (1979), *Conservation of Coinage, Monetary Exploitation and Restraint in France, Catalonia and Aragon*, c.*1000–1125 A.D.*, Oxford: Clarendon Press.

Kindleberger, Charles P. (1986), *The World in Depression, 1929–1939*, revised edn, Berkeley: University of California Press.

Nurkse, Ragnar (1949), "Balance-of-Payments Equilibrium," in American Economic Association, *Readings in the Theory of International Trade*, Philadelphia: Blakiston, pp. 1–25.

Vaubel, Roland (1977), "Free Currency Competition," *Weltwirtschaftliches Archiv*, vol. 113, no. 3, pp. 435–59.

Warren, George F. and Frank A. Pearson (1933), *Prices*, New York: Wiley.

14

The panic of 1873

The panic of 1873 fits somewhat uneasily into a discussion on crashes in the American stock market. In the first place, the panic was international, as many others including those of 1890, 1929 and 1987, have been. The title of this paper might properly be called "The panics of 1873," since there were panics in Vienna and Berlin, as well as in New York. Secondly, the United States end of the troubles was felt in the bond market, more than that for equities, and even in the market for urban building sites, especially in Chicago. These differences or extensions, do not seem to me to be sufficient reason to abandon the study. The panics of 1873, 1890 and 1929 are of particular interest for their international character and because each was followed by fairly deep depression on a global scale. That of 1873 is thus worth re-examination.

The international connections of the crash are of particular interest. National observers repeatedly insist that financial crises within their borders are of purely local origins and consequences. This has been claimed especially for the Overend, Gurney failure in London, and the *corso forzoso* (forced circulation or abandonment of the silver standard) in Italy, both of 1866, on the one hand, and for the 1890 Baring crisis and its 1893 aftermath in London, Argentina, Turin, Melbourne, New York, and probably also Johannesburg, on the other. The connections among Vienna, Berlin, Frankfurt and New York in 1873 were more

*Paper prepared for a Conference on Financial Panics held on October 19, 1988 at the Salomon Brothers Center for the Study of Financial Institutions, New York University, first published in 1990 in *Crashes and Panics in Historical Perspective*, a Salomon Brothers Center Book.

readily recognized (except by Emden, 1938, p. 183, who claims the Jay Cooke failure to be independent of the Viennese *Krach*). Friedman and Schwartz (1963) insist that the 1920–1 and 1929 stock-market crashes originated solely in the United States, pointing to the gold inflows of the periods as proof. But connections between financial markets and macro-economies extend beyond those running solely through money flows. Booms and busts can both be spread by money movements, to be sure, but also by arbitrage in internationally-traded commodities and securities, through the foreign-trade multiplier connecting incomes in two countries through trade between them, and especially by psychological responses in one or more markets to trouble in another. The market (or markets) that follows marks down its prices along with prices in the originating one, shifting both demand and supply curves, if one needs to think in those terms, without transactions between the markets necessarily taking place. Especially of relevance to 1873, one market may precipitate a recession, a depression and even a crash in another by halting lending to it at a time when the earlier recipient had come to depend on a regular inflow. The events of 1873 provide a striking example of a dictum of R.C.O. Matthews (1954, p. 69), applied by him to 1836–9, in the question whether the trouble started in Britain or in the United States: "It is futile to draw any hard-and-fast rule assigning to either country causal primacy in the cycle as a whole or its individual phases."

I start with a model which is perhaps familiar to those who know my book *Manias, Panics and Crashes: A Study of Financial Crises* (1989). There is a "displacement" or autonomous event or shock that changes investment opportunities. Some old lines of investment may be closed down, but especially some new are opened up. Prices in the new lines rise. Gains are made. More investment follows. The process can cumulate, accelerate, pick up speed, become euphoric, and verge on irrationality. To quote from the *Chicago Tribune* of April 13, 1890, on the contemporary land boom:

> In the ruin of all collapsed booms is to be found the work of men who bought property at prices they knew perfectly well were fictitious, but who were willing to pay such prices simply because they knew that some still greater fool could be depended on to take the property off their hands and leave them with a profit. (Quoted in Hoyt 1933, p. 165)

A stage of "overtrading" or "overshooting" equilibrium levels may be reached. After a time, expectations of continued price rises in the asset weakens and may even be reversed. The period in which expectations are weakening is known as "distress." The expectations that had led to a crescendo of movement out of liquid assets such as money into long-term or equity assets reverse themselves, gradually or precipitously. If the reversal is precipitous, there is a crash and perhaps a panic.

In this history of manic episodes followed by market collapse it is often clear what the displacement was. The period leading up to 1873, on the other hand, had a great many, making it difficult to rank them in importance. In chronological order they were:

1. The end of the Civil War in the United States.
2. The Prussian–Austrian war of 1866.
3. The Overend, Gurney crash in Britain, again in 1866.
4. The *Wunderharvest* in wheat in Austria in 1867, a year when the rest of Europe experienced short crops, that gave a life to Austrian railroad traffic and exports.
5. The opening of the Suez canal in 1869.
6. The Franco-Prussian War of 1870–1.
7. The astounding success of the Thier *rentes*, issued in 1871 and 1872 to recycle the 5-billion-franc indemnity paid by France to Prussia.
8. The Chicago fire of October 1871.
9. The mistake of German monetary authorities in paying out gold coins minted from a portion of the indemnity payment before the silver coins to be withdrawn had been retired.
10. Relaxation of German banking laws.

There were also a number of lesser but still disturbing events:

11. The Crédit Mobilier scandal in the finance of the Erie and Union Pacific railroads.
12. The US claims against Britain for having outfitted and supported the Confederate naval vessel *Alabama* that preyed on Northern shipping.
13. The Granger movement in the West with farm groups fighting the expanding railroads regarded as avaricious monopolies by legislating limits on the rates charged for handling, storing, and shipping farm products.

Of particular importance in the relations between Europe and the United States was that different countries in Europe participated in the boom at its height in 1872–3 in varying degrees. France was relatively depressed as it sought to raise a portion of the indemnity through taxation. Britain had already been through a railway mania in 1847, with a moderated reprise in 1857, so that it was not caught up in domestic-investment euphoria in the same way as Germany, Austria and Hungary. Moreover, it had just experienced the Overend, Gurney panic of 1866, largely associated with foreign investment in the Mediterranean, especially Egypt and Greece, and in shipping, and was in consequence wary of investment excitement. Britain functioned in fact to a degree as a balance wheel between central Europe and the United States, absorbing US government and railroad bonds sold by German investors to acquire funds for investment at home (Simon, 1979, pp. 101, 127, 145), and fine-tuning the short-term capital market as the French indemnity transfer took place to a large extent through sterling bills. It did so by frequent changes of the Bank of England discount rate – 24 in 1873 alone.

Foremost among the displacements in 1871–2 in Europe was the payment of the 5-billion-franc indemnity of France to Prussia which the latter shared with other German states as the Reich was founded. Significant monetary changes followed from the payment of 512 million francs in gold and silver, plus the drawing of gold from London with sterling exchange. This part of the payment was connected with German monetary reform, the adoption of the gold standard, and the expansion of the money supply through the issuance of gold coin before calling in the silver, widely noted as a mistake (Åkerman, 1957, p. 341; Wirth, 1968, pp. 456–8; Zucker, 1975, pp. 68–9). In three years the circulation of thalers, later renamed marks, tripled from 254 millions to 762 million (Wirth, 1968, p. 438).

The bulk of the rest of the indemnity was paid off by September 1873 recycling. The French raised two massive bond issues at home (the Thier *rentes*) in June 1871 and July 1872 that were subscribed to by French investors, some of whom sold their European securities to acquire the money to do so, and by investors, banks and speculators all over Europe. The real transfer occurred later as French investors reconstituted their portfolios of foreign securities, and foreign purchasers of the *rentes* sold them to take their profit and repatriated the funds.

The proceeds of the indemnity in Germany were used to pay off the debts of the German states, debts both at home and abroad. One billion marks of German state securities were estimated to have been held in Austria and the redemption of this amount led to a new boom in Austrian railroads. The Austrian railroad system had already been expanded by 16 percent in mileage and 38 percent in traffic between 1864 and 1867, the latter largely the result of the *Wunderharvest*. The liquidation of German securities led Austrian investors to a new wave of railroad investment that spread to the related industries of iron and steel and rolling stock, and especially to a major expansion in financial institutions, both general banks and a specialized type, the *Maklerbank* or broker's bank, which loaned to purchasers of securities.

In Germany itself there was a boom in banking, in railroads, and especially in construction. The formation of the Reich with Berlin as its capital attracted large numbers of people to that city and, in due course, banks that had originated in other places. Along with mixed banks like the Deutsche Bank, formed in 1872 to compete with London in the finance of German foreign trade but inevitably drawn into domestic lending by the boom, there was created a class of so-called *Baubanken*, or construction banks, that ostensibly financed building but more than anything else financed speculation in building sites. A class of millionaire peasants developed that sold their farm land in the periphery of cities, especially Berlin, and so-called "tent-cities" were built, along with barracks to accommodate the workers that poured in. Rents in Berlin doubled and trebled in a short time, and calculable reality gave way to fantasy (Pinner, 1937, pp. 202–4). Among the foremost of the *Baubanken* was one Quistorpische Vereins-Bank of Berlin, with 29 subsidiaries in the field of real estate, construction and transport. Its shares went from 191 marks on April 1, 1873, to 25½ marks the following October 10 (ibid, p. 205; Oelssner, 1953, p. 257). After paying out dividends of 20, 30 or 40 percent per annum in 1872 the prices of *Baubanken* shares fell after September 1873 to 50, 20, 10 or 5 percent of nominal capital (Pinner, 1937, p. 203). In the early years Berlin was called "Chicago on the [River] Spree" (Stern, 1977, p. 161). (I come later to the 1873 real-estate boom in Chicago, the third of five in a century, which evokes Chicago as the standard of real-estate manias (Hoyt, 1933)).

The period from 1871 to 1873 is called the *Gründerzeit*. For a time I thought this term derived from the founding of the German Reich, as in *Reichgründungszeit* (Böhme, 1966). It refers, however, to the founding of companies, companies of all kinds but especially of banks (Good, 1984, p. 164). In Austria 1,005 companies with a nominal capital of 5,560 million gulden were chartered between 1867 and 1873, including 175 banks with a nominal capital of 1.4 billion gulden, and 604 industrial firms with nominal capital of 1,337 millions. Many of these never got started, and only 516 with a nominal capital of 1,555 million gulden survived to 1874. In North Germany 265 companies with a nominal capital of 1.2 billion marks were founded in 1871; in Prussia, which made up most of North Germany, 481 firms with a capital of 1.5 billion marks were chartered in 1872, followed in 1873 by 196 companies with a nominal capital of 166 million thalers (Wirth, 1968, pp. 466–71). The data are partial and incomparable. Detailed data for Prussia in 1872 include 49 "Banks and credit institutions," with 345 million marks in capital, and 61 *Baubanken* with a capital of 227 million.

The boom in the new Reich and in Austria had the usual characteristics: widespread participation in speculative investments; service of distinguished names – largely of nobility – as members of company boards as shills to engender investor confidence; swindles of all kinds.

Wirth (1968, pp. 502–9) observes that there was an epidemic desire to become rich, and that the easy credibility of the public was never greater in any epoch. To get high returns many people "would throw their money out the window." Edmund Lasker, a member of the Prussian House of Delegates from Magdeburg, called attention in February 1873 to a series of scandals in railroad and financing involving German nobility, most notably the Arnim affair, "the most celebrated scandal of the 1870s," involving a professional ambassador to France at the time of the indemnity who was accused of arranging his negotiations so as to affect the stock market in which he had a position. Lasker also denounced collusion in the manipulation of securities between railroad promoters and officials of the Ministry of Commerce (Stern, 1977, pp. 234–42).

Distress appeared in the late summer and early fall of 1872. Wirth (1968, p. 508) observed that the bow was stretched so taut in the fall of 1872 that it threatened to snap. In Austria trade and speculation had been triumphant in 1871 and most of 1872 but at the first sign of trouble railroad securities receded into the background and more speculative bank, construction and industrial companies moved to the foreground. Already in the second half of 1872 textile firms found themselves in difficulty.

In the fall of 1872 the magic word, according to März (1968, p. 172), was the *Weltaustellung* (World Exhibition) to open on May 1, 1873, in Vienna to celebrate the twenty-fifth anniversary of the accession to the imperial throne of Francis Joseph. Hotels, cafés and places of amusement were built in abundance for the Exhibition which was expected to attract hundreds of thousands of people from all over Europe and to promote widespread prosperity. These hopes were widely exaggerated.

The Creditanstalt pulled back from participation in the market to ready itself to provide help if it were needed (ibid., pp. 177–8) – an action of a major bank getting ready to serve as a lender of next-to-last resort, and paralleling other action by money-center banks at other times, especially the largest New York banks under the National Bank Act (Sprague, 1968, pp. 15, 95, 147, 153, 230, 236–7, 239, 253, 273–4; summarized in Kindleberger, 1989, pp. 188–90), and the action of the New York banks in the spring of 1929 in cutting down brokers' loans to prepare to fill in for "out-of-town banks" and "others" when they withdrew in crisis (Kindleberger, 1986, Table 9, p. 100). Stock-market near-panic broke out in the fall of 1872, and again on April 10, 1873, but the market held on, waiting for the *deus ex machina* sought in the opening of the Exhibition (Wirth, 1968, p. 519). This period of distress has been called "a silent moratorium" (ibid., p. 508). On May 1, 1873, the Exhibition duly opened. No brilliant success was evident for the first week and on May 9 the stock market collapsed, one of a series of Black Fridays.

Berlin hung on until September 1873 when it collapsed simultaneously with the failure of Jay Cooke and Co. in Philadelphia and the closing of the New York Stock Exchange. *Baubanken* continued to lend; prices to rise. The wholesale price level rose from 107 in 1870 (1880 = 100) to 133 in 1872 and 141 in 1873. For industrial materials alone the price level went from 121 in 1870 to 159 in 1872 and 167 in 1873 (by 1879 the two indexes had fallen to 93 and 95, respectively) (Jacobs and Richter, 1935, p. 81). Wirth (1968, p. 513) observed that the writing on the wall should have been clear to all after the revelation of the scandals of Strousberg in 1872, the failure of the Deschauer Bank in Munich, and the Lasker speech of February 1873, but capital continued to be withdrawn from the solid paper of the Reich to be invested in new ventures. Interest rates tightened. In September the bourse collapsed.

The financial crises in Austria and Germany were primarily asset-market phenomena with little or nothing to do with constriction of the money supply (ibid., p. 515). Money in circulation in Austria rose slightly in the second quarter of 1873 (ibid., p. 537). The course of the money supply in Germany in 1873 is too difficult to pin down. Reichsbank figures for gold reserves and circulation do not begin until 1876 (Deutsche Bundesbank, 1976, Sections A and B.1). In 1870, before the founding of the Reichsbank in 1875, there were 38 banks of issue, with notes in circulation rising from 300 million thaler in that year to 450 million in 1872 (Zucker, 1975, p. 78). As already noted, coins in circulation rose from 250 million to three times that amount between 1870 and September 1873. When the last payment on the French indemnity had been paid on September 5, 1873, it is true, the foreign exchanges turned against Germany and it lost several hundred million marks in a few months, says Wirth (1968, p. 459), because Berlin was the dearest city in the world. How much of this occurred before the stock-market crash of September 15 is not evident, but the accounts place no stress on the gold outflow as a precipitant of the collapse. As in Austria, there was no remarkable internal drain.

The relevance of this negative information is to Anna Schwartz's (1986) attempted distinction between "real" and "pseudo" financial crises, echoed by Michael Bordo (1987, p. 3), who calls the former "true" financial crises. Real or true financial crises have bank panics that produce runs out of ordinary money into high-powered money such as bank notes, or, in the circumstances of the development of banking at the time, gold coin. Pseudo-crises do not have such drains. Both Schwartz and Bordo are convinced monetarists, and seem to need to fit financial crises into a monetarist framework. It is not clear that they get much support from the central European crisis of 1873. Bordo's (1987, pp. 2–3) agreement with Schwartz seems a little forced since a reduction in the money supply is sixth in his list of ten elements of a financial crisis, following behind, presumably in the order of importance although possibly chronologically, a change in expectations, fear of insolvency of financial institutions, attempts to convert real and/or illiquid assets into money, threats to the solvency of commercial banks and other financial institutions, and bank runs.[1] The crises in Germany, Austria (and the United States) seemed real to contemporaries, conformed to Bordo's elements and Goldsmith's definition, and produced a depression lasting to 1879, even though on Schwartz's monetarist definition it would have to be scored as a pseudo-crisis.

The theme of my work on the 1930s and on financial crises generally is that when there is no lender of last resort to halt the collapse of banking institutions they lead to extended depression (Kindleberger, 1986, ch. 14; 1989, ch. 10). In 1931 the lenders of last resort, the United States and France, were too little and too late. In the 1890 Baring crisis, the position was belatedly saved by the rapidly-rising production of gold in South Africa, but only after financial crises in Australia and the United States in 1893 and a depression that extended to 1896. In 1873, a feeble effort was made to staunch the wound to the financial system in Austria: a support fund (*Aushilfsfond*) of 20 million gulden was established, with the national bank contributing 5 million, the state 3 million and the Creditanstalt 2 million to be lent on solid securities. Suspension of the Bank Act, on the analogy of Bank of England action in 1847, 1857 and 1866, was discussed on Sunday, May 11, 1873, and put into effect the next day, but the limit to the issuance of uncovered gulden notes was set at 100 million, a limit that violated the Bagehot prescription that the lender of last resort should lend freely. März (1968, p. 179) comments that the suspension of the Bank Act was awkward in meeting the needs of the moment because the crisis was due to overproduction, not to a scarcity of money.

Money shrank after Black Friday. In October, following the German crash, it became apparent that the Bodenkreditanstalt and its associated banks were in trouble. This time the government helped on a more generous scale because much of the lending by the group had been on domain lands (owned by the emperor) and was regarded abroad as equivalent to government debt. März (1968, p. 181) hints that the greater governmental energy in saving this banking group may have been the consequence of the felt need to protect highly-placed persons who had gambled with the Bankverein's money (ibid., p. 181). The lender-of-last resort function tends as a rule to raise the insider–outsider problem of who should be saved, an inescapable political aspect.

In a passage that evokes the plight of the thrift institutions in

California and the southwest United States today, März (1968, p. 179) observes that the Creditanstalt tried (in vain) to rescue the *Baubanken*, including among its tools the device of merging them.

Lender-of-last-resort steps in Germany were virtually excluded by the transitions getting under way from the thirty-odd principalities and free cities to the Reich, from 38 banks of issue – although only one of them, the Prussian National Bank, was of any size – to the Reichsbank which opened its doors in 1876. There was also the clumsily handled transition from bimetalism to the gold standard. Transitions, it is generally recognized, make decisive action in crises difficult. In the great depression in the United States there were three such, from the monetary leadership of the Federal Reserve Bank of New York to that of the Federal Reserve Board in Washington, from the retiring president, Herbert Hoover, to Roosevelt who was elected in November 1932 but took office only six months later, and from the international economic leadership of Britain, which yielded it in the summer of 1932, to that of the United States which picked up the burden piecemeal between 1936 and perhaps the Lend-Lease Act of 1941 or the Marshall Plan of 1947. In addition to the major transitions in Germany, there were financial innovations that confused matters – continuous legislation with regard to coinage, the retirement of small notes and of foreign coins (Borchardt, 1976, pp. 6ff.), and financial deregulation which stimulated the formation of the *Baubanken.* Innovation in banking tends to be underpriced, according to the Cross Report (Bank for International Settlements, 1986, ch. 10), and to lead to what Adam Smith and the classical economists call "overtrading." The German economy was suffused with vigor partly as a consequence of the founding of the German empire, and eventually pulled itself out of the slump. It is hard to find in the literature, however, a recognition of the role of the lender of last resort.

One tragic aspect of the German depression from 1873 to 1879 is that it turned German public opinion against liberalism (Lambi, 1963, ch. vi). Some observers attribute the shift of Bismarck's trade policy from one of low tariffs to the notorious tariff of rye and iron to this shift. Agriculture, in particular, had not been helped by the boom, except for peasants around cities, and was prepared to desert free trade when its exports gave way to import competition from new lands. In addition, the depression gave rise to a wave of anti-Semitism on the ground that Jewish speculators had been prominent among the beneficiaries on the boom, and among the swindlers (ibid., p. 84; Good, 1984, p. 163).

Connections between economic conditions in Germany and Austria and those in the United States went back to the end of the Civil War in 1865. Central Europe was depressed from 1866 to 1869, partly as a result of the Prussian war against Austria, and this, combined with recovery in the United States, produced a large-scale movement of capital westward to New York from Cologne, Berlin and especially Frankfurt. Matthew Simon (1979) estimates the total capital inflow into the United States from June 1865 to June 1873 as roughly $1 billion, starting relatively slowly at about $100 million a year, picking up to $175 million in 1869 and reaching a peak of $259 million in 1872, before declining to $114 million in 1873 and $100 million in each of 1874 and 1875 (all fiscal years, ended June 30).

Most of this investment up to 1870 was in US government bonds issued during and after the war, notably the 5-20s (5 percent, 20-year bonds) issued in 1862, 1865 and 1867. Immediately after the war these bonds fell in price to very low levels and were bought speculatively. Later, as the US government ran sizable budget surpluses from 1866 to 1871 and reduced its gross debt from $2.7 billion at the end of fiscal 1865 to $2.3 billion six years later, and the gold agio declined from a high of 185 percent in 1865 to 25 percent in 1869–70 and 11 percent in 1874–5, there were assured opportunities for gain (Simon, 1979, pp. 34, 113). The flow from central Europe slowed down in 1866 with the Prussian attack on Austria, and again in July 1870 at the outbreak of the Franco-Prussian War. Panics such as Overend, Gurney and war scares produce two effects on capital movements, according to Simon (1979, p. 92): capital flight which stimulated the purchase of American securities; and building up cash on hand, "the liquidity motive," to be ready for any eventuality, that leads to selling foreign assets. Which motive dominates in a given situation may depend on other factors. From 1866 to 1869 depression in Europe resulted in a greater outflow than the mobilization of cash (ibid., p. 97). In 1870, however, the liquidity motive prevailed (ibid., p. 101). The rise in the prices of US government bonds and the possibilities of a boom in railroad also played a part in the earlier period, a pull as opposed to a push. In 1870 the disturbed market in Europe meant that the US Treasury's attempt to refinance outstanding debt by issuing $200 million of 10-5s, $300 million of 15-4½s and $1 billion of 30-4s, resulted in failure (ibid., p. 105).

The proceeds of bonds sold by US investors to Europe or redeemed by the US government were largely invested in US railroads, pushing their way west. The railroad network expanded rapidly after the Civil War, from 35,000 miles at the end of 1865 to 53,000 miles five years later, and 70,500 miles at the end of 1873 (Bureau of Census, 1949, p. 200).

Jay Cooke and Co. got its financial start by a major innovation in the marketing of US war bonds in aggressive domestic sales campaigns designed to appeal to mass support rather than merely established financial circles. His success did not make him a favorite of established bankers like Drexel in Philadelphia and Morgan in New York. Like the Pereire brothers in France who failed in 1868, he was an "active" banker, rather than a passive one like the Drexels, Morgans and Rothschilds in Paris (Gras, 1936, p. xi; Larson, 1936, pp. 86–7, 433). The financial history of the nineteenth century is sometimes written in terms of bankers' quarrels, and the distinction between active and passive bankers is echoed in the current controversy whether bankers lending to the Third World in the 1970s were "loan pushers" or "wall flowers, waiting to be asked to dance" (Darity and Horn, 1988).

Cooke's success in marketing US government bonds at home meant that he was late in moving in two other directions, in selling bonds abroad and in entering the market for railroad bonds. When he did move in the latter direction, the eastern railroads such as the Baltimore and Ohio banked by the Brown Brothers, the Chesapeake and Ohio by Alexander Brown, and the Pennsylvania by Drexel already had established connections, as did some newer lines – the Rock Island (Henry Clews), the Union Pacific (the Ciscos) and the Central Pacific (Fisk and Hatch) (Larson, 1936, pp. 245, 257). In addition the Central Pacific and the Union Pacific had governmental subsidies (ibid., p. 259). Like latecomers in many businesses, Jay Cooke was forced to take what was left over, and palpably more risky in his case, the Northern Pacific. This led westward from Duluth, Minnesota, through sparsely settled country. It was hoped to sell land from the abundant grant as the lines reached further west, though the terms would produce little cash, and to sell more bonds in the United States and in Germany as progress was made. Land offices were opened in Germany, Holland and Scandinavia in the hope of attracting settlers. But selling Northern Pacific bonds proved slow, especially when Missouri Pacific bonds through more settled territory were available at around $90 and Union Pacific at $84. European investors held US railroad bonds in considerable disrepute, especially after the Erie and Union Pacific Crédit Mobilier scandals of 1868 and 1872. Cooke failed to enlist the support in Europe of the Rothschilds or Bleichröder, and was forced to form a connection with a new house, Budge, Schill & Co. of Frankfurt. When the Franco-Prussian war broke out the prospect of selling Northern Pacific bonds in Germany evaporated.

Cooke had many other troubles: an absentee president of the line who incautiously bought supplies with cash well in advance of need rather than inducing suppliers to grant long credits or accept bonds. His brother Henry, who ran the Washington lobbying office, lived high and was a drain. Substantial investments in advertising and support of newspapers in Europe failed to pay off in the light of US railroad scandals. Bit by bit, Jay Cooke and Co. found itself advancing capital to the Northern Pacific for construction. In the fall of 1872 the London partner, Fahnestock, observed that it was cruel to the depositors to use their money to support Northern Pacific bonds, and that the railroad should go to the market to borrow at any price. The near-panic in the market of September 1872 made this impossible. Both Northern Pacific and Southern Pacific pushed for Congressional subsidy of $40,000 a mile, but the scandals in Erie and the Union Pacific made Congress leery.

The scramble to keep Northern Pacific and Jay Cooke and Co. afloat lasted until September 1873, when the storm broke in the second week. The Granger movement in the West attacked railroad rates. Money was tight as funds were withdrawn from the East to finance an early heavy harvest. The New York Warehouse and Security Company suspended on September 8. Formed to lend on grain and other farm produce, like Jay Cooke it had been induced into lending to the Missouri, Kansas and Texas railroad. On September 13 the banking house Kenyon, Cox & Co. failed as a result of endorsing a note of the Canada Southern railroad for $1.5 million which the latter could not pay. Jay Cooke and Co. closed its doors on September 18, and Fisk and Hatch the next day (Black Friday), followed by the Union Trust Company and the National Bank of the Commonwealth on Saturday, September 20. The stock market was closed that day and remained so for ten days, a move later agreed to have been mistaken in so far as it induced a panic withdrawal of brokers' loans in October 1929 for fear of a closing of the exchange. The *Commercial and Financial Chronicle* of September 20, 1873, blamed the crash on the excessive tightness of the money market that prevailed without interruption from September 1872 to May 1873, making it impossible for railroad companies to borrow on bonds and leading several banking houses negotiating large railroad loans or intimately connected with the building of the roads to become responsible by endorsement of loans or by borrowing on call loans collateralized by railroad securities. "In this delicate situation, the equilibrium was liable to be violently disturbed" (quoted in Sprague, 1968, p. 36). The newspaper account makes no reference to the decline in foreign lending from Europe, but it is clear that the tightness of money rates in the market from September 1872 to the following May is associated with the decline in foreign funds.

The collapse of the bond and stock market in New York in September 1873 also put paid to the land boom in Chicago. Public participation in land buying, according to Hoyt (1933, p. 100), began about 1868 when many cases of large profits made in land since 1861 became common knowledge. In 1871 one writer claimed that every other man and every fourth woman had an investment in lots. The Chicago fire of October 8, 1871 destroyed 17,450 of the 60,000 homes in the city, but the fire accentuated rather than slowed down the growth of the city, with a year of "hectic borrowing" from the East, and the spending of $40 million for new construction (ibid., p. 102). Population in a belt within three to five miles of the center grew from 8,000 in 1860 to 55,000 in 1870 and nearly 100,000 in 1873. Land prices went from $500 to $10,000 an acre between 1865 and 1873 in the fashionable residential area of the South Side, and some land near the village of Hyde Park from $100 an acre to $15,000 (ibid., pp. 107–9). The euphoric aspect of the boom and the dangerous position of land speculators in the summer of 1873 is described by Hoyt (1933, p. 117) in terms of

> municipal extravagance, excessive outlays on magnificent business blocks built at high cost on borrowed money, lavish expenditure on street improvements in sections where they were not required, overextended subdivision activity, and a disproportionately large amount of real estate purchases on small down payments – all these had been the result of the extreme optimism of the times.

In the summer of 1873, the upward movement of land values stopped as a consequence of limited cash resources of prospective buyers as wages fell. Moreover, Hoyt (1933, ch. XIV) comments, as land values cease to rise the desire to purchase it falls off sharply as expectations of a fall replace those of a rise. There was a lull in activity from May to September 1873 when the Jay Cooke failure was make known, and then a collapse in land values and building prices.

At first on such occasions that occurred in 1837, 1857, 1873, 1893 and 1929, the stock-market crash shatters the hopes of gain, but has no other result. Debts contracted to purchase land or buildings are for a term, not on demand. There has been no short selling, and no forced liquidation. Owners of real estate, indeed, tend to congratulate themselves that they escaped more lightly than the owners of stocks or of defaulted bonds. There follows, however, a process of attrition (ibid., p. 400). The decline of industry lowers prices. Unemployment induces recent arrivals to return to the country. Gross income from rentals declines sharply, but expenses of interest and taxes remain the same. Landholders retain their ownership until the constant attrition of interest charges, taxes and penalties or the inability to renew mortgages brings foreclosures that squeeze out the equities above the mortgage. Hoyt (1933, pp. 119, 124) comments that it takes about four or five years to complete this process and thoroughly to deflate land values. The process often cripples banks. In Chicago in 1933, 163 out of 200 banks suspended, and a footnote (Hoyt, 1933, p. 401) observes that real estate was the largest single factor in the failure of 4,800 banks in the period 1930–3.

It would be useful to have a comparable study of land values in Berlin and Vienna in the years after the crash of 1873. I call attention to the spread of deflation from the bond and stock market in New York to the market for real estate in Chicago, as it may furnish food for thought about the delayed effects of the October 19, 1987 decline in the stock market on the markets for office buildings, condominia, shopping malls, hotels and the like, including especially luxury housing. There is, of course, the major difference that real estate today has built-in lenders of last resort in the Federal Deposit Insurance Corporation and the Federal Savings and Loan Insurance Corporation, troubled as those institutions are.

Notes

1. Compare Goldsmith's (1982, p. 42) definition that includes no mention of money: "a sharp, brief, ultracyclical deterioration of all or most financial indicators – short-term interest rates, asset (stock, real estate, land) prices, commercial involvements and failures of financial institutions." Goldsmith regards financial troubles of the 1960s and 1970s in the United States as at most potential or near-crises, and does not regard foreign-exchange difficulties as a necessary concomitant of financial crises.

References

Åkerman, Johan (1957), *Structure et cycles économiques*, vol. II, Paris: Presses Universitaires de France.

Bank for International Settlements (1956), *Recent Innovations in International Banking* (Cross Report), Prepared by a Study Group established by the Central Banks of the Group of Ten Countries, Basle: Bank for International Settlements.

Böhme, Helmut (1966), *Deutschlands Weg zur Grossmacht. Studien zum Verhältnis von Wirtschaft und Staat während der Gründungszeit, 1848–1861*, Cologne: Kiepenheuer & Witsch.

Borchardt, Knut (1976), "Währungs- und Finanzpolitik von der Reichsgründung bis zum 1. Weltkrieg," in Deutsche Bundesbank, *Währung und Wirtschaft in Deutschland, 1876–1975*, Frankfurt am Main: Fritz Knapp.

Bordo, Michael D. (1987), "Financial Crises: Lessons from History," unpublished paper presented to the 5th Garderen Conference on International Finance, Erasmus Universiteit, Rotterdam.

Bureau of the Census, Department of Commerce, (1949), *Historical Statistics of the United States, 1789–1945*, Washington, DC: US Government Printing Office.

Darity, William Jr. and Bobbie L. Horn (1988), *The Loan Pushers: The Role of Commercial Banks in the International Debt Crisis*, Cambridge, Mass.: Ballinger.

Deutsche Bundesbank (1976), *Deutsches Geld- und Bankwesen in Zahlen, 1876–1975*, Frankfurt am Main: Fritz Knapp.

Emden, Paul H. (1938), *Money Powers of Europe of the Nineteenth and Twentieth Centuries*, London: Sampson, Low, Marston & Co.

Friedman, Milton and Schwartz, Anna J. (1963), *A Monetary History of the United States, 1867–1960*, Princeton, NJ: Princeton University Press.

Good, David (1984), *The Economic Rise of the Habsburg Empire, 1750 to 1914*, Berkeley: University of California Press.

Goldsmith, Raymond W. (1982), "Comment" on Hyman P. Minsky, "The Financial Instability Hypothesis: Capitalist Processes and the Behavior of the Economy," in C.P. Kindleberger and J.-P. Laffargue, eds, *Financial Crises: Theory, History and Policy*, Cambridge: Cambridge University Press.

Gras, N.S.B. (1936), "Editor's Introduction" to Henrietta M. Larson, *Jay Cooke, Private Banker*, Cambridge, Mass.: Harvard University Press.

Hoyt, Homer (1933), *One Hundred Years of Land Values in Chicago: The Relationship of the Growth of Chicago to the Rise in Its Land Values, 1830–1933*, Chicago: University of Chicago Press.

Jacobs, A. and H. Richter (1935), "Die Grosshandelspreise in Deutschland von 1792 bis 1934," *Sonderhefte des Instituts fur Konjunkturforschung*, no. 37.

Kindleberger, Charles P. (1986), *The World in Depression, 1929–39*, revised edn, Berkeley: University of California Press.

Kindleberger, Charles P. (1989), *Manias, Panics and Crashes: A History of Financial Crises*, revised edn, New York: Basic Books.

Lambi, Ivo Nikolai (1963), *Free Trade and Protection in Germany, 1868–1879*, Wiesbaden: Franz Steiner.

Larson, Henrietta M. (1936), *Jay Cooke, Private Banker*, Cambridge, Mass.: Harvard University Press.

März, Eduard (1968), *Österreichische Industrie- und Bankpolitik in der Zeit Franz Joseph I. am Beispiel der k. k. priv. Österreischischen Creditanstalt für Handel und Gewerbe*, Vienna: Europa.

Matthews, R.C.O. (1954), *A Study in Trade-Cycle History: Economic Fluctuations in Great Britain, 1832–1842*, Cambridge: Cambridge University Press.

Oelssner, Fred (1953), *Die Wirtschaftkrisen*, vol. 1, *Die Krisen im vormonopolistischen Kapitalismus*, Berlin: Dietz.

Pinner, Felix (1937), *Die grossen Weltkrisen im Lichte des Structurwandels der Kapitalistischen Wirtschaft*, Zurich and Leipzig: Max Niehans.

Schwartz, Anna J. (1986), "Real and Pseudo Financial Crises," in F. Capie and G.E.G.E. Wood, eds, *Financial Crises and the World Banking System*, London: Macmillan.

Simon, Matthew (1979), *Cyclical Fluctuations and the International Capital Movements of the United States, 1865–1897*, New York: Arno Press; first published 1955.

Sprague, O.M.W. (1968), *History of Crises under the National Banking System*, for the National Monetary Commission, New York: August M. Kelley; first published 1910.

Stern, Fritz (1977), *Gold and Iron: Bismarck, Bleichröder and the Building of the German Empire*: London: Allen & Unwin.

Wirth, Max (1968), *Geschichte der Handelskrisen*, 3rd edn, New York: Burt Franklin; first published 1890.
Zucker, Stanley (1975), *Ludwig Bamberger*, *German Liberal Politician and Social Critic*, *1823–1899*, Pittsburgh, Pa.: University of Pittsburg Press.

15

Capital flight: A historical perspective

It is difficult – perhaps impossible – to make a rigorous definition of capital flight for the purpose of devising policies to cope with it. Do we restrict cases to domestic capital sent abroad, or should foreign capital precipitously pulled out of a country be included? What about the capital that emigrants take with them, or send ahead of them, especially when the people involved are being persecuted – Huguenots from France following the revocation of the Edict of Nantes in 1685, noble *émigrés* after the French Revolution of 1789 and especially the Reign of Terror in 1793, German Jews or Jews in the countries neighboring Germany during the decade of National Socialism? Does it make a difference whether the emigration is likely to be permanent or temporary, to the extent that one can tell *ex ante*? And what about the cases where there is no net export of capital, but capital is sent abroad to be returned to the country as foreign investment – French investors buying bonds of the Chemin de Fer du Nord issued in London in the 1840s (Platt, 1984, ch. 2), or Argentinian investors buying their country's own securities issued in London both before 1914 and in the 1920s? Is there a valid distinction to be made between capital that is expatriated on a long-term basis for fear of confiscatory taxation, and domestic speculation against the national currency through buying

* Published as Chapter 2 of Donald R. Lessard and John Williamson, eds, *Capital Flight and Third World Debt*, Washington, DC: Institute for International Economics, 1987, the proceeds of a conference held at the Institute in October 1986. The paper was written when I was a United Nations University scholar at the World Institute for Development Economic Research (WIDER) in Helsinki in the summer of 1986. I express gratitude to WIDER for their support, and to Carl-Ludwig Holtfrerich and Eric S. Schubert for helpful comments on an earlier draft.

foreign exchange that is ostensibly interested in short-term profits? The distinctions are elusive, and it is not clear how much they matter to the questions of how to prevent capital flight or to attract it back, except perhaps in the case of refugees escaping persecution who manage to take some or all of their capital with them.

In his article on capital flight at the depth of the great depression, Machlup (1932) left the inference that capital flight was unimportant provided that the monetary authorities pursued proper policies. If the authorities refused to accommodate the attempt to raise liquid funds at home, capital flight would raise interest rates, lower prices and start a transfer process automatically. Difficulty might be encountered if the funds were not invested abroad but hoarded, since transfer is assisted by expansion in the receiving country as well as contraction in the sending. Machlup recognized that the deflation in the sending country might have serious consequences in bank failures and the like, but at the time professed an Austrian view of macro-economic policy that blamed the troubles of any bank in difficulty from falling prices on its own misuse of credit.[1]

I started to write this paper as a series of historical episodes, concentrating on the following cases:

France

- 1685 (and earlier) to 1700: revocation of the Edict of Nantes.
- 1720: safeguarding the profits of the Mississippi bubble.
- 1789–97: capital flight from the French Revolution, the *assignats*, and the Terror, and the return.
- French purchases of French bonds issued in London in the 1840s.
- The speculative attack against the franc in 1924 and the successful "squeeze."
- The 1926 Poincaré stabilization following the extreme depreciation of May–June 1926.
- The 1936 middle-class strike against the Front Populaire.
- The 1968 middle-class strike against the Accord de Grenelle.
- The 1981–2 middle-class strike against the Mitterrand socialist campaign of nationalization.

Italy

- 1866 and the onset of the *corso forzoso* that was finally halted in 1881.
- Foreign-exchange controls of the 1930s.
- The 1961–3 flight of banknotes smuggled into Switzerland, representing a middle-class strike against the nationalization of the electricity industry.

Germany

- The outflow of German capital during the hyperinflation of 1919–23.
- 1931 outflow leading to the Standstill Agreement.
- Foreign-exchange control with the death penalty for evasion in the 1930s.

Latin America

- Some comments on international financial intermediation through Latino purchases of bonds issued abroad for Latin American account.
- One or two comments on the present capital outflow.

After an extended false start, I changed to an analytical approach. Before presenting it in outline, I note that my background is in European financial history, and I lack all but the most superficial knowledge of Latin American capital flight. One should further observe that there are no English or Scandinavian episodes of an outstanding nature to draw on, despite speculation against sterling at various times through leads and lags and the purchase of Kaffirs in London and their sale in Johannesburg.

The analytical outline conforms to taxonomies of the means of capital escaping a country, on the one hand, and of measures to prevent it or entice it back, on the other. The outflow of flight capital can be financed by the following means:

- Outflow of specie, especially important regarding the Huguenots, safeguarding the profits on the Mississippi bubble, the *émigrés* of the French Revolution, and in the outflow from Italy in 1866.
- Real transfer, through deflation; through the export and sale of valuables or in hyperinflation short-circuiting the exchange market by shipping goods abroad directly and retaining the proceeds; and through exchange depreciation, particularly relevant to France in the 1920s.
- Various types of countervailing inflow, including: governmental borrowing abroad (the case where domestic investors subscribe to foreign issues of their government or major domestic borrowers may not qualify as capital flight, but in any event arises from somewhat similar motivation); loss of foreign-exchange reserves; central-bank borrowing; monetary constriction at home to raise interest rates and attract a capital inflow; depreciation of the currency, leading to foreign speculative purchases betting on revaluation; dumping of currency in foreign markets purchased by foreigners for speculation or use.

While these various means of financing a capital outflow are analytically distinct, they may, of course, occur together, either simultaneously or in series. The price-specie-flow mechanism, for example, in principle starts with an outflow of specie that leads to deflation.

The taxonomy of measures to prevent capital flight or entice it back overlaps to some degree with the means of financing it. For example, deflation helps finance real transfer of capital exports, and at the same time, by making it more expensive, tends to cut it off. Again, the various measures are in many cases possible complements as well as substitutes.

The following alternatives are available to the country losing the capital:

- Ignore it. It sometimes pays to let a movement based upon a swing of sentiment burn out, holding various policies steady. This is especially relevant to the intermediation cases – the French buying bonds issued by French entities in London, or Argentinian investors buying Argentinian bonds issued abroad. The intermediary function of the foreign-bond underwriter often leads, after learning, to direct dealing.
- Deflate through monetary and fiscal measures to the extent possible within political constraints, and lengthen the term structure of government debt to lock in possible flight capital and entice that abroad back through high yields. The French government's inability to refund at long term the short *bons de le défense nationale* in the 1920s was the key weakness in its weaponry.
- Use exchange-rate policy, including: holding the rate, with own funds or swaps, or both; devalue to a credible rate and exhibit determination to hold it; with own or borrowed funds run the rate up to "squeeze" those with a short position, as in the 1924 French operation and the US dollar action of October 1978; impose exchange control with prohibitions or a multiple exchange-rate system, possibly with separate rates for the current and the capital accounts (though these are virtually impossible to operate even when backed by the death penalty, and certainly not without inspection of mail and regulation of credit terms on trade and service transactions that are difficult of public acceptance).
- Implement a monetary reform of sufficient scope and determination to win credibility, for example, the replacement of the mark by the Rentenmark and then the Reichsmark in 1923 and 1924.

Receiving countries have also sought to repel hot money from abroad by a variety of expedients:

- They may allow the currency to appreciate. The classic instance is the rise of the pound sterling to a high of well over $5.00 in 1936 to divert French capital from London to New York.

- They may set special reserve requirements against foreign bank deposits, a technique developed especially by Switzerland and the Federal Republic of Germany.
- They may threaten to report foreign owners of capital to their home governments. This is not only unattractive commercially, but is readily frustrated by the use of domestic nominees.
- The usual tactic is to ignore the influx and regard the problem as one for the authorities in the country from which the capital comes. In the "Golden Avalanche" of 1937, stimulated by the prospect of a reduction of the US gold price, the American authorities hung on, until the likelihood of a policy change vanished with the September recession.
- Other means of limiting inflows of capital through reporting mechanisms have been explored, especially in such cases as communications companies where foreign investment is limited by law (for example, ITT in the 1930s), or where the Securities and Exchange Commission (SEC) rules call for the identification of individual holders with more than 5 percent of the stock of a given company. Such regulations are difficult and probably impossible to apply generally.

Financing capital flight mainly through specie

It is perhaps only of antiquarian interest to explore the three French cases of capital flight in the seventeenth and eighteenth centuries with a somewhat primitive monetary system, but some interesting points emerge. The revocation of the Edict of Nantes, it will be recalled, took place in 1685 but was foreshadowed several years earlier by a policy of quartering dragoons on Protestants who refused to abjure and embrace Catholicism. A short, sharp outflow of capital took place, mainly in the form of coin, but also in jewelry and plate, wine, and bills of exchange bought from Catholic bankers in all large cities, from government agents in Paris and elsewhere, from the Swiss in Lyons and from foreign diplomatic representatives in France (Scoville, 1960, p. 296). Scoville's discussion of the "Effects of the Revocation on Finance and Agriculture" gives a great deal of anecdotal detail concerning individual escapes with and without valuables, but is unable to pin down an estimated loss between the extreme estimates of 1 billion livres (say £40 million) and a derisorily low figure of 5 million or 1.25 million livres, depending upon whether the emigrants amounted to 200,000 persons at 25 livres a head or 50,000 (ibid., p. 291). Other estimates are offered of 150 million livres, and, by a scholar whom Scoville characterizes as less cautious, 360 million. Incidentally, Scoville accepts the estimate of approximately 200,000 emigrants out of a total of 2 million Protestants, divided roughly between 40,000 to 50,000 to England, 50,000 to 75,000 to Holland, and to Switzerland (largely Geneva) 60,000 gross and 25,000 net,[2] with others to Germany, Ireland and overseas (ibid., pp. 120–7). Louis XIV made an attempt to bring back the sailors among these numbers to strengthen the French navy, but I do not see that any systematic attempt was made to woo others. Many remained in close touch with their 1,800,000 coreligionists who had abjured, mostly insincerely.

Some evidence concerning the loss of specie is available in the receiving countries. The London mint is reported to have coined 960,000 louis d'or (of 23 livres or approximately one pound sterling each) as a consequence of the influx (ibid., pp. 292, 299). In the early eighteenth century, the Huguenots contributed some 10 percent of the wealth of Britain in the funded debt of England and Bank of England shares, having wider and deeper financial experience gained from dealing in *rentes* (Carter, 1975, esp. ch. 7). The annual figures available for the Bank of Amsterdam for January 31 show an increase in deposits – for the most part specie – from 5.17 million guilders (approximately £465,000) in 1676 to 8.28 million guilders in 1681, 12.71 million guilders in 1689 and a peak of 16.75 million guilders in 1699. Assuming, for the sake of argument, that the Bank of Amsterdam's dealings with other customers than French canceled out, and that the increase of 11.58 million guilders or over 23 million livres was entirely due to the Huguenots, the amount was about £1 million or roughly the same as the louis d'or minted in London (Van Dillen, 1964, p. 119). In any event, refugee funds were said to inundate the Dutch market and led to financiers begging for borrowers at 2 percent (Scoville, 1960, p. 292).

France was depressed for three decades at the end of the reign of Louis XIV, but neither Scoville nor other writers are ready to ascribe the major blame to the revocation of the Edict of Nantes, citing, in addition, the two wars fought after 1685 against the British and bad harvests. In an early passage, Scoville states that the revocation "may well have been responsible for the long depression" (ibid., p. 129). At the end of his intensive study, however, he notes that there is not enough evidence to estimate how much the loss of specie was responsible (ibid., p. 446) and concludes that it did much less harm than most historians of the nineteenth and twentieth centuries believed (ibid., p. 446). Another channel for harm, of course, was the loss of skilled artisans in glass, silk, and paper.

The Mississippi bubble was a "system" promoted by John Law to achieve prosperity in France through the issue of paper money that additionally bid up the price of the shares of the Compagnie d'Occident operating in the French colony of Louisiana through which the Mississippi River flowed, along with other places world-wide. The Compagnie, under John Law's aggressive push, also took over a series of monopolies in France. Initially, the Banque Générale was restricted in note issue. In 1717 it gave way to the Banque Royale, which was not. Frenzied speculation in shares of the Compagnie by French investors and by hordes of foreigners who flocked to Paris drove the price from an initial value of about 200 livres, when the moribund company was reformed, to 500 in early 1719, when Law offered to buy them at that price, to 1,000 in early September, and 5,000 later in the month, from which they rose to 10,000 in November, 15,000 at the end of the year, and nearly 20,000 at the peak early in 1720 (Carswell, 1960, p. 93). These prices are, however, open to considerable question. Eric S. Schubert (1986, Table 3.1, p. 131) has compiled prices of Compagnie des Indes stock from the daily London press from October 1719 to April 1720 which show them rising from 1,000 percent of par (500 livres) or 5,000 livres to 2,000 percent or 10,000 livres on December 9, 1719, and again on April 9, 1720.

Major profit-taking by the "anti-system" – French merchants and bankers who were opposed to Law – began in the fall of 1719, although Chaussinand-Nogaret (1970, p. 143) cites a company formed in July 1718 to transfer money to Cadiz by way of Amsterdam. Keeping profits in notes was risky because they were depreciating, and even buying real property in France – although many including John Law did – was dangerous since most financial troubles in France, and ends of reigns, had been followed by *Chambres de Justice* in which excess profits – what we would perhaps call today "undue enrichment" – were examined and fined or confiscated. The problem was to get foreign assets or specie abroad. Lüthy (1959, p. 347) notes that most complicated schemes with forward markets and the like proved illusory either because of the failure of the counter-parties, the cancellation of paper money and bank accounts, or the disastrous decline of the exchange for those who tried to shift their profits abroad late. The rate (ostensibly on Swiss francs) fell from 290 in March 1720 to between 1,200 and 1,300 at the end of September (ibid., p. 367). As an example of the difficulties faced by some, Swiss bankers and merchants in Lyons complained that they were "forced to receive in paper and pay in specie, a thing which one does not practice either at Tunis or Algiers" (ibid., p. 344).

Some did get specie out despite the facts that the Swiss frontier was closed for three months because of plague in Marseilles, and that silver, more readily available than gold, was too heavy. Various routes were used for shipment of specie, including Leghorn and Genoa, as a means of sending it to Amsterdam and London (ibid., p. 369). Lüthy (ibid.) tells of the triumphs of one Jacques Huber, who won large profits speculating successively in the Mississippi bubble, the South Sea bubble and in the stock of the Dutch East India Company, each time telling his agents that he wanted to remit *espèces sonnantes* (money that would ring on the table). Mackay's (1980, p. 29) colorful account of the Mississippi scheme, written in 1852, has one Vermelet, a jobber, procuring gold and silver coin to the extent of nearly 1 million livres and taking it in a cart, covered with hay and cow dung, across the border into Belgium and ultimately Amsterdam, he dressed as a peasant. On one unspecific report, there was said to be a sudden doubling of the creditors of the Bank (Chaussinand-Nogaret, 1970, p. 172).

I can find no account of a return flow of capital to France after the liquidation of the Mississippi bubble. There was first a Chamber of Justice (called Visa II, Visa I having been the settlement after the death of Louis XIV) in which local ill-gotten gains were fined in whole or in part, although those with political protection, including a number who had used their profits to buy *offices*, were spared (Chaussinand-Nogaret, 1970, pp. 138, 149). Economic recovery had been proceeding from 1717, with the inflationary impact of the Mississippi bubble offsetting any deflationary impact of the loss of specie. After the Visa, there was some gain in confidence, it would appear, from the slim evidence furnished by the decline in deposits of the Bank of Amsterdam, which fell from 28.89 million guilders on January 31, 1721, to 15.24 million in 1727. Of particular importance was the fixing of the price of gold in France in 1726, following the similar action of Britain in 1717. France remained on the bimetallic standard, with wartime interruptions, until 1885 when the shift was made to gold, but adjustments in the bimetallic ratio were made entirely in the silver price, and the gold price, officially, was unchanged until 1928. As a further remark, it may be noted that, unlike the revocation of the Edict of Nantes, the Mississippi bubble did not involve extraordinary emigration.

The French Revolution

The French Revolution produced another flight of capital accompanied by emigration. Again for information it is necessary to look outside France. The class composition of some 87 percent of the 17,000 executed inside France has been studied by Greer (1935). Six and one-half percent were clergy, 8 percent were nobles, and 14 percent upper class according to a necessarily arbitrary categorization. The percentages of *émigrés* in these classes were doubtless much higher, as the peasants and laborers executed for their part in the counter-revolutionary movement in the Vendée, or the artisans of the uprising against the Revolution in Lyons, did not have significant *émigré* counterparts. The clergy did not bring much money with them, judging by their poverty in England, which required support from the British government, and the nobles spent what they took out freely until they, too, required subventions (Weiner, 1960). But the movement of specie to Britain beginning in 1789 picked up with the *assignats* and the Reign of Terror. The mint that normally received £650,000 a year acquired £3¾ million in 1793 and 1794 (Hawtrey, 1919, p. 261).

Seen from England, the mass of refugee money pouring into the Bank of England from France between 1789 and 1791 led to a rapid increase in the number of note-issuing country banks, and financed the canal mania (Ashton, 1959, p. 168). The panic of 1793 when the canal bubble collapsed occurred despite a continued inflow. But after the end of the Terror following the fall of Robespierre in July 1794 and the collapse of the *assignats*, a return movement of specie to France took place to provide some means of payment. The *assignats* survived somewhat longer in Paris than in the countryside, where they were refused. Even in Paris, however, prices began to be quoted in gold. Hawtrey notes that there was an enormous profit to be made on importing gold, as the premium on the louis d'or in the fall of 1795 was 20 percent higher than the premium on foreign bills (ibid., pp. 247–8). The Bank of England gold stock was also drained by British government expenditures during the war, and declined from £6¾ million in August 1794 to £2½ million in December 1796 and £1 million in February 1797 (ibid., p. 258). With the panic engendered by a trivial military incident, the Bank of England suspended payment of its notes in coin – a suspension that lasted until 1819.

The Corso Forzoso

The Italian incident of 1866 was perhaps less capital flight by Italians than a halt to French lending and an attempt to repatriate advances to Italy that led to some Italian outflow and abandonment of the silver standard following a heavy outpouring of specie. Part of the occasion was the crisis in northern Europe caused by Prussian mobilization against Austria, the Overend, Gurney crisis, and a French banking liquidity crisis caused by the collapse of cotton prices following the close of the Civil War. There had also been an internal Italian railroad and other public works boom, loosely financed. The outpouring of silver contributed to the troubles of that metal which ended in the abandonment of bimetallism everywhere. Of particular interest is that fiscal and monetary policy was orthodox, exchange depreciation moderate, and by 1881 the lira was reestablished at the old parity with a stabilization loan and a return flow of capital.

Real transfer: through deflation

This is the therapy that Machlup (1932) prescribed for capital flight. Moreover, he and Viner thought that the success of the German payment of reparations after 1928 until breakdown in 1931 showed how malleable the balance of payments was in response to an "abnormal" capital transfer such as reparations or capital flight (Machlup, 1950; Viner, 1952, p. 182). Machlup finally recanted on the ground that the political price – the breakdown of the Weimar Republic and the coming of National Socialism – was too high (Machlup, 1980, pp. 128–31).

Deflation is strong medicine not only in terms of the possibility of political breakdown. It may be institutionally difficult or impossible. French fiscal policy was strongly contractionary in so far as the deficit was wiped out and replaced with a small surplus in the period to 1925, but it was impossible for the authorities to follow up with the appropriate debt policy. They were, that is, unable to lock in French capitalists with their short-term *bons de la défense nationale* by refunding them into long-term bonds that would halt the capital outflow by driving bond prices down, and interest rates up, every time wealth-holders tried to liquidate bonds to get money with which to buy foreign exchange. Each week a sizable amount of short-term bonds became due, and the market could insist on obtaining cash for these. A fiscal program of running substantial surpluses to pay off debt was impossible, given the widespread resistance to heavier taxes. The alternative was exchange depreciation, discussed below, which effected the real transfer of capital flight.

Deflation at home may also raise interest rates to such an extent that, given the appropriate expectations, flight capital is attracted back. In the process, some continuing capital flight may be transferred by a countervailing return flow, discussed below. The conditions to assure credibility are doubtless stringent: the establishment of confidence in the stability of money, the budget, the exchange rate, plus the possibility of the one-way option that the currency can only appreciate.

Deflation may be the orthodox neoclassical remedy. It is one, however, that calls for a great many necessary conditions and it is difficult to think of a clear-cut example of its implementation. The

Poincaré stabilization of July 1926, for example, lowered taxes on the upper-income groups rather than raised them.

Real transfer: through direct export of valuables or other merchandise

It was mentioned earlier in connection with the Huguenots and the *émigrés* that escapees took valuables with them, along with specie. Valuables may also be dumped at home to get currency for transfer through the exchanges: Tiffany's moved from selling paste jewelry to real diamonds when the price of the latter fell precipitously in Paris after the fall of the Orleanist monarchy in 1848.

The more interesting case, however, is that, when a currency is breaking down in hyperinflation and virtually infinite depreciation, the exchanges may be short-circuited by those exporting capital abroad. Goods are bought at home, shipped and sold abroad, with the proceeds retained in foreign currency. This was notably true of Germany in 1922 and 1923. The later development of foreign-exchange control, of course, tries to frustrate this method of escape by requiring exporters to turn in the receipts of foreign sales. Underinvoicing of exports and overinvoicing of imports provide one means of evading such control.

Real transfer: through exchange depreciation

Typically an attempt is made to prevent capital exports by letting the exchange rate go. This may lead to speculative purchases of the currency – a countervailing inflow, such as occurred in Germany before about June 1922. Or, if it does not, the depreciation as capital pushes abroad is apt to lead to undervaluation of the exchange rate and an export surplus, such as occurred after June 1922. (The statement rejects the McCloskey and Zecher 1976 notion that purchasing-power parity is always automatically achieved.)

Other classic cases in point are the French depreciation of the 1920s, the capital flight of 1936 reacting against the Front Populaire of socialist Premier Blum, and the French outflow in the fall of 1968. Each of these was halted by devaluation to a lower level that provided profits to returning capital, requiring the rate to be set at levels, and accompanied by measures, that inspired confidence that the rate would be held. In the instant cases these were the Poincaré stabilization of July 1926, the Tripartite Monetary Agreement of September 1936, and the August 1969 devaluation agreed to by Germany.

Exchange depreciation raises the question of a possible squeeze to reverse the expectations of speculators and capital exporters. The classic instance is probably the squeeze engineered by Lazard Frères for the French government in March and April 1924, with the help of a stabilization loan from J.P. Morgan and Company in the amount of $100 million. The details have been written up by Phillippe (1931). Initially the squeeze was put into effect when the franc was 123 to the dollar. This rate was held with difficulty in the first week of the operation, after which the level was raised to 84.45 on March 19, 78.10 on March 24, and 61 at the end of April. At this last rate the authorities stopped buying francs and sold them to the badly beaten shorts – French, German, Dutch, and Austrian – who had to repay borrowed francs. The short-term gain was lost over time, however, as a left-wing government won election in June 1924, and measures to stabilize the position judged adequate by the market were not taken. The rate sagged to between 80 and 85 in June, and the decline resumed thereafter until it reached a low of 249 in early July 1926 just before the Poincaré stabilization.

Other squeezes against short speculation on the part of investors, though perhaps not involving capital flight, have been put in place by Italy in 1964, the United Kingdom in 1976, and the United States on October 31, 1978.

Countervailing inflow: purchase of local bonds in foreign capital markets

As already noted, this is not a net export of capital so much as a search for an intermediary in order to lend to one's own government or nationals. It can be a natural stage in the education of investors and the acquisition of trust in their national borrowers. Platt (1984), for example, observes that most estimates of UK nineteenth-century lending are too high because they fail to take account of the extent to which investors in the borrowing countries acquired bonds issued in London; while the investors wanted to invest at home, they wanted to do so by means of obligations that the local government or borrower would hold in higher esteem than those owed locally, and perhaps wanted the added liquidity that a bond traded on an international market would command. He noted initially that the bonds issued in London for the Chemin de Fer du Nord in the 1840s were largely bought by the French. It is well known that Argentinian and Brazilian investors bought Argentinian and Brazilian bonds, respectively, issued in London and Paris. As the New York market gradually started to issue bonds for European borrowers after World War II, substantial percentages of these were bought by investors in the issuing countries (Kindleberger, 1971).

Platt makes the point that many borrowing countries have a lot of capital at home to invest at home but prefer to do it through the intermediation of investment bankers abroad. Whether this should be called capital flight depends, of course, on what happens next: whether it is followed, as in the French 1840 case, by the development of a French capital market which obviated the necessity for such intermediation, or whether distrust of domestic creditors grows and intermediation is followed by true capital flight.

Countervailing inflow: loss of foreign-exchange reserves

The revocation of the Edict of Nantes, the expatriation of Mississippi bubble profits, and the flight of capital during the French Revolution occurred before central banks had been established on the Continent. After the establishment of central banks, capital flight could still be effected through gold losses, and in addition, where the central bank held foreign exchange in its reserves, with a loss of foreign exchange. It is perhaps stretching matters to call this a countervailing capital inflow, although technically such is the case. The issue is clearer where monetary authorities borrow abroad, a subject we are about to discuss, but it frequently happens that the loss of foreign-exchange reserves or gold is an early means of accommodating capital flight, followed, after the flight has proceeded for some time, by borrowing.

Countervailing inflow: official borrowing abroad

The monetary authorities can borrow abroad in a variety of ways: through swaps in the case of the Group of Ten (G10), through selling foreign exchange forward, through arranging for parastatal bodies to borrow abroad rather than at home and sell the proceeds to the authorities.

A classic swap case occurred in the Italian lira in 1963 following the nationalization of the electricity-generating industry and a middle-class strike that took the form of capital flight. The Italian authorities chose to meet the crisis not by depreciating the currency, which would have raised domestic prices in irreversible fashion, but by entering into swaps, primarily with the US government. This seems to me to have been wise. The irritation of the Italian capitalists did not last long when they learned that the socialist terms for compensation were generous – overgenerous, as a number of mainstream economists told me. By financing the outflow and hanging on, the position was restored – although again in the long run the inflation was not cured, and the exchange rate ultimately declined.

The French have gotten themselves into a bind, in my judgment, by holding on to their gold and borrowing foreign exchange through such parastatal bodies as Electricité de France to meet balance-of-payments losses and capital flight in 1968–9 and again as a response to the Mitterrand policy of nationalization in 1981. Gold is illiquid today if attempt be made to sell it in large amount. While the French dollar debt has been reduced in real terms by the fall of the dollar and the easing of interest rates, the overall position remains unstable.

Countervailing inflow: through macroeconomic policy

Deflation to attract private inflows through higher interest rates and depreciation to attract capital inflow through speculation may be discussed together since their possibilities of success turn on similar criteria. The relevant instances are provided by Germany. In the 1920s, exchange depreciation up to June 1922 encouraged a sufficient speculative capital inflow to finance reparation payments, the current-account deficit, and some unestimated volume of capital flight. The inflow was based on inelastic expectations, the belief, that is, that the mark would one day return to par. There are many estimates of the amount of capital that flowed to Germany in 1919–23 and 1924–31 (Holtfrerich, 1977; 1980; 1986; Schuker, 1978), amounts said to be larger than American assistance to Germany under the Marshall Plan after World War II, but no reliable estimates of how much capital the Germans managed to export in the period before the Dawes Plan. At French insistence, a committee parallel to the Dawes Committee had been appointed under McKenna to determine the amount of capital exported by Germany, just as, at the time of standstill in 1931, a Layton Committee was established alongside the Wiggin Standstill Committee for the same purpose. It is clear on theoretical grounds that after the shift in expectations from inelastic to elastic, usually ascribed to June 1922, when the American holders of marks and German securities tried to liquidate them, that German mark holders were on the same side of the market. But it is not readily estimated how much capital flight by Germans took place before that time. Schuker (1978, p. 350) says that German exporters left their foreign earnings abroad, just as Holtfrerich (1986, p. 286) notes that the earlier movement in the other direction consisted partly of American exporters leaving the mark proceeds of sales in German banks waiting for the price to rise.

The central point is expectations. Higher interest rates and exchange depreciation will each attract foreign capital and help provide the counterpart of capital flight to the extent that they inspire confidence that the authorities are in full command and have every intention of restoring the position in the case of higher interest rates, and of appreciating the currency in the case of depreciation. Holtfrerich writes me that the return flow of German capital to Germany in the spring of 1924 was owing to tight money on the part of the Reichsbank. This forced business to repatriate hoarded exchange, especially after the establishment of the Golddiskontbank by Schacht strengthened confidence in the long-term stability of the currency, all this even before the adoption of the Dawes Plan. He went on to say that the stringent requirements of the Dawes Plan strengthened confidence still more and assisted that return movement. When such confidence is absent, however, and expectations are inelastic, raising interest rates leads to increased flight by foreigners and domestic holders alike, and the same is true in the case of depreciation.

Countervailing inflow: dumping of currency abroad

One method of capital flight is to buy foreign currency. In 1940 in Switzerland, I met a man who had arranged to receive five $100 bills from New York each week, which he sold for about $650. He then sent $500 back by draft each week and lived on the difference. A large capital inflow to the United States – outflow from Europe – took place through currency movements reported by banks, but more – much more – contributed to the residual debit in the US balance of payments through covert mail exports of US currency, and through purchases of currency through intermediaries in New York that were hidden in safe-deposit boxes. The counterpart of this US inflow, to the extent it was reported, was European capital flight, i.e. the increase in European holdings of US currency.

In addition to buying currency at home, capital can be exported by selling domestic currency abroad. Various German, Italian, and especially Russian foreign-exchange controls were evaded by smuggling currency abroad and selling it – in Amsterdam and Zurich for the Reichsmark in the Nazi period, in Helsinki and Istanbul for the ruble. The countervailing party that bought the currency in the foreign market effected the capital outflow. If no one had bought it, the price would have gone to zero. There is, of course, no evidence on the point but the supposition is that most of it was bought to be smuggled back, for example to pay for German exports. One anecdotal suggestion is that the British secret service was a substantial demander of Reichsmark currency in Amsterdam.

A further anecdote is of interest because of the echoes it conveys of the export of the capital of Huguenots after the revocation of the Edict of Nantes through "Catholic bankers, government agents in Paris . . . and foreign diplomatic representatives" (Scoville, 1960, p. 296) the perfection of markets that made the prices of estates in London vary with South Sea stock at the time of the South Sea and Mississippi bubbles (Carswell, 1960, p. 159), and of real estate in Geneva move in consonance with the notes of the Banque Royale (Lüthy, 1959, p. 364). In (I believe) 1937, on a train from Amsterdam to Paris, Emile Despres fell into conversation with a man who said his business had been getting capital out of Germany. There were, he said, three methods. One could buy a Reichsbank official and get sterling in London; this was expensive but sure. Or one could bribe a bank clerk to get currency for deposits in large amounts, and get it out of Germany through the pouches of diplomatic officers of a number of small states. Or one could smuggle it out by train. The risk–return payoffs by each method were related, and what was especially notable was that when there was a coup by the German authorities that temporarily blocked one method the cost of using the others rose. An analogous result materialized in the Italian export of capital to Switzerland in 1963: highway robbers gathered along the main road from Milan to Lugano to prey on those exporting capital in bundles of banknotes disguised as packages of butter (*Die Zeit*, October 15, 1963). Some part of the countervailing reflow of these notes to Italy, according to a tax accountant I interviewed in Milan in 1972, came from Italian companies repatriating "black cash" accumulated abroad through overinvoicing to get it back on their books to make good losses. These appeared as foreign purchases of the company's newly issued shares.

Means to contain capital flight or to entice it back

Only a few loose ends remain to cover the list set forth above, since many of the options have already been covered in connection with the means of financing the outflow, notably: ignoring, deflating, depreciating, stabilizing at a devalued rate, operating a squeeze with or without stabilization loans, and, implicitly, monetary reform. A word or two may be useful, however, on forward operations, foreign-exchange control, and steps that might be taken abroad. I happen not to be sanguine about any of them.

It has been suggested by Keynes and others, notably John Spraos

(1959), that central banks need not lose gold or foreign exchange, since they can create the equivalent by selling foreign exchange forward, roll the contract over as it matures, and keep going virtually to infinity. A domestic holder of, say, sterling, who wants protection against depreciation, can in capital flight either demand dollars – I write as if the system were one of a movable peg – or be content with a contract to be provided with dollars against sterling at a set price in the future. The subject merits extensive exposition for which space is lacking. In short, however, it may be said that when the market believes that the authorities' commitments to deliver foreign exchange are likely to exceed their available reserves, the market may be unwilling to renew its forward engagements by rolling them forward, and demand fulfilment (Spraos, 1969). This is broadly what happened in Britain in 1967. Again, the question turns on credibility.

Exchange control is another subject deserving extended treatment. Systems differ markedly in their approaches,whether they use prohibitions and enforced collection, differentiation by price, or some combination. All are porous to greater or lesser degree, depending to a considerable extent on the elusive concept of national character. Thus Britain in the 1950s managed to develop a wide spread between ordinary sterling and security sterling, whereas in France and Belgium the spread between current-account and capital-account foreign exchange never diverged beyond a few percent before being contained by arbitrage. As the Despres anecdote in the previous section indicates, moreover, even the death penalty in Germany – an efficient country in policing transactions – failed to make the system of control tight. As a rough guess, I have suggested that at one extreme Germany might restrain 95 percent of the attempts to evade foreign-exchange controls whereas a typical Latin country might achieve success only in the range of 60–75 percent. In times of war or other national emergency that pulls a country together, the ratio rises.

The point of exchange control, of course, is to prevent the public from buying in the cheapest market and selling in the dearest. It attempts to override basic economic incentives.

A particularly instructive example of the futility of halfhearted exchange control is US experience in the 1960s with the interest equalization tax, Gore Amendment, Voluntary Credit Restraint Program, and Mandatory Control Program. The administration tried to prevent capital outflow one conduit at a time, when the US capital market was tied to markets abroad through many. As each link was cut off, the flow was diverted to others.

In the postwar period, Switzerland and Germany have at various times tried to keep out foreign funds by requiring banks to maintain special reserves against foreign deposits. The best-known example is the German *Bardepot.* I am not a deep student of the experience, but I think it was, on the whole, only partially successful. Nominees can be used to disguise foreign ownership, although there are risks that the fiduciary will fail to live up to commitments.

My own rather thin files from the period when I was working at the Federal Reserve Bank of New York include two memoranda addressed to Mr Sproul, one with E. Despres, of June 28, 1937, entitled "Would American and British Support for the Franc bring French Capital Home?" and one with E.G. Collado, dated April 18, 1938, on "Hot Money." The first is a little bizarre, as the purpose of inducing capital repatriation to France was to induce the French authorities to buy gold and relieve some of the pressure on the United States from the "Golden Avalanche." The critical issue, it was stated, was whether French capital abroad was primarily a hedge against further depreciation or restrictions, or was held chiefly because of fear of expropriation. The conclusion was that the former was the primary motive, and that a US–UK announcement of an intention to stabilize the French currency would be effective in inducing capital repatriation.

The Kindleberger–Collado memorandum explored the possibility of limiting the capital inflow to the United States by taxation, thought to be unenforceable, and various means of limiting the inflow through short-term banking funds, such as a requirement of 80 percent to 100 percent reserves, taxes, widening of the gold points, and a lowering of the gold price. All but some widening of the gold points were rejected. A new method was proposed, simple in theory but deemed complex in practice, to limit foreign purchases of US securities, so as to create two prices after the limit was reached, one for foreign-held shares, and another lower one for those in American hands. The proposal came from recognition that this had already happened to ITT stock, because of limitations on foreign ownership of US communications. As I reread the memorandum now, however, I have the feeling that youthful optimism won out over practicality.

The crucial condition for capital repatriation

The historical record indicates that the crucial aspect inducing repatriation after capital flight is a return of confidence – confidence in the capacity of the country to maintain the exchange rate, in the safety of capital, in economic recovery. This criterion makes it unlikely, in my judgment, that capital repatriation will take place gradually over a long period of time, as contemplated, for example, in the report of the Inter-

American Dialogue (1986). This report argues (p. 12) that Latin American recovery depends on an inflow of $20 billion a year, made up of $12 billion a year from the commercial banks, $4 billion from the multilateral agencies, $1 billion to $1.5 billion each from foreign direct investment and bilateral lending, and $1 billion to $2 billion in recaptured flight capital. This estimate of the return of flight capital, which the report considers "a reasonable goal" is too little if confidence is restored, and algebraically far too high if it is not, since the capital flight will continue. If I may quote once more from my files, a contribution of January 12, 1937 to a Federal Reserve Bank of New York Research Department collection, on "Some General Implications of Recent Currency Developments," laid heavy emphasis on the restoration of confidence. Such restoration, it was thought, might precede or follow renewed domestic investment and economic recovery (in France), but excluded further depreciation of the franc. The same conclusion is central to Michael Bruno's (1985, p. 868) judgment about stabilization of the monies of the Latin American Southern Cone, i.e. the necessity of building "credible expectations." This essentially means that short-run measures in the foreign-exchange market, such as a stabilization or a squeeze, must be buttressed by long-run macro-economic stabilization that is seen to be politically supportable. It is quite an order.

Notes

1. For an analytical account of capital flight of a half century ago, see Chapter 10 of my *International Short-Term Capital Movements* (1937), treating the literature by Machlup (1932), Iversen (1935), Nurkse (1935), and Fanno (1935). It covers all capital movements not based on normal income-induced flows, and includes such "abnormal" flows as reparations.
2. I presume that the difference between the gross and net of Huguenots going to Switzerland represents not a return to France but moves from Switzerland to other refuges.

References

Ashton, T.S. (1959), *Economic Fluctuations in England, 1700–1800*, Oxford: Clarendon Press.

Bruno, Michael (1985), "The Reforms and Macroeconomic Adjustments: Introduction," *World Development*, vol. 13, no. 8 (August), pp. 867–9.

Carswell, John (1960), *The South Sea Bubble*, London: Cresset Press.

Carter, Anne Clare (1975), *Getting, Spending and Investing in Early Modern Times: Essays on Dutch, English and Huguenot Economic History*, Assen, the Netherlands: Van Gorcum & Co.

Chaussinand-Nogaret, Guy (1970), *Les Financiers de Languedoc au XVIII siècle*, Paris: SEVPEN.

Fanno, Marco (1939), *Abnormal and Normal Capital Transfers*, Minneapolis: University of Minnesota Press; Italian original published in 1935.

Greer, Donald (1935), *The Incidence of the Terror during the French Revolution: A Statistical Interpretation*, Cambridge, Mass.: Harvard University Press.

Hawtrey, Ralph G. (1919), *Currency and Credit*, London: Longmans, Green.

Holtfrerich, Carl-Ludwig (1977), "Internationale Verteilungsfolgen der deutschen Inflation, 1918–1923," *Kyklos*, vol. 30, pp. 271–92.

Holtfrerich, Carl-Ludwig (1980), *Die deutsche Inflation, 1914–23*. Berlin: de Gruyter. Published in English as *The German Inflation, 1914–1923*, New York, NY: de Gruyter (1986).

Holtfrerich, Carl-Ludwig (1986), "U.S. Capital Exports to Germany 1919–23 Compared to 1924–29," *Explorations in Economic History*, vol. 23, pp. 1–32.

Inter-American Dialogue (1986), *Rebuilding Cooperation in the Americas*, Washington, DC: Inter-American Dialogue.

Iversen, Carl (1935), *Aspects of the Theory of International Capital Movements*, Copenhagen: Einar Munksgaard.

Kindleberger, Charles P. (1937), *International Short-term Capital Movements*, New York: Columbia University Press.

Kindleberger, Charles P. (1971), "The Pros and Cons of an International Capital Market," in Kindleberger, *International Money*, London: George Allen & Unwin, pp. 225–42.

Lüthy, Hubert (1959), *La Banque protestante en France de la révocation de l'édit de Nantes à la révolution*, vol. 1, *Dispersion et regroupement (1685–1730)*. Paris: SEVPEN.

Machlup, Fritz (1932), "Theorie der Kapitalflucht," *Weltwirtschaftliches Archiv*, vol. 36, pp. 512–29.

Machlup, Fritz (1950), "Three Concepts of So-called Dollar Shortage," *Economic Journal*, vol. 60, no. 237, pp. 46–68.

Machlup, Fritz (1980), "My Early Work in International Monetary Problems," *Banca Nazionale del Lavoro Quarterly Review*, no. 133, pp. 113–46.

Mackay, Charles (1980), *Extraordinary Popular Delusions and the Madness of Crowds*, New York: Harmony Books, first published 1852.

McCloskey, Donald N. and J. Richard Zecher (1976), "How the Gold Standard Worked, 1880–1913," in J.A. Frenkel and H.G. Johnson, eds, *The Monetary Approach to the Balance of Payments*, Toronto: University of Toronto Press.

Nurkse, Ragnar (1935), *Internationale Kapitalbewegungen*, Vienna.

Phillippe, Raymond (1931), *Le Drame financier de 1924–1938*, Paris: Gallimard.

Platt, D.C.M. (1984), *Foreign Finance in Continental Europe and the USA, 1815–1870: Quantities, Origins, Functions and Distribution*, London: George Allen & Unwin.

Schubert, Eric S. (1986), "The Ties that Bound: Market Behavior in Foreign Exchange in Western Europe during the Eighteenth Century," Ph.D. dissertation, University of Illinois at Urbana-Champaign.

Schuker, Stephen A. (1978), "Finance and Foreign Policy in the Era of the German Inflation: British, French and German Strategies for Economic

Reconstruction after the First World War," in Otto Busch and Gerald D. Feldman, eds, *Historische Processe der deutsche Inflation, 1914 bis 1924*, Berlin: Colloquium Verlag.

Scoville, Warren C. (1960), *The Persecution of Huguenots and French Economic Development, 1680–1720*. Los Angeles: University of California Press.

Spraos, John (1959), "Speculation, Arbitrage and Sterling," *Economic Journal*, vol. 69, no. 1 (March), pp. 1–21.

Spraos, John (1969), "Some Aspects of Sterling in the Decade 1957–66," in Robert Z. Aliber, ed., *The International Market for Foreign Exchange*, New York: Praeger.

Van Dillen, J.G. (1964), "The Bank of Amsterdam," in Van Dillen, ed., *History of the Principal Public Banks*, London: Frank Cass, pp. 79–124.

Viner, Jacob (1952), *International Economics*, Glencoe, Ill.: The Free Press.

Weiner, Margery (1960), *The French Exiles, 1789–1815*, London: John Murray.

PART 5
Conclusion

16

Conclusion

It is presumptuous to offer a conclusion to this pot-pourri of papers of and about economic history. I return, however, to the discussion of methodology of the first two chapters and argue that economic history belongs in the curriculum of the economist from which it is being squeezed out and replaced by more mathematics and more econometrics. The trend seems to me mistaken. I argue not that graduate students should *do* economic history beyond the exercise of writing term papers on conventional subjects in class, but rather that they should be exposed to substantial doses of it so as to bring a historical perspective to economic questions. I favor, that is, historical economics.

There is a widespread view in the profession that formalism in economics has gone too far and that more attention should be paid to policy issues, institutions, rhetoric, perhaps economic history. The emphasis on history is generally confined not to practice, as in the preceding essays, but to preaching. Kenneth Arrow (1986) and Robert Solow (1986), undeniably economic theorists with strong mathematical capacities, lend their authority to support for arresting the decline in the teaching of economic history. The Oxford econometrician, Terence Gorman (1984), and Michio Morishima (1984), a mathematical economist, both think that the mathematicization of economics has lost all sense of balance and urge that curricula include more history. Gorman (1984, p. 286, n. 29) observed, however, that an attempt to put forward a combined program of technical economics and economic history at the London School of Economics when he taught there failed because of "the single-mindedness which is the besetting sin of much modern economics." Commenting on the Gorman experience, Morishima (1984, pp. 69–70) expressed doubt that economics and history can be taught simultaneously: "Heaven does not bestow more than one gift, and those that like history tend to dislike mathematics."

Martin Shubik, a professor of mathematical economics and institutions at Yale University, is a specialist in game theory. He has told me that the unusual combination of designations in his title derives from the fact that games are played with rules, and that rules are typically embodied in institutions. To study the way rules evolve in evolving institutions, he reads economic history (Shubik, 1986).

I suspect that Professor Gorman was trying to train students to be both technical economists and economic historians. This goes well beyond any ambition of mine. I would argue that interdisciplinary exercises of the sort offered in Chapter 7 on the postwar resurgence of the French economy can be undertaken only midway in an economist's development and after a firm grounding in economic theory and perhaps in an economic special field. My interest is not in producing economic historians but rather in diluting the rigor of modern technical economics through exposure to a fairly broad range of human economic experience. Gorman (1984, p. 274) notes that the great economists of our generation – he mentions Arrow, Hahn and Samuelson – have a wide and perhaps deep knowledge of economic and general history. The same is true of course of most of the great economists of the past – Adam Smith, John Stuart Mill and Alfred Marshall, though there may be doubt about Ricardo and Keynes.[1]

An attempt to understand the past through the application of standard economic models, as called for by rational expectations, should persuade the budding economist of the necessity to have a host of models in his or her toolbox, along with a readiness to change models frequently as called for by circumstances, and the capacity for pattern recognition sufficient to judge when to use which model. There is a debate in artificial intelligence over whether computers can ever be programmed consistently to defeat grand masters at chess, or to distinguish at a glance between a squirrel and a rabbit. Art, instinct, intuition, hunch and pattern recognition may be among the missing ingredients of the economic tyro and the unrecognized asset of the magisterial one. Exposure to economic history, if necessary at some cost in giving up courses in advanced mathematics in the economics curriculum, will push the student a slight distance in the development of these capacities.

Economic history can do more. It can test economic models for generality. In William Parker's symposium, *Economic History and the Modern Economist*, I held (Kindleberger, 1986) that tariff history that relied solely on the Stolper–Samuelson theorem (1941), along with knowledge of whether the scarce or the abundant factor of production had political dominance, beautifully explained some, but not all, of the historic experience in movements toward protection or toward freer trade. A scarce factor with political clout may impose a tariff when threatened with massive imports in the products it readily produces, or it may not: it may emigrate, as in the case of labor engaged in Italian wheat farming in the 1880s and thereafter, violating a usual assumption of international-trade theory of mobile goods and immobile factors. It may wish to impose a tariff but be overruled in the interest of higher political goals, as Napoleon III, anxious to win English support for his Italian campaign against Austria, overrode the claims of French manufacturing by lowering tariffs in the Cobden–Chevalier treaty of 1860. It may even convert to an entirely new industry through a burst of innovation – Danish farmers who had exported wheat, shifting to dairy products, eggs and bacon, and importing grain as feed in a dynamic rather than a static model. (Violation of an assumption of the theory of international trade – or of any other branch of economic theory – in the real world is anathema to the theorist but occurs occasionally as a fact of life.) In other research (Kindleberger, 1961), I have noted that the relations between foreign trade and national economic growth are complex: increased imports can depress growth or under certain circumstances stimulate it, and the same is also true of decreased imports, increased exports and decreased exports. Specialists in either trade or economic growth or both without some acquaintance with the range of possibilities exemplified by history may generalize from a single case or a few cases, and fail to appreciate the need for care in the choice of assumptions and models, along with the frequent need to change them.

Let me illustrate this in a different connection, based on the paper on Spanish silver above (Chapter 3). The usual model of balance-of-payments adjustment postulates a tendency to equilibrium. In the price-specie-flow analysis it works fairly rapidly. If gold or high-powered money is lost, the system contracts, prices decline, imports decline, producers of exportables turn from domestic to foreign markets, and exports rise. The same is broadly the case with foreign-trade-multiplier models as income changes produced by trade change restore equilibrium – a decline in income from an increase in imports or decrease in exports, for example, reducing domestic expenditure, lowering imports directly, and freeing up goods for exports. The case of Spanish silver illustrates a different possibility, that equilibrium in the balance of payments may not be restored in the short run or the long. It is true, as economists emphasize, that a person or an economy cannot run balance-of-payments deficits forever. Sooner or later one runs out of credit and assets. Classical economics leans heavily on celestial mechanics, and equilibrium, like Halley's comet, must catch up at the end, if only in quasi-death for the economy, such as Spain experienced after 1750, or in a person dying bankrupt. I do not claim that history repeats itself or that those who know no history repeat old mistakes, merely that history is helpful in suggesting the range of possibilities. The persistent deficits of Spain and surpluses of India and China in the early modern period evoke the current persistent deficits of the United States and surpluses of Japan, Taiwan, Germany and Switzerland, even when all these countries try ineffectually to correct the disequilibria by macro-economic policy, including exchange-rate changes, and worse, such micro policies as tariffs and quotas.

I have no intention of going through the remaining Chapters from 4 to 16 to suggest the relevance of history to current economic problems, but a few sentences on one or two of the chapters may be apposite. Thomas Mun's remark that the foreign-exchange rate cannot be controlled by "confederacie" should provide food for thought for government and central-bank officials trying to stabilize foreign-exchange rates today (Chapter 4). The present fashion of chaos theory which states in vulgar formulation that virtually anything can happen, starting small and leading in unexpected directions, is supported by Adam Smith's failure to recognize the onset of the industrial revolution happening around him as *The Wealth of Nations* appeared in 1776 (Chapter 5). It equally relates to the resurgence of the French economy after World War II at a time when the analysts, including economic historians, were busy explaining French economic retardation (Chapter 7). The essays on commercial policy between the wars (Chapter 6) and US foreign economic policy over two centuries (Chapter 8) are rather more descriptive than analytical, but Chapters 9 and 10 pose a salient question of the present day, whether the growth processes of an economy can be extended by policy measures readily available to governmental bodies. The issue is posed in acute form by the decline in the rate of personal savings in the United States since the 1970s, and especially after tax reductions favoring the higher-income groups were adopted for the ostensible purpose of raising saving rates. It arises also in other areas related to the aging process: declines in the rates of gain in labor and factor productivity; loss of innovation activity, outside the narrow area of finance; increasing consolidation of interest groups – "distributional coalitions" in Mancur Olson's (1982) terminology – with their effective resistance to increases in taxation or reduction in benefits, including in the latter for the "military-industry complex," a reduction in military expenditure. As economies age, unrejuvenated by the losses of major wars, they have no trouble in willing the ends, but find it increasingly difficult to will the means, which implies recognizing and distributing the costs. The trauma of defeat in war, as Olson points out, may dissolve these vested interests and make possible appropriate technical policies under effective leadership. But the best-designed policies, political economists should recognize, may not be available for application when the forces of resistance are organized and powerful.

The relevance of historical perspective of the five financial chapters (11–15) should be clear enough, all having been written in the last few years troubled by problem loans and bad debts, exchange-rate crises, capital flight from Third World countries, and the stock-market collapses of October 19, 1987 and October 13, 1989.

It is doubtless unseemly for older scholars to bewail present fashions in the subjects they profess, and to wax evangelical for a mode of learning that has been virtually discarded. It may be right, moreover, as M.M. Postan has somewhere stated, that economic history is for economists in their dotage. I cannot be cheerful, however, about the direction in which modern economics is going, with more and more relentless mathematics, and less focus on the facts of the real world.

Donald McCloskey (1986) asserts that all economists, in fact all scientists, use rhetorical devices, prominent among which is appeal to authority. I have already invoked the authority of Arrow, Gorman, Morishima and Solow, not to mention Adam Smith, John Stuart Mill and Alfred Marshall. I conclude, however, with three quotations, one from a minor deity in economics, one from a novelist, and one, metamorphized, perhaps unfairly, by substituting "economics" for "foreign policy" and "mathematical economists" for "ideologues," from a historian with whose political views I am not altogether sympathetic:

> Political economy is an abstract science which labours under a special hardship. Those who are conversant with its abstractions are usually without a true contact with its facts; those who are in contact with its facts have usually little sympathy with and little cognizance of its abstractions. (Walter Bagehot, 1978, p. 227)

> There is no great harm in the theorist who makes up a new theory to fit a new event. But the theorist who starts with a false theory and then sees everything as making it come true is the most dangerous enemy of human reason. (Chesterton 1914, p. 103)

> The seizure of economics by a boarding party of mathematical economists invites a host of dangers. Most of all you tend to get things wrong. Where the past empirical approach sees the present as emerging from the past and preparing for the future, mathematical economics is counter-historical. Its besetting sin is to substitute models for reality. No doubt the construction of models – logically reticulated, general principles leading inexorably to particular outcomes – is an exercise which helps the delineation of problems – but not when the artificial constructs are mistaken for a description of the real world. This is what Alfred North Whitehead calls the "fallacy of

> misplaced concreteness" . . . The error of (some) mathematical economics is to prefer essence to existence, and the result, however gratifying logically and psychologically, undermines the reality principle itself. (Schlesinger, 1983, p. 5).

Historical economics, I contend, can bridge the chasm between abstractions and facts, test theories against the course of events, and ensure the discard of models that are unuseful in illuminating concrete situations.

Notes

1. Raymond DeRoover (1949, p. 287n.) stated that Keynes on mercantilism in Chapter 26 of *The General Theory* "is full of inaccuracies and misinterpretations."

References

Arrow, Kenneth J. (1986), "History: the View from Economics," in William N. Parker, ed., *Economic History and the Modern Economist*, Oxford: Blackwell, pp. 13–20.

Bagehot, Walter (1978), "The Postulates of English Political Economy, No. I," in Norman St John-Stevas, ed., *The Collected Works of Walter Bagehot*, vol. xi, London: The Economist, pp. 222–54; first published 1880.

Chesterton, G.K. (1914), *The Flying Inn*, New York: John Lane.

Raymond DeRoover (1949), *Gresham on Foreign Exchange*, Cambridge, Mass.: Harvard University Press.

Gorman, Terence (1984), "Toward a Better Economic Technology," in Peter Wiles and Guy Routh, eds, *Economics in Disarray*, Oxford: Blackwell, pp. 260–88.

Kindleberger, Charles P. (1961), "Foreign Trade and Economic Growth: Lessons from Britain and France, 1850–1913," *Economic History Review* (2nd series) vol. 14, no. 2 (December), pp. 289–305.

Kindleberger, Charles P. (1986), "A Further Comment," in William N. Parker, ed., *Economic History and the Modern Economist*, Oxford: Blackwell, pp. 83–92.

McCloskey, Donald N. (1986), *The Rhetoric of Economics*, Madison: University of Wisconsin Press.

Morishima, Michio (1984), "The Good and Bad Uses of Mathematics," in Peter Wiles and Guy Routh, eds, *Economics in Disarray*, Oxford: Blackwell, pp. 51–73.

Olson, Mancur (1982), *The Rise and Decline of Nations*, New Haven, Conn.: Yale University Press.

Schlesinger, Arthur, Jr. (1983), "Foreign Policy and the American Character," *Foreign Affairs*, vol. 16, no. 1 (Fall), pp. 1–16.

Shubik, Martin (1986), private conversation, March 5.

Solow, Robert M. (1986), "Economics: Is Something Missing?" in William N. Parker, ed., *Economic History and the Modern Economist*, Oxford: Blackwell.

Stolper, Wolfgang F. and Paul A. Samuelson (1941), "Protection and Real Wages," *Review of Economic Studies*, vol. 9 (November), pp. 58–73.

Acknowledgements

Chapter 1: an abridged version of this article appeared in *Liberal Education* 75:1 (May/June 1989), 7–9. Copyright Association of American Colleges, Washington, DC.

Chapter 3: is reprinted by permission of the Asean Economic Research Unit of the Institute of Southeast Asian Studies, Singapore.

Chapter 4: was originally published in a German translation in "Klassiker der Nationalökonomie," H.C. Rechtenwald, (ed.), *Thomas Muns Werk in moderner Sicht*. Düsseldorf, Verlag Wirtschaft und Finanzen, 1989. It appears here with kind permission of the publishers.

Chapter 5: was originally published in *The Market and the State: Essays in Honour of Adam Smith* edited by Thomas Wilson and Andrew S. Skinner, © Oxford University Press 1976.

Chapter 6: was originally published in *The Cambridge Economic History of Europe*, vol. VIII, *The Industrial Economies: The Development of Economic and Social Policies* edited by Peter Mathias and Sidney Pollard, Cambridge University Press 1989.

Chapter 7: reprinted by permission of Harvard University Press, Cambridge, Massachusetts.

Chapter 8: reprinted by permission of the Council on Foreign Relations, Inc. New York.

Chapter 9: reprinted by permission of the Institut für Weltwirtschaft, Kiel, Federal Republic of Germany.

Chapter 11: reprinted by permission of Elsevier Science Publishers, Physical Sciences and Engineering Division, Amsterdam.

Chapter 13: reprinted by permission of The MIT Press, Massachusetts Institute of Technology, Cambridge, Massachusetts.

Chapter 14: reprinted by permission of the Salomon Brothers Center for the Study of Financial Institutions, New York University, New York.

Chapter 15: reprinted by permission of the Institute for International Economics Washington, DC.

Index